Dear Julia,

Thank you for all of your
support these last 8 years.
You're a great role model,

Yael

The Political Psychology of Israeli Prime Ministers

This book examines leaders of the seemingly intractable conflict between Israel and its Palestinian neighbors. It takes as an intellectual target of opportunity six Israeli prime ministers, asking why some of them have persisted in some hard-line positions, whereas others have opted to become peacemakers. The author argues that some leaders do change, and explains why and how such changes come about. She goes beyond arguing simply that "leaders matter" by analyzing how their particular belief systems and personalities can ultimately make a difference to their country's foreign policy, especially toward a long-standing enemy. Although no hard-liner can stand completely still in the face of important changes, only those with ideologies which have specific components that act as obstacles to change and who have an orientation toward the past may need to be replaced for dramatic policy shifts to occur.

Yael S. Aronoff is the Michael and Elaine Serling Chair in Israel Studies and associate professor of International Relations in James Madison College and Jewish Studies at Michigan State University. She is a recipient of the Michigan State University 2011 Teacher Scholar Award and is also Associate Director of Jewish Studies at Michigan State University. Professor Aronoff's work has been published in *Israel Studies*, *Israel Studies Forum*, and the *Political Science Quarterly*. She serves as the book review editor for the journal *Israel Studies Review* and is on the Board of Directors of the Association of Israel Studies. She served as Assistant for Regional Humanitarian Programs at the Pentagon's Office of Humanitarian and Refugee Affairs under the Office of the Secretary of Defense in 1994, and she was a Jacob K. Javits Fellow with the Senate Foreign Relations Committee in 1992–1993.

The Political Psychology of Israeli Prime Ministers

When Hard-Liners Opt for Peace

YAEL S. ARONOFF

Michigan State University

CAMBRIDGE
UNIVERSITY PRESS

CAMBRIDGE
UNIVERSITY PRESS

32 Avenue of the Americas, New York, NY 10013-2473, USA

Cambridge University Press is part of the University of Cambridge.

It furthers the University's mission by disseminating knowledge in the pursuit of education, learning, and research at the highest international levels of excellence.

www.cambridge.org
Information on this title: www.cambridge.org/9781107669802

© Yael S. Aronoff 2014

First published 2014

A catalog record for this publication is available from the British Library.

Library of Congress Cataloging in Publication data
Aronoff, Yael, 1968–
The political psychology of Israeli prime ministers : when hard-liners opt for peace / Yael S. Aronoff.
  pages   cm
ISBN 978-1-107-03838-7 (hardback)
1. Prime ministers – Israel.   2. Peace – Israel – Psychological aspects.
3. Israel – Politics and government – 20th century.   4. Israel – Politics and government – 21st century.   I. Title.
DS126.5.A8637   2014
956.9405'40922–dc23

2014002754

ISBN 978-1-107-03838-7 Hardback
ISBN 978-1-107-66980-2 Paperback

Dedicated to Rita, Mike, Eric, Maya, and Aidan Aronoff

Contents

Preface

There is no more fundamental concern in international relations than war and peace. Although much has been written about why states go to war, there is insufficient attention to why they make peace. This is particularly the case for long-standing conflicts in which the opposing leaders hold apparently irreconcilable positions. This book examines leaders dealing with the seemingly intractable conflict between Israel and its Palestinian neighbors. It takes as an intellectual target of opportunity six Israeli prime ministers and asks why some of them have persisted in their hard-line positions, whereas others have opted to become peacemakers.

There is perhaps no situation in which the knife-edge between peace and war is more precarious and for which the impact of a leader's decisions – regarding the populations in the immediate area as well as global geopolitics – is more profound than the Middle East, and specifically the Israeli-Palestinian conflict. Stretching over the past sixty-five years, this conflict has consumed the energies (and lives) of generations of Israelis and Palestinians and has been a thorn in the side of every U.S. administration dealing with the Middle East. If the Israeli-Palestinian conflict is a powder keg, this book argues that political leaders can either light the fuse or extinguish the fire and engage in peace negotiations. The Israeli case is particularly fruitful for such an examination, both because of the geopolitical importance of the conflict and its passionate intensity, and because it forms an excellent laboratory in which to examine the differences leaders make. All six prime ministers considered here were responding to similar changes on the part of the Palestine Liberation Organization (PLO) starting in 1988. By focusing on the Israeli leaders, I examine how different leaders operate in and respond to similar circumstances.

Some theorists imagine politics as a chess match, with rational calculations governing moves on both sides of the board, making individual personalities and psychologies irrelevant. I, however, analyze the differences leaders *do* make in determining war and peace by examining six Israeli prime ministers and their attitudes toward their long-standing enemy, the PLO. At the same time, even those international relations scholars who use constructivist approaches and *do* give great importance to agency, tend to focus their analyses at the level of international structure and interstate norms. At the state level, the focus is on changing identities and interests, but specific leaders and their worldviews often get ignored. A political-psychological approach focusing on leaders needs to be brought back into this discussion. At the same time, those scholars who do study leaders tend to assume that the leaders have stable political predispositions that make them resistant to change. From this it would follow that a change of leadership is necessary for a nation to shift from a hard-line strategy to a strategy of peacemaking.

This book argues against the formulation that leaders have to be replaced for enduring rivalries to be resolved. It shows that some leaders do change, and above all it explains why and how such changes come about. I go beyond arguing that "leaders matter" by analyzing how their particular belief systems and personalities can ultimately make a difference to their country's foreign policy, especially toward a long-standing enemy. Although no hard-liner can stand completely still in the face of important changes, only those whose ideologies have specific components that act as obstacles to change and who have an orientation toward the past may need to be replaced for dramatic policy changes to take place.

The book is informed by a political-psychological framework which stipulates that although changes in the opponent and the environment may be necessary to alter a leader's image of an enemy, the following conditions make it more likely that this image will change: (1) a weak link to an ideology that is inconsistent with change or the absence of such an ideology, (2) a present or future time orientation, (3) a flexible cognitive system, (4) emotional intelligence, and (5) a propensity for risk. It further stipulates that the following four aspects of ideology may inhibit change: (1) ideological goals that contradict those of the enemy; (2) a long, optimistic time horizon which prevents a belief that peace is urgent or that a policy has failed; (3) a perception that the world is permanently hostile; and (4) the view that security is possible without peace or territorial compromise. These variables inform the case studies of the Israeli prime ministers who appear in Chapters 2 through 7. The differences in ideology and personality among these six Israeli prime ministers have had significant impacts on their image of the enemy, their perception of and reaction to the intifadas (Palestinian uprisings) and the Gulf War, and ultimately on their ability to reach an agreement with the Palestinian Authority.

This book builds on a broad literature stressing the importance of domestic politics for understanding international relations, but it focuses on the importance of leaders' perceptions in explaining how conflict can lead to cooperation. It also builds on the literature connecting perceptions to policy preferences and even behavior, but it focuses on *change* in views and desired policies. Much of the literature dealing with the impact of beliefs on policy preferences has dealt with why individuals are unlikely to change their attitudes regarding an enemy. Therefore, it is especially interesting to investigate how and why some leaders eventually shift their images of an enemy while others do not.

I explore why certain leaders are more likely than others to perceive changes in their opponent and in the regional environment. I describe the Israeli prime ministers in terms of their ideologies, time horizons, and cognitive flexibility. Time orientation refers to the degree to which an individual focuses on the past, present, or future. Cognitive flexibility accounts for the degree to which an individual fits incoming information into existing categories and maintains these categories. I also analyze the effects of risk propensity and emotional intelligence, the ability to understand and be sensitive to other people, especially regarding prime ministers for whom these factors are most influential.

I situate a leader's individual cognitive makeup within a larger, cultural context. Varied ideological goals among leaders who belong to different political parties explain the extent to which each leader changes, whereas the leaders' individual traits not only explain the probability of change, but the different rates and ways in which attitudinal change occurs in leaders who hold the same ideology.

The case studies proceed from prime ministers who most strongly resisted change to those who changed the most. In Chapter 2 I analyze how and why Yitzhak Shamir remained a hard-liner throughout his life. Shamir, Israel's prime minister from 1983 to 1984 and from 1986 to 1992, often said, "The sea is the same sea and the Arabs are the same Arabs." Shamir's image of the Palestinians did not change for more than seventy years. He maintained that "the Arabs" wanted to conquer Israel and throw the Jews into the sea.

A significant reason why Shamir did not soften his position toward the PLO was that he was an ideologue – one for whom ideology is the sole basis for policy making. His ideology was founded on the Revisionism of Vladimir Jabotinsky in the 1920s and 1930s, but was even more extreme than Jabotinsky's. This ideology, which has greatly influenced the ideology of the Likud Party, contains certain basic assumptions key to my concerns here: that time is on Israel's side in regard to its conflict with the Palestinians; that Israel has a right to the Greater Land of Israel (including the West Bank); that it faces a hostile world; and that peace is unlikely and does not require territorial compromise with the Palestinians. Shamir's lifelong dedication to this ideology resulted in policies that rejected territorial compromise in exchange for peace with the Palestinians, his refusal to negotiate with the PLO, and a continued building of Jewish settlements on the West Bank, in defiance of significant pressure from the United States.

Shamir's ideological barriers to recognizing the PLO were strengthened by his preoccupation with past conflict – not only with the Palestinians, but also with the centuries of conflict between Jews and their enemies – which strengthened his view that the Palestinians were unchangeable. Shamir's cognitive rigidity reinforced his resistance to changing his image of the PLO and influenced him to ignore signals of its increasing moderation. His tendency to disparage opposing views and to perceive people and ideas in black-and-white terms prevented him from perceiving change among the Palestinians.

Chapter 3 focuses on the complex and perplexing leader Benjamin Netanyahu, Israel's prime minister from 1996 to 1999 and its current prime minister since March 2009. He has remained a mystery to many observers: Some argue that he is an ideologue representing the Revisionist Zionist roots of the Likud Party who defies international and U.S. pressure, whereas others insist that he is merely an opportunist who has no deeply held beliefs. Does his support for a two-state solution (starting in 2009) represent a dramatic shift in his image of the Palestinians? Or is it a tactical and symbolic acquiescence to American pressure that will not translate into his working hard to accomplish this stated goal?

Chapter 3 argues that although public opinion plays a larger role in influencing Netanyahu's policies than it does for any other leader analyzed, his ideology still has a strong effect on the extent and timing of his compromises. During Netanyahu's first term, he remained true to his ideology by trying to keep as much territory as possible, and the tactical changes he made – agreements with the Palestinians and meeting with Yasser Arafat – were designed to maintain this ideology. Strategically, he remained only formally committed to the Oslo agreement, while he tried to undermine it by slowing down its implementation and minimizing its effects. Netanyahu's ideology restricted him from conceding nearly as much land as Labor leaders were willing to give and constrained him from implementing all of the withdrawals. In addition to his ideology, Netanyahu's focus on the past, his cognitive rigidity, and his lack of emotional intelligence also prevented him from changing his hostile image of the Palestinians. He was emotionally involved in the historic conflict, did not respect or listen to opposing opinions, and was suspicious of his own advisors as well as of the Palestinians.

In his second and third terms, Netanyahu largely remains a hard-liner who holds a monolithic and hostile image of the Palestinians and remains deeply skeptical about the chances for peace. Netanyahu's policies, however, have softened. Despite his vehement opposition to the Oslo Accords, he argued that he would abide by them if the Palestinians honored their commitments. He signed the Wye and Hebron Agreements, granting additional land and jurisdiction to the Palestinians in order to improve his chances of getting reelected. In 2009, he accepted a two-state solution under American pressure; he then largely froze settlements in the West Bank for ten months in 2009–2010 in order to facilitate peace negotiations. Although he refused to renew the settlement freeze, in the summer of 2013 he agreed to release Palestinian prisoners to facilitate renewed negotiations with the Palestinian Authority.

Chapter 4 examines the enigma of Ariel Sharon, who fought in all of Israel's wars, beginning with the War of Independence. Sharon served as prime minister from February 2001 until January 4, 2006, when he suffered a severe hemorrhagic stroke. By the time he was struck down by the stroke, Sharon had overseen the withdrawal of all Israeli troops and settlers from the Gaza Strip and was setting the stage for a unilateral withdrawal of Israeli troops and settlers from much of the West Bank. Would Sharon have completed this withdrawal, thereby making a political change as dramatic as Richard Nixon's trip to China? Or was Sharon's Gaza withdrawal a cynical ploy to hang on to the West Bank by a hardliner who had not undergone any real change? What can explain the decision of one of the architects and strongest supporters of settlements in the West Bank and Gaza to unilaterally withdraw from the Gaza Strip and four West Bank settlements and pursue a new strategy of unilateral disengagement?

Unlike Shamir and Netanyahu, Sharon was a nominal member of the Labor Party in his youth, as were his parents. Not having grown up steeped in Revisionist ideology, he did not rigidly toe the ideological line and publicly accepted the idea of a Palestinian state. He took the risk of unilateral withdrawal from the Gaza Strip, just as he had taken risks in the military realm throughout his career. However, adopting other elements of Likud ideology, Sharon believed that time was on Israel's side, that the Arabs' relative military strength would diminish, and that peacemaking could be put off for another twenty years while Israel built other settlements and increased immigration. Sharon believed that Israel's enemies could be "walled off" to ensure security and that in time the Palestinians would acquiesce to Israel's greater strength and significantly reduce their demands.

Chapter 5 traces Yitzhak Rabin's transformation from hawk to Nobel Prize peacemaker. Rabin, prime minister from 1974 to 1977 and from 1992 to 1995, is one of the most dramatic examples of a hard-liner opting for peace with a long-standing enemy. In 1988 he was a hawkish defense minister who cracked down on the intifada through force. Thousands of Peace Now activists demonstrated, demanding Rabin's resignation. Yet, only five years later, this same man reluctantly shook the hand of his mortal enemy Yasser Arafat, after signing the Oslo Accords, which provided for mutual recognition between the PLO and Israel. Only two years from that moment, he stood on a stage, singing a peace song in front of tens of thousands of Peace Now members and other supporters of the Oslo Accords, who were now cheering him on. On that same night, an assassin's bullet tore through the lyrics of the song, which he had placed in his breast pocket, and pierced his heart.

Rabin's dramatic shifts can be explained by aspects of his ideology and his personality. His Labor Party ideology emerges as a permissive variable that enables its adherents to perceive change in the opponent and in the regional environment. Labor ideology does not have an extended, optimistic time frame with regard to winning the conflict with the Palestinians; therefore, Rabin increasingly believed that time was not on Israel's side and peace had to be promoted with greater urgency. Labor ideology also did not hold that world hostility toward Israel was permanent, and this enabled Rabin to be open to changes on the part of the Palestinians and to be influenced by world opinion. Labor ideology focused on security and viewed territory more pragmatically than its right-wing rivals. Therefore, it was always willing to compromise territory for peace. Finally, Labor leaders were more likely to risk political solutions, as they did not view long-term security as possible without peace.

Although most Labor members, like Rabin, underwent a softening of their positions toward the Palestinians, not all members changed at the same rate or through the same mechanisms. Rabin's cognitive rigidity and his focus on the present led to his changing more slowly than Shimon Peres, learning from events as opposed to trends, and reacting to daily occurrences as opposed to initiating dramatic changes.

Chapter 6 critically examines Ehud Barak's all-or-nothing approach to peace negotiations. Prime minister from July 1999 to March 2001 and defense minister from March 2009 to March 2013, Barak pledged to follow in the footsteps of his mentor Yitzhak Rabin and provide Arafat with sufficient concessions to "test" his desire to reach an agreement with Israel. Barak started his term after winning an unprecedented majority with a broad coalition and a close relationship with U.S. President Bill Clinton. Yet, despite these advantages and his making more far-reaching concessions than any previous prime minister, Barak lasted only eighteen months and was unable to reach peace with the Palestinians and Syrians as he had hoped.

Barak is also a hard-liner who underwent significant change. He not only started out against a Palestinian state, but he also opposed the Oslo Accords as chief of staff in 1993 and abstained from the vote on Oslo II as a member of the cabinet in 1995. However, during talks at Camp David, he became the first Israeli prime minister to break the taboo against negotiating the division of Jerusalem. Barak was ideologically open to compromise, but his personality played a part in the ultimate failure of these negotiations. Barak fully admits that he lacks sensitivity to others' emotions and believes that everyone's thinking is merely made up of logical steps that he can anticipate based on his own logic.

Chapter 7 analyzes the transformation of Shimon Peres from a security hawk to a leading supporter of the peace process. Prime minister from 1984 to 1986 and 1995 to 1996 and president of Israel since 2007, Peres changed from a hard-liner, relying on military force to deter Israel's foes and initiating Israeli's nuclear military facility in Dimona in the 1950s, to signing the Oslo Accords with the Palestinians in 1993. Although Peres still believes that Israel's military has to be strong, he now relies to a greater degree on political and economic solutions to resolve conflict with the Palestinians. Peres's changes in attitude are reflected in the titles of his books: In 1970, he wrote *David's Sling*, in which he emphasized Israel's defense buildup and his primary role in it. In contrast, in the late 1980s and early 1990s, he wrote *Battling for Peace* and *The New*

Middle East, emphasizing Israel's need to take the initiative in making peace with its neighbors. Peres believes that the world has changed, and that borders and territory have grown less important in relation to global economic cooperation.

Labor ideology made Peres's shift to a more dovish position possible. Peres believes that time is working against Israel and that new options for achieving peace have to be considered. Labor ideology's unlinking of security and territory allowed Peres to contemplate territorial compromise, whereas the view that sustainable security cannot be achieved without peace reinforces Peres's willingness to risk political solutions. Labor ideology enabled Peres to think not only that neighbors' perceptions of Israel are open to change but also that Israel needs to be more sensitive to world and U.S. opinion.

Whereas Peres's flexible ideology fostered change, his orientation toward the future influenced his rate and mechanisms for change. Peres was influenced by a perception of what evolutions *would* occur – such as changes in the relative importance of economic cooperation, rather than territory, in fostering peace – than by specific events such as the intifada. Finally, Peres's cognitive flexibility allowed him to listen to a variety of opinions and to think creatively with staff about possible solutions to the Israeli-Palestinian conflict. This in turn enabled him to alter his image of the PLO more quickly than Rabin, whose mind was relatively less open and whose ideas were less differentiated.

Thus Peres changed his view of the Palestinians and the PLO a decade earlier than Rabin, and to a more extensive degree, as well as through different mechanisms (perceived trends as opposed to events). Although both leaders increased their propensity to favor political over military solutions to conflict, Peres's changes in his notion of security were more extensive, encompassing a new focus on regional economic development and cooperation. As president today he is still urgently pursuing peace and declared, "I'm willing to go by air, land, sea, even to swim, to achieve peace."

Chapter 8 relates the implications of the case studies to the scholarly literature on the psychology of political conversion. The analysis of these Israeli prime ministers strongly suggests that although changes within the enemy and in regional and international contexts are necessary to explain the change in a leader's image of the adversary, they are not sufficient. The perceptions of leaders make a significant difference in reaching agreements such as Oslo and in influencing the success or failure of a peace process. This study refutes the main alternative explanation that leaders react to the changes in the regional environment and in the opponent similarly, and, thus, there is no need to examine leaders to explain their nation's foreign policy. The differences in ideology and personality among the six Israeli prime ministers have had a significant impact on their images of the enemy, their perception of and reaction to the intifadas, the Gulf War, the Arab Peace Initiative, the uprisings in the Middle East over the past three years, and ultimately on their ability to reach an agreement with the Palestinians.

The evidence in this book suggests that risk-tolerant leaders may also be more likely to make peace, complicating Daniel Byman and Kenneth M. Pollack's hypothesis that risk-tolerant leaders are more likely to cause wars.[1] Moreover, the analysis of the leaders' individual time orientations provides greater empirical verification that individuals who focus to a greater extent on the past are less likely to reevaluate a hostile image of an enemy.[2] The findings here also suggest that those leaders who are emotionally attached to and focus on a violent, conflict-ridden past are less likely to be able to reach durable peace settlements because they are less able to forge a new image of a past opponent as a partner.

This finding is also relevant with regard to current debates over how groups move toward reconciliation in the face of past injustices, suggesting that a certain amount of "forgetting of the past" may be necessary in order first to establish a "cold" peace, while an engagement with the past injustices may be necessary in the future to establish a "warmer" peace. Leaders who focus mostly on the present, receiving information about ongoing changes in small increments, are slower to perceive overall shifts and to implement changes. This builds on Jervis's notion that information arriving gradually is more likely to be dismissed or lead to slight modifications by arguing that a focus on the present and its immediate events likewise leads to the perception of information arriving gradually and has the same consequences.[3] However, unlike leaders who focus on the past, those leaders who have a present time orientation are capable of change, although their rate of change is slower than those leaders oriented toward the future.

Two of the prime ministers analyzed in this book continue to be major players. Benjamin Netanyahu is prime minister and Shimon Peres is president. The question on everyone's mind is whether Netanyahu, a hard-liner, will make dramatic shifts or need to be replaced through elections for a peace agreement to be achieved. My analysis also has implications for U.S. foreign policy, as the United States continues to play a significant role not only in mediating the conflict between Israelis and Palestinians, but also in engaging in preventive diplomacy to contain conflicts around the world before they erupt into large-scale violence. Analyzing leaders by the criteria used in this book will also help guide policy makers to the best methods for persuading leaders to end enduring conflicts and to prevent other conflicts from erupting.

---

[1] Daniel L. Byman and Kenneth M. Pollack, "Let Us Now Praise Great Men: Bringing the Statesman Back In," *International Security* 25, no. 4 (Spring 2001), 137.

[2] See Robert Jervis, *Perception and Misperception in International Politics* (Princeton, NJ: Princeton University Press, 1976); Charles W. Kegley, Jr., and Gregory A. Raymond, *How Nations Make Peace* (New York: St. Martin's Press, 1999), 230–9.

[3] Jervis, *Perception and Misperception in International Politics*, 308–9.

Acknowledgments

I would like to especially thank Robert Jervis and Fred Greenstein, my mentors. I thank Bob for introducing me to and piquing my interest in political psychology; the idea of this book emerged in conversation with him. I benefited immensely from his suggestions, input, and continuous support. Fred provided invaluable suggestions and feedback throughout the progress of this manuscript and has also been a true mentor. I would also like to thank Richard Betts, Jack Snyder, and Barbara Farnham for reading and commenting on earlier chapters of this book. A yearlong Lady David Fellowship at the Hebrew University provided me with the means to conduct field research there and gave me valuable access to faculty, such as Reymond Cohen and Yaakov Bar Siman Tov.

I also would like to thank my colleagues at James Madison College at Michigan State University for the supportive intellectual environment I have enjoyed as I brought this project to fruition. Kenneth Waltzer and Linda Racioppi gave me valuable suggestions and read parts of the manuscript. Dean of James Madison College Sherm Garnett, and Kenneth Waltzer in his capacity as director of Jewish Studies, provided invaluable support in the form of a semester sabbatical and course releases to complete this project, as well as funding for field research in Israel over several summers. I would also like to thank my students at James Madison College who contributed their own suggestions to the manuscript, in particular Rebecca Farnham, Megan Holland, Mark Houser, Geoffrey Levin, Sarah Oliai, Grant Rumley, and Kareem Seifelden. I would also like to thank my research assistants Brian Palmer and Ariana Segal.

I thank Lewis Bateman of Cambridge University Press for his steadfast belief in and support of this book and the anonymous reviewers whose suggestions made the manuscript even stronger.

I would also like to thank Berghahn Journals for allowing the publication of material from my article "From Hawks to Peacemakers: A Comparison of Two Israeli Prime Ministers," *Israel Studies Forum* 24, no. 1 (Summer 2009), and

Indiana University Press for giving me permission to publish parts of my article "From Warfare to Withdrawal: The Legacy of Ariel Sharon," *Israel Studies* 15, no. 2 (Summer 2010).

I would especially like to thank my family. My mom, Rita Aronoff, was always a great teacher who provided endless inspiration and support and was a tremendous believer in the value of education. Her loving childcare during parts of the process both enabled my work and were formative experiences for her grandchildren, which they will never forget. She created a heaven on earth for her family, and she continues to be my inspiration. My dad, Myron (Mike) Aronoff, piqued my interest in Israel Studies through his own expertise in, contribution to, and love for the field, and he read and commented on several drafts of the manuscript, providing valuable suggestions, encouragement, and support. I am honored to follow in his footsteps. I would like to thank my sister, Miriam Aronoff, for translating and transcribing a few of the interviews and for her continual support and encouragement. I would like to thank my husband and soul mate, Eric Aronoff, for being willing to follow me to Israel for lots of field research and for being an equal partner, for editing parts of the manuscript, and for providing the love, support, and harmony that made it possible to pursue this. Finally, I would like to thank our amazing children, Maya and Aidan, for the joy and happiness they bring, for being sports about tagging along to do field research, for understanding why their mother is too often in front of a computer, and for their own intellectual interest and engagement.

I

Introducing the Conceptual Framework

The history of peacemaking between Israel and her Arab neighbours showed that it was the change of mind of the hawks and the shift in their positions, not the preaching of the doves, that allowed Israel to exploit chances of peace at vital crossroads. The major breakthroughs in peacemaking were made and legitimized by the hawks.

– Shlomo Ben-Ami, Israeli Foreign Minister at Camp David negotiations, 2000[1]

Why do leaders make peace? Why do some leaders who defiantly vow that they will never negotiate, never make concessions to an enemy, sometimes dramatically shift course and do precisely that? How does this shift in perception happen – a shift from seeing your adversary as an enemy deserving a bullet to a partner deserving a handshake? This book analyzes the conversion of leaders from hardliners to negotiators of peace, and the way these conversions influence the timing and probability that peace can be achieved. Although changes within the enemy and in the regional and international context are necessary elements in explaining decisions to negotiate, the perceptions of individual leaders make a significant difference in determining if and when a peace agreement will end a conflict.

Changes in the international and regional balance of power are often insufficient to explain accommodation with a long-standing enemy. There can be generation-long gaps between these changes and eventual cooperation. Just as important as the actual changes in the structural environment is the recognition of such changes by leaders. This engenders the debate between the more deterministic structural adjustment model of adaptation to environmental change, in which actors will respond similarly to environmental change, and the learning model that expects that different perceptions of changes in the environment will lead to varied reactions. I necessarily ask questions put forth in the literature on

[1] Shlomo Ben-Ami, *Scars of War, Wounds of Peace: The Israeli-Arab Tragedy* (Oxford: Oxford University Press, 2006), 313.

I

learning: Are some types of people more likely to learn than others? Through what processes do political leaders learn? How quickly do they learn? From what types of events do they learn?[2]

Richard Ned Lebow and Janice Gross Stein point out that the field of foreign policy analysis knows "surprisingly little about why, how, and when leaders initiate dramatic change in foreign policy."[3] Despite the gravity of elite decisions in foreign policy change, the scholarly literature typically either ignores the impact of individual leaders, or underestimates the complexity of their roles by positing that hard-liners will always respond objectively to new information concerning changes on the part of their opponent or changes in domestic and international circumstances. Rose McDermott argues that "[t]he dominant paradigm, rational choice, does not tend to focus on individual leaders except to the extent that they are seen as similarly calculating men whose main desire is to stay in power."[4] Other scholars have concluded that hard-liners are resistant to change and, therefore, need to be replaced for change to occur.[5]

[2] Jack S. Levy, "Learning and Foreign Policy: Sweeping a Conceptual Minefield." *International Organization* 48, no. 2 (1994): 311; George W. Breslauer and Philip Tetlock, eds., *Learning in U.S. and Soviet Foreign Policy* (Boulder, CO: Westview Press, 1991), 27–31, 297.

[3] Richard Ned Lebow and Janice Gross Stein, "Afghanistan, Carter, and Foreign Policy Change: The Limits of Cognitive Models," in *Diplomacy, Force, and Leadership: Essays in Honor of Alexander L. George*, eds. Dan Caldwell and Timothy J. McKeown (Boulder, CO: Westview Press, 1993), 95.

[4] Rose McDermott, *Political Psychology in International Relations* (Ann Arbor, MI: The University of Michigan Press, 2004). For a forceful argument against scholars ignoring leaders, see Daniel L. Byman and Kenneth M. Pollack, "Let Us Now Praise Great Men: Bringing the Statesman Back In," *International Security* 25, no. 4 (Spring 2001). Also see Fred I. Greenstein, *Personality & Politics: Problems of Evidence, Inference, and Conceptualization* (Princeton, NJ: Princeton University Press, 1987); Greenstein argues that rational-actor analyses have difficulty explaining the variance in goals and behavior of different leaders.

[5] Ernest May, *Lessons of the Past: The Use and Misuse of History in American Foreign Policy* (New York: Oxford University Press, 1973); Graham T. Allison and Morton H. Halperin, "Bureaucratic Politics: A Paradigm and Some Policy Implications," *World Politics* 24, Issue Supplement: Theory and Policy in International Relations (Spring 1972), 66, 76; Gordon A. Craig and Alexander L. George, *Force and Statecraft: Diplomatic Problems of Our Time* (New York: Oxford University Press, 1990), 233; Robert Randle, "The Domestic Origins of Peace," *The Annals of the American Academy of Political and Social Science* 392 (November 1970): 11; Roy Licklider, "What Have We Learned and Where Do We Go from Here?" in *Stopping the Killing: How Civil Wars End*, ed. Roy Licklider (New York: New York University Press, 1993), 306; I. William Zartman, "The Unfinished Agenda: Negotiating Internal Conflicts," in *Stopping the Killing: How Civil Wars End*, ed. R. Licklider (New York: New York University Press, 1993), 20–34; Zeev Maoz and Ben D. Mor, "Enduring Rivalries: The Early Years," *International Political Science Review* 17, no. 2 (1996): 141–56. Fred Charles Ikle does not delineate whether and why hawks might be capable of change; see his *Every War Must End* (New York: Columbia University Press, 1971). Richard Ned Lebow is an exception, arguing that leaders do not necessarily need to be replaced, and that resolution requires a reorientation in thinking by leaders; see his "Transitions and Transformations: Building International Cooperation," *Security Studies* 6, no. 3 (Spring 1997): 154–79. He sets up useful conditions for possible transformation but does not elaborate on the reasons why leaders will adopt particular goals and lessons that will prompt them to seek accommodation.

Given that the psychological literature regarding balance theory states that people will manipulate information to fit beliefs, rather than adapt beliefs to new information, many psychologists would agree with this conclusion.[6] However, the fact that some hard-liners *do* shift their attitudes, whereas others do not, is contrary to both expectations and calls for explanation.

In contrast to the argument that leaders necessarily need to be replaced in order to reach accommodation, I engage in a theory-building exercise analyzing which types of hawkish leaders are more likely to convert into peacemakers. Fred Greenstein has suggested that a leader's personal variability will have a heightened effect under a specific set of criteria: First, he argues, personal attributes will become more decisive in highly ambiguous environments, in which there is unclear or even contradictory data that is open to multiple interpretations. Second, the leader must be in a strategic position, such that decisions made have systematic strategic impact. Third, the leader is emotionally involved in the subject. The six Israeli prime ministers I examine in this book meet all of these criteria.[7] All of these leaders were working in such environments, as the Middle East was undergoing, and continues to undergo, dramatic changes with ambiguous consequences; each was strategically positioned, and each was emotionally involved in the foreign policies discussed.[8] All the prime ministers started out as hawks who were opposed to recognizing the Palestine Liberation Organization (PLO) and against the creation of a Palestinian state. Yet their differences in ideology and core attributes significantly affected their perception of events and their subsequent desire and ability to reach an agreement with the Palestinians.

Although much scholarship on Israeli foreign policy has usefully explained the influence of its security culture and the military bureaucracy, these approaches fail to adequately explain the reversals of policy by some prime ministers toward the Palestinians. Ilan Peleg argues that the beliefs of leaders are especially important to the formation of foreign policy in deeply divided societies such as Israel.[9] Aaron

---

[6] Keith L. Shimko, *Images and Arms Control: Perceptions of the Soviet Union in the Reagan Administration* (Ann Arbor, MI: University of Michigan Press), 29.

[7] Greenstein, *Personality & Politics*, vii, 144, and "The Impact of Personality on Politics: An Attempt to Clear Away Underbrush," *The American Political Science Review* 61, no. 3 (September 1967): 634, 639. Also see Fred I. Greenstein and Michael Lerner, eds., *A Source Book for the Study of Personality and Politics* (Chicago: Markham Publishing Company, 1971). Peter Katzenstein agrees that in times of profound change, ambiguous signals allow for variability in how states define their security interests; see his *Cultural Norms and National Security: Police and Military in Postwar Japan* (Ithaca, NY: Cornell University Press, 1996), 201.

[8] Some studies have examined American leaders who had less knowledge of or less interest in foreign policy issues, and thus the results concerning change have been more ambiguous. See Shimko, *Images and Arms Control*, 111. John R. Zaller argues that the more informed a person, the less susceptible he or she is to attitude change; see his, *The Nature and Origins of Mass Opinion* (Cambridge: Cambridge University Press, 1992), 19.

[9] Ilan Peleg, "Israeli Foreign Policy Under Right-Wing Governments: A Constructivist Interpretation," *Israel Studies Forum* 19, no. 3 (2004): 102. For a particularly useful analysis of

Klieman has argued that "the student of Israeli decision making is advised to pay greater attention to the biographies of national leaders than to formal organizational charts."[10] The constant state of crisis regarding war and peace issues often increases the influence of the prime minister.

Hawks and doves are, of course, idealized types at the ends of a continuous spectrum. "Hawks," or "hard-liners," have a high threat perception, a low sense of urgency to resolve a dispute, a high predilection to use force, and a belief that the probability of peace is low. They are afraid that accommodations will be interpreted as weakness which will be exploited, and they view the opponent as a monolithic enemy – unchanged throughout the history of the conflict and, as importantly, *unchangeable*, having permanently aggressive and unrealistic goals and no justified motives. "Doves," or peacemakers, on the other hand, see the adversary's – or at least a faction of the adversary's – aims as limited and somewhat legitimate, and have a lower threat perception. They also believe that accommodation will be reciprocated – whereas aggressive moves can escalate the conflict – thus, accommodative moves should at least be tried before coercive ones. They place a higher value on settlement per se.[11]

I do not claim that leaders "should" have learned a particular lesson from the events under examination; rather, I assess whether new information presented by the events was entirely ignored, or how it was interpreted. It is not always prudent for hard-liners to change. In some cases, information may be ambiguous or their image of the enemy as hostile may indeed be accurate. However, when new information is ignored or misinterpreted, it inhibits adaptation to a more "reality-oriented" strategy. Nonrational resistance to change is often at the root of cases in which leaders fail to notice events of obvious importance that contradict their beliefs, and thus they maintain constant policies in the face of changing circumstances.[12]

the influence of the military bureaucracy, see Yoram Peri, *Generals in the Cabinet Room: How the Military Shapes Israeli Policy* (Washington DC: United States Institute of Peace Press, 2006).

[10] Aaron Klieman, *Israel & the World After 40 Years* (New York: Pergamon-Brassey's International Defense Publishers, 1990), 89.

[11] Alexander L. George, *The "Operational Code": A Neglected Approach to the Study of Political Leaders and Decision-Making* (Santa Monica, CA: The Rand Corporation, 1967), 21; Holsti, "The Operational Code as an Approach to the Analysis of Belief Systems: Final Report to the National Science Foundation Grant SOC75-15368" (December 1977), 48, 96, 105–6; Efraim Inbar, *War and Peace in Israeli Politics: Labor Party Positions on National Security* (Boulder, CO: Lynne Reiner Publishers, 1991), 15; Glenn H. Snyder and Paul Diesing, *Conflict Among Nations: Bargaining, Decision Making, and System Structure in International Crises* (Princeton, NJ: Princeton University Press, 1977), 297–310. Often hard-liners see their most extreme counterparts as reflecting what everybody on the other side thinks or as inherently dictating the policy of the opponent.

[12] Snyder and Diesing, *Conflict Among Nations*, 392; Robert Jervis, *Perception and Misperception in International Politics* (Princeton, NJ: Princeton University Press, 1976), 307; Alexander George, *Presidential Decisionmaking in Foreign Policy* (Boulder, CO: Westview Press, 1980), 63.

ANALYTIC APPROACH

This study explores explanations as to why certain leaders are more likely than others to perceive changes in the opponent and in the regional environment. I move among five separate but related ways to describe individual cognition and attitude: ideology (drawing on Alexander George's work on the operational code), individual time orientations (derived from Robert Jervis's use of the rate and magnitude of incoming information), cognitive openness, emotional intelligence, and risk propensity. Ideology is key to explaining the varied goals pursued by different leaders, which in turn influences the extent to which each leader changes. To explain the different rates and ways in which attitudinal change occurs in leaders who hold the same ideology, however, it is necessary to analyze the leaders' perceptions of time, their cognitive rigidity, emotional intelligence, and risk propensity.

I conclude that although a change in both the opponent and the environment is necessary for leaders to change their image of an enemy, a combination of five additional elements makes change more probable: (1) a weak commitment to an ideology that would prevent responsiveness to changing circumstances, or a commitment to a pragmatic ideology that is more responsive to shifts in the environment; (2) a present or future time orientation; (3) either a flexible cognitive system or exposure and openness to a significant advisor who has a different view of the opponent; (4) emotional intelligence, which increases the possibility of being exposed to diverse opinions; and (5) risk propensity, which can increase the probability of making concessions to an enemy. Ideologies that do not act as obstacles to change in image may act as permissive causes. This type of ideology may permit change but will not necessarily lead to change without other factors – changing conditions, a time horizon that is not immersed in the past, or an advisory system that exposes the leader to different points of view. Advisory systems can both reflect cognitive style and, in combination with ideology, explain change or lack thereof.

DETERMINANTS OF CONVERSION: THE INFLUENCE
OF IDEOLOGY AND COGNITIVE STYLE ON PERCEPTIONS
OF THE ENEMY

Ideology

The degree of commitment to the ideology and the content of the ideology are important in explaining subsequent behavior. Ideologies filter and shape the perception of "facts" to fit a particular outlook on the world. Similarly to George's concept of the "operational code," ideology refers to a general belief system about the nature of history and politics, the political environment, the fundamental character of one's political opponents, the prospects for the eventual realization of one's fundamental political values and aspirations, and the predictability of the future.[13] I also use Myron Aronoff's definition; that is, ideology is "a more concrete, rationalized, and systematized version of the general political culture articulated by groups and regimes to give legitimacy to their identities and justify their goals."[14] Holsti argues that ideology can serve "as a direct guide to action, as a framework for definition of the situation ... or as a set of operationally-useful symbols."[15] Those whose ideology is a direct call to action will be less likely to change, as they are more likely to reject information that does not conform to their ideology. Psychological experiments show that raising ideological differences makes it harder for decision makers to achieve a resolution.[16]

Since all six Israeli prime ministers discussed in this text were highly influenced by their respective ideologies, I also focus on the ideologies' *content*, as opposed to the intensity of the leaders' beliefs alone. I analyze both Likud and Labor ideologies as different Zionist ideologies, with different "linked beliefs" that define different "identities and political projects." Ideology is key to explaining the different goals pursued by leaders and the extent to which each leader changes. I suggest that the ideological components that thwart a change in attitude toward an enemy include a long, optimistic time horizon preventing adherents from recognizing the urgency of peace or policy failure; specific, rigid goals contradicting those of the enemy; the perception that the world is hostile; and the belief that security is possible without peace.[17]

1. Is Time on Israel's Side?

I define ideology's "time horizon" as the relationship between time and the achievements of central goals built into the logic of the ideology itself. An ideology with an optimistic, extended time horizon – one that perceives its struggle as extending into the distant future – encourages a perception that a strategy "failing" in the short term will win "in the next hundred years." If one believes that time is on one's side and is optimistic about reaching one's goals, one is less likely to reassess strategies that do not seem to be working in the short

---

[13] George, *The "Operational Code,"* vi–vii.

[14] Myron J. Aronoff, "Ideology and Interest: The Dialectics of Politics," in *Political Anthropology Yearbook I*, ed. Myron J. Aronoff (New Brunswick, NJ: Transaction, 1980), 8. Also See Myron Aronoff and Jan Kubik, *Anthropology and Political Science: A Convergent Approach* (Brooklyn, NY: Berghahn Books, 2012).

[15] Ole Holsti, "Cognitive Dynamics and Images of the Enemy: Dulles and Russia," in *Enemies in Politics*, eds. David J. Finlay, Ole R. Holsti, and Richard R. Fagen (Chicago: Rand McNally & Company, 1967), 49.

[16] Zaller, *The Nature and Origins of Mass Opinion*, 28; D. Druckman and K. Zechmeister, "Conflict of Interest and Value Dissensus," *Human Relations* 23 (1970): 431–38.

[17] In order to verify whether the leader genuinely believes the ideology or is only using it instrumentally, I analyze when the ideology was introduced, how it was reinforced, and whether leaders' ideological beliefs kept them from achieving other important goals.

run, compromise goals, or change images of an enemy.[18] One is also more apt to perceive inaction as bearing a lower risk than action. If, as scholars such as Jerel Rosati have argued, change is motivated by perceived failures, then leaders who are less likely to perceive strategies as failing due to their extended time frames will be less likely to change.[19] In addition, when a destructive stalemate prompts peace negotiations, a leader with a long-term, optimistic time horizon may not perceive the stalemate, or at least perceive it as one that will not last.[20]

2. Ideological Goals: General and Adaptable, or Specific and Rigid?

The second proposition in regard to the content of ideology is that hard-liners whose ideological goals are directly in conflict with those of the enemy are less likely to change their image of an adversary. If they revise their perception of an opponent, this reconsideration threatens the attainment of their ideological goals.[21] For instance, if security is central to an ideology, differing interpretations over time as to what is needed to maintain security will arise. The more abstract the stated general goals of an ideology, the more variety there may be in policy preferences that could meet the goals. The more specific the ideological goal, the less maneuverability there is for vastly different policy preferences that might achieve the goal. In addition, if the goal of the ideology requires as a matter of faith that territory has to be maintained, it, according to prospect theory, would further explain the greater weight put on conceding land as it is interpreted as a loss that would be traded for an uncertain gain.[22]

3. Is the World With Us or Against Us?

The third proposition regarding ideological content is whether the world is perceived as being inherently hostile; if so, one is more likely to perceive conflict

---

[18] Holsti discusses philosophical beliefs concerning "On whose side is time?" He builds on Alexander George's questions concerning the prospects for the eventual realization of one's fundamental political values; George, *The "Operational Code,"* 23.

[19] Rosati argues that failures often trigger change; Jerel Rosati, "The Power of Human Cognition in the Study of World Politics," *International Studies Review* 2, no. 3 (Fall 2000): 67; Mikhail Gorbachev's "new thinking" about foreign policy resulted from trial and error and the failure of the Afghanistan war; see Janice Gross Stein, "Political Learning by Doing: Gorbachev as Uncommitted Thinker and Motivated Learner," *International Organization* 48 (1994): 155–83.

[20] I. William Zartman, *Ripe for Resolution: Conflict and Intervention in Africa* (New York: Oxford University Press, 1985).

[21] George argues that signals may not be recognized due to the "rewards and costs" associated with them. See his *Presidential Decisionmaking in Foreign Policy,* 73; Philip E. Tetlock, "Content and Structure in Political Belief Systems," in *Foreign Policy Decision Making: Perception, Cognition, and Artificial Intelligence,* eds. D. A. Sylvan and S. Chan (New York: Praeger, 1984), 107–28, and "Cognitive Style and Political Ideology," *Journal of Personality and Social Psychology* 45 (1983): 74–83.

[22] Rose McDermott, *Political Psychology in International Relations,* 269. Also see Rose McDermott, *Risk Taking in International Politics: Prospect Theory in American Foreign Policy* (Ann Arbor, MI: The University of Michigan Press, 1998).

with an opponent as unstoppable.[23] International pressure is ineffective, since such an actor already sees these international voices as adversaries. This exemplifies the ideological perception of heightened threat, which magnifies the enemy's goals to their most extreme form – the destruction of one's nation. Conversely, if one does not perceive the world as hostile, then one will be more open to the idea that one has allies – to whom one can turn for aid and assistance, and whose suggestions need to be considered seriously – and that even one's adversaries can change over time.

4. *How Much Will Peace Contribute to Security? Does Peace Require Territorial Compromise?*

Finally, my fourth proposition is that leaders adhering to ideologies which posit that security can be attained without peace will be less inclined to take risks to achieve peace. For instance, Likud ideology has traditionally called for an iron wall of military defense that would eventually force the Arabs to accept Israel's existence in the Greater Land of Israel. Peace was seen as a long-term prospect, entailing Palestinian acquiescence to Israeli rule, with limited autonomous rights. Vladimir Jabotinsky, in his 1923 essay "On the Iron Wall," argues that "the only way to reach an agreement [with the Arabs] is an Iron Wall – that is to say, strength and security in Eretz-Israel whereby no Arab influence will be able to undermine its foundations."[24] Israel would have to continually protect this iron wall from repeated attacks, until continued military successes would prove that Israel could not be eliminated. As Jacob Lassner and S. Ilan Troen argue, "The Zionist Right demands more convincing proof than the Zionist Left before being willing to relax the logic of the iron wall."[25] Although on the one hand Jabotinsky paid lip service to the idea that Israel would "negotiate" with the Palestinians, his understanding of negotiation was quite narrow, encompassing ideas of limited political autonomy within the Israeli polity. It did not entail compromise on an independent Palestinian state in any part of Greater Israel and did not see a point of trying to reach an agreement until Palestinians were willing to recognize Israeli sovereignty in the whole of the land.[26] This idea – that there was no point to negotiations while Israeli sovereignty in Judea and Samaria was challenged – provided a framework in which peace was not urgent and a relatively high degree of security could be provided without peace.

---

[23] This relates to the nature of political life. George, *The "Operational Code,"* 21.

[24] Vladimir Ze'ev Jabotinsky and Mordechai Sarig, *The Political and Social Philosophy of Ze'ev Jabotinsky: Selected Writings* (London: Vallentine Mitchell, 1999), 102–5.

[25] Jacob Lassner and S. Ilan Troen, *Jews and Muslims in the Arab World: Haunted by Pasts Real and Imagined* (New York: Rowman & Littlefield Publishers, 2007), 338.

[26] Ian Lustick, "To Build and to Be Built By: Israel and the Hidden Logic of the Iron Wall," *Israel Studies*, 1, no. 1 (Spring 1996): 196–223.

Cognitive Style

Ideology deals with a leader's participation in collective ways of viewing the world. Leaders with the same political ideology, however, will differ in the ways and rates at which they change their image of an enemy in similar circumstances. To explain these differences, one must turn to elements of cognitive style, such as an individual's time orientation, the structure (as opposed to the content) of his or her beliefs – the person's position on a continuum from cognitive flexibility to cognitive rigidity – emotional intelligence, and risk propensity. Time orientation and cognitive style can be characterized as components of personality as they are tendencies or characteristics that vary by individual.[27] Although Philip Tetlock finds that ideology is correlated with levels of cognitive rigidity, my case studies reveal variance in cognitive rigidity among leaders who hold the same ideology.[28]

1. Time Orientation

In discussing leaders' time orientations, I analyze two separate but related ways in which individuals think about time in relation to events and goals. The first kind of time horizon, as discussed earlier, is the way the ideology views time in relation to the achievement of its goals. The ideological analysis of the time frame looks at optimism only as it relates to winning a conflict with an enemy, even in the distant future. The second kind of time orientation is an element of personality and pertains to the relative amount of time each leader devotes to thinking about the past, present, or future. Although underanalyzed in the scholarly literature, an individual's perception of time is a core element of cognitive style.[29] As Rose McDermott states, "Some people remain preoccupied with the past, others manage to stay focused in the present, while still others concentrate on the future."[30] Ilona Bobiewee and Philip Zimbardo argue that time perspective "is one of the most powerful influences on virtually all aspects of human behavior" and that each individual's time perspective varies and influences individual choices.[31] Whether a leader refers more to the past, present,

---

[27] James David Barber, *The Presidential Character: Predicting Performance in the White House*, 2nd ed. (Englewood Cliffs, NJ: Prentice Hall, 1977), 7; Fred I. Greenstein, "The Impact of Personality on Politics: An Attempt to Clear Away Underbrush," *Political Science Review* 61 (1967): 641; Fred I. Greenstein, "Can Personality and Politics Be Studied Systematically?" *Political Psychology* 13, no. 1 (1992): 107.

[28] Philip E. Tetlock, "Cognitive Style and Political Ideology," *Journal of Personality and Social Psychology* 45, no.1 (1983), 118–26.

[29] Milton Rokeach and Richard Bonier, "Time Perspective, Dogmatism, and Anxiety," in *The Open and Closed Mind: Investigation into the Nature of Belief Systems and Personality Systems*, ed. Milton Rokeach (New York: Basic Books, 1960).

[30] Rose McDermott, *Presidential Leadership, Illness, and Decision Making* (New York: Cambridge University Press, 2008), 10. Also see J. Hornik and D. Zakay, "Psychological Time: The Case of Time and Consumer Behavior," *Time and Society*, 5 (1996): 385.

[31] Ilona Boniwell and Philip Zimbardo, "Time to Find the Right Balance," *The Psychologist* 16, no. 3 (2003): 129–31; Ilona Boniwell and Philip G. Zimbardo, "Balancing Time Perspective in Pursuit

or future in trying to understand events and to shape decisions can influence whether or not that individual changes his or her image of an enemy, as well as the rate and mechanisms of any change. It is certainly the case that individuals have varied interpretations of the past. As Lassner and Troen persuasively argue, a variety of "interpretations of the past contribute to how Jews assessed present and future relations."[32] Therefore, my argument concerning individual time orientation not only rests on a preoccupation with the past, but also on one's interpretation of that past and the extent to which the present is conceived of as mirroring the past. I argue that leaders who are emotionally attached to and focused on a violent, conflict-ridden past, who view that violent history as repeating itself, and who view this past as a living reality, will be less likely to change their perception of the opponent even if the balance of power changes or the enemy becomes more moderate.[33]

This hypothesis has most often been analyzed at the level of groups and states, with the conclusion that an excessive reliance on the particular history of a dispute, at the expense of analysis of changes and future possibilities, may inhibit reconciliation among groups. This study confirms the findings of several scholars who have pointed to the detrimental effects of focusing on the past. For example, Charles W. Kegley, Jr. and Gregory A. Raymond conclude that peace agreements must look forward rather than backward, and Roy Licklider argues that some forgetting is necessary for reconciliation after civil wars.[34] Yaacov Vertzberger argues that some individuals have a greater propensity than others to view the past as a living reality with which to evaluate the present, whereas Jervis has argued that some individuals use what he calls "the representativeness heuristic" to find similarities between present and past events and make (often misplaced) generalizations.[35] Therefore, one could argue that the more the past informs one's present – especially when one has an emotional attachment to a history of conflict with an enemy – the more one would expect the enemy's past behavior to be reflected in its present behavior.

An excessive reliance on the particular history of a dispute, to the detriment of an analysis of the present changes and possibilities for future changes, can be

of Optimal Functioning," in *Positive Psychology in Practice*, eds. P. Alex Linley and Stephen Joseph (Hoboken, NJ: John Wiley & Sons, 2004), 165.

[32] Jacob Lassner and S. Ilan Troen, *Jews and Muslims in the Arab World*, 325.

[33] Although people can view the past as multivaried and contested, the prime ministers who have a past orientation with the implications I analyze do not perceive the past as continuous and uniform. They tend to view a Hobbesian past in which present enemies are perceived as analogous to previous different enemies across centuries of history.

[34] Charles W. Kegley, Jr. and Gregory A. Raymond, *How Nations Make Peace* (New York: St. Martin's Press, 1999), 230–39; Roy Licklider, "Memory and Reconciliation After Civil Wars: The U.S. and Nigerian Cases," presentation for the Center for Historical Analysis at Rutgers University, February 14, 1995.

[35] Yaacov Vertzberger, *The World in Their Minds: Information Processing, Cognition, and Perception in Foreign Policy Decisionmaking* (Stanford, CA: Stanford University Press, 1990), 321; Jervis, *Perception and Misperception*, 145, 203, 331.

debilitating. As Richard Betts argues, failures to anticipate surprise attacks happen because "extrapolations from past behavior and incremental changes are poor bases for anticipating dramatic shifts."[36] Deborah Larson argues that "the 'heavy hand of the past' keeps states from recognizing potential gains from agreements."[37] The more one focuses on the history of a dispute and "who is to blame," the more one is likely to keep questioning the other side's motives. This is why peace negotiations often specifically prohibit participants from discussing the past, as was the case in the Oslo negotiations.

When the individual not only dwells on the past, but also has an archaic or totemic (as opposed to linear) notion of time, he or she associates the present enemy with all other enemies, even in the ancient past. The past is an immediate part of the present, whereas the future may be perceived in almost messianic terms, very distant and separated from the present by dramatic rupture.[38] Individuals who operate under this notion of time are less likely to expect and thus perceive change, and the image of a hostile enemy is magnified to mythic proportions. Dwelling on a history of conflict to which one is emotionally attached may present an obstacle to perceiving change in a former enemy, because present behavior is filtered through memories of past behavior. As Jervis suggests, too narrow a conception of the past and a lack of recognition of changed circumstances can lead to "the tyranny of the past upon the imagination."[39] Psychologists have shown that a past orientation leads an individual to be extremely conservative and resistant to change.[40]

Whereas a focus on the past inhibits change, a present or future orientation enables leaders to change their perception of the opponent and helps explain differing rates and mechanisms of change for leaders holding the same ideology. Leaders who focus primarily on the present do change; however, if they receive information about ongoing changes in small increments, they are slower to perceive overall shifts and to implement changes of their own. This builds on Jervis's notion that information arriving gradually is more likely to be dismissed or lead to only slight modifications. Focusing on immediate events makes any changes seem incremental and, thus, less important.[41] Focused on the present, a leader is more likely to react to events than to initiate change and will be more

---

[36] Richard K. Betts, *Surprise Attack: Lessons for Defense Planning* (Washington, DC: The Brookings Institution, 1982), 96.

[37] Deborah Welch Larson, *Anatomy of Mistrust: U.S.-Soviet Relations During the Cold War* (Ithaca, NY: Cornell University Press, 1997), 25.

[38] Myron J. Aronoff, "The Politics of Collective Identity: Contested Israeli Nationalisms" in *Terrorism, Identity and Legitimacy*, ed. Jeean Resefeld (Oxford: Routledge, 2010), 168–87; Aronoff, *Israeli Visions and Divisions: Cultural change and political conflict* (New Brunswick, NJ: Transaction Publishers, 1989), 137.

[39] Jervis, *Perception and Misperception*, 217.

[40] Boniwell and Zimbardo, "Balancing Time Perspective in Pursuit of Optimal Functioning," 169.

[41] Jervis, *Perception and Misperception*, 308–9.

influenced by particular dramatic events than by broader trends of change than is a leader who emphasizes the future.

Alternatively, leaders who dwell on the future and perceive the future to be different from the past are more likely to respond quickly to perceived changes and even initiate change, while particular dramatic events will be subsumed within a vision of broad future trends and, thus, be less influential. If a leader spends a greater percentage of time thinking of a future that is different from the past, that leader is more likely to view the opponent as changeable. Not only will that leader react incrementally to daily changes in the environment, but will more likely create dramatic changes in response to perceived future trends. At the same time, individual dramatic events may be downplayed in importance in favor of these perceived broad trends.[42]

2. Risk Propensity

Political psychologists such as Alex Mintz and Rose McDermott have found that the individual risk propensity of leaders influences their foreign policy decisions. Certain individuals may generally be risk averse, risk acceptant, or risk neutral. Of course this personality trait might not always be consistent regardless of the conditions or issue area, as prospect theory would suggest that everyone tends to be more risk averse with perceived losses than gains. There are many conditions that might exacerbate the perception of something as a loss, and different triggered emotions might enhance the framing of something as a loss.[43] Alexander George agrees that more analyses are needed of leaders' different types of motives, beliefs, and attitudes toward risk taking, in order to better assess the appropriate strategies for replacing or resocializing these leaders.[44] The evidence in this book suggests that risk-tolerant leaders may also be more likely to make peace, qualifying Daniel Byman and Kenneth M. Pollack's hypothesis that risk-tolerant leaders are more likely to cause wars.[45] The difference may lie in the degree of risk tolerance, as well as in the fact that different individuals may be prepared to take different kinds of

---

[42] This personal orientation toward the future is different from the "extended time horizon" contained in some ideologies discussed earlier. The personal orientation toward the future does not necessarily contain the sense that "time is on one's side" in regard to a conflict with an enemy – if anything, it seems to require constant vigilance lest one be overtaken or left behind by shifting trends. In the extended time horizon of an ideology, an individual could still see the past as persisting in the present, while believing that time is on one's side in the future.

[43] Alex Mintz and Karl DeRouen, Jr., *Understanding Foreign Policy Decision Making* (Cambridge: Cambridge University Press, 2010), 28; McDermott, *Political Psyhology in International Relations*, 217; McDermott, *Presidential Leadership: Illness, and Decision Making*, 194–95.

[44] Alexander George, "The Need for Influence Theory and Actor-Specific Behavioral Models of Adversaries," in *Know Thy Enemy: Profiles of Adversary Leaders and Their Strategic Cultures*, eds. Barry R. Schneider and Jerrold M. Post (Maxwell Air Force Base, AL: United States Air Force Counter Proliferation Center, November 2002).

[45] Byman and Pollack, "Let Us Now Praise Great Men," 137.

risks. Also, risk propensity may make leaders more likely to initiate peace negotiations and territorial withdrawal, as opposed to cautiously accept ongoing processes initiated by others.

3. Cognitive Flexibility

I analyze the influence of the *structure* (as opposed to content) of individual thinking on attitude change. A person's system is open to the extent that he or she can evaluate information based on its own merit, apart from preexisting beliefs or outside factors. The rigid mind is strongly committed to the mutual exclusivity of mental categories that are distinguished by an either/or logic that does not tolerate gray areas among these binary categories. Related to relative rigidity is cognitive complexity, which refers to the degree of differentiation in classifying ideas, people, and policies, with the least cognitively flexible not allowing for ambiguity and classifying ideas and people as good or bad.[46] A leader who is cognitively rigid is less likely than one who is more flexible to change attitudes because he or she will tend to dismiss information that challenges previous stereotypes. Relative cognitive flexibility is determined by looking at a broad range of a leader's attitudes on a variety of issues throughout his or her life.

Rigid minds that prefer the status quo will especially cling to it during times of change. Thus, contrary to neorealist expectations, rather than states adapting to changes in the balance of power, rigid leaders may become even more entrenched in their old policies. It takes fewer signals for a more cognitively flexible individual to trust the other side, and he or she has a greater tendency toward conciliation during negotiations. The more closed the cognitive system, the less likely are decision makers to pay attention to new information and change their attitudes.[47]

4. Emotional Intelligence

Emotional intelligence can enhance or impede a leader's ability to listen to advice and contrasting opinions, and can also contribute to the success or failure of peace negotiations. Emotional or interpersonal intelligence is the "ability to understand other people: what motivates them, how they work, how to work

[46] Milton Rokeach, *The Open and Closed Mind* (New York: Basic Books, 1960), 57; Eviatar Zerubavel, *The Fine Line: Making Distinctions in Everyday Life* (New York: The Free Press 1991), 34; Margaret G. Hermann, "Handbook for Assessing Personal Characteristics and Foreign Policy Orientations of Political Leaders," Mershon Center, Ohio State University, May 1987, 12.

[47] Zerubavel, *The Fine Line*, 55; David J. Finlay, Ole R. Holsti, and Richard R. Fagen, *Enemies in Politics* (Chicago: Rand McNally & Company, 1967), 23; Margaret G. Hermann and Thomas W. Milburn, eds., *A Psychological Examination of Political Leaders* (New York: The Free Press, 1977), 472; Larson, *Anatomy of Mistrust*, 32; Vertzberger, *The World in Their Minds*, 133, 134; Arie W. Kruglanski and Donna M. Webster, "Motivated Closing of the Mind: 'Seizing' and 'Freezing,'" *Psychological Review*, 103, no. 2 (1996): 265.

cooperatively with them," skills that many politicians have.[48] However, not all leaders share these skills, and some have difficulty responding appropriately to the moods and temperaments of others. They lack the ability to nurture relationships and keep friends and the ability to resolve conflicts. Leaders who are "emotionally tone deaf" lack empathy, or the ability to take another person's perspective; are insensitive to others' feelings; and are unable to listen to others.[49] In contrast, leaders who are emotionally intelligent are more likely to maintain relations even with those who have diverse views, and therefore be exposed to information challenging their beliefs. Leaders who are more likely to maintain loyal advisors who work effectively together also are more able to implement changed preferences since they have established relations across the political spectrum. Finally, leaders may be more likely to change perceptions after the adaptation of policies as self-perception theory would expect.

Advisors

The more a leader is exposed to the dominant influence of an advisor who suggests a different image of an enemy, the more likely the leader is to change. John Burke and Fred Greenstein suggest that one ask, "To what extent does he have qualities that lead him to receive a rich stream of advice and information?"[50] When a leader is dependent on a single channel of information, and that one source is slow to recognize changes on the part of the opponent or in the regional and international environment, that leader will be less likely to adapt to these changes. Decision-making groups will offer better advice to a leader when they disagree and this diversity of views will also be more likely to alter the leader's point of view.

THE INFLUENCE OF IDEOLOGY AND COGNITIVE STYLE ON PERCEPTIONS AND PREFERENCES

In order to judge the effects of the variables outlined here, I examine the changes – or lack thereof – in leaders' images of, and strategies for dealing with, the enemy. The enemy image fosters the "fundamental attribution error," or the belief that any good behavior on the part of an opponent was forced by situational factors, whereas the opponent's "bad" behavior springs from negative dispositions.[51] It

---

[48] Daniel Goleman, *Emotional Intelligence: Why It Can Matter More Than IQ* (New York: Bantam Books, 1995), 39.

[49] Ibid., 96, 284.

[50] John P. Burke and Fred I. Greenstein, with the collaboration of Larry Berman and Richard Immerman, *How Presidents Test Reality: Decision on Vietnam, 1954 and 1965* (New York: Russell Sage Foundation, 1989), 266.

[51] George, *Presidential Decisionmaking in Foreign Policy*, 59.

is especially important to examine how leaders break out of this cycle and revise their perceptions.

An alternative hypothesis to be tested is whether leaders may in fact undergo similar quantitative changes in perception, but that these quantitative shifts, measured from different starting points, may result in different qualitative effects on policy. As Jervis writes, "If we consider views on waging war as forming a continuum from strongly in favor to strongly against, the presence of uniform movement in one direction is as significant as the absence of shifts over the midpoint."[52] Rather than measuring change as a binary process – "change" or "no change" – this approach views change as a continuum, on which only a certain threshold would produce the promotion of actual policy changes. Whereas in the previous approach, all hard-liners begin from a similar position – for example, nonrecognition of the opponent – this approach postulates a continuum *within* this position.

An additional aspect of change to be examined is the differing rate of change for those who have the same qualitative shifts in attitude. It has been established that "images of other states as hostile or untrustworthy tend to lag behind changes in their behavior." These time lags are important in that they "themselves may lead to missed opportunities, simply because the other side responds too late."[53] The length of the time lag can be crucial to the success of cooperation, and it is therefore helpful to study why certain leaders have longer perceptual time lags than others.

The book also analyzes the different mechanisms for change for the different leaders. Some leaders may change due to specific events, others may perceive changing trends, and others learn from personal experience.[54] Larson suggests that "beliefs do not change incrementally in response to each new piece of evidence, but all at once as in a religious conversion."[55] These case studies investigate whether leaders changed their images of an enemy and policy preferences immediately after a dramatic event, whether the process was more gradual and a result of trial and error and incremental learning from events over a period of years, or whether learning occurred as a result of a perception of changing future trends.

The first section of each case study chapter examines the effect of ideology, cognitive style, and advisors on a leader's capacity to change enemy images; the latter sections explore how these perceptions produced concrete policy preferences and functioned in the context of particular events. The case studies illuminate to what extent enemy images influenced policy preferences, and to what extent changes in policy altered images. One of the hypotheses I will be

---

[52] Jervis, *Perception and Misperception in International Politics*, 289.
[53] Larson, *Anatomy of Mistrust*, 5, 247.
[54] Ole R. Holsti, "The Operational Code as an Approach to the Analysis of Belief Systems: Final Report to the National Science Foundation Grant NO. SOC75–15368," December 1977, 93–94.
[55] Larson, *Anatomy of Mistrust*, 14.

testing is that, the more strongly one identifies with an ideology, the more likely one's principles will guide policy preferences. On the other hand, self-perception theory would predict that leaders first set their foreign policy and only then develop the image and attitudes that could support such a policy.[56] The more a leader is motivated by public opinion, the greater the chances that policies could lag behind changes in image of an enemy.[57] Finally, international pressure may lead to policy revisions that were not the original preference of the leader. Based on the case studies analyzed here, I suggest that policies of reconciliation toward an enemy may be more dramatic when accompanied by a revised image of the enemy, as cooperation often involves building trust. However, international pressure may lead to revisions in policy preferences and, subsequently, in attitudes.

METHOD

I suggest that certain types of leaders are more likely to adjust to changing structures or help create these changes, but this is not the basis on which one can accurately predict a leader's actions. An actor's belief system, however, sets the boundaries within which a leader may perceive different types of situations and assess a variety of policies.[58] I broadly follow Alexander George's procedures of congruence and process tracing in order to show the explanatory power of beliefs. This entails establishing the consistency between beliefs and decisions, and tracing the steps by which beliefs influence the assessment of incoming information, the definition of the situation, and the evaluation of options: "If the characteristics of the decision are consistent with the actor's beliefs, there is at least a presumption that the beliefs may have played a causal role in this particular instance of decision making."[59]

This book uses qualitative content analysis, as opposed to quantitative analysis (which assumes that the more frequently a word is used, the more important it is to the speaker).[60] I agree with Alexander George that "one mention of a

[56] Robert Jervis, "Political Decision Making: Recent Contributions," *Political Psychology* 2 (1980): 95; Daryl Bem, "Self-Perception Theory," in *Cognitive Theories in Social Psychology*, ed. L. Berkowitz (San Francisco, CA: Academic Press, 1978), 228; Jack L. Snyder, *Myths of Empire: Domestic Politics and International Ambition* (College Station, TX: Texas A&M University Press, 2005), 2. According to Snyder, leaders may come to believe the rationalizations for their policies.

[57] Margaret G. Hermann, "Leaders, Leadership, and Flexibility: Influences on Heads of Government of Negotiators and Mediators," *ANNALS, AAPSS* 542 (November 1995), 152; Holsti, "The Operational Code," 78; Barbara Farnham, "Political Cognition and Decision-Making," *Political Psychology* 2, no. 1 (1990): 94.

[58] George, The *"Operational Code,"* 15–16.

[59] Alexander George, (1979). The Causal Nexus between Cognitive Beliefs and Decision Making Behavior: The "Operational Code," in *Psychological Models in International Politics*, ed. L. Falkowski (Boulder, CO: Westview Press, 1979) 105–6.

[60] Hermann, "Handbook for Assessing Personal Characteristics and Foreign Policy Orientations of Political Leaders," 1.

topic or characteristic may be as important as 25; it all depends on its salience to the political leader," and that "some characteristics can only be inferred from what is spoken or written; there is no explicit mention of them to count."[61] Analyzing a leader at a distance through coding speeches might be necessary in a less transparent society where one does not have access to leaders, their family members, and advisors, as well as to archives – none of which is the case with the Israeli leaders I treat here.

Since Israel is a transparent society, interviews and archival research were possible. In order to assess leaders' degree of commitment to their ideology, cognitive style, and perceptions of the Palestinians, I rely on more spontaneous communications by the leaders in interviews and meetings, as opposed to prepared speeches, as the latter are less likely to reveal "genuine" attitudes.[62] Thus, I rely on approximately eighty of my own interviews, as well as television and newspaper interviews, minutes from party central committee meetings, and other forums for more spontaneous dialogue in which there was less time for strategic preparation or input from advisors and speechwriters. I have conducted these interviews over sixteen years, from 1997 to 2013, and have interviewed many leaders and advisors (e.g., Shimon Peres and Yossi Beilin) as often as three times during different intervals. I could therefore determine whether and how they have adapted their positions and or shown sustained ideological and personality characteristics. Some of the interviews have been extensive, as in full-day interviews of Yitzhak Rabin's sister, and a three-hour interview of Ehud Barak. I also draw from memoirs, biographies, and secondary academic literature.

I assess how the same events were perceived differently by each leader, how these perceptions shaped enemy images, and whether attitudes and policies were revised as a consequence of these events. I take note of their reactions to or changes after the following events: Sadat's visit to Jerusalem; the first intifada, which began in 1987 and gradually declined by 1993; the 1988 PLO Proclamation; the end of the Cold War; the Gulf War in 1991; the cycle of violence during the second intifada from 2000 to 2005; the Saudi 2002 Peace Plan; reactions to the ongoing uprisings in the Middle East that began in December 2010; and the Palestinian bid for statehood at the United Nations in September 2011 and November 2012. Changes in policy preferences are measured along the following categories: willingness to make territorial concessions and the depth of those concessions; advocating a Jordanian solution for the Palestinian people; advocating functional autonomy for the Palestinians; advocating autonomy for the Palestinians under the leadership of non-PLO leaders; and negotiating with the PLO over the future of the territories, advocating a

[61] Alexander George, "Quantitative and Qualitative Approaches to Content Analysis," in *Trends in Content Analysis*, ed. I. deS. Pool (Urbana, IL: University of Illinois Press, 1959), 7–32.
[62] Hermann and Milburn, *A Psychological Examination of Political Leaders*, 460; Greenstein, "The Impact of Personality on Politics," 637.

Palestinian state and a willingness to divide and share Jerusalem in a peace agreement. The book will start with the case study of Yitzhak Shamir, who remained a hard-liner, and end with Shimon Peres, who underwent the most dramatic and consistent changes, analyzing the myriad reasons for the degrees of change that the prime ministers have experienced. The conclusion will analyze the broader question of conversion on the part of hard-liners.

2

Yitzhak Shamir: Once a Hawk, Always a Hawk

The sea is the same sea and the Arabs are the same Arabs.[1]
— Yitzhak Shamir, October 27, 2000

Yitzhak Shamir maintained a hostile image of the Palestinians throughout his long life, thinking until his death at age ninety-six in July 2012 that "the Arabs" want to conquer Israel and throw the Jews into the sea. Unlike Yitzhak Rabin, Shimon Peres, and Ehud Barak, who tried to obtain peace with the Palestinians, Shamir remained a hawk unwilling to compromise any of the Greater Land of Israel for peace or to negotiate with the Palestinian Authority directly, and he vehemently opposed a Palestinian state. Shamir strongly criticized Benjamin Netanyahu's and Ariel Sharon's compromises.

Shamir was speaker of the Knesset from 1977 to 1980, foreign minister from 1980 to 1983 and from 1984 to 1986, and prime minister from 1983 to 1984 and from 1986 to 1992. In these positions, he significantly shaped Israel's policies toward the Palestinians and continued to have influence within the Likud Party after leaving office.

Shamir did not soften his image of, or positions toward, the PLO because he was a self-described ideologue – one for whom ideology is the sole basis for policymaking and evaluation and who adheres to his ideology dogmatically.[2] He, like many hard-liners, perceived the enemy in monolithic terms and considered concessions to be a sign of weakness. Shamir based his ideology on the Revisionist Zionism founded by Vladimir Jabotinsky in the 1920s and 1930s, but he was even more extreme than Jabotinsky. Revisionism contains certain basic assumptions: time is on Israel's side in regard to its conflict with the

---

[1] Deborah Sontag, "Suicide Attack in Gaza Strip Increases Tension in Mideast," *The New York Times*, October 27, 2000, A6.

[2] Arye Naor, "Greater Israel in Likud Governments: Begin, Shamir, and Netanyahu," (presented at the 15th Annual Meeting of the Association for Israel Studies, Washington, D.C., May 1999, 2).

Palestinians; Israel has a right to the Greater Land of Israel (including the West Bank); Israel faces a permanently hostile world; security can be provided without peace with the Palestinians; and peace with the Palestinians does not require territorial compromise. Therefore, Shamir refused direct negotiations with the PLO, rejected territorial compromise, and supported building Jewish settlements on the West Bank.

Shamir's ideological barriers to recognizing and making concessions to the PLO were strengthened by his preoccupation with past conflict – not only with the Palestinians, but also with centuries of conflict with other enemies. Having personally experienced violent conflict from an early age, Shamir's history directly informed his present. Focusing on such an emotionally charged history makes it more difficult to see shifts in position by a former enemy, because the perception of present behavior is filtered through memories of past behavior.

Shamir remained staunchly hard-line not only because he was an ideologue who was immersed in the past, but also because of his cognitive rigidity. Shamir disparaged opposing views and categorized people in stark black-and-white terms. The intifada (Palestinian uprising) and the Gulf War only strengthened Shamir's portrayal of Palestinians as hostile. Although Shamir remained a hard-liner, he could not stand completely still in the face of change. International pressure led to tactical changes that had broader, unintended consequences.

DETERMINANTS OF CONVERSION

Ideology

Shamir was a self-described ideologue who openly romanticized the life of uncompromising commitment to a cause: "From ideology," he said, "there are no retreats."[3] Born in Poland in 1915, Shamir became actively involved in Zionist politics at the age of fourteen when he joined the Betar Zionist Youth. From this group, he received a paramilitary education with all the symbols and ceremonies of military life because Jabotinsky insisted that countries were won by blood and iron. In 1935, the Revisionists seceded from the World Zionist Organization to protest that organization's refusal to declare a Jewish state its immediate aim and formed the New Zionist Organization, which elected Jabotinsky as its president.

Shamir left Poland for Palestine in 1935 at age twenty. In 1937, Shamir joined the Irgun Zvai Leumi (IZL, Hebrew for the National Military Organization). The IZL, a pre-state defense organization, split from Haganah in 1931 in opposition to Haganah's policy of self-restraint, minimizing offensive military operations, and insisting that no innocent life be sacrificed. The Irgun was

---

[3] Interview with Hemi Shelev, Israeli journalist for the newspaper *Maariv*, May 24, 1998, Jerusalem; Haim Misgav, *Sichot Im Yitzhak Shamir* [Conversations with Yitzhak Shamir] (Tel Aviv: Sifriat Poalim Publishing House, Ltd., 1997), 164.

commanded by Jabotinsky and was described by Shamir as "a combat formation made up of volunteers bound by a nationalistic and militant idealism."[4]

The development of Shamir's career was likewise determined by ideological disputes. He later joined and then helped lead the even more extreme Lochemei Herut l'Israel (Israel Freedom Fighters) or Lehi, also pejoratively known as "the Stern Gang," which split off from the Irgun in order to engage in an underground war against the British in Palestine. By joining Lehi, Shamir in effect rejected the authority of the democratically elected, Labor-dominated institutions. Lehi members believed that both Britain and Germany were the prime enemies. An internal Lehi document reads, "There will yet arise neither one Hitler nor two, but rather a large number of Hitlers, or executioners. If we desire to solve thoroughly the question of anti-Semitism, we must uproot it. And its root is none other than that which is ruling our beloved land, our homeland."[5]

Shamir believed that ideological differences were worth breaking ties with former allies and mentors. Lehi was more extreme than the Irgun in its belief in the centrality of the Greater Land of Israel as the future Jewish state, and in the means justified for bringing about that state. It criticized Israel's army, the Israel Defense Force, for only defending against attack, arguing instead that the organization should liberate the whole of Israel. Shamir was not only enamored by the particular Lehi ideology, but also writes that "in conspiratorial life ... everything – rules, regulations, proscriptions, discipline – is totally directed towards serving the cause" and that when Lehi ceased to exist after independence, he needed an "emotional and psychological substitute for the intensity to which we had all been addicted for so long ... It was the whole-heartedness and the completeness of commitment to an ideal for which I hankered."[6]

A rare exception to Shamir's uncompromising stance toward ideology was his reluctant acceptance of a proposal by Zionist leaders in 1945 that 100,000 Jews would be allowed to immigrate to Palestine, and in return, the underground organizations would end their battle with the British government. Shamir agreed, believing that the British would never accept the proposal (which they did not). He did not want Lehi to be accused of having stopped 100,000 Jews from entering Israel. Shamir was willing to contemplate compromising his ideology only when he thought that the other side would balk, and thus he would not need to compromise. This tendency is important in assessing Shamir's "pseudo-compromises" with the Palestinians in the Madrid conference.[7]

---

[4] Yitzhak Shamir, *Summing Up: An Autobiography* (New York: Little, Brown, 1994), 19. See also Rael Jean Isaac, *Party and Politics in Israel: Three Visions of a Jewish State* (New York: Longman, 1981), 36–37, 41.

[5] Isaac, *Party and Politics in Israel*, 43; Joseph Heller, *The Stern Gang: Ideology, Politics and Terror, 1940–1949* (London: Frank Cass, 1995), 5, 108, 116–17, 137.

[6] Heller, *The Stern Gang*, 115; Israel Eldad, *The Jewish Revolution: Jewish Statehood* (New York: Shengold Publishers, 1971), 143; Shamir, *Summing Up*, 36, 49, 76.

[7] Shamir, *Summing Up*, 56–58. Shamir's family was murdered in Europe, and not to go along with this deal would have given Shamir indirect responsibility for 100,000 deaths.

In modern Israel, the Likud Party is the inheritor of the basic philosophies of the Irgun. The Irgun evolved into the Herut ("Freedom") Party, led by Menachem Begin after the establishment of Israel. Herut adopted the Irgun emblem – a hand holding a rifle on the background of a map of Palestine, which stretched over both banks of the Jordan River. Herut became the Gahal Party after a merger with the Liberal Party and then the Likud Party in 1973 as a result of a merger with three small nationalist splinter groups. Shamir joined Herut in 1970 because it supported the idea of an Israel "from the Nile to the Euphrates" and because Begin, whom Shamir had known during his student days in Poland, led the party. Shamir claimed, "Jabotinsky's name and spirit are kept alive mostly through the Likud Party, which, to a significant degree, represents and articulates his basic philosophy and is, so to speak, executor of his political testament." He argued, "of all the Zionist leaders, only Jabotinsky … succeeded in leaving behind him so well-defined a political entity … and so clear-cut an ideology."[8]

Shamir gave up his position as prime minister rather than compromise Likud ideology – testifying to the exceptionally strong ties Shamir felt to that ideology. Rather than stop settlements on the West Bank, Shamir gave up loan guarantees from the United States, despite public opinion polls showing that the majority of Israelis were willing to halt settlements and concede land for peace. The withdrawal of loan guarantees contributed to the defeat of the Shamir government in June 1992. Shamir refused to concede an inch of the Greater Land of Israel.[9] Shamir said, "I am not willing to give up my principles for the power to govern …. The main principle should be that Eretz Israel is the land of the Jewish people. That's it. From here I can't move."[10]

Shamir also lost popular support because of his ideologically motivated rejection of an American peace plan. He dismissed Shimon Peres as finance minister despite the plan's support by a majority of Likud ministers and Labor counterparts. Labor then forced a vote of no confidence in the Knesset and the government fell. Shamir prided himself on adhering to his ideology and criticized Netanyahu for abandoning his ideology in order to save his political future by signing the Wye Agreement.[11] In contrast, Shamir was willing to concede power rather than compromise.

---

[8] Shamir, *Summing Up*, 9; Colin Shindler, *Israel, Likud and the Zionist Dream: Power, Politics and Ideology from Begin to Netanyahu* (New York: I. B. Tauris, 1995), 174–86.

[9] Glenn Frankel, *Beyond the Promised Land: Jews and Arabs on the Hard Road to a New Israel* (New York: Simon and Schuster, 1996), 221; Galia Golan, "Arab-Israeli Peace Negotiations: An Israeli View," in *The Arab-Israeli Search for Peace*, ed. Steven L. Spiegel (Boulder, CO: Lynne Rienner, 1992), 42–44; James A. Baker, *The Politics of Diplomacy: Revolution, War and Peace 1989–1992* (New York: G. P. Putnam's Sons, 1995), 541; interview with Hemi Shelev, May 24, 1998, Jerusalem; Shamir, *Summing Up*, 171.

[10] Interview with Yitzhak Shamir, July 5, 1998, Tel Aviv.

[11] Deborah Sontag, "Netanyahu Stakes Out Israel's Political Center," *The New York Times*, October 24, 1998, A9.

The ideology of the Israeli prime ministers analyzed here has four central components that influence the likelihood of its adherents changing their perceptions of the Palestinians.

1. *Is Time on Israel's Side?*
Likud ideology emphasizes that "time is on our side" with respect to Israel's conflict with the Palestinians. Israel Eldad suggests that if adherents truly believe in their ideals, their vision would be realized in the face of historical probability. As Arye Naor points out, Likud ideology incorporated strong elements of political theology in which "Greater Israel was perceived as a supra-historical entity embodying eternity."[12] Raised to such mythic levels, the messianic vision of Greater Israel promoted by Likud ideology achieved a status beyond time and above historical contingency.

This infinite time horizon in turn radically alters the frame within which one judges the success or failure of a particular policy. Shamir did not judge policy as having failed if it did not yet appear to be successful. Since he perceived time to be working in Israel's favor, the more time that went by, the more Israel could expand its control of the territories. From this perspective, there is no urgency to engage in negotiations with an enemy because in time this adversary would be defeated. Shamir believed that the PLO would have been defeated in 1981 had it not been for the cease-fire on the Israeli-Lebanese border.[13]

This aspect of Likud ideology shaped Shamir's perceptions throughout his life. He often portrayed the opposing political party as being short-sighted, as he did the Yishuv policy of Havlagah. Much later, Shamir wrote that he told U.S. Secretary of State George Shultz to go slowly with his peace initiatives and that Shultz and Peres were impatient for peace. In contrast, Shamir did not know if peace was possible: "The Americans, when they see a problem, they think the solution should come in a week. They don't have time.... In the Middle East we have time.... If we stand by our beliefs ... [t]he Arabs might understand that we will never accept their view." Shamir argued that in 1992 the PLO would have broken apart in six months. When Peres replied that the country's size was not the most significant issue since Hamas used suicide bombers, Shamir responded that Israel could have finished off Hamas.[14]

Shamir was an expert at delay tactics. He believed that Israel's resolve would prove to be stronger in the long term. This belief in the eventual defeat of the enemy was coupled with the belief that with time, Israel could alter the demographics in the West Bank through increased settlement of 5 million Jews who would immigrate to Israel. Shamir believed that what was thought improbable in the past had been realized. He argued that just a small number of people were

---

[12] Naor, "Greater Israel in Likud Governments," 14, 26.

[13] Interview with Yitzhak Shamir, July 5, 1998, Tel Aviv.

[14] Ibid.; Shamir, *Summing Up*, 18, 168, 177; interview with Yitzhak Shamir, Israeli Broadcasting Authority, Channel One, program entitled "Popolitika," December 7, 1997.

able to fight the British Empire. Also, although in 1967 nobody thought tens of thousands of Russians would immigrate to Israel, within twelve years, 150,000 Russians came. Shamir was proud of his faith and efforts that proved to be successful.[15]

2. Ideological Goals: General and Adaptable, or Specific and Rigid?

The Greater Land of Israel is central to Likud ideology and has directly influenced Shamir's refusal to concede land to the Palestinians. Jabotinsky was adamant that Israel keep Judea and Samaria (the West Bank), and the Revisionists opposed partitioning the land in 1948. Jabotinsky's New Zionist Organization offered membership to anyone who would commit to the statement "My aim is a Jewish state on both sides of the Jordan" and reject the validity of the Churchill White Paper of 1922, which removed Transjordan from the provisions of the Mandate relating to the Jewish National Home.[16] Shamir interpreted Zionism to mean a return to the entire Greater Land of Israel and called those who did not share this goal "semi-Zionists." Lehi's ideology centered on a Land of Israel reaching from the River Euphrates to the River Nile, the ancient Kingdom of David at its height, whereas the Revisionist Party "settled" for the territory of the twelve tribes, which was largely included in the original British Mandate for Palestine. According to Herut's founding document, "The partition statelet will give no freedom, neither to the few in it or the many who will be compelled to remain outside. If we do not expand we will be thrown into the sea, not right away but in the course of time."[17]

A cardinal Likud principle is that Judea and Samaria remain under Israeli control with unlimited right of Jewish settlement. Shamir wrote that in 1948 much of the Land of Israel had been severed from the Jewish State and "I have done all I could, in various ways, in the intervening years to help rectify this distortion to which I can never be reconciled ... Nothing has ever mattered to me more, nor matters more now, than the unity of the people of Israel and the wholeness of their Land."[18]

Prime Minister Menachem Begin was able to concede the Sinai to Egypt as it was not part of historical Judea and Samaria, which he pledged to never cede to a Palestinian state.[19] Begin did not perceive the withdrawal from Sinai to be the precedent for future withdrawals, but rather as a means to secure Israeli control

---

[15] Dan Margalit, "Interview with Yitzhak Shamir" (Hebrew), *Ma'ariv*, September 21, 1979; Shamir, *Summing Up*, 30, 35, 83.

[16] Joseph B. Schechtman and Yehuda Benari, *History of the Revisionist Movement, 1925–30* (Tel Aviv: Hadar Publishing House Ltd., 1970), 281; Isaac, *Party and Politics in Israel*, 36, 44.

[17] Eldad, *The Jewish Revolution*, 106–7, 114; Isaac, *Party and Politics in Israel*, 136.

[18] Shamir, *Summing Up*, 26, 60.

[19] Ilan Peleg, "The Israeli Right," in *Contemporary Israel: Domestic Politics, Foreign Policy, and Security Challenges*, ed. R. O. Freedman (Boulder, CO: Westview Press, 2009), 27.

over the West Bank.[20] Begin defined the "eternal patrimony of our ancestors" as "Jerusalem, Hebron, Bethlehem, Judea [and] Shechem [Nablus]" in the West Bank and declared to a group of Jewish settlers in 1981 "I, Menachem, the son of Ze'ev and Hasia Begin, do solemnly swear that as long as I serve the nation as Prime Minister we will not leave any part of Judea, Samaria [or] the Gaza Strip."[21]

3. Is the World With Us or Against Us?

Shamir's personal experiences and ideology reinforced each other in influencing him to perceive the world as permanently hostile. With this perception came a tendency to lump enemies together rather than to differentiate among them. Shamir's perception of a hostile world made him more resistant to U.S. pressure and world criticism because he attributed anti-Israel motives to explain the criticism of Israeli policies by foreign leaders.

Central to the Likud ideology is the view that the world is permanently hostile to Jews. Shamir did try to cultivate relations with other countries, and sent his deputy director of the Mossad, Efraim Halevy, to talk to the leaders of Morocco, Oman, Qatar, and Algeria.[22] However, Likud supporters have often turned the biblical prophecy of Balaam – "Lo, it is a people that shall dwell alone and shall not be reckoned among the nations" (Num. 23:9) – from a curse into a blessing. Former Prime Minister Menachem Begin, its most articulate spokesman, wrote a letter on August 2, 1982, to President Ronald Reagan, in which he compared Beirut to Berlin and Yasser Arafat to Hitler. Eldad spoke of the wickedness of the Gentiles, especially the British and the Arabs in obstructing the creation of Israel before the Holocaust. Shamir recalled that the members of Lehi were "well aware that our enemies vastly outnumbered our friends"; even in 1979 Shamir suspected that "the whole world is against us."[23] When asked by a reporter in 1979 whether he still perceived anti-Semitism in the West in the same manner as it existed in Poland in the 1930s, he responded that Jews in France believe that anti-Semitism there is permanent and that he believes that support for the Palestinians in France reflects anti-Semitism.[24]

---

[20] Avi Shlaim, "The Likud in Power: The Historiography of Revisionist Zionism," *Israel Studies* 1, no. 2 (Fall 1996), 283.

[21] As Quoted in Jonathan Rynhold and Dov Waxman, "Ideological Change and Israel's Disengagement from Gaza," *Political Science Quarterly* (Spring 2008), 15.

[22] Interview with Efraim Halevy, August 6, 2013, Ramat Aviv, Israel. Halevy was deputy director of the Mossad when Shamir was prime minister. He worked for the Mossad for forty years, eventually becoming its director 1998–2002.

[23] Ilan Peleg, "Israeli Foreign Policy Under Right-Wing Governments: A Constructivist Interpretation," *Israel Studies Forum* 19, no. 3, 111; Myron J. Aronoff, *Israeli Visions and Divisions: Cultural Change and Political Conflict* (New Brunswick, NJ: Transaction Publishers, 1989), 135–36; Eldad, *The Jewish Revolution*, 149; Shamir, *Summing Up*, 38.

[24] Dan Margalit, "Interview with Yitzhak Shamir," *Ma'ariv*, September 21, 1979.

Lehi ideology also tended to minimize differences among the various threats that faced Jews. For instance, its members did not differentiate between the British and the Germans. Shamir also perceived all Arabs as wanting to push Israel into the sea and did not differentiate among them. When asked who he thought was the most threatening enemy, Shamir replied that it is not important for him to analyze who poses the greatest threat as he views them as all threatening.[25] The perceived threat of the Palestinians acquiring large parts of the Greater Land of Israel was close in gravity to the threats emanating from Iran and Iraq. Shamir also perceived the PLO and Hamas to be working hand in hand.

Shamir's personal experiences were interwoven with Revisionist Zionism's depiction of a hostile world. When attending university in Warsaw in 1932, Shamir faced gangs of anti-Semitic youths and was forced to carry a knife. Shamir writes that he and Menachem Begin had "our adult lives, and thus many of our attitudes, permanently affected by the Holocaust ... in Poland ... among the millions who were abandoned, tormented and slaughtered was my entire family. I cannot forget and will not forgive."[26] Shamir's whole being was focused on the need to be rid of the British in Palestine since they barred European Jews from entering Palestine. Shamir's belief that the world did not care about the Jews was substantiated when in the summer of 1938, President Roosevelt called together the representatives of thirty governments to find arrangement for Jewish refugees, but only the Dominican Republic offered to take any in.[27]

To Shamir, his experiences later in life confirmed his perception of a hostile world. He argued that the European media hated Israel. In 1979, Shamir criticized European leaders for thinking that they could moderate the PLO by holding talks with its officials and argued that there was no chance that the PLO would change its desire to annihilate Israel. He also claimed that Western opposition to Israel's position regarding its borders not only predated 1968, but also predated the establishment of Israel. Of his time as foreign minister, he writes, "almost wherever I went, the Arab states, their Third World friends and an unsavory collection of their anti-Semitic helpers seemed to have been there before me, 'preparing' the ground" and declared that Lord Carrington, Britain's foreign minister, "belongs to that British school of thought we fought against [during the Mandate period]."[28] In 1997, he still argued that there is no place in the world that does not have the seeds of anti-Semitism that can grow and, under

---

[25] Shindler, *Israel, Likud and the Zionist Dream*, 175; interview with Yitzhak Shamir, July 5, 1998, Tel Aviv.

[26] Shamir, *Summing Up*, 5, 7, 86.

[27] Ibid., 28–29; Shlaim, "The Likud in Power," 286.

[28] Dov Goldstein, "Raayon Hashavooah Eem Yitzhak Shamir" [The Week's Interview with Yitzhak Shamir], *Ma'ariv*, December 21, 1979; Hagi Eshed, "Hemonot Shel Yitzhak Shamir" [The Faith of Yitzhak Shamir], *Davar*, December 21, 1979; Shamir, *Summing Up*, 112, 116; Leon Hadar, "Quiet Diplomacy," *The Jerusalem Post*, October 2, 1981.

certain conditions, lead to catastrophe. In 1998, he stated that Israel had more enemies than friends.[29]

Shamir's belief that Israel faced an inherently hostile world led him to discount world opinion and even American pressure. Shamir was more skeptical of American intentions than were Labor leaders, even calling U.S. Secretary of State James Baker a new "hangman" for the Jewish people. Shamir backed the striking of the Iraqi nuclear installation, since "not for the first time nor the last, it was clear that it would be up to us to remove the threat since no one else was going to do it for us ... no punishment meted out to Israel would be comparable to the peril awaiting us if we let world opinion overrule our sense of self-preservation."[30]

Baker was angered by Shamir's lack of sensitivity to U.S. concerns. Shamir refused to compromise with the Palestinians, even if it meant the collapse of his government and a sharper conflict with the United States. According to Baker, "In what we took as a calculated slap at the United States, the acting Shamir government had kept building settlements ... I could scarcely control my anger with Shamir and his colleagues." Having "been burned repeatedly by Shamir," he thought that peace negotiations required a new Israeli prime minister.[31]

Since Shamir believed that many people did not support Israel's true interests and were also probably anti-Semitic, he argued that granting concessions would only lead to demands for more. He argued that Netanyahu mistakenly went along with the Oslo Accords, but that this "didn't help him at all. No one is for him. He is in conflict with the U.S., with Europe, with the Arabs of course, and with part of the Jews."[32] Shamir was suspicious of other countries' motives and interests and therefore was less willing to bend to their pressure.

4. How Much Will Peace Contribute to Security? Does Peace Require Territorial Compromise?

Integrated with the beliefs that time is on Israel's side, that it faces a hostile world, and that the desire to keep the West Bank is an article of faith, is the notion that peace with the Palestinians as well as Israel's security do not require territorial compromise. Likud ideology has traditionally called for an iron wall of military defense that would eventually force the Arabs to accept Israel's existence in the Greater Land of Israel. Peace was seen as a long–term prospect, entailing Palestinian acquiescence to Israeli rule, with limited autonomous rights. Jabotinsky believed that "the only way to reach an agreement [with the Arabs] is an Iron Wall – that is to say, strength and security in Eretz-Israel

---

[29] Misgav, *Conversations with Yitzhak Shamir*, 57; interview with Yitzhak Shamir, July 5, 1998, Tel Aviv.

[30] Shlaim, "The Likud in Power," 290; Moshe Arens, *Broken Covenant* (New York, Simon and Schuster, 1995), 54, 60; Dov Goldstein's interview with Yitzhak Shamir, *Ma'ariv*, January 2, 1979; Shamir, *Summing Up*, 125.

[31] Baker, *The Politics of Diplomacy*, 25, 123–32.

[32] Interview with Yitzhak Shamir, July 5, 1998, Tel Aviv.

whereby no Arab influence will be able to undermine its foundations."[33] Israel
would have to continually protect this iron wall from repeated attacks until its
military victories would prove that Israel could not be eliminated. Although
Jabotinsky paid lip service to the idea that at that point, Israel would "negotiate"
with the Palestinians, his understanding of "negotiation" was quite narrow,
encompassing ideas of limited political autonomy within the Israeli polity. It did
not entail compromise on an independent Palestinian state in any part of Greater
Israel and did not see a point of trying to reach an agreement until the
Palestinians were willing to recognize Israeli sovereignty in the whole of the
land.[34] This idea provided a framework in which peace was not urgent, and a
relatively high degree of security could be provided without peace.

In response to Labor peace initiatives, Shamir wrote that "peace" will lead
only to greater demands for all of the land, including Jerusalem. When asked
whether Israel could exist if it were a little smaller because it is so strong, Shamir
responded:

> No. No … We won't be able to sustain ourselves, won't be able to bring more Jews
> here.… The power of a nation is not just the army. It is also population. If there are
> more Jews there will be more in the army. I think that [the] 5 million Jews we have
> now is not enough … we need at least 10 million. We can't accept the immigration
> of millions of Jews if we give up parts of our territory.[35]

Even if Shamir perceived Israel as very strong, he would have opposed compromise because he believed that security could be achieved through military means
alone.

Cognitive Style

1. Time Orientation
In addition to the ideological obstacles to revising his image of the PLO or
making territorial concessions to it, Shamir's focus on a conflictual past also
prevented any such reevaluation. Because his view of Jewish history was one of
perennial persecution, and he believed that the world would continue to be
hostile to Israel, he did not expect a former enemy to give up aspiring to destroy
Israel. Shamir criticized the text of the Camp David Accords as "written in a style
which reveals nothing of the past, as though the conflicts referred to were equally
the fault of all sides and recent."[36] In defending his opposition to recognizing or
negotiating with Arafat, Shamir stated, "We have to learn a lesson from our
ancient history dating back to the period before the destruction of the Second

[33] Mordechai Sarig, *The Political and Social Philosophy of Ze'ev Jabotinsky: Selected Writings*
(London: Vallentine Mitchell, 1998), 102, 105.
[34] Ian Lustick, "To Build and To Be Built By: Israel and the Hidden Logic of the Iron Wall," *Israel
Studies* 1, no. 1 (Spring 1996), 196–223.
[35] Interview with Yitzhak Shamir, July 5, 1998, Tel Aviv; Shamir, *Summing Up*, 168.
[36] Shamir, *Summing Up*, 104.

Temple in the days of Simon when Hasmoneans tried to assist the Romans against the Greek regime in our land. In the end, it was the Romans who destroyed the Jewish State."[37] Shamir proudly wrote that Betar, his youth movement, was named after the last stronghold of Jewish resistance against the Romans during the three-year revolt led by Shimon Bar Kochba, which ended in AD 135 with the murder and the expulsion of the surviving Jews from Judea. When Shamir was a prisoner of the British, he said, "I thought often, too, of the deadly conflicts that had flared among the Jews in the years preceding the fall of Jerusalem to the Romans."[38]

Shamir often referred to a past of persecution and rejection that repeated itself. In 1979, when visiting Australia, Shamir was asked about the Palestinians and he shifted the conversation to Poland in the 1930s. Although many Israelis perceive their history as one of persecution, for Shamir it also represented his personal experiences; therefore, it was not only an intellectual understanding, but also a deeply emotional one. At Shamir's funeral, Benjamin Netanyahu recalled that on Holocaust Remembrance days Shamir would always talk about his parents and siblings who had been murdered by the Nazis.[39] Shamir wrote,

> I had long followed, with horror and pain, the communist attempt to finish off what the Tsars had begun. . . . The persecution of Jews, the accusations and mock trials that led to execution of hundreds of thousands, the Government-directed anti-Jewish campaigns that let hooligans loose to pillage, desecrate, torture and kill, the murder of Jewish leaders, writers, doctors and poets sent to the their deaths on absurd charges or imprisoned and subjected to brutality, were not items I merely read in the paper and sighed over. They were wounds within me.[40]

For Shamir, his past was a living part of his present, much more so than for Rabin, Barak, and Peres. He often argued that others pay too little attention to history. When he visited Germany as foreign minister and went to Dachau, he "cried, pierced by sorrow for the perished multitudes – and my family – feeling for a moment that the weight of the memories was almost too much to bear. But the brief ceremony over, the inadequate acknowledgment to history made, we went on to Bonn." For Chancellor Helmut Kohl, he continues, "the Holocaust is history, long over, an enormity that happened when he and his generation were young or not yet born and thus not guilty, not to be blamed, not emotionally involved."[41]

Shamir's focus on the past directly shaped his reluctance to engage in peace negotiations. He admitted that part of the reason that he did not like the

---

[37] Yitzhak Shamir, "Israel and the Middle East Today," *The Brown Journal of World Affairs* 3, no. 2 (Summer/Fall 1996), 69.

[38] Shamir, *Summing Up*, 9, 56.

[39] Greer Fay Cashman, "Parting from Shamir," *The Jerusalem Post*, July 6–12, 2012.

[40] Shamir, *Summing Up*, 83, 69; Margalit, "Interview with Yitzhak Shamir."

[41] Shamir, *Summing Up*, 114.

peace-making processes of the 1980s and the 1990s, was that the fiasco of 1939 echoed in his mind. Shamir thought that the Chamberlain government accomplished nothing in inviting Jewish and Arab leaders to a conference in London. He often emphasized the cases in history in which countries used "the slogan of peace as a deliberate lie, a camouflage for the true objective which was conquest and occupation," in order to argue that the Arabs are not to be trusted. Shamir argued that Hitler claimed he wanted peace after he had conquered territory; Chamberlain had announced "peace in our time" before World War II; and Lenin said he wanted peace, but his objective was the conquest of land.[42]

Shamir argued that "history proves many times over" that concessions do not produce a friendlier stance toward Israel. Whereas the Americans thought that Israel's returning Taba (a border town) to Egypt would make the Egyptians friendlier, according to Shamir the return of Taba changed nothing and "the absence of cultural exchanges, the minimal trade relations, the often totally unbridled attacks made against Israel, and me, in the Egyptian press – along with blatantly anti-Semitic caricatures – the virtual quarantine imposed on Israel's Ambassador, all went on Taba or not."[43] Drawing upon these perceived lessons, Shamir saw no benefit in making concessions to the Palestinians.

Because Shamir was immersed in the past, and thought that not much had changed, he was also less likely to perceive changes in the regional environment, much less in an opponent. In 1992, Shamir addressed a memorial meeting of the Fighters for the Freedom of Israel. His theme was that nothing had changed since the War of Independence: "We need to accept that war is inescapable, because, without this, the life of the individual has no purpose and the nation has no chance of survival."[44] Although one could argue that Israel has gained much strength and some of its neighbors have become more moderate and accepting of Israel over time, Shamir emphasized the continuing centrality of war.

2. *Risk Propensity*

Shamir was willing to take personal risks, but was risk averse when it came to the possibility of losing any part of Greater Israel under Israeli control. He risked his leadership position by refusing to freeze settlements on the West Bank, and he said that he was willing to die for the Greater Land of Israel.[45] He also took the risk of leaving Poland at age twenty in 1935 to go to Palestine to create the state of Israel. This reveals, perhaps, the complexity of personality and the willingness to take risks: issues that are core ideological values might generate risk-taking at opposite ends of the spectrum – a willingness to take great risks to secure that value, and an extreme aversion to taking risks that would then threaten that value.

[42] Ibid., 27; Shamir, "Israel and the Middle East Today," 66.
[43] Shamir, *Summing Up*, 171–72; Naor, "Greater Israel in Likud Government," 28.
[44] As quoted in Shlaim, "The Likud in Power," 289.
[45] Interview with Ami Ayalon, August 4, 2010, Herzliya.

3. Cognitive Flexibility

Not only did Shamir's emphasis on a past of conflict and persecution hinder him from changing his image of the Palestinians, but so too did his cognitive rigidity. Shamir viewed ideas and people in categorical negative and positive terms, was often unreceptive to new or disconfirming information, and was reluctant to change his mind on issues central to his ideology. Over the past sixty years, Shamir often was less willing to compromise than other leaders with the same ideology: "[Shamir] was generally unreceptive to the idea of bargaining and compromise, his natural instinct being to stand firm in the face of external pressure."[46] Shamir argues that while he was prime minister, he was rigid over issues that were central to him:

> I was totally opposed ... to the idea that the Israel-Arab problem could be solved via an international conference, then that was that: in such matters I felt that I knew best, that I was right, that my obligations to the country ... lay in a given direction and nothing could or did ever budge me from this position.[47]

Shamir believed that his mission in life was to fight for the Greater Land of Israel and he did not change his mind much during his lifetime.[48]

Shamir's rigidity led him to ignore the opinions of those with whom he disagreed. He stated that, although his father believed that one should respect the opinions of others, he had not always done so. Shamir judged a Jew who did not move to Israel as self-hating; "You can't," he said, "understand it any other way."[49] Shamir walked out on speeches and dismissed opinions with which he disagreed. Peres argued, "I'm leading the opposition not for the first time, and it is the first time that I'm in a situation in which during a speech of the opposition leader the prime minister [Shamir] leaves.... The problem is that there is no one to talk to."[50] As speaker of the Knesset in the late 1970s, Shamir felt that heckling during Knesset discussions was acceptable behavior.[51] When Jewish intellectuals called upon him to accept the Shultz Plan, Shamir claimed that they added nothing except inexpert opinion, and he denounced James Baker's remarks before the American-Israel Public Affairs Committee as "useless."[52]

---

[46] Yaacov Vertzberger argues that the greater the centrality of a belief, the greater the rigidity, and the greater the emotional intensity of a belief, the greater its resistance to change. Yaacov Y. I. Vertzberger, *The World in Their Minds: Information Processing, Cognition, and Perception in Foreign Policy Decisionmaking* (Stanford, CA: Stanford University Press, 1990), 118, 134–37; Shlaim, "The Likud in Power," 286.

[47] Shamir, *Summing Up*, 149, 157.

[48] Interview with Hemi Shelev, May 24, 1998, Jerusalem; interview with Yitzhak Shamir, July 5, 1998, Tel Aviv.

[49] Interview with Yitzhak Shamir, July 5, 1998, Tel Aviv; Shamir, *Summing Up*, 4.

[50] Shimon Peres, Labor Party Leadership Bureau, August 9, 1990, Document #182, 19.

[51] Aryeh Rubinstein, interview of Yitzhak Shamir entitled, "Coping with Parliamentary Pandemonium," *The Jerusalem Post Magazine*, August 24, 1979.

[52] Shamir, *Summing Up*, 179; Baker, *The Politics of Diplomacy*, 119, 122.

Throughout his political career, Shamir often dismissed the opinions of those who disagreed with him.

In the pre-state era, Shamir not only ignored opposing views, but also advocated assassinations of "traitors" and some leaders advocating compromise, as well as British officers. In 1948, after the UN enforced a cease-fire in the War of Independence, the Swedish Count Bernadotte tried to mediate and advocated that Jerusalem be an international city. According to Shamir, he came up with a new partition that would have opened the way to putting an end to the Jewish state. In response, he, Israel Eldad, and Yellin-Mor decided that Bernadotte should be assassinated – a plan that was carried out by Yehoshua Cohen on September 17, 1948, in Jerusalem. Shamir also did not show remorse for the bombing of the King David Hotel that killed a hundred people, including British senior staff as well as Jewish officials and others who simply happened to be on the spot. He was also proud of ordering the assassination in Cairo of Lord Moyne, Britain's resident minister in the Middle East. He claimed that the two men who carried out the assassination and were subsequently hanged died as heroes, and he delivered their eulogy when their bodies were brought to Israel in 1975. Because Shamir perceived both the actors and the goals in absolute terms, he justified the violence: the "terror" was against those who wanted to "hurt us" and it succeeded in gaining a Jewish state.[53]

Shamir refused to acknowledge political realities that would complicate the attainment of his ideological goals. For instance, he denied that there are far more Palestinians than Jews in the West Bank and that birthrates would only widen the demographic gap, thus making it impossible to annex the territory (offering citizenship to Palestinians) and to maintain a democratic Jewish state. Shamir described the "so-called demographic problem," as an intellectual abstraction raised by despairing defeatists and declared that there was no change for the worse in the demographic balance between Jews and Arabs. Claiming that scholars at the Hebrew University misperceived reality, he declared, "Let the scientists and pursuers of analytical examination descend from Mt. Scopus and dive into the depths of the emotions, experiences and dreams of the people."[54] As Arye Naor accurately explains, "[E]motions, experiences and dreams will replace analytical examination; faith will replace knowledge; and the dream will replace proof." Therefore, it is possible to continue to believe that "time is on our side."[55]

Shamir ignored the contradictions between democracy and retaining a Jewish state when analyzing the idea of giving Israeli citizenship to Palestinians in the

[53] Interview with Yitzhak Shamir, July 5, 1998, Tel Aviv; Shamir, *Summing Up*, 22–29, 38, 51–61, 70–75; Heller, *The Stern Gang*, 252; Shindler, *Israel, Likud and the Zionist Dream*, 179. Lehi was responsible for 71 percent of all political assassinations carried out by Jewish underground groups between 1940 and 1948, and 48 percent of its killings were of Jewish informants to the British.

[54] Yitzhak Shamir, *For the Sake of Zion, Vision and Faith: Addresses and Speeches* (Hebrew) (Tel Aviv: Beit Yair-Stern House, 1993), 40, 41, 274; Naor, "Greater Israel in Likud Governments," 25.

[55] Naor, "Greater Israel in Likud Governments," 26.

territories. He claimed that Palestinians would reject an offer of Israeli citizenship. However, when pushed, he admitted that he would rather have the West Bank than democracy, true to Lehi ideology. Shamir argued,

> For democracy I will not give up on Eretz Israel. Eretz Israel is a tiny country, a very tiny country, as you know, and if we give up Yehuda and Shomron, and they want more, also Jerusalem, we won't have anywhere to bring in Jews. We will be such a tiny, tiny country we won't be able to exist ... of course this is more important than democracy.[56]

Shamir was reluctant to consider trade-offs for security that would acknowledge a disadvantage to a policy preference emanating from his ideology. For instance, when asked whether the loans that he did not receive from the United States because of his building of settlements on the West Bank could have been used for the Israeli Defense Force to enhance security, Shamir said "for money you don't give up your land."[57]

Because Shamir categorized countries as "good" and "bad," he was unable to accept the fact that Israel, a "good" nation, could be responsible for wrongdoing. The Commission of Enquiry after the Sabra and Shatilla massacres by Phalangists during the Israeli 1982 war in Lebanon concluded that Shamir had not fulfilled his duties as foreign minister because he did not verify the report from the communications minister or bring it to the attention of the prime minister or the defense minister. Shamir claimed that he heard that the Phalangists were running wild and that since everyone was running wild in Lebanon, it did not seem that there was any special significance in what the communications minister said. He lamented the haste with which Israel was condemned by the international media as malicious and often anti-Semitic. Likewise, Shamir did not acknowledge that during the War of Independence, Israeli forces massacred villagers of Dir Yassin, arguing that it was not a premeditated massacre. He also claimed that it was not important if the Arabs of Lod and Ramle in 1948 were expelled or left of their own accord, because it was advantageous to the demographics of a Jewish state that they leave.[58]

4. Emotional Intelligence

Shamir's cognitive rigidity was matched with a low degree of emotional intelligence. His wife described him as very closed and as someone who made decisions alone.[59] Shamir was a suspicious person and Joel Singer, who worked in the Israeli Defense Force under Shamir, maintained, "Shamir continued to live in the

---

[56] Interview with Yitzhak Shamir, July 5, 1998, Tel Aviv.

[57] Ibid.

[58] Shamir, *Summing Up*, 71, 133–34. The Israeli Kahan Commission found that Israeli Defense Minister Ariel Sharon was indirectly responsible for the massacres in that the Phalangists were not stopped from killing Muslim Palestinian refugees.

[59] David Landau, "Moderate Extremist ... and His Very Discreet Wife," *Jerusalem Post Magazine*, January 16, 1981; interview with Joel Singer, August 6, 1999, Washington, D.C.

underground while Prime Minister."[60] He was never comfortable with the public and was not sensitive to people.[61] When Leah Rabin was in the hospital having an angioplasty after Rabin was elected to his second term, she said she received a floral arrangement from President Mubarak, but not a word from Yitzhak Shamir. Although he had worked closely with Rabin in a unity government and Rabin was the first and only Israeli prime minister to be assassinated, he never said a single word of condolence to Leah Rabin."[62]

Shamir not only was unable to muster empathy for those whose policies he did not agree with, but he also did not form friendships with advisors and often did not fully trust them to represent his policies. David Levy, the Israeli foreign minister, was more flexible than his boss. Part of the reason he had joined Herut in the 1960s was that, as a Sephardi leader, he had been repelled by Labor's paternalism toward Sephardim (Jews from Middle Eastern and north African countries); he had not been particularly attracted to the Likud Party's revisionist ideology. Levy agreed to Baker's proposal that Israel could obtain the loan guarantees if it agreed not to use the funds for settlement activities – an agreement that Shamir then retracted. Levy was supposed to represent Israel in Madrid along with the other foreign ministers, but Shamir did not trust his more moderate minister and went himself.[63]

Advisors

Shamir's cognitive rigidity and weak emotional intelligence made him reluctant to accept advice. Shamir argued that he consulted with his fellow Likud members such as the foreign minister and the defense ministers, Moshe Arens and Ariel Sharon; the government's legal consultant, Elyakim Rubenstein, the manager of the office of the prime minister, Yosi Ben Aharon, and Moshe Nisum, treasury minister.[64] Although Shamir consulted with his cabinet members, he was reluctant to take their advice. David Levy, Moshe Arens, and Dan Meridor were also influenced by Likud ideology, but under much American pressure and recognition that the intifada had made the Palestinian issue more central, they were willing to hold municipal elections in the West Bank to allow some degree of autonomy.[65] Shamir's greater reluctance to

[60] Ibid.

[61] Interview with Ami Ayalon, August 4, 2010, Herzliya.

[62] Leah Rabin, *Our Life, His Legacy* (New York: G. P. Putnam's Sons, 1997), 220.

[63] Interview with Hemi Shelev, May 24, 1998, Jerusalem; Shindler, *Israel, Likud, and the Zionist Dream*, 172; J. Rynhold, "Identity, Values, and Cultural Change: Israel, the United States and the Palestinian Question Since Camp David" (PhD diss., London School of Economics, International Relation Dept, 1999), 188, 198; interview with Aliza Goren, June 26, 1998, Mevasseret.

[64] Interview with Yitzhak Shamir, July 5, 1998, Tel Aviv.

[65] Jonathan Rynhold makes a distinction between the conservative beliefs of Arens, Meridor, and Levy and the ultranationalist beliefs of Shamir, arguing that although they all adhered to maintaining Greater Israel and the settlements, these conservatives have less of a conviction that the

compromise in comparison to these advisors resulted from his holding their common ideological beliefs more dogmatically, as well as his cognitive rigidity.

Secretary of State Baker regarded Shamir as a man of principle who was incapable of being practical. Shamir used the word *pragmatist* as a pejorative. He speculated that he would not have given up as much in Camp David "however irate the U.S. President, however demanding the Egyptians, however pragmatic and pressing my own advisers."[66] Moshe Arens, a hard-line pragmatist, found that Shamir had become a prisoner of his own ideology and called him the "reluctant dragon." When Arens tried to convince Shamir to enter negotiations with Palestinians in Cairo, he said that Shamir was not willing to hear him out. Arens also tried to persuade Shamir to call for democratic elections in the territories so that there would be an alternative to the PLO. Arens wrote, "I felt that I was talking to the wall."[67]

Although occasionally Shamir's advisors could, after much resistance, influence him tactically, nobody had any influence over him on strategy.[68] Shamir defied the advice of most of his advisors and refused to stop building settlements in the West Bank in exchange for billions of dollars in loans from the United States, which played a role in his losing the 1992 election. It is probable that he would have continued building settlements in the West Bank even if the United States had threatened to withdraw all of its aid from Israel, believing "Settlement is Zionism."[69]

IMAGE OF THE ENEMY

Shamir's staunch adherence to Likud ideology, his cognitive rigidity, and his orientation toward the past enabled him to maintain his hostile image of the Palestinians. He viewed them as having destructive goals, as being monolithic, and as having no justified claims. This image was shaped by Jabotinsky, who argued that Israel was claiming only 1/170 of the Middle East and that "[i]f ours is a righteous demand, then anything that threatens its implementation loses the right to cloak itself with lofty phraseology such as 'self-determination' or 'liberty.' Its true name is none other than – criminal."[70] Shamir likewise argued that there are no distinct Palestinian people and they do not differ in character, culture, and language from the Jordanian or Saudi people. Shamir perceived

world is hostile. I find the commonalities of these beliefs to be greater than their differences. Rynhold, "Identity, Values and Culture Change."

[66] Baker, *The Politics of Diplomacy*, 119; Shamir, *Summing Up*, 105.

[67] Shlaim, "The Likud in Power," 288; Arens, *Broken Covenant*, 52, 60, 126–28.

[68] Interview with senior civil servant in Shamir's government who met with him at least once a week, but who wanted to remain anonymous, May 5, 2010, Toronto.

[69] Interview with Yitzhak Shamir, July 5, 1998, Tel Aviv; Dan Margalit, "Interview with Yitzhak Shamir" (Hebrew), *Ma'ariv*, September 21, 1979.

[70] Sarig, *The Political and Social Philosophy of Ze'ev Jabotinsky*, 96.

Palestinian opposition to partition, as well as Palestinian violence against Jews in the 1930s, as motivated by hatred for Jews alone.[71]

Shamir believed that the Palestinians perceived compromise as a short-term necessity and that they would never give up on their optimal goal of replacing Israel with a Palestinian state. Since Shamir emphasized history and the lack of change over decades, in 1994 he wrote that the *Jerusalem Post* "quoted a statement that might, I realize as I re-read it, have been made only yesterday – though this was in the autumn of 1974." This is the statement:

> The dominant element in the Israel-Arab relationship is that those Arab groupings which do not recognize our right to live in the Land of Israel [i.e., the entire historic area] also do not recognize our right to live in part of the Land of Israel ... it was time we learned to believe our enemies when they say that they wish to destroy us. Who, after all, believed Hitler when he wrote in *Mein Kampf* that he would destroy all the Jews of Europe if he ever got the chance? ... Not enough has changed since then, how tragic.[72]

According to Shamir, "nothing has changed" since the Palestinian attempt to prevent Jewish immigration to and settlement of the Land of Israel in the 1920s: "They want to get rid of us ... they fight for a Palestinian country that will be instead of Israel."[73]

Shamir declared that Hamas and the PLO shared the same goals and that they had a division of labor whereby Hamas murdered and the PLO got concessions from Israel. Shamir argued on Israeli television that "they all want to destroy us" to which Shimon Peres answered, "[T]here are those and there are others." Shamir replied, "[T]here are no others, they all want to destroy us."[74] He thought that over many decades, the Palestinians would give up these aspirations.[75]

INITIAL POLICY PREFERENCES

Opposition to Camp David Peace Agreement Between Israel and Egypt

The degree to which Shamir was influenced by his ideology and his personality was exhibited by opposition to the Camp David Accords. Shamir said that if it had not been for this agreement, he might have tried to annex Judea and Samaria when he was prime minister. Although Shamir admitted that the Sinai was not part of the Greater Land of Israel, he objected to the precedents it might set for

---

[71] Misgav, Conversations with Shamir, 155–56; Shamir, *Summing Up*, 19, 70.

[72] Interview with Yitzhak Shamir, July 5, 1998, Tel Aviv; Shamir, *Summing Up*, 93; Rubinstein, interview of Speaker Yitzhak Shamir, "Coping With Parliamentary Pandemonium," *The Jerusalem Post Magazine*, August 24, 1979.

[73] Interview with Yitzhak Shamir, July 5, 1998, Tel Aviv; Shamir, *Summing Up*, 19.

[74] Interview with Yitzhak Shamir, July 5, 1998, Tel Aviv; [Shamir: When we return to the government we'll find a way to change the agreement], *Chazash*, November 24, 1993; interview of Shamir on Israeli Television, December 7, 1997.

[75] Interview with Yitzhak Shamir, July 5, 1998, Tel Aviv.

the future for the forcible evacuation of Jewish settlements and for greater autonomy for the Arabs in Judea, Samaria, and Gaza; had he been prime minister, he claimed, he would not have signed the Camp David Accords. However, he abstained from the 1978 vote on the Accords and from the 1979 vote on the Israel-Egypt Peace Treaty, rather than vote against them, out of respect for Begin. Shamir saw Sadat as an exception to the general Arab rejection of Israel who was then murdered for making peace.[76]

Opposition to 1987 Secret Agreement Between Shimon Peres and King Hussein

Although the Labor Party favored the Jordanian option in the 1980s – territorial compromise over the West Bank negotiated with King Hussein of Jordan – the Likud opposed it. When in 1987 Shimon Peres and King Hussein of Jordan conducted secret negotiations in London and were on the verge of agreeing on a framework for peace, Shamir refused to go along with the plan because Palestinians living or working in East Jerusalem would have participated in the negotiations. Peres ruefully writes that, Shamir would negotiate "only with Palestinians who had not yet been born" – he refused the delegations that met with Baker and refused anyone from Jerusalem. Shamir derailed the agreement out of fear that it might open the door to territorial compromise.[77] He defied the advice of his advisor on terrorism, Rafi Eitan, who tried to persuade him to accept the London Agreement so that the Palestinian issue would have been resolved through Jordanian sovereignty over the West Bank.[78] Shamir feared that the Palestinians would eventually demand more than autonomy; he also resented Peres for having conducted the negotiations, and for having sent Yossi Beilin to meet with U.S. State Department officials in Scandinavia without his knowledge.[79]

REACTIONS TO THE INTIFADA, 1988 PLO PROCLAMATION, AND THE GULF WAR

To continue to study the role that ideology and personality played in explaining Shamir's image of the Palestinians and his policy predispositions, it is revealing to analyze his perceptions of and reactions to the intifada, the 1988 PLO Proclamation, and the Gulf War. The intifada that started on December 7, 1987, and gradually declined by 1993, served to strengthen Shamir's view that the Palestinians sought to destroy Israel. Because he emphasized the hostility of the past, he was less able to differentiate the uprising from previous uses of force by the Palestinians:

---

[76] Shamir, *Summing Up*, 100–5, 109, 129, 143; Landau, "Moderate Extremist"; interview with Yitzhak Shamir, July 5, 1998, Tel Aviv.

[77] Labor Party Central Committee, March 27, 1991, Document #1053, 12; Shlaim, "The Likud in Power," 287.

[78] Cashman, "Parting from Shamir."

[79] Interview with senior civil servant in Shamir's government who met with him at least once a week, but who wanted to remain anonymous, May 5, 2010, Toronto.

Ultimately, it was a continuation of the war against Israel's existence, its immediate purpose to push us back to the 1967 lines and to establish another Palestinian state in the areas we leave ... the Intifada changed nothing in our basic situation. ... It proved to me once more that the conflict was not over territory but over Israel's right to exist.[80]

Shamir's ideologically held conviction that time was on Israel's side in relation to its conflict with the Palestinians influenced him to neglect to see that the strategy of trying to quell the uprising by force was failing. He believed that the past had proven that Israel would succeed, and that Israel's will would prove to be stronger over time, despite the continuation of the uprising: "We have had ... 100 years of intifada. When did the Arabs and Palestinians not fight us? In the 20s before the state, in the 30s in the 40s ... Each time we beat them." He continued that had Peres not saved the PLO through recognizing it, the PLO would have been broken within another six months.[81]

On September 5, 1988, Salah Khalaf announced that the PLO was ready to recognize Israel if Israel recognized the PLO and the right to Palestinian self-determination. The Palestine National Council (PNC), on November 15, 1988, accepted United Nations Resolution 242. The United States announced that it would engage in direct talks with the PLO. Shamir's image of the PLO was so ingrained that he called PLO statements that it might recognize Israel and renounce terrorism criminal lies by enemies who cannot be trusted. He was ready to present evidence to Washington that the PLO continued its terrorist activity. Shamir threatened to imprison Arafat if he flew to Israel to talk peace and said, "Hitler and Arafat belong to the same family of demagogues, enemies of the Jewish people who think nothing of killing millions in order to achieve their objective."[82] Shamir's equation of Arafat with Hitler reflected his cognitive difficulty with differentiating among enemies.

Saddam Hussein invaded Kuwait on August 2, 1990, and the Gulf War began in January 1991. This war, like the intifada, did not lead Shamir to question his image of the PLO. Palestinian support for Saddam Hussein and their celebrations as missiles hit Israel, only strengthened Shamir's perception that given the opportunity, they would try to destroy Israel. His ideological barrier to conceding territory made him reluctant to perceive regional changes after the Gulf War that might be conducive to negotiations. When asked if the Gulf War had led to changes in the region that had increased the chances for peace, Shamir responded:

Would the US be willing to give up part of her territory? Even one kilometer! No they would never be willing. Would England give anyone else one kilometer? No.

---

[80] Shamir, *Summing Up*, 180, 182.

[81] Interview of Yitzhak Shamir on Israeli Television, December 7, 1997.

[82] Shamir, as quoted in "The 50 Years War: Israel & the Arabs," directed by Dai Richards and Norma Percy (PBS Video, 2000); Arens, *Broken Covenant*, 56; Shlaim, "The Likud in Power," 286.

Germany, would it agree that the land of Sudetenland belongs to Czechoslovakia? It never changes.[83]

Shamir refers to Germany's position in 1938 as if it were the present: Germany did, in fact, concede Sudetenland after 1945. This is an indication of the extent to which the past is part of his present.

CONSEQUENT POLICY PREFERENCES

Continued Opposition to Cultivating an Internal Palestinian Leadership
Whereas the Gulf War and the intifada only strengthened Shamir's image of Palestinian hostility toward Israel and his determination not to concede land, these events mobilized U.S. pressure on Israel to negotiate with the Palestinians. After much pleading by Moshe Arens that therefore Israel had better choose its own peace plan to further its interests, Shamir finally agreed to propose elections in the territories for leaders who would negotiate self-government. But to the astonishment of Arens and Dan Meridor, he told the Knesset Foreign Affairs and Defense Committee that it was a public relations ploy and refused to put the plan to a vote in the party's Central Committee. Instead, he argued against negotiation as long as the violence of the intifada continued, rejected Palestinian sovereignty in the West Bank and Gaza, rejected negotiations with the PLO or a Palestinians state, and continued settlements. In March 1990, Arens and Meridor advised Shamir to acquiesce to American pressure that Shamir meet with Palestinians in Cairo. Shamir refused to go to Cairo because they were going to "break our bones" there and claimed he would resign over the issue. Arens concluded, "I could not – and do not to this day – understand how he envisioned a resolution of the Arab-Israeli conflict without meaningful contact with the Palestinians."[84]

Shamir defied the advice of his more pragmatic Likud ministers, and engaged in delaying tactics. Baker writes, "The haggling seemed endless to me, a calculated exercise in obfuscation to play for time and avoid coming to grips with the hard choices required."[85] Shamir had used these tactics as a Lehi prisoner. In response to a British proposal to the prisoners, "we put together a counter-proposal, designed not to be accepted but rather to gain us enough time so that we could go ahead with planning our escape."[86] Likewise, Shamir reluctantly came up with proposals that he thought would be rejected by the Palestinians in order to play for time in response to tremendous pressure to negotiate in the wake of the intifada and the Gulf War.

---

[83] "The 50 Years War: Israel & the Arabs"; interview with Yitzhak Shamir, July 5, 1998, Tel Aviv.
[84] Myron J. Aronoff, *Power and Ritual in the Israel Labor Party: A Study in Political Anthropology*, rev. ed. (London: M. E. Sharpe, 1993), 210; Shindler, *Israel, Likud, and the Zionist Dream*, 256–58; Arens, *Broken Covenant*, 128.
[85] Baker, *The Politics of Diplomacy*, 127, 450.
[86] Shamir, *Summing Up*, 40.

Meeting with the Palestinian Delegation at the Madrid Conference, 1991

Shamir's delaying tactics, and his strategy of setting preconditions he knew would not be agreed to for negotiations, finally caught up with him. Although he had vowed to never negotiate with "PLO terrorists" and likened an international conference to being as "bad as a pig in a temple," he agreed to participate in the Madrid Conference in October 1991.[87] According to Uzi Landau, a member of Shamir's delegation to Madrid, "Shamir went to Madrid due to American blatant pressure."[88] Shamir did not expect Syria to agree to negotiate. When the United States successfully pressured the Syrians to participate, Baker writes, "Shamir seemed genuinely shocked, almost thunderstruck, and quite suspicious, over [Syrian President Hafez al-] Assad's acceptance" and "his countenance betrayed an inner turmoil. Shamir looked as though he'd bitten into an unripe persimmon," but he had no choice but to say yes as Israel had pressed for years for face-to-face direct negotiations.[89] Shamir's lifelong strategy of delay and then agreeing to proposals he was convinced the other side would not accept backfired.

Madrid did not represent a shift in his image of the Palestinians or a compromise of his ideological principles because Shamir had no intention of conceding land. He confessed, "In my political activity I know how to display the tactics of moderation, but without conceding anything on the goal – the integrity of the Land of Israel . . . I would have carried on autonomy talks for ten years and meanwhile we would have reached half a million [Jewish] people in Judea and Samaria."[90] He reiterated this to Ehud Barak, his head of intelligence at the time, believing he could maintain the status quo despite having to participate in negotiations.[91] Shamir never directly compromised his ideology but succumbed to some extent to U.S. pressure.

Opposition to Oslo Accords and to a Palestinian State

Shamir's tactical decision to go to Madrid was neither motivated by nor ever followed by a change in his view of the Palestinians. He did think that he was negotiating from a position of strength as he thought that increased Soviet immigration had made Arafat anxious about the future demography in the West Bank if there would be continued immigration.[92] However, when Peres told Shamir that Arafat signed a letter recognizing Israel in front of the whole world, Shamir retorted that Arafat could not be trusted and thought it

[87] Shamir, quoted in "The 50 Years War: Israel & the Arabs"; Rynhold, "Identity, Values, and Cultural Change," 188.

[88] Interview with Uzi Landau, July 5, 2007, Raanana.

[89] Interview with Yitzhak Shamir, July 5, 1998, Tel Aviv; Richard Haass, as quoted in "The 50 Years War: Israel & the Arabs"; Baker, *The Politics of Diplomacy*, 125, 493–96.

[90] Yosef Harif's interview with Shamir, in *Ma'ariv*, June 26, 1992.

[91] Interview with Ehud Barak, June 28, 2004, Tel Aviv; interview with Hemi Shelev, May 24, 1998, Jerusalem.

[92] Interview with Efraim Halevy, August 6, 2013, Ramat Aviv.

impossible that the PLO was willing to settle for an area next to Israel. Shamir claimed that if he returned to government, he would find a way to change the agreement and opposed Netanyahu's decision to agree to the essence of the Oslo Accords: "We have to stop Oslo ... That was a big mistake, a terrible mistake. In Oslo we had a disaster for Israel. Anyone going on that path will fail, will cause Israel to lose everything she has."[93]

Shamir consistently opposed negotiations with PLO officials and recognition of the PLO because he never waivered from his belief that the Palestinian Authority was a terrorist organization intent on obliterating Israel through violence and the right of return of refugees. Shamir's distrust of the PLO was so strong that when he was prime minister, he fired Science Minister Ezer Weizman for contacting a spokesperson for Yasser Arafat. Shamir continued to believe that the Palestinians would not be satisfied "as long as we're here" and that a Palestinian state would threaten Israel's survival.[94] The continuity of Shamir's beliefs in his 76 years in Israel was facilitated by his focus on a past of persecution and conflict, his ideological conviction that the world was hostile, his tendency to view groups in black-and-white terms, and his ideological barrier to conceding land.

CONCLUSIONS AND IMPLICATIONS

Shamir's ideology and personality reinforced each other, making it more difficult for him to change his perceptions of the PLO or significantly change his policy preferences, which he never did, despite changes in the PLO and in the regional environment, public opinion, and Israel's increased military strength. Shamir adhered more strictly to this ideology than did other Likud members in his cabinet. The long-term, optimistic time horizon built into Likud ideology predisposed Shamir to hope for increased Jewish immigration and for the Palestinians to give up on statehood. He did not perceive Israel's military response to the intifada as a failure requiring political solutions, as he expected a future Israeli victory.

Likud ideology's emphasis on the territorial Greater Land of Israel inhibited Shamir from perceiving change in the Palestinians, since to do so would lead to a conflict of goals. Both Shamir's ideology and personal background emphasized the hostility of the surrounding world, which strengthened his hostile image of the Palestinians. Since he did not differentiate between degrees of belligerence – for instance, between Hamas and the PLO or between Iraq and the PLO – he never regarded the PLO as a possible bulwark against more threatening groups. In addition, Shamir's perception of an antagonistic world made him more

---

[93] Interview with Yitzhak Shamir, July 5, 1998, Tel Aviv; interview with Yitzhak Shamir, "Popolitika" on Israeli Television.

[94] Shamir, *Summing Up*, 123, 173; interview with Dan Meridor, June 18, 1998, Jerusalem; interview with Yitzhak Shamir, "Popolitika," on Israeli Television.

distrustful of and resistant to U.S. pressure. Finally, Shamir's ideology led him to believe in the possibility of security without peace, therefore rendering peace inessential for security.

Bolstering Shamir's ideological barriers to change was his orientation toward the past that reinforced his image of a hostile enemy. Shamir thought of present events most readily in terms of the past and thus viewed the enemy as unchangeable. He did not reassess his image of the PLO as a consequence of the intifada, the 1988 PLO Proclamation, the Gulf War, or even the PLO's formal recognition of Israel in the Oslo Accords. The Gulf War and the intifada only emphasized to Shamir the hostility of the Palestinians and did not lead him to think that a solution was possible or urgent.

These factors were reinforced by Shamir's cognitive rigidity and lack of emotional intelligence, which restricted his ability to listen to more pragmatic advisors who pleaded with him to negotiate with the Palestinians, led him to view compromise as unprincipled, and reinforced his image of Israel as the "good" actor who could do no wrong. Shamir's inability to differentiate grey areas in his ideas also led him to ignore or explain away problems inherent in achieving his ideological goals. He denied the problematic nature of the overwhelming number of Palestinians relative to Jews on the West Bank and dismissed potential security costs to turning down American loans in order to continue settlements.

Shamir's strong commitment to his ideology, cognitive rigidity, suspicion of even his own advisors, and past time orientation contribute to his lifelong hostile image of the Palestinians and his opposition to dialogue with the PLO and the creation of a Palestinian state. Shamir claimed that he did not feel inhibited by his coalition from doing what he wanted as prime minister, and the Israeli policy toward the Palestinians reflected his own preferences.[95] Although it is clear that Shamir would not have been able to make the concessions necessary to reach an agreement with the Palestinians, as a response to American pressure he did negotiate in Madrid with Palestinians (as participants in a Jordanian delegation) receiving instructions from the PLO. Shamir made shifts that, although not producing dramatic foreign policy change, kept him from standing completely still. This tactical change ultimately had significant, if unintended, political consequences, since it paved the way for broader public support for negotiating with Palestinians.

---

[95] Interview with Yitzhak Shamir, July 5, 1998, Tel Aviv.

3

Benjamin Netanyahu: Battling the World

A PLO state on the West Bank would be like a hand poised to strangle Israel's vital artery along the sea.[1]

– Benjamin Netanyahu, 1993

Who are we, they ask, to resist the entire world? That it is sometimes – and in the case of Israel, often – necessary to dissent from and resist prevailing opinion seldom crosses their minds.[2]

– Benjamin Netanyahu, 2000

Jerusalem Isn't a Settlement, It's Our Capital[3]

– Benjaming Netanyahu, 2011

Benjamin Netanyahu, Israel's longest serving prime minister since David Ben-Gurion, has been an enigma to many observers. He was prime minister from 1996 to 1999, from March 2009 to January 2013, and after receiving the most votes in January 2013, formed his third government in March 2013. Some argue that he is a hard-line ideologue representing the Revisionist Zionist roots of the Likud Party who needs to be replaced if peace is to be secured. Others insist that he is an opportunist who has no deeply held beliefs, and therefore will make a peace agreement if he believes it will keep him in office. Netanyahu's actions over time underscore this enigma, as he has swerved between maintaining hard-line positions and taking small steps toward compromise, negotiation, and peace. He has, on the one hand, vehemently opposed the Oslo Accords since their inception. On the other hand, during the 1996 campaign to become prime

---

[1] Benjamin Netanyahu, *A Place Among the Nations: Israel and the World* (New York: Bantam Press, 1993), 282.
[2] Benjamin Netanyahu, *A Durable Peace: Israel and Its Place Among the Nations* (New York: Warner Books, 2000), 373.
[3] Netanyahu speech to AIPAC, May 2011, in Helene Cooper, "Obama and Netanyahu, distrustful Allies, to Meet," *The New York Times*, May 19, 2011.

minister, he argued that he would abide by the agreements if the Palestinians honored their commitments. After becoming prime minister, though, he undermined the Oslo process by slowing it down and minimizing its effects.[4] Although not ceding territory is a central part of Netanyahu's ideology, he granted additional land and jurisdiction to the Palestinians in the Hebron and Wye Agreements in order to improve his chances of getting elected again in 1999. Most of the withdrawals agreed to at Wye, however, were not implemented. This pattern continued through Netanyahu's second term in office: in June 2009, under intense pressure from the United States, Netanyahu publicly agreed in principle to something he had rejected his entire life – the establishment of a Palestinian state alongside Israel under certain conditions. However, as with previous agreements, he has continued to implement policies that have effectively brought the process to a standstill: he continues building in East Jerusalem and the West Bank except for a 10-month settlement freeze in the West Bank in 2009–2010; refuses to negotiate over Jerusalem; demands the Palestinians recognize Israel as a "Jewish state"; and demands that the Israeli military will maintain a presence in the Jordan Valley.

This chapter analyzes Netanyahu's ideology and personality traits in order to explain both his tactical shifts of policy and the limitations of these changes. It examines Netanyahu's ideological commitments – in particular Likud ideology's commitment to territory, its long-term time horizon that sees time "on Israel's side," and its conception of the world as a hostile place fundamentally set against the Jewish state – alongside his particular personality traits such as cognitive rigidity, sense of time, and emotional intelligence. Although Netanyahu's perception of the conflict and his policy preferences are strongly influenced by Likud ideology, I argue that he is willing to make tactical compromises in order to secure his political future.[5] When Netanyahu makes these pragmatic compromises, however, the strong influence of his ideology constrains and delays them.[6] For Netanyahu, ideology is a point of departure that shapes particular decisions, whereas his day-to-day operations are consumed with preoccupations with reelection and concerns over maintaining his coalition.[7]

---

[4] Ilan Peleg, "The Right in Israeli Politics: The Nationalist Ethos in the Jewish Democracy," in *Israel's First Fifty Years*, ed. Robert O. Freedman (Gainesville: University Press of Florida, 2000), 146, 154, 156; interview with Shlomo Brom, June 21, 2004, Tel Aviv. Brom was Chief of Strategic Planning Division of the Israeli Defense Forces under the Netanyahu government in his first term.

[5] Interview with Efraim Halevy, August 6, 2013, Ramat Aviv, Israel. According to Halevi, Netanyahu is a tactician. Halevy worked for the Mossad for forty years, was its director 1998–2002, and was the head of the National Security Council 2002–2003.

[6] Interview with Dore Gold, June 2, 1999, New York. Gold was Netanyahu's main policy advisor until he became Israel's permanent representative to the United Nations 1997–1999; he was present at the Wye negotiations.

[7] Interview with Dennis Ross, August 6, 1999, Washington, DC; Ross was the U.S. State Department's special coordinator for the Middle East during Netanyahu's first term as prime minister and National Security Council member during Netanyahu's second term. Interview with Hemi Shelev, journalist for *Ma'ariv*, May 24, 1998, Jerusalem.

DETERMINANTS OF CONVERSION

Ideology

Netanyahu is heavily influenced by an ideology inherited from his father, Ben-Zion Netanyahu, who was a historian of the Spanish Inquisition and ideologue of Revisionist Zionism. His mother has also been a lifelong supporter of Revisionist Zionism. Netanyahu's grandfather, Nathan Mileikowsky, was a supporter of Vladimir Ze'ev Jabotinksy, founder and leader of the Revisionist movement. Ben-Zion joined the Revisionist party in 1928 and in 1939 worked in the United States as Jabotinksy's personal assistant until Jabotinksy's death in 1940. He was also co-editor of the Revisionists' daily newspaper *Ha-Yarden*. Territory was always a central tenet in Ben-Zion's philosophy, and he steadfastly opposed any territorial compromise. In November 1947, Ben-Zion and his friends put out an ad in the *New York Times* opposing the UN's decision for partition of Palestine, and he later thought that Menachem Begin had endangered the existence of Israel by signing the Camp David Accords with Egypt.[8]

Ben-Zion Netanyahu's ideology and politics in turn shaped his son's thinking throughout his career. Netanyahu keeps several volumes of Jabotinsky's works in his office and frequently consulted with his father until his father passed away on April 30, 2012. During his 1996 campaign, Netanyahu shifted the focus of major policy speeches at his father's urging. Even those around Netanyahu have been shaped by Ben-Zion's hand: Moshe Arens – Netanyahu's political mentor who made Netanyahu second in command when he was ambassador to the United States from 1982 to 1984 and advocated on Netanyahu's behalf for his appointment as Israel's UN ambassador from 1984 to 1988 – was a member of the Betar (Revisionist) youth group led by Ben-Zion.[9]

While the ideology represented by his father profoundly influences Netanyahu, public opinion also influences his campaign strategies and policy platforms. During the 1996 campaign, his researchers found that 70 percent of voters were willing to concede settlements for peace; consequently, Netanyahu toned down his statements.[10] Similarly, public opinion was a decisive factor in reaching the Wye accords. Throughout the campaign, the pollster Shai Reuveni

---

[8] Ben Caspit and Ilan Kfir, *Netanyahu: The Road to Power* (Secaucus, NJ: Carol Publishing Group, 1998), 14–31; Ronit Vardi, *Mi Ata Adoni Rosh Hamimshala?* [Benjamin Netanyahu: Who Are You, Mr. Prime Minister?] (Jerusalem: Keter Publishing House Ltd., 1997), 52, 54, 85; David Remnick, "The Outsider," *The New Yorker*, May 25, 1998, 86.

[9] Yossi Klein Halevi, "His Father's Son," *The Jerusalem Report*, February 5, 1998, 12; Vardi, *Netanyahu*, 70.

[10] Interviews with Dennis Ross, August 6, 1999, Washington, DC; David Bar Ilan, June 9, 1998, Jerusalem, Israel. Bar Ilan was communications director in the first Netanyahu government; he began working with Netanyahu in 1983 and was one of his closest advisors. Interviews with Dore Gold, June 2, 1999, New York; and Hemi Shelev, May 24, 1998, Jerusalem; Remnick, "The Outsider," 80, 81; Vardi, *Netanyahu*, 249, 306, 314.

monitored public reaction, passing the data to Netanyahu in a weekly folder stamped "highly secret." When the Wye negotiations intensified, Reuveni's polls revealed that Netanyahu's projected lead over Ehud Barak would increase if he signed the accord. He did so in the face of overwhelming opposition from within his Likud party.[11] In another example, after months of asking the U.S. to suspend emergency aid to Moscow until Russia stopped selling nuclear materials to Iran, Netanyahu personally asked the International Monetary Fund to give the Russians the $4.8 billion loan they were seeking – in order to court the Russian immigrants' votes in the 1999 election. Although he did suspend a $50 million agricultural loan to Russia originally promised in 1997 because of Moscow's aid to Iran, he visited Russian Prime Minister Yevgeny Primakov to receive an endorsement from him, despite Defense Minister Arens's objection that this weakened Israel's struggle against the Iranian threat and hampered U.S.-Israeli relations.[12] Although concerns regarding public opinion prompt Netanyahu to compromise, they are constrained and moderated by his ideology.[13]

1. Is Time on Israel's Side?

Like many other members of Likud, Netanyahu believes that in Israel's conflict with the Palestinians, "time is working in our favor." Netanyahu's father gave his sons history lessons about the Christians' war of independence in Spain, which lasted more than two hundred years before the Muslim occupiers were finally expelled. His lesson was that you have to be ready to fight for hundreds of years in order to protect your rights. Netanyahu argued that in the long term, there would be more Jews than Palestinians in the West Bank – Palestinian birth rates would continue to decline, and that thousands of Palestinians each year would emigrate.[14] Although in his second and third terms he began to take more seriously demographic projections that question this initial prognosis (described herein), he continues to feel no urgency to make peace.

---

[11] Naveh, *Executive Secrets* (Tel Aviv: Miskal, Yedioth Ahronoth Books and Chemed Books, 1999), 203–8.

[12] Thomas L. Friedman, "Russian Roulette," *New York Times*, April 13, 1999.

[13] Interview with Rueven Rivlin, July 26, 2007, Jerusalem. Rivlin has served in the Knesset as a representative of the Likud party since 1988. He served as Speaker of the Knesset 2003–2006 and 2009–2013. Moshe Arens, *Broken Covenant* (New York: Simon & Schuster, 1995), 269; interview with Dennis Ross, August 6, 1999, Washington, DC. Ilan Peleg, "The Likud Under Rabin II: Between Ideological Purity and Pragmatic Readjustment," in *Israel Under Rabin*, ed. Robert O. Freedman (Boulder, CO: Westview Press, 1995), 158.

[14] Yoel Marcus, "Hannibal Is at the Gate," *Ha'aretz*, December 19, 2000; Vardi, *Netanyahu*, 81; Netanyahu, A *Place Among Nations*, 303. This is also supported by other members of the Knesset such as Michael Kleiner, who calls himself a scholar of Jabotinksy. Interview with Michael Kleiner, June 30, 1998, Jerusalem.

2. Ideological Goals: General and Adaptable or Specific and Rigid?

In his book, *A Place Among the Nations*, Netanyahu laid out his ideology, "Revisionism for the 1990's," which focused on the exclusive Jewish rights to all of Eretz Israel. Jabotinsky had envisioned a state as originally defined in the British mandate, which included land on both sides of the Jordan River. Netanyahu's books contain the same deeply held ideological belief in the historical right to the land.[15] Netanyahu's ideological connection to the Greater Land of Israel explains his initial vehement opposition to the Oslo Accords, and then his efforts to minimize land concessions. Although Netanyahu realizes that Israel will have to concede land to move toward a two-state solution, the Knesset established the Land of Israel Caucus in January 2010 to strengthen Israel's hold on the West Bank. The caucus included all Likud Knesset members and ministers, with the exception of Minister of Improvement of Government Services Michael Eitan, Deputy Prime Minister Dan Meridor, and Netanyahu.[16] In addition, the Likud became a more right-wing party as the hard-line faction was successful in the November 2012 primaries. Therefore, members of Likud in the Knesset after the January 2013 elections included hard-liners such as Danny Danon, Miri Regev, and Moshe Feiglin, while more moderate longtime Likud Knesset members such as Dan Meridor, Benny Begin, and Michael Eitan were too low on the list to make it into the 19th Knesset. This strengthened the faction within Likud that opposes territorial concessions on the West Bank and opposes a two-state solution.

3. Is the World With Us or Against Us?

Central to Likud ideology is the view that the world is permanently hostile to Jews.[17] Netanyahu's view of a menacing world is particularly shaped by his father's Revisionist ideology, which perceives Jewish history in terms of holocausts and enduring anti-Semitism. In his *The Origins of the Inquisition in Fifteenth Century Spain*, Ben-Zion Netanyahu showed that, even if Jews had converted, they would have been forced into exile or murdered.[18] Benjamin Netanyahu continues to see Israel as facing existential danger. In

---

[15] Benjamin Netanyahu, *A Place Among the Nations*, 353.

[16] Jonathan Rynhold and Dov Waxman have persuasively pointed to the ideological changes within Likud that accommodate the emerging consensus that Israel will not be able to keep all of the West Bank, but the Land of Israel Caucus and the November 2012 Likud primaries also point to the limits of this ideological change. Rynhold and Waxman, "Ideological Change and Israel's Disengagement from Gaza," *Political Science Quarterly* (Spring 2008): 11–38. See also Yossi Verter, "Likud Minister to Rightists: Give Up Dream of Greater Israel," *Haaretz*, November 8, 2010; Nadav Shelef, *Evolving Nationalism: Homeland, Religion, and Identity in Israel 1925–2005* (Ithaca, NY: Cornell University Press, 2010). Shelef also argues that tactical compromises can lead to policy change under certain conditions.

[17] Peleg, "Israeli Foreign Policy Under Right-Wing Governments: A Constructivist Interpretation," *Israel Studies Forum* 19, no. 3 (2004): 111.

[18] Ben-Zion Netanyahu, *The Origins of the Inquisition in Fifteenth Century Spain* (New York: Random House, 1995); Remnick, "The Outsider," 84, 85; Halevi, "His Father's Son," 12.

a speech at Auschwitz, for example, he reminded the world that the lesson to be learned from the Holocaust is to unite against evil before it can realize its schemes. With implied references to Iran, he pledged that he would not allow a "new Amelek" to destroy the Jewish nation, a reference to a biblical king who waged war against the Jews.[19]

According to Dennis Ross, the strongest ideological influence on Netanyahu is his perception that the world is filled with enemies and that there are few countries one can trust: Netanyahu, Ross argues, feels that "Israel has to constantly look over her shoulder because it is constantly being threatened. The world is shaped with enemies and one has to safeguard against them."[20] Naomi Chazan agrees that Netanyahu thinks that "the whole world is out to get us."[21] U.S. President Barack Obama's chilling of relations with Israel in 2009 fed into Netanyahu's view that the whole world was against Israel. Unlike most Israelis, Netanyahu was so wedded to a hostile perception of the world that he did not even rejoice at Anwar Sadat's visit to Jerusalem. Rather, Netanyahu arrived at a party looking as if he were attending a funeral, since the Sinai would have to be given up. Netanyahu claims that Israel faces criticism because even Israel's friends have a difficult time coming to terms with Jewish power. In this light, Netanyahu sees those who want to freeze settlements on the West Bank as saying "no Jews."[22]

This perception of a hostile world is magnified in the case of the Palestinians. The Israel Government Press Office under Netanyahu published tracts emphasizing Palestinian hatred toward Israel. One booklet was entitled "A Compendium of Hate: Palestinian Authority Anti-Semitism Since the Hebron Accord." On the front cover was a picture of an Israeli flag with a swastika drawn on it that was being burned at a Hebron rally. The table of contents included violations of the Oslo Accords and Hebron Protocol's provisions against the use of anti-Semitic stereotypes, comparisons of Israelis with Nazis and Fascists, Holocaust denial, and the de-legitimization of Israel and the Jewish people. Other handouts included Government Press Office bulletins entitled "Arafat Tells Palestinians: Burn the Ground Under the Feet of the Invaders!" and "Arafat Invokes 1974 Phased Plan Calling for Israel's Destruction, Compares Oslo to Temporary Truce." (As it turns out, many of these quotes

---

[19] Cnaan Lipshiz, "Netanyahu at Auschwitz: World Must Unite to Confront New Threats," *Haaretz*, January 27, 2010.

[20] Interview with Dennis Ross, August 6, 1999, Washington, DC.

[21] Interview with Naomi Chazan, July 17, 2007, Jerusalem.

[22] Netanyahu, *A Place Among the Nations*, 177, 397, 398. See also Jonathan Rynhold, "Identity, Values and Culture Change: Israel, the United States and the Palestinian Question Since Camp David" (PhD diss., London School of Economics, International Relations Department, 1999), 244. Rynhold differentiates Netanyahu's conservatism from his father's and Shamir's "ultra-nationalism." He argues that although Netanyahu inherited a hostile image of the world, it was less extreme than Shamir's. I argue that they shared the same beliefs, only Netanyahu was less dogmatic about those beliefs because of personal political ambition.

were not from Yasser Arafat, but from clerics, students, and others.) The energies given to collecting and disseminating this material far outweighed any such efforts taken by a Labor government. Dore Gold claims that this focus on Palestinian violations was influenced by Netanyahu's ideological prism, which led him to oppose Oslo. He perceived Arafat to be a permanent enemy. According to Dennis Ross, Netanyahu "was constantly campaigning against the Palestinians who he supposedly wanted to deal with."[23]

Netanyahu continued this strategy in his second term. After eighteen months of no negotiation, on the very day of the establishment of proximity talks, Netanyahu's Security Cabinet met to hear a report on Palestinian incitement, and to discuss the establishment of an incitement index that would monitor and quantify incitement episodes on a regular basis. They highlighted incidents such as a square in Ramallah being named after Dalal al-Mughrabi, who took part in a 1978 terrorist attack on a bus in Israel. A senior official in Netanyahu's office said, "[I]f the Palestinian leadership is putting extremists and terrorists on a pedestal as national heroes, it does not have a commitment to peace."[24] Deputy Foreign Minister Daniel Ayalon also invited the foreign press corps to hear about Palestinian incitement against Israel from the director of Palestinian Media Watch, a politically right-wing nongovernmental organization.[25]

Netanyahu tends to lump enemies together. In the early 1990s, he claimed that the goals of Hezbollah, the PLO, Hamas, Fatah, and Syria were all the same – to expel the Jews from every area of the country. Netanyahu largely views Fatah and Hamas as one and the same: he thinks that both have the same goals but differ in strategy – one is content to work in stages, while the other wants victory all at once. Both, though, are willing to use terrorism, which leads him to challenge the notion that members of Fatah are the "moderates" and those of Hamas are the "extremists." Benjamin Tempkin, a Knesset member of the Meretz Party, said to Netanyahu, "[F]or you all the Arabs are the same."[26] Netanyahu believes that the PLO uses Hamas and terrorism as bargaining chips to gain negotiating leverage against Israel. For instance, when Israel suspended further withdrawals from the West Bank required by the Wye Agreement, Arafat lifted the house arrest on Hamas leader Sheik Ahmed Yassin, who called for a holy war against Israel. In contrast, Dan Meridor was surprised at the extent to which the Palestinian Authority was curtailing terror and Brigadier General Yaakov Amidror, head of the research

---

[23] Interview with Dore Gold, June 2, 1999, New York; interview with Dennis Ross, August 6, 1999, Washington, DC.

[24] Herb Keinon, "Cabinet to Discuss Incitement-Monitoring," *The Jerusalem Post*, May 5, 2010.

[25] Barak Ravid, "Foreign Ministry Working with Rightists Against Palestinian Incitement," *Haaretz*, May 7, 2010.

[26] Netanyahu and Benjamin Tempkin, *Knesset Minutes*, April 18, 1994, 6247, 6251; Vardi, *Netanyahu*, 206; Netanyahu, *A Place Among the Nations*, 102; Netanyahu, *Knesset Minutes*, October 26, 1992, 23.

department of military intelligence, praised Arafat for battling against Hamas's terrorist infrastructure.[27]

Netanyahu argues the Arabs' hostility stems from Pan-Arab nationalist rejection of any non-Arab sovereignty in the Middle East, the Islamic fundamentalist drive to cleanse the region of non-Islamic influences, and the bitter resentment against the West, none of which Israel can control. Moreover, he states that Arabs were killing Jews before the establishment of Israel and the acquisition of the West Bank, so Arab hostility does not depend on Israeli policies. He believes that "the Arab campaign against Israel is hence rooted not in a negotiable grievance but in a basic opposition to the very existence of Jewish sovereignty."[28]

If Netanyahu tends to lump Palestinian adversaries together, he often also includes the international community in this group. He believes that he can do nothing right in world opinion. Israel, he argues, was not rewarded by the world for the Hebron Agreement, but rather the UN continued to pass resolutions that were hostile to Israel.[29] Likewise, he believes that he has continued to bear the brunt of American and international criticism despite freezing settlements on the West Bank for ten months in 2009–2010, removing many roadblocks and checkpoints on the West Bank during his second term, and releasing Palestinian prisoners who had been imprisoned for killing Israelis in his third term.

Netanyahu's perception of the world and his actions have had serious consequences. In his first term in office, Jordan's King Hussein severed their personal relationship primarily because of Netanyahu's attempt to have Khaled Meshaal, a senior member of the political wing of Hamas, assassinated in Jordan; Egyptian President Hosni Mubarak and Yasser Arafat did not trust him; and he alienated President Bill Clinton and Secretary of State Madeleine Albright.[30] In his second term, the tensions between Netanyahu and Obama were palpable.

Netanyahu's perception that Israel is vulnerable in a world that is against it has led him to publicly challenge the United States more than did Yitzak Rabin, Shimon Peres, or Ehud Barak. He thinks that if Begin had been more forceful, he would have had to give fewer concessions at Camp David – especially autonomy to the Palestinians – and may have avoided the precedent for total withdrawal. In his first term as prime minister in 1996, Netanyahu courted international

---

[27] Interview with Dore Gold, June 29, 1998, Jerusalem; interview with Dan Meridor, June 29, 1998, Jerusalem. Meridor was minister of intelligence and atomic energy in the second Netanyahu government. Deborah Sontag, "Freed Palestinian Militant Leader Calls for Holy War Against Israel," *New York Times*, December 28, 1998; Naveh, *Executive Secrets*, 110; Rosenblum, M., "Netanyahu and Peace: From Sound Bites to Sound Policies?" in Robert O. Friedman (ed.) *The Middle East and the Peace Process: The Impact of the Oslo Accords* (Gainesville: University Press of Florida, 1998), 60.

[28] Netanyahu, *A Place Among the Nations*, 125, 389.

[29] Interview with David Bar Ilan, June 9, 1998, Jerusalem; interview with Dore Gold, June 2, 1999, New York.

[30] Madeleine Albright, *Madam Secretary: A Memoir* (New York: Miramax Books, 2003), 298; Caspit and Kfir, *Netanyahu*, 269.

condemnation for planned building on Har Homa, a controversial settlement in municipal Jerusalem; when Dennis Ross pressured Netanyahu to stop the construction, Netanyahu pronounced that if it were a choice between Jerusalem and the U.S. government, he would choose Jerusalem. In his second term, Netanyahu made the same calculation: In August 2011, while trying to convince the United States and the EU to oppose the impending Palestinian efforts to have the United Nations vote to recognize a Palestinian state, he approved building 900 new housing units in Har Homa.[31] According to Ross, "Netanyahu always emphasized that he was not afraid of a fight with us ... he was constantly on guard, constantly in battle, and trying to head off things we would do."[32] When Netanyahu, as prime minister, had his first meeting with President Clinton in July 1996, he did not behave, according to Clinton, in a way that showed that he knew that Clinton was the president of a friendly superpower and that Netanyahu was the leader of a small nation that needed the superpower's support. He visited leading Republicans, Christian fundamentalists, and Jewish groups before meeting with Clinton, in hopes of influencing Clinton to tone down his pressure on Israel.[33]

Robert Freedman perceptively argues that it was almost inevitable that Netanyahu and Obama would clash as they had "different worldviews" and "different Middle East priorities."[34] Netanyahu's priority is the perceived existential threat posed by Iran, and he wants the United States to not only pressure Iran, but be more specific about publicly setting a red line for what would merit military strikes against Iranian nuclear facilities. Obama's priority is U.S. standing in the region, and he believes that solving the Israeli-Palestinian conflict will take ammunition away from anti-American forces. These divergent priorities have set the stage for what has been a fraught relationship between the two leaders. Netanyahu initially resisted the freeze on settlements demanded by President of the Palestinian Authority Abu Mazen, and President Obama; he later accepted a two-state solution (with certain conditions) and a ten-month freeze on settlements on the West Bank. Rumors flew that Netanyahu believed that Obama wanted his government to collapse, that the Jews in Obama's inner circle were self-haters, and that Obama

[31] Akiva Eldar, "EU Slams Israel's Decision to Build New East Jerusalem Housing Project," *Haaretz*, August 6, 2011.

[32] Interview with Dennis Ross, August 6, 1999, Washington, DC; see also, Netanyahu, *A Place Among the Nations*, 371, 392.

[33] Vardi, *Netanyahu*, 67, 85, 124; Remnick, "The Outsider," 95; Steven Erlanger, "Israel Urges U.S. to Keep Peace Plan Quiet, but It's Already Out," *The New York Times*, March 5, 1998, A11; Ilan Kfir, *Barak: Biography* (Israel: Alfah Communications, 1999), 399. Netanyahu is the most "American" Israeli leader. For many years he held dual Israeli and American citizenship. He lived in America between the ages of eight and ten and during his high school years; he attended M.I.T. and then Sloan Business School after serving in the Israeli army. He considered staying in America and changing his name to Benjamin Nitai.

[34] Robert O. Freedman, "George W. Bush, Barack Obama, and the Arab-Israeli Conflict," *Israel and the United States: Six Decades of US-Israeli Relations*, ed. Robert O. Freedman (Boulder, CO: Westview Press, 2012), 57.

was using criticism of Israel to improve the relationship between the United States and the Muslim world.[35]

4. How Much Will Peace Contribute to Security? Does Peace Require Territorial Compromise?

Echoing Jabotinsky's key metaphor of the "iron wall," Netanyahu entitles one of his chapters in *A Place Among the Nations* "The Wall." In it, he argues that "the incontrovertible need for the protective wall" of the Samarian and Judean mountains "rules out another Arab state injected in between Israel and Jordan"; "to survive," he argues, "Israel must keep [them] in its control forever."[36] Peleg writes that Netanyahu's militaristic attitude is similar to Jabotinksy's and that he does not view peace as a product of mutual recognition and accommodation, "but a function of strength, deterrence, and domination."[37] Netanyahu thinks that when the Arabs recognize Israel's strength, they will make concessions.

According to Netanyahu, not only does peace not require deep territorial compromise; a peace agreement will not significantly enhance security. In a Knesset meeting after the Oslo Accords, Netanyahu accused Rabin of deluding himself about the peace process. Netanyahu does not think that treaties with Syria or the Palestinians would make them any more likely to remain neutral if Israel were attacked by Iraq or Iran. Formal peace does not eliminate the possibility of future wars because the Arabs will remain hostile and "you cannot end the struggle for survival without ending life itself."[38]

Since hostility between Israel and the Palestinians is permanent, regardless of a peace agreement, Netanyahu focuses on deterrence and believes that concessions are perceived as acts of weakness, encouraging further demands. For instance, in 1992, he used the word *weakness* ten times in a single paragraph in referring to the Labor Party's misguided readiness to make concessions. He believes that Israel is in danger of moving quickly from a superior military position to one of extreme weakness. After his defeat in May 1999, he warned that "if Israel complies with their [Palestinian] demands, it will soon find itself dwarfed, shrunken, with its back to the sea. Such a state will be a constant temptation to threats of aggression and terror." Therefore, Israel will never reach a sufficient level of security and "that is why we exert constant efforts to magnify our power, to expand, and not to limit, the IDF's [Israeli Defense Force] scope of action. We seek to strengthen, not weaken, our hold on the land."[39]

---

[35] Gil Hoffman and Herb Keinon, "Ya'alon Tells PM He Was Misunderstood," *The Jerusalem Post*, August 20, 2009.

[36] Netanyahu, *A Place Among the Nations*, 353.

[37] Peleg, "The Likud Under Rabin II," 155.

[38] Netanyahu, *A Place Among the Nations*, 337, 376; see also Caspit and Kfir, *Netanyahu*, 139; confirmed by interview with Bar Ilan, June 9, 1998, Jerusalem, Israel; Vardi, *Netanyahu*, 206; Benjamin Netanyahu, *Knesset Minutes*, April 18, 1994, 6251.

[39] Joel Greenberg, "Resigning from Parliament, Netanyahu Hints at Return," *The New York Times*, May 28, 1999; see also Benjamin Netanyahu, *Knesset Minutes*, October 26, 1992, 23; Netanyahu,

Cognitive Style

The way in which Netanyahu's ideology shapes his perceptions of the Palestinian leadership, the urgency for peace, or the desirability of a Palestinian state, is reinforced by his cognitive style. His orientation toward the past, his lack of emotional intelligence, and his low propensity for risk, also worked to limit the degree to which he has changed his views.

1. Time Orientation

If Netanyahu's ideology encourages his hostile image of the Palestinians, this ideology is reinforced by his psychological propensity to focus on past conflicts with enemies in general, and with the Palestinians in particular. Netanyahu's many references to the past in *A Place Among the Nations*, and his derision for the "fashionable ahistoricism prevalent today," reflect this thinking.[40] He argues that the Jews have struggled for 3,000 years for the land, and the situation has not changed: mocking Peres in the Knesset, he retorted, "[Y]ou wrote a book about the new Middle East, but what can be done, the old Middle East is exploding in your face."[41]

Netanyahu not only looks to the ancient past, but views it as part of the present. His father inculcated the lesson that, even though the Muslims conquered Spain for 800 years, they could not claim that it was theirs; the Spanish retained their right to independence. Likewise, Netanyahu argues that "it was not the Jews who usurped the land from the Arabs, but the Arabs who usurped the land from the Jews" when they conquered the land in the seventh century. Historical accuracy aside – the Romans in fact were responsible for most of the Jewish expulsions – for Netanyahu the ancient past is neither ancient, nor past.[42]

Netanyahu frequently uses Czechoslovakia before World War II as a historical analogy for Israel, in which the West Bank is the Sudetenland, the pretext used by Hitler to overrun the entire country. He draws parallels between German and Arab aggression, between Hitler and Arafat. Right after the Oslo agreement was announced, Netanyahu published an op-ed piece in the *New York Times* entitled "Peace in Our Time?" referring to British Prime Minister Neville Chamberlain's infamous statement after his Munich "agreement" with Hitler. Netanyahu refers to this statement in his book as well.[43] Thus Netanyahu exhibits a strong tendency to turn to the past – a past characterized by violence and conflict – to shape his view of the present.

A Place Among the Nations, 244–48; interview of Benjamin Netanyahu by Tsvi Gilat, *Yediot Ahronot*, September 3, 1993; Netanyahu, *Knesset Minutes*, September 21, 1993, 143.

[40] Netanyahu, *A Place Among the Nations*, 25, 29; interview with Dore Gold, June 2, 1999, New York.

[41] Benjamin Netanyahu, *Knesset Minutes*, April 18, 1994, 6248. See also Benjamin Netanyahu, [Only the People Are Entitled to Decide], *Ma'ariv*, September 3, 1993, B2.

[42] Netanyahu, *A Place Among the Nations*, 25; see also Vardi, *Netanyahu*, 130.

[43] Netanyahu, "Peace In Our Time?" E11; Netanyahu, *A Place Among the Nations*, 157; Vardi, *Netanyahu*, 204.

2. Risk Propensity

Netanyahu tends to be risk averse, particularly when it comes to retaining his political position.[44] He does not want to risk the breakup of his coalition. When he signed the Wye accord, he did so to decrease the risk to his public support vis-à-vis potential political opponents like Barak; he did not foresee that his coalition would collapse. In his second term, he was so adamant about retaining the coalition that he risked much friction with the world and especially the United States, and also was willing to bear criticism and the loose cannon of his foreign minister, Avigdor Lieberman, who did not refrain from publicly defying and contradicting Netanyahu's stated policies. Even though he was expected to win a future election if he were to complete his second term, he again showed risk aversion by calling for early elections when there was no clear challenger, and forming a bloc with Likud and Yisrael Beitenu in order to circumvent the threat from the right and preempt the center-left from forming a bloc. On the one hand, this risk aversion might be seen to express itself in Netanyahu's relative reluctance to take significant military risks in either term. Unlike other prime ministers, he did not invade Lebanon, and did not reoccupy major portions of the West Bank. In November 2012 Netanyahu launched Operation Pillar of Defense to end rocket attacks against Israel; he ended the operation after eight days of fighting without introducing Israeli ground troops or tanks into Gaza. The operation was far more limited than the three-week-long Operation Cast Lead under a Kadima government in December 2008/January 2009. Also, despite his many declarations that the Iranian threat is existential and that it may commit genocide against Israel, Netanyahu refrained from taking the risk of bombing Iran's nuclear facilities during his second term in office and during the first year of his third term. This kind of risk aversion might be seen as conducive to peace (since it avoids war). On the other hand, this risk aversion also expresses itself in his great reluctance to take the risks that he perceives are inherent in peace agreements.

3. Cognitive Flexibility

In addition to Netanyahu's focus on the past, his cognitive rigidity also reinforces his hostile image of the Palestinians, as he evaluates the world in stark contrasts.[45]

---

[44] This has been affirmed by many who have had frequent interactions with and interviews of Netanyahu. For instance, David Makovsky and Ghaith al-Omari both claimed this in a conversation I had with them on September 13, 2012, at Michigan State University. Makovsky is the Ziegler Distinguished Fellow and Director of the Project on the Middle East Peace Process at the Washington Institute for Near East Policy. Al-Omari is Executive Director of the American Taskforce on Palestine. Likewise, Natasha Mozgavaya – who headed the Washington Bureau of the Israeli newspaper *Haaretz* from 2008 to 2012, and worked for the Israeli newspaper *Yedioth Ahronot* from 2000 to 2008 and had interviewed Netanyahu ten times – also attested to his risk aversion in an interview I had with her on March 31, 2013, at Michigan State University.

[45] Shaul Kimhi, "Benjamin Netanyahu: A Psychological Profile," in *Profiling Political Leaders: Cross-Cultural Studies of Personality and Behavior*, eds. Ofer Feldman and Linda Valenty (London: Praeger, 2001). Kimhi codes 170 Israeli newspapers and magazines from 1985 to 1997, books written by Netanyahu, and books about Netanyahu; He also concludes that Netanyahu exhibits a rigid personality.

Although Netanyahu is capable of compromise, he often ignores opinions that differ from his own. According to those who have worked with him, Netanyhu tends to believe that those who disagree with him do not understand historical/political processes correctly, and therefore to ignore their opinions. Several of his best childhood friends found it hard to hold a conversation with him: As one put it, "Anyone who didn't agree with him was automatically wrong. He would end his speech by determining that we were all wrong and that was it."[46]

Netanyahu resembles U.S. President Richard Nixon in his distrust in and antipathy for "the establishment" – those perceived as controlling the corridors of power and influence through their political affiliations. Netanyahu acquired this antipathy from his father, who was convinced that the Hebrew University did not hire him because of his right-wing activism. Embittered toward the Labor Party–dominated "establishment," he took his family to the United States where he taught for fifteen years. When Netanyahu considered running for prime minister, his father retorted that those Bolsheviks would not let him win. To defeat the Bolshevik establishment was a family mission. The Oslo Accords were the ultimate expression of the Left's immorality because they were willing to put the country's security in the hands of the Arabs. Hagi Ben-Artzi, Netanyahu's brother-in-law, argues that "the Netanyahus were obsessed with Ben-Zion's persecution which created a paranoid atmosphere toward outsiders" and a deep resentment of the Labor establishment.[47]

Netanyahu perceives Israel's cultural and media institutions as part of this leftist establishment that opposes him. The press's criticism led him to identify with his father's persecution. After the botched Mossad attempt to kill Khaled Meshaal, a senior member of the political wing of Hamas in Jordan, on September 25, 1997, Netanyahu – who had ordered the attack – accused the press of a campaign to overthrow him. Just a few days before his 1999 election defeat, Netanyahu claimed that the media set aside professional ethics for Barak's victory. Always feeling the outsider, he hates the elite/leftists/media in a visceral way, thinks that they view him as an illegitimate usurper, and fights against them.[48]

---

[46] Caspit and Kfir, *Netanyahu*, 34, 89; see also David Margolick, "Star of Zion," *Vanity Fair* (June 1996), 63; Arye Naor, "Greater Israel in Likud Governments: Begin, Shamir, and Netanyahu," (presented at the 15th Annual Meeting of the Association for Israel Studies, Washington, D.C., May 23–25 1999); Kimhi, "Benjamin Netanyahu," 155.

[47] Interview with Hemi Shelev, journalist for *Ma'ariv*, May 24, 1998, Jerusalem; Remnick, "The Outsider," 86, 88, 94; Kimhi, "Benjamin Netanyahu," 155; Vardi, *Netanyahu*, 56, 87, 225; Halevi, "His Father's Son," 13; Serge Schemann, "Outside In," *New York Times Magazine*, November 23, 1997, 56, 58.

[48] Remnick, "The Outsider," 86, 88, 95; interview with Hemi Shelev, May 24, 1998, Jerusalem; Halevi, "His Father's Son," 13; Deborah Sontag and William A. Orme, Jr., "With Prospects Bleaker, Netanyahu Lashes Out," *New York Times*, May 14, 1999, A3; Schemann, "Outside In," 56–58.

Netanyahu not only inherited from his father a sense of persecution from and hatred for the Labor Party establishment, but also for the "establishment" in the Revisionist movement and the Likud Party. After Jabotinsky's death, Ben-Zion was treated as an outcast by Israel's right-wing politicians because he believed that Likud leaders had betrayed Jabotinsky's teachings. Netanyahu regards his Likud colleagues with that same contempt. After Netanyahu accused Likud leader David Levy of blackmailing his wife, one of Netanyahu's advisors said that Netanyahu first fires and then aims.[49] In 1993, when Netanyahu took over the Likud Central Committee, the Likud became a party of a single opinion – his. Previously, the word *traitor* had never been used in internal political disputes, but Netanyahu deployed it against Benny Begin and other rivals in the Likud Party.[50]

4. *Emotional Intelligence*

Netanyahu's rigidity is magnified by his deep-rooted suspicion of others, which deters him from listening to advice. Netanyahu resembles Rose McDermott's description of Richard Nixon as a deeply suspicious person, who like Netanyahu fired many officials and wanted to be surrounded by yes-men.[51] He perceives others as enemies or potential enemies and thereby is reluctant to compromise, even at political costs to himself. Milton Rokeach argues that "an enduring state of threat in the personality is one condition giving rise to closed belief systems" and that "the correlations between closed belief systems and anxiety are always positive."[52] This correlation between a feeling of threat and a closed mind seems to hold for Netanyahu.

Netanyahu was so suspicious of even his closest advisors that as a result of leaks to the press, he had his whole office – top officials in the foreign ministry as well as his top advisors – undergo polygraph tests in February 1998. Dan Naveh felt humiliated and told Netanyahu that it was not the way to handle his mistrust of people. Media affairs advisor Shai Bezek's test results were unclear (despite what Naveh describes as many years of hard work and loyalty); Bezek was exiled to Miami to work in the Israeli consulate.[53]

Netanyahu's deep suspicion led him to adopt uncompromising stances, even at the risk of weakening his own coalition. Netanyahu firmly believed in privatizing the economy, but he moved control of the privatization program to his office in order to minimize the influence of the popular Likud finance minister, Dan Meridor. Meridor resigned on June 18, 1997, after an annual economic forum in which the participants, along with the Bank of Israel, criticized

---

[49] Orit, Galili, "Let's Not Talk About It," *Haaretz*, December 31, 1993.

[50] Halevi, "His Father's Son," 14; Caspit and Kfir, *Netanyahu*, 178, 195.

[51] Rose McDermott, *Presidential Leadership, Illness, and Decision Making* (Cambridge: Cambridge University Press, 2008), 157–96.

[52] Rokeach, *The Open and Closed Mind* (New York: Basic Books, 1960), 403.

[53] Naveh, *Executive Secrets*, 178–79.

Netanyahu's monetary policy and recommended that interest rates be cut. Netanyahu ignored this advice and did the opposite. Netanyahu was convinced that Meridor was behind the media criticism of his policies and did not talk to him for a year.[54] Netanyahu acted in the same rigid, uncompromising manner in regard to Foreign Minister David Levy's budget requests, leading to Levy's resignation on January 4, 1998. Although Levy had warned that he would resign unless more funds were allocated for social welfare, and Netanyahu depended on his political support and the support of the four other Gesher Party members of the coalition who would leave with Levy, Netanyahu would not compromise. Ironically, after the budget passed, Netanyahu announced that he would propose amendments to the budget to allocate $98 million for poor cities and other social projects, which Levy had demanded before his resignation. Netanyahu risked the downfall of his coalition, which then rested on only 61 seats in the 120-member Knesset, at a time when a Gallop poll showed that in a new election Ehud Barak would win.[55]

According to Dennis Ross, Netanyahu failed to understand that his extreme suspiciousness created a self-fulfilling prophecy by turning those who should have been his natural allies into enemies.[56] If he had returned phone calls from Shamir, who had helped him get elected, perhaps Shamir would have toned down his criticism of Netanyahu. If he brought Arens, who was responsible for developing and encouraging Netanyahu's career, closer to him, as well as his defense minister Yitzhak Mordechai, they might not have turned into adversaries. Netanyahu was suspicious that Mordechai was going to run against him for prime minister and fired him on January 30, 1999. Of those ministers who did not resign or were not fired, most did not bother greeting him when he entered the room for Sunday morning meetings. After one opening speech at a new Knesset session, not one minister came forward to give him the traditional congratulatory handshake.[57]

The degree to which Netanyahu categorized people as his enemies is also exhibited by his participation in rallies against Rabin before Rabin's assassination. In July 1995, Netanyahu headed a mock funeral procession in which Rabin's coffin and a hangman's noose were borne on high and people cried

54　Neill Lochery, *The Difficult Road to Peace: Netanyahu, Israel and the Middle East Peace Process* (Reading, England: Garnet Publishing, 1999), 14; Nahum Barnea, *Yemey Netanyahu* [*Bibi Time: Political Columns, 1993–1999*] (Tel Aviv: Lezmorah-Beitan, 1999), 428; Nehemia Strasler, "Meridor One Year Later: Netanyahu Operates by 'Cynicism, Manipulation, Image-Building,'" *Ha'aretz*, June 22, 1998.

55　Naveh, *Executive Secrets*, 16–18, 64; Serge Schmemann, "Despite Defection, Israeli Premier Wins Budget Vote," *New York Times*, January 6, 1998; Serge Schemann, "Suspense Is Rising in Israel Over Impasse on the Budget: No Progress on Netanyahu's Rival's Demands," *New York Times*, January 3, 1998.

56　Interview with Dennis Ross, August 6, 1999, Washington, DC.

57　Yoel Markus, "Remarks on the Situation," *Ha'aretz*, March 7, 1997; Halevi, "His Father's Son," 16; Susser, "How Vulnerable Is Bibi?" *The Jerusalem Report*, November 27, 1997.

"death to Rabin!" After the rally, Carmi Gilon, the head of internal security, informed Netanyahu about a plot to assassinate Rabin and asked him to tone down his rhetoric. Instead, Netanyahu ordered Uri Aloni to step up the protests. In October, when the Knesset voted in favor of the second Oslo Accord, there was a mass rally in Jerusalem at which protesters held simulated photographs of Rabin in a Nazi SS uniform, while others charged "Rabin is a murderer!" and "Rabin is a traitor!" and set fire to Rabin's picture. Netanyahu spoke to the crowd while standing right next to a poster reading "Death to Rabin."[58] Netanyahu's involvement in these protests was in part attributable to a combination of his rigidity, which led him to view Rabin in such starkly negative terms, and a political calculation that these character assassinations could help his own campaign. After the assassination, some accused his campaign of contributing to an atmosphere that facilitated violence; Netanyahu's response was to accuse the Labor Party of McCarthyism and the press with conducting a witch hunt against him.[59]

Advisors

Netanyahu is reluctant to rely on cabinet members and bureaucrats since he is suspicious of their loyalty. He tried to minimize the influence of the Foreign Ministry, headed by his archrival David Levy, and to downgrade the influence of the minister of defense, Yitzhak Mordechai. Yoram Peri persuasively argues that because of his reliance on young aides who agreed with him, and his belief that the senior military establishment was sympathetic to the Labor Party, Netanyahu often ignored the military's advice. Major General Oren Shchor claimed that "there is an atmosphere of acute paranoia and witch hunting on the part of the prime minister, directed at the IDF's high echelons."[60] In early August 1996, Netanyahu excluded his generals from the peace process. Although Yitzhak Mordechai, Chief of Staff Amnon Shahak, and the Internal Security Chief Ami Ayalon all agreed that unilaterally opening a second entrance to the Hasmonean tunnel running along the side of the Temple Mount without first consulting with the leader of the Waqf – the Muslim religious leadership in Jerusalem – could cause serious rioting in the city, Netanyahu ignored their advice. In the riots that followed, more than twenty-six Israeli soldiers and one hundred Palestinians died, and hundreds were injured.[61] Netanyahu also

58 Yitzhak Rabin, *Knesset Minutes*, April 18, 1994, 6244; Benjamin Netanyahu, *Knesset Minutes*, February 28, 1994, 4910; Vardi, *Netanyahu*, 293; Caspit and Kfir, *Netanyahu*, 213, 216.
59 Jonathan Mendilow, "The Likud's Double Campaign: Between the Devil and the Deep Blue Sea," in *The Elections in Israel 1996*, eds. Asher Arian and Michal Shamir (Albany: State University of New York Press, 1999), 195.
60 Yoram Peri, *Generals in the Cabinet Room: How the Military Shapes Israeli Policy* (Washington DC: United States Institute of Peace Press, 2006), 87.
61 Interviews with Bar Ilan and Hemi Shelev, May 24, 1998, Jerusalem; Neill Lochery, "The Netanyahu Era: From Crisis to Crisis, 1996–1999," *Israel Affairs* 6, nos. 3 & 4 (Spring/Summer

ignored Chief of Staff Amonon Shahak's warning that if the peace process slowed down, the army would have to prepare for a Palestinian uprising and possibly even war. In 1998, Netanyahu dismissed an Internal Security assessment that the Palestinian Authority was making a serious effort to fight terror. Netanyahu's relationship with the military got so bad that in mid-October 1996, Internal Security ordered Israeli troops to appear without their rifles when the prime minister visited their army base.[62]

Netanyahu's suspicion of people, including experienced politicians, and his conviction that he is always right led him to often work alone and rely only on a few inexperienced yes-men and close family members. Because Netanyahu's suspicion of outsiders carried over to his staff, there was little coordination or exchange of ideas among them. He relied on one advisor for each area, which meant he got only one opinion. David Bar Ilan and Dore Gold both attest to the fact that meetings with a large number of participants, in which different opinions were aired, were rare because of Netanyahu's fear of leaks. Netanyahu is a loner with no close friends or constant inner circle of trusted advisors with whom he has maintained long-term relationships. He continually changed advisors because of his great mistrust of people. Bar Ilan considered himself to be one of Netanyahu's two or three closest confidants but that even with him, Bibi was very closed: "Netanyahu is a close to the chest player, he relies on very few people, and even on them he relies only for certain things."[63]

Ministers continued to resign, and those who stayed had tense relationships with Netanyahu. He was deprived of more moderate voices when David Levy and Dan Meridor resigned, and he fired Defense Minister Mordechai. Benny Begin resigned and Netanyahu had the worst confrontations with his new foreign minister, Ariel Sharon, who suspected that he was left out of decisions. The break between Netanyahu and Natan Sharansky, the leader of the main party representing Russian immigrants (Israel in Aliya), led Sharansky to vote for Barak.[64] Although Netanyahu's coalition initially held 68 seats in the Knesset, by the end of his first administration he was supported by only 61 of the 120 Knesset seats. Netanyahu was preoccupied with what the coalition would bear. In order to appeal to his right-wing base, he had to make it clear that he would hold out longer and give up less than Labor would have done.[65]

2000): 225, 226; Mark Rosenblum, "Netanyahu and Peace: From Sound Bites to Sound Policies?" in *The Middle East and the Peace Process: The Impact of the Oslo Accords*, ed. Robert O. Freedman (Gainesville: University Press of Florida, 1998), 67; Caspit and Kfir, *Netanyahu*, 260, 261.

[62] Leslie Susser, "History Repeating Itself?" *The Jerusalem Report*, June 22, 1998, 15–16; Rosenblum, "Netanyahu and Peace," 68.

[63] Interview with David Bar Ilan; also confirmed by interview with Dore Gold, June 2, 1999, New York; and Hemi Shelev, May 24, 1998, Jerusalem; Halevi, "His Father's Son," 16; Vardi, *Netanyahu*, 14, 184.

[64] Naveh, *Executive Secrets*, 196–97, 200.

[65] Schmemann, "Outside In," 58; interview with Dennis Ross, August 6, 1999, Washington, DC.

In his second term Netanyahu created the largest cabinet in Israel's history, and pragmatically brought Begin and Meridor, with whom he had quarreled in his first term, into his government, and did not face as many resignations. However, the prime minister's bureau was perceived as dysfunctional for having internal dissent and ill-defined responsibilities. He moved to appoint a chief of staff after he replaced bureau director Ari Harrow after only one year. Bureau chief Natan Eshel was criticized for not being familiar with defense, state, and economic affairs, and was widely believed to have been appointed because of his close ties to Sara Netanyahu, with whom he had to maintain contact as part of his job.[66]

IMAGE OF THE ENEMY

Netanyahu's ideology intensified his perception of the hostility that Israel faces, and his emphasis on the past conflict with the Palestinians. His cognitive rigidity reinforced his deep suspicion of advisors and ministers while the "yes-men" with whom he surrounded himself confirmed the validity of this image. Throughout his political career, Netanyahu has not significantly altered his image of the Palestinians. He believed, and continues to believe, that Palestinians are bent on Israel's destruction and continue to support terrorism, with the 1974 phased plan calling for Israel's destruction still in effect. According to Netanyahu, the "PLO is committed, sinews and flesh, tooth and nail, to the eradication of Israel by any means" and therefore peace is merely a "tactical intermission in a continuing total war."[67] Netanyahu omits or dismisses moderate PLO pronouncements and quotes only its more radical statements. Before meeting with President Clinton on January 20, 1998, Netanyahu's cabinet issued a document detailing fifty Palestinian violations of the peace accords to be corrected ahead of any further withdrawals. Netanyahu claims that the only way that the PLO will change is if it ceases to exist.[68] After Netanyahu succeeded in having the PLO formally amend its Covenant, he still was unconvinced that its goals were limited to the West Bank and Gaza because some officials would refer to UN resolution 181, which also includes places in Israel proper. In 2010, he continued to say that he saw no signs of moderation among the Palestinians.[69] In 2012, he often

---

[66] Barak Ravid, "Netanyahu Seeks Chief of Staff to Fix His Dysfunctional Bureau," *Haaretz*, March 14, 2010.

[67] Netanyahu, *A Place Among the Nations*, 210, 232–33, 329, 337, 344. Confirmed by interviews with Bar Ilan and Michael Kleiner, June 30, 1998, Jerusalem; Hemi Shelev, May 24, 1998, Jerusalem; see also interview of Benjamin Netanyahu by Tsvi Gilat, *Yediot Ahronot*, September 3, 1993.

[68] Interview of Benjamin Netanyahu by Tsvi Gilat, *Yediot Ahronot*, September 3, 1993; Peleg, "The Likud Under Rabin II," 157; Leslie Susser, "Unity Finale for Netanyahu's Three Stage Balancing Act," *The Jerusalem Report*, February 5, 1998; Deborah Sontag, "Netanyahu Sees Enemies All Around Him," *The New York Times*, April 23, 1999, A13.

[69] Interview with Dore Gold, June 2, 1999, New York; Barak Ravid and Anshel Pfeffer, "Is a Serious Israel-EU Crisis in the Works?" *Haaretz*, March 20, 2010.

challenged Abu Mazen as not a genuine peace partner. For example, in one televised interview he claimed, "When Abu Mazen embraces Hamas and allows Hamas protests to take place in the West Bank that call for the elimination of Israel I ask myself, is he a partner for peace? You need to ask a simple question – why has Abu Mazen been refusing for four years to enter negotiations? Why is he posing preconditions?"[70]

Netanyahu's image of the enemy is intensified by strong emotions. Netanyahu was closest to his brother Yonatan, and he holds Arafat accountable for Yonatan's death while leading the successful hostage rescue in Entebbe, Uganda, in 1976. Netanyahu subsequently established the Jonathan Institute for the study of terrorism and edited the book *Terrorism: How the West Can Win*.[71] Netanyahu's role in directly combating terrorism while in the military, and his focus on terrorism after his brother's death, led him to be even more inclined to view the PLO as an organization with a history of denying terrorism while engaging in it.[72] Yonatan's death also made Netanyahu less inclined to release Palestinian suspects, as demanded by the Palestinian Authority. When Netanyahu eventually did release prisoners as required by agreement with the Palestinians, his mother told the press that if prisoners are released with blood on their hands, then her son died for nothing (since the Entebbe raid was conducted instead of releasing prisoners as demanded by the hostages.) She influenced her son to prevent further releases until her death in 2000 and said that the notion of peace with the Arabs was absurd.[73] However, in 2011, under immense domestic pressure, Netanyahu released 1,027 Palestinian prisoners as a result of indirect negotiations with Hamas to achieve the release of captured Israeli soldier Gilad Shalit. In 2013, as a result of American pressure, Netanyahu agreed to release 104 Palestinian prisoners as a good faith measure to begin negotiations with the Palestinian Authority.

Netanyahu rejected a suggestion that Likud recognize the PLO in 1994, and had it not been for the reality created by Oslo, Netanyahu never would have dealt with the PLO.[74] Netanyahu's decision to negotiate with the PLO was not preceded or followed by a change in his image of the organization. After he won the 1996 election, Netanyahu did not call Arafat. Even Naveh, who shared Netanyahu's hostile image of the Palestinians and his ideology, claims that Netanyahu was mistaken in not forming a relationship with Mohamed

---

[70] Channel 2 News Interview of Benjamin Netanyahu, December 24, 2012.

[71] Benjamin Netanyahu, *Terrorism: How the West Can Win* (New York: Farrar Straus & Giroux, 1986).

[72] Vardi, *Netanyahu*; Margolick, "Star of Zion," 64; interview with Hemi Shelev, May 24, 1998, Jerusalem; address by Prime Minister Benjamin Netanyahu to a Joint Session of the United States Congress, Washington, DC, July 10, 1996, 3; Netanyahu, *A Place Among the Nations*, 207.

[73] Shalom Yerushalmi, "Lo Solahat, Lo Motset Nehama" [Does Not Forgive, Does Not Find Consolation], *Ma'ariv*, March 11, 1997.

[74] Interview with Dennis Ross, August 6, 1999, Washington, DC. See also Caspit and Kfir, *Netanyahu*, 197; Mendilow, "The Likud's Double Campaign," 201.

Rashid, a member of the Palestinian Authority with a strong influence on Arafat. Even after losing office, Netanyahu continued to insist that time was on Israel's side and that all military means should be used to attack Arafat and his supporters, even if it meant the collapse of Arafat's regime. In 2010, he continued to tell his cabinet that there were no signs of moderation among the Palestinians.[75]

Reaction to the Intifada, 1988 PLO Proclamation, the Gulf War, and the End of the Cold War

Netanyahu's ideology led him to believe that ultimately time was on Israel's side regarding the Palestinians who were permanently hostile to Israel. This ideology, combined with his focus on the history of the conflict and his relatively rigid mind, prevented Netanyahu from reassessing his image of the Palestinians or his policies toward them even in light of dramatic events in the region. He felt no need to seize what some saw as a window of opportunity for peace after the Soviet Union collapsed, or after the PLO was weakened following the first Gulf War.[76]

As with Shamir, Netanyahu's ideological conviction that time was on Israel's side also shaped his reaction to the first intifada from 1986–1993: he believed that the intifada would lose momentum on its own, that Arafat was defeated, that the economic hardship emanating from the intifada led many Palestinians to want to emigrate, and that Israel could wait it out without trying to reach a peace settlement. The Labor government's release of prisoners would only reinvigorate the intifada because the Arabs would perceive it as a sign of weakness. Netanyahu had learned from his father that a hundred years of war are nothing in the life of a nation, and thus that the intifada did not require new policies.[77]

Netanyahu equated the intifada with past uses of violence and argued that "a rock the size of a baseball hurled into a car traveling at sixty miles per hour is a weapon at least as deadly as a knife or an ax" and bemoaned the international community's separate standards for judging Israel's actions. Netanyahu's focus on the history of the conflict convinced him that the intifada was not about fighting occupation in the West Bank, but about driving "the Jews from every inch of Israel." He continues to decry "the campaign of delegitimization that has challenged the right of Jews to live in the heartland of Israel," and claims that this is due to "historical amnesia."[78] Jews, he argues, had lived for millennia in places such as Hebron and Jerusalem, and the historical rights of Jews to live on

[75] Naveh, *Executive Secrets*, 24, 27; Vardi, *Netanyahu*, 99; Thomas L. Friedman, "Israel at 50," *The New York Times*, February 14, 1998; Marcus, "Hannibal"; Barak Ravid, "Is a Serious Israel-EU Crisis in the Works?" *Haaretz*, March 29, 2010.

[76] Interview with Dore Gold, June 2, 1999, New York.

[77] Benjamin Netanyahu, *Knesset Minutes*, October 26, 1992, 23, 24; Moshe Arens, "From Oslo to the Al Aqsa Intifada," *Ha'aretz*, November 14, 2000; Vardi, *Netanyahu*, 252.

[78] Netanyahu, *A Place Among the Nations*, 165–78, 229, 303.

the West Bank was recognized by the world in the Balfour Declaration, the Treaty of Versailles, and the League of Nations Mandate.

Although the 1988 PLO statement could be read as recognizing Israel and abrogating terror, Netanyahu interpreted it as showing the deviousness of the PLO rather than moderation. Netanyahu's analysis of the statement was that, "leaving aside the peculiar view that words alone suffice for the political redemption of tyrants and terrorists, a view contradicted by a long list of despots in this century who have habitually lied to achieve their ends, it must be noted that these words, which the Americans extracted from the PLO the way one pulls a tooth, did not amount to much."[79] Netanyahu, then the Israeli ambassador to the United Nations, ignored Peres's directive from the Foreign Office for all Israeli ambassadors to cease verbal attacks on Arafat, and continued to call Arafat a terrorist with blood on his hands. Immediately after the signing of the Oslo Accords, he argued that "since [Arafat's] 'breakthrough' promise in 1988 to stop PLO terror, his own Fatah faction has launched more terrorist attacks against Israel than any other Palestinian group."[80]

Rabin and Peres interpreted the post–Cold War environment in the Middle East as more conducive to peace because the PLO and Syria had lost support from the Soviet Union and were more dependent on the United States; in contrast Netanyahu found it more dangerous. As he saw it, whereas the Soviet Union was sometimes able to control the aggressive impulses of its clients, now there was no one in the region to check their ambitions other than Israel. Netanyahu believes that the East-West conflict has been replaced with the Arab-Western conflict.[81] Therefore, he does not perceive there to be any incentive for the PLO to moderate its stance toward Israel in order to gain the favor of the only superpower, and perceives the chances for peace to be even lower than they were before.

The Gulf War strengthened Netanyahu's hostile image of the Palestinians, and he did not perceive it to be a window of opportunity for peace. According to Netanyahu, the Gulf War tore down the myth that the heart of the conflict in the Middle East was the Palestinian problem. Decisive in this narrative was Palestinian sympathy and support for Saddam Hussein. An opinion poll following Iraq's invasion of Kuwait suggested that 80 percent of Palestinians supported Saddam. This strengthened Netanyahu's view that the Palestinians were out to destroy Israel, and that Israel should not make any concessions to them. For him, this proved that a Palestinian state would work with Iran and Iraq to endanger Israel's existence.[82] When he was deputy foreign minister, in the beginning of March 1990, Netanyahu surprised his political mentor Moshe Arens by opposing Arens' plan to work with U.S. Secretary of State James Baker's strategy for

[79] Ibid., 212, 214.
[80] Benjamin Netanyahu, "Peace In Our Time?" See also Caspit and Kfir, *Netanyahu*, 126, 127.
[81] Netanyahu, *A Place Among the Nations*, 391; Peleg, "The Likud Under Rabin II," 156.
[82] Netanyahu, *A Place Among the Nations*, 91–129, 313; Colette Avital, "It's Time to Talk to Fatah," *The Jerusalem Post*, August 19, 2009.

negotiating with non-PLO Palestinians.[83] Despite this, he went with Shamir to Madrid, but like Shamir had no intention of making any territorial concessions.

CONSEQUENT POLICY PREFERENCES (FIRST TERM, 1996–1999)

None of these events – the first intifada, the 1988 PLO declaration, the end of the Cold War, or the first Gulf War – caused Netanyahu to reevaluate his image of or policies toward the Palestinians; indeed, they served only to confirm his prior convictions. Thus, following the Madrid conference, he argued that Israel should annex Gaza and the West Bank, giving autonomy to four Palestinian urban centers.[84] What did affect eventual changes in his policy preferences was not his reassessment of regional conditions or a perception of increasing moderation on the part of the PLO, but his desire to get elected and to remain in office.

From Total Opposition to Oslo to Tactical Acceptance

Netanyahu did not change his antipathy toward the Oslo Accords, but support for him plummeted after Rabin's assassination, and he was forced to recognize the public's preference for peace in order to win the election. Therefore, in late April 1996, he publicly declared that he would recognize the provisions of the Oslo Accords, against his father's advice. Initially, Netanyahu declared that when he became prime minister, there would be no additional territorial concessions. He ended up accepting "the new reality," but without genuine change in attitude. In Likud Party Central Committee Meetings two years into his term, he continued to refer to Oslo as a horrible and irresponsible agreement.[85]

To the regret of the American administration, the mantra of "reciprocity" was the new centerpiece and ultimate weapon of Netanyahu's policy toward the Palestinians during his first term as prime minister. Since he did not believe that the Palestinians would live up to their commitments, he had an excuse for Israel not fulfilling its Oslo obligations.[86] David Bar Ilan explained that "Netanyahu [was] doing everything in his power to reverse what the previous government [had] done." Reciprocity became the exclusive criterion for policy evaluation.[87]

---

[83] Remnick, "The Outsider," 89; interview with Netanyahu family member who did not wish to be identified, 1998, Jerusalem; Arens, *Broken Covenant*, 121.

[84] Netanyahu, *A Place Among the Nations*, 351–52.

[85] Interview with Dan Meridor, June 29, 1998, Jerusalem; Peleg, "The Likud Under Rabin II," 159; Likud Party Central Committee Meeting, December 27, 1998, Document #166/2, 27.

[86] Interviews with Netanyahu family member who did not wish to be identified; Michael Kleiner, June 30, 1998, Jerusalem; and Dore Gold, June 2, 1999, New York; Mendilow, "The Likud's Double Campaign," 201–3; Israel Government Press Office Press bulletin, "Four Years of Israeli Concessions and Palestinian Violations," May 4, 1998; Rosenblum, "Netanyahu and Peace," 55–56.

[87] Interview with David Bar Ilan; Naor, "Greater Israel in Likud Governments," 37–38.

Ian Lustick persuasively argues that Netanyahu treated the Oslo Accords "not as a basis for an evolving partnership, but as an array of legalist and public relations weapons that can free Israel of its commitments, prevent further transfers of territory to Palestinian control, and delegitimize Arafat and the idea of a Palestinian state in the mind of Israeli public opinion."[88]

Hebron Agreement, January 1997

The Oslo II agreement mandated that Israel concede most of Hebron. After much delay and despite Netanyahu's reluctance (he referred to Hebron as the "first Jewish community in history"), he signed the Hebron Agreement, which became the first agreement between a Likud government and the PLO. The IDF had pressed hard to relinquish control of Hebron and wanted to complete the process of Palestinian self-rule. The head of Internal Security told Netanyahu that without a peace process the Palestinians would not cooperate on security matters. Netanyahu was afraid of the possibility of war and that he would be blamed for it. But he faced strong resistance even in his own family. Netanyahu's brother-in-law, Hagi Ben-Artzi, publicly criticized Netanyahu for signing the agreement and went to live in Hebron, arguing that keeping the entire land was a holy principle in the family. Netanyahu's father was also critical of the agreement for betraying Revisionist principles.[89]

Netanyahu justified the deal with several arguments: the Oslo Accords, he said, had already committed Israel to a withdrawal; there was tremendous international pressure; he made a better deal than Labor would have; Israel was not leaving Hebron but rather redeploying in part of the city. He argued in meetings of the Likud Party Central Committee that Oslo was an accordion that had inflated Palestinian expectations to believe they would get 90 percent of the West Bank; he had compressed the accordion so that Palestinians would receive 10 percent plus an extra 3 percent for a nature preserve. He promised that he would not concede more than 1 percent in a third redeployment.[90] Ariel Sharon and Benny Begin opposed the agreement, and Begin resigned over the issue. Thus, while obeying in principle the Oslo Accords and fulfilling the commitment to withdraw from Hebron, Netanyahu took every opportunity to resist the process, and clearly had not changed his view on either the PLO or the peace process itself. In September 2013, in response to an Israeli soldier being killed in Hebron, he announced that settlers should be allowed to reenter

---

[88] Ian S. Lustick, "The Oslo Agreement Used as an Obstacle to Peace." Presented at the American Political Science Association Annual Meeting, Washington, DC, August 28–31, 1999.

[89] Interview with Uzi Landau, July 5, 2007, Raanana; interview with anonymous family member of Netanyahu; David Makovsky, "Hebron: Signed, Sealed, and . . .," *Jerusalem Post*, January 23, 1997; Caspit and Kfir, *Netanyahu*, 162; Remnick, "The Outsider," 84.

[90] Interview with Dennis Ross, August 6, 1999, Washington, DC; Naor, "Greater Israel in Likud Governments," 38; Likud Party Central Committee Meeting, October 10, 1998, Document #165/2, 44–46.

a contested home in Hebron. "Anyone who tries to uproot us from the city of our patriarchs will achieve the opposite," he said. "We will continue to fight terrorism ... with one hand, while strengthening the settlement with the other."[91]

Wye Agreement, October 23, 1998

This pattern of ideological resistance coupled with incremental concessions in the name of electoral politics continued with the Wye Agreement. After eighteen months of stagnation in the peace process, Netanyahu compromised by agreeing to concede part of the Greater Land of Israel. The cabinet was split over ratifying the agreement, and Netanyahu exercised the determining vote. Israel was obligated to make additional withdrawals to implement the second stage of the 1995 Oslo Accords, but Netanyahu conceded less land than the Labor Party would have, and refused to implement most of the withdrawal. Rabin and Peres had withdrawn from 27 percent of the West Bank and Netanyahu agreed to an additional 13 percent. If all provisions were implemented, Arafat would have 41 percent of the land and Israel would retain 59 percent of the land before the start of the final negotiations. In return as an additional incentive, Netanyahu also received a Memorandum of Strategic Understanding from the United States that would strengthen Israel's ability to deter long-range missiles.[92]

Netanyahu was attempting to fulfill his own ideological aims, satisfy the demands of his like-minded coalition partners, *and* improve his popularity with an electorate that seemed to favor peace negotiations. A significant reason for Netanyahu's signing of the agreement was his concern over his own political future. A Gallup poll commissioned by the newspaper *Maariv* indicated that if elections were held before Wye, 41 percent would vote for Barak and 33 percent for Netanyahu. He argued that, by signing, he had reduced what could have been a massive redeployment, to a withdrawal of no more than 1 percent in the third-stage of implementation of the Oslo Accords.[93] Netanyahu, arguing that the Palestinian Authority had not confiscated illegal weapons or stopped incitement against Israel, withdrew from only 2 percent of the 13 percent of land he had agreed upon, despite enormous American pressure.[94] Knesset member Michael Kleiner, arguing that a Palestinian state would eventually try to dismantle Israel, threatened to bring down the government if the planned

[91] Chaim Levinson, "Netanyahu Orders Settlers Be Allowed Back Into Contested Hebron House, *The Jerusalem Post*, September 23, 2013.

[92] Naveh, *Executive Secrets*, 91, 99, 103; Rynhold, "Identity, Values and Culture Change," 266, 267.

[93] Interview with Dore Gold, June 2, 1999, New York; David, Makovsky, "Winding Road to Wye," *Ha'aretz*, April 12, 1998.

[94] Schemann, "Suspense Is Rising in Israel Over Impasse on the Budget"; Naveh, *Executive Secrets*, 138–45; Ministry of Foreign Affairs Information Release No. 16, "Wye River Memorandum: Status of Implementation as of February 1, 1999."

withdrawals in Wye were implemented. Netanyahu attributes the downfall of his government to contradictory demands from the Left to implement Wye and from the Right to tear up the Wye accords.[95] At the same time, Netanyahu made statements that seemed to indicate a shift in stance. In 1993, Netanyahu refused to accept the idea of "land for peace" with regard to the West Bank. In April 1999, he claimed that "territory for peace" might work with reciprocity.[96] This signals a concession on ideological principle, in order to remain politically viable, but with the clear intent of using the idea of "reciprocity" to minimize territorial concessions.

West Bank Settlements

During his first term as prime minister, Netanyahu showed his ideological commitment by doubling construction in the territories, despite 1996 polls showing that 70 percent of the electorate rejected the Likud line on settlements, and despite public rebukes from the United States. This buildup was not based primarily on realpolitik since the military did not think that settlements were needed in order to protect Israeli security interests.[97] Instead, Netanyahu was willing to defy Israeli public opinion and American pressure in order to promote his ideological goals, and because he thought that he could count on the Israeli public to blame the Palestinians for the deadlock in the peace process. Only in his second term, starting in March 2009, did he acquiesce to strong American pressure and agree to a ten-month settlement freeze on the West Bank – but he refused to make such an official freeze for East Jerusalem. He also refused to extend the settlement freeze, despite strong U.S. inducements, which reputedly included an offer of twenty F-35 fighter planes to Israel.[98] During his second term in office, Netanyahu had 6,867 units in settlements built, with more than one-third in settlements to the east of the planned route of Israel's security barrier. Breaking the commitment of several previous governments not to build new settlements, Netanyahu built sixteen new settlements. Netanyahu also established a new settlement in East Jerusalem, which no Israeli government had done since he was last prime minister in the late 1990s.[99]

[95] Interview with Michael Kleiner, June 30, 1998, Jerusalem; Jeff Barak and Danna Harman, "Interview with Prime Minister Benjamin Netanyahu," *The Jerusalem Post*, May 11, 1999.

[96] Sontag and Orme, "With Prospects Bleaker, Netanyahu Lashes Out," A3; Netanyahu, *A Place Among the Nations*, 293; Benjamin Netanyahu, "Looking Forward," *Jerusalem Post*, April 20, 1999.

[97] Mendilow, "The Likud's Double Campaign," 198; Rynhold, "Identity, Values, and Culture Change," 252; Naveh, *Executive Secrets*, 84–85, 93–94.

[98] Freedman, "George W. Bush, Barack Obama, and the Arab-Israeli Conflict," 73. Although certainly a significant portion of blame for the friction in American-Israeli relations can be placed on Netanyahu, Robert Freedman also suggests that perhaps President Obama intentionally cooled ties with Israel. He cites as evidence of this cooling the fact that Obama delayed visiting Israel until March 2013, despite strong suggestions by American Jewish supports like the dovish J-Street Lobby as early as July 2009.

[99] Lara Friedman, "Laying Bare the Facts About Netanyahu and the Settlements," *Daily Beast*, January 18, 2013.

CONSEQUENT POLICY PREFERENCES (SECOND TERM,
2009 – PRESENT)

A Two-State Solution

It was only during his second terms as prime minister that Netanyahu, in June
2009 during a speech at Bar-Ilan University, announced his acceptance of the
eventual establishment of a conditional Palestinian state – an announcement that
came only under heavy American pressure. His vision of a Palestinian state did
not include East Jerusalem, demanded Palestinian recognition of Israel as a
Jewish state, and depended on a continued Israeli military presence in the
Jordan Valley. Therefore, it was unacceptable to Abu Mazen. However,
Netanyahu's concessions appeared to be significant because they ran counter
to his previous ideological convictions. He had previously opposed Oslo because
he interpreted it as promising Palestinian statehood. After he formally accepted
Oslo, Netanyahu continued to oppose the word *state*. He believed that, even if
there were "another" Palestinian state (in addition to Jordan, which he considers
a Palestinian state because its majority population is Palestinian), the struggle
would never end because "a PLO state on the West Bank would be like a hand
poised to strangle Israel's vital artery along the sea."[100] As for demilitarization,
he had previously claimed that the Palestinians would never abide by demilitarization, since one could not be partially sovereign any more than one could be
partially pregnant.[101] Netanyahu's apparently significant shift regarding
Palestinian statehood seems reminiscent of his shift in accepting Oslo before
his 1996 election. It does not reflect a change in attitude about the urgency of
establishing a final agreement, or a belief that such a peace agreement would
enhance Israeli security, or a change in perception of the Palestinian leadership.
Therefore, just as he knew that the mantra of reciprocity would delay, if not stop,
the Oslo process, he also knew that the conditions that he put on statehood, in
combination with continued settlement in East Jerusalem, would make it difficult for the Palestinians to engage in serious negotiations. Indeed, there were no
negotiations for three years before their resumption in July 2013, under heavy
pressure from U.S. Secretary of State John Kerry. Although Netanyahu's calls for
demilitarization are not significantly different from those of previous Israeli
Labor Party leaders, his conditions regarding Israeli military presence within
the Palestinian state, Palestinian recognition of Israel as a Jewish state, and an
insistence that no parts of East Jerusalem be conceded had not been shared by the
Barak or Olmert governments during their negotiations with Abu Mazen.

---

[100] Netanyahu, *A Place Among the Nations*, 389, 282; see also Benjamin Netanyahu, Statement to
the Knesset, September 21, 1993; confirmed by interview with David Bar Ilan.
[101] Interview with Dore Gold, June 2, 1999, New York; Benjamin Netanyahu, "Autonomy not
Statehood," *Yediot Ahronot*, February 18, 1994; [If You're Going to Make Peace, Then Now],
Al Hamishmar, November 19, 1993.

Response to U.S. Pressure

The friction between Netanyahu and the Obama administration escalated to such an extent that Nadav Tamir, Israeli consul in Boston, sent a letter warning that the posture of the Israeli government was damaging its strategic interests with the United States. He related Aaron Miller's description of the meeting between Obama and Netanyahu as a meeting "between Obama 'yes we can' and Netanyahu 'no you won't.'" Tamir argued that Israel should "dramatically change [its] conduct regarding the Obama Administration. . . . I suggest that we talk of our ambition for peace and our support of the two state solution more convincingly, and not like we are bowing to American pressure, but like those who understand that this is first and foremost an Israeli interest."[102] Netanyahu did not heed Tamir's advice. As Ilan Troen has argued, "[T]he dismissive way in which Tamir's cable was received in the Prime Minister's Bureau is a product of a contempt for criticism."[103]

In stark contrast to Tamir's advice, Netanyahu's announcement during Vice President Biden's visit to Israel in March 2010 of plans to build an additional 1,600 housing units in East Jerusalem led the Obama administration to declare that it had been insulted. According to Alon Pinkas, a former Israeli consul in New York, "the Americans feel that the prime minister has been toying with them for a year, and their strong reaction to the Ramat Shlomo building announcement was meant to signal that enough is enough."[104] When, however, the United States demanded a settlement freeze in Jerusalem, Netanyahu publicly equated construction in Jerusalem with construction in Tel Aviv, and argued in a speech to the American Israel Public Affairs Committee (AIPAC) that Jerusalem was not a settlement but Israel's capital; he also encouraged Elie Wiesel to put an ad in the newspapers claiming that Jerusalem would remain Israeli – all to counter President Obama's pressure.[105] He has resisted tremendous American and international pressure to freeze Jewish settlement in East Jerusalem both because he believes that Jerusalem should remain the unified capital of Israel, and because his coalition would not allow or support such a freeze.[106] Although Netanyahu largely froze settlement building in the West Bank for ten months, he defiantly and publicly made it clear that he would not fully accommodate American demands.

---

[102] Ori Nir, "Israeli Envoy Reprimanded for Asking Netanyahu to Support Obama's Peace Push," *Americans for Peace Now*, August 12, 2009.

[103] Ilan Troen, "The Consul Who Dared," *Haaretz*, July 18, 2011.

[104] Quoted in Leslie Susser, "Crunch Time for Netanyahu," *The Jerusalem Report*, April 15, 2010, 11.

[105] Barak Ravid, "Netanyahu: Building in Jerusalem Is Like Building in Tel Aviv," *Haaretz*, March 21, 2010; "Prime Minister Benjamin Netanyahu's Speech to AIPAC Conference," March 23, 2010.

[106] Barak Ravid, "U.S. Demand for Israel Building Freeze in East Jerusalem," *Haaretz*, August 27, 2009.

Three weeks before the September 26, 2010, Israeli cabinet deadline for the
ten-month freeze, President Obama succeeded in getting Palestinian Authority
leaders – who had refused to directly negotiate with Israeli officials during the
first nine months of the freeze because it did not include East Jerusalem – to come
to the table. During these talks, Netanyahu had a very small negotiating team for
fear of leaks. Only one member had negotiating experience: attorney Yitchak
Molcho, who negotiated with Yasser Arafat during Netanyahu's first term.
Deputy Premier Dan Meridor immediately claimed that indirect talks would
lead nowhere.[107] They lasted three weeks and were followed by three years
without negotiations before their resumption in July 2013. While Obama and
Netanyahu clearly supported each other's rivals in both of their elections in
2012/2013, the reality that they are both staying in office for an additional term
has caused the friction to diminish and a better working relationship to develop.
As David Miller suggests, a better relationship between Netanyahu and Obama
is needed, where each is not trying to undermine the other, for peace negotiations
to succeed.[108]

REACTIONS TO THE PALESTINIAN UPGRADED STATUS AT THE UN, EFFORTS AT RECONCILIATION BETWEEN HAMAS AND FATAH, AND THE UPRISINGS IN THE MIDDLE EAST BEGINNING IN 2010

Despite Netanyahu's conditional acceptance of a Palestinian state during his
June 14, 2009, speech, his pessimism in regard to its probability, if not also its
desirability, grew between 2010 and 2013. His bureau chief, Ari Harrow, who
left in 2010, captured Netanyahu's concerns when he wrote,

> [W]ith the Middle East ablaze, Iran racing unchecked toward nuclear capability
> and its proxy Hamas back in the Palestinian government, the world must be told
> that 2011 is not 2009 ... he must bluntly tell Congress that talk of Palestinian
> statehood is simply off limits ... With northern Israel in the crosshairs of Hezbollah
> rockets, Egypt's future uncertain at best to our south, and Syria on the brink of
> chaos, we cannot possibly conduct talks over relinquishing land to another perilous
> unknown in the shape of a Palestinian state. The reality of the Fatah-Hamas
> coalition and its current refusal to abandon violence or recognize the Jewish State
> of Israel makes principled inaction imperative. Any negotiations at this point would
> be an act of masochism at best, and simply suicidal at worst.[109]

Whereas Hamas and Fatah had been separate entities controlling different parts
of the territories since 2007, in May 2011 they reached an agreement to form an

---

[107] Herb Keinon, "Meridor: Talks Won't 'Yield Results,'" *The Jerusalem Post*, May 5, 2010; see
also Barak Ravid and Avi Issacharoff, "Israel to Open Peace Talks with Security, Water
Demands," *Haaretz*, May 3, 2010.

[108] Aaron David Miller, "Memorandum to the President," *Pathways to Peace: America and the
Arab-Israeli Conflict*, ed. Daniel C. Kurtzer (New York: Palgrave Macmillan, 2012), 148.

[109] Ari Harrow, "The PM's Speech: History in the Making?" *The Jerusalem Post*, May 21, 2011.

interim national unity government to prepare for elections (an agreement that as of March 2014 has not been implemented). This only increased Netanyahu's suspicions as to the long-term intentions of the Palestinian Authority, as Hamas continues officially to seek the destruction of Israel, opposes all previous agreements with Israel, and supports the use of terror. In March 2011 Hamas fired a rocket at an Israeli school bus, killing a sixteen-year-old student. Netanyahu declared that, given Hamas's policies, Abu Mazen had chosen making peace with Hamas over peace with Israel and that the two were mutually exclusive.

Netanyahu's deep suspicion of Abu Mazen's "true intentions" was also magnified by the Palestinian president's public international diplomacy to gain support for his bid for Palestinian statehood in 2011 and 2012, finally succeeding in gaining an upgraded status in the fall of 2012. Netanyahu claims that the 1967 borders are unacceptable and understands the UN bid as reflecting the Palestinian goal of getting an Israeli withdrawal without conceding anything in return in regard to refugees, recognition of a Jewish state, or an end to attacks on Israel.[110] Also, in contrast to Ehud Barak's fear that the UN bid could pose a "diplomatic tsunami" for Israel, Netanyahu argues that the implications of the UN bid should not be exaggerated. He dismissively says that the General Assembly could also decide that the world is flat. Abu Mazen's refusal to negotiate without a total settlement freeze before July 2013, and his UN bid, are themselves the product of his deep distrust of Netanyahu, given Netanyahu's record during his first term. Abu Mazen also knows that Netanyahu would put forth a less generous peace offer than Prime Minister Olmert had in 2008. Saeb Erekat told U.S. diplomat David Hale that "Abbas will not allow Netanyahu to do to him what he did to Arafat."[111]

As Netanyahu's deep suspicions of the Palestinian leadership were, in his mind, being confirmed, the seismic shifts in the region in 2011–2014 only served to confirm his ideological conviction that peace agreements do not enhance security. His reaction to demonstrations in Tunisia was to point out that the region was unstable, and that therefore it was uncertain whether future peace treaties would be honored.[112] He began to question whether Israel's thirty-year peace with Egypt and its seventeen-year-long peace with Jordan would unravel as the Muslim Brotherhood gained more power. Mubarak had favored Fatah and penalized Hamas; the Egyptian regime that replaced Mubarak was already making overtures to Hamas, opening the border with the Gaza Strip, and renewing diplomatic relations with Iran. This underscored his previous concern about making tangible concessions to the Palestinian Authority,

[110] Barak Ravid and Natasha Mozgavaya, "Netanyahu: Palestinians Not Interested in Solution Based on 1967 Borders," *Haaretz*, June 5, 2011.

[111] Barak Ravid, "Leaked Document Shows What the Palestinian Authority Really Thinks of Netanyahu," *Haaretz*, January 24, 2011. See also Jonathan Lis, "Netanyahu: Israel Cannot Prevent UN Recognition of Palestinian State," *Haaretz*, May 30, 2011; Barak Ravid, "Netanyahu Mulling West Bank Pullout to Stave Off Diplomatic Tsunami," *Haaretz*, April 12, 2011.

[112] Barak Ravid, "Netanyahu: Tunisia Turmoil Shows Instability of Entire Mideast," *Haaretz*, January 16, 2011.

which could likewise be torn up by a future government in which Hamas gained greater control. In addition, growing Hezbollah influence in Lebanon and an increasingly challenged and brutal Syrian government also increased his uncertainty concerning regional threats. These regional changes serve to confirm Netanyahu's opinion that peace agreements are not urgent and that one has to proceed slowly and with great caution. Netanyahu increased defense spending in his second term and sped up the construction of a fence along the Egyptian border. One of his close associates described Netanyahu's mood as "Masada."[113]

Preempting Netanyahu's planned speech to the U.S. Congress, President Obama made a speech broadcast nationwide on May 19, 2011, in which he addressed the developments of the Arab Spring, and in that context, put forth a formula for Palestinian-Israeli peace negotiations: the future Israeli-Palestinian border, he said, should be based on 1967 lines with mutually agreed upon land swaps. He also deviated from his and previous presidents' attempts to deal with security, borders, Jerusalem, and refugees simultaneously, to concentrate first on borders and security.

Although President Obama's formula was not entirely new and had been agreed to by the Barak and Olmert governments in previous negotiations, Netanyahu publicly rebuked Obama's formula. Netanyahu was angry that he had not been sufficiently consulted, that the reference to 1967 borders would suggest that Israel either has to concede East Jerusalem or compensate the Palestinians for it by giving other land within the 1967 borders, and that in return for an agreement on borders, the Palestinians were not necessarily required to give up on their claim to refugee return, or to recognize Israel as a Jewish state. One of Netanyahu's key messages in his 1996 campaign was that Peres was going to divide Jerusalem, and every night his televised campaign ads showed Peres and Arafat dividing Jerusalem in two. In his first address to the U.S. Congress as prime minister in 1996, Netanyahu argued that there have been dangerous efforts to re-divide Jerusalem and "there will never be such a re-division of Jerusalem. Never."[114]

If Obama's proposed plan seemed to touch on one of Netanyahu's ideological principles – negotiating over Jerusalem – then the reaction of both close supporters and the world community seemed to trigger Netanyahu's view that "the world is against us," and the corresponding reactions of suspicion and dismissal that characterize much of his interactions. World Jewish Congress President Ronald Lauder, who had been one of Netanyahu's biggest donors, and who had supported Netanyahu in all of his campaigns, publicly criticized Netanyahu's policies in the wake of Obama's speech, arguing that Netanyahu should present a diplomatic plan to regain international support and block

[113] Aluf Benn, "Israel's Lost Chance," *The New York Times*, July 29, 2011.
[114] Address by Prime Minister Benjamin Netanyahu to a joint session of the U.S. Congress, Washington, DC, July 10, 1996. See also Caspit and Kfir, *Netanyahu*, 229, 231.

Palestinian attempts to gain UN recognition of its statehood in September, even if it meant political suicide for Netanyahu. Lauder's reaction followed Netanyahu's refusal to attend the World Jewish Congress annual meeting because he was furious with Lauder for allowing the Channel 10 television station – of which Lauder was a major shareholder – to broadcast a series of investigative reports about overseas trips the Netanyahus took, financed by private individuals or organizations.[115]

CONCLUSIONS AND IMPLICATIONS

Netanyahu has remained a hard-liner, maintaining a relatively monolithic view of the Palestinians, who he believes retain the ultimate goal of destroying Israel; he believes the probability of peace is low or even nonexistent. His cognitive rigidity and his belief that he is surrounded by enemies, that time is on Israel's side, that security can be attained without peace, as well as his focus on a past of persecution against Jews, have been and continue to be obstacles to his perceiving greater moderation on the part of the PLO. His cognitive rigidity has led him to surround himself with only those who agreed with him, and his deep suspicion of others combines to create a situation in which information that might contradict his beliefs never reaches him, or is ignored.

However, Netanyahu has been unable to stay completely still in the face of regional changes and the reality created by the Oslo Accords. As a result of his sensitivity to public opinion and his political ambition, he abandoned his previous ideological purity by signing the Hebron and Wye Agreements, which gave up small parts of the Greater Land of Israel. In his second term, he claimed that he supported the establishment of a Palestinian state (under his specific conditions), he froze settlements on the West Bank for ten months, and reduced road blocks in the West Bank from forty-two to fourteen.[116] In his third term, he agreed to release 104 Palestinian prisoners, most of whom had served more than twenty years for having killed Israelis, as a good faith measure to rekindle peace negotiations with the Palestinian Authority. Despite the fact that he has not undergone the dramatic changes that Rabin and Peres went through, he did make significant policy changes in relation to his starting point – total opposition to conceding any of the Greater Land of Israel. However, these changes were motivated by personal ambition rather than changed attitudes. His changed policies also did not in turn lead him to change his image of the PLO, as self-perception theory would suggest.

Despite having made considerable concessions in relation to his starting point, Netanyahu does not merely represent an opportunist who abandons all principles in order to further his political ambitions. Netanyahu has strong

[115] Barak Ravid, "Top Jewish Leader and Close Netanyahu Ally Blasts PM for Lack of Diplomatic Plan," *Haaretz*, June 29, 2011.
[116] Roger Cohen, "Sunny Days in Israel," *The New York Times*, May 6, 2010.

principles based on Revisionist Zionist doctrine and tries to pursue these ideological goals under considerable domestic and international constraints. He was motivated by ideology to give less land than a Labor government (or even his former party colleague Ehud Olmert) would have been willing to give, and he never implemented the majority of the Wye Agreement that he signed. He successfully used the tool of reciprocity to put a stop to the momentum of the peace process and to the atmosphere of increased trust that had been established under Rabin and Peres. Instead, an atmosphere of constant accusations and delays was created. In his second term, Netanyahu reinforced the previous theme of reciprocity and that peace is not a one-way street in which only Israel makes concessions.[117]

Whereas Netanyahu went along with Oslo formally, he continually tried to torpedo it in practice. His "tactical concessions" unintentionally broke the dominance of the ideological purists in the Likud Party. Netanyahu helped break down the wall between the Labor and the Likud parties, but he did so by backing into it, all the time denying what he was doing.[118] Oslo turned the debate from *whether* to concede land in the West Bank to *how much* to concede. Netanyahu both legitimized the Oslo process by formally accepting the reality it established, and created an atmosphere that helped lead to the situation today in which many claim that "Oslo is dead." He used formal acceptance of Oslo as a tactic in a continued battle against the Palestinians, just as he believes Arafat signed the agreement as a tactic in his eventual pursuit of the destruction of Israel. Although ideological and personality factors acted as barriers to Netanyahu's changing his image of the Palestinians and from making as many concessions to the Palestinians as Peres and Rabin would have been ready to make, his concerns for attaining and retaining power enabled him to make some compromises in his policy preferences.

David Bar Ilan argues that Netanyahu often agrees with the saying that "politics is the art of the possible," but that he has not changed his essential attitude toward the Palestinians or his essential goals. He keeps his focus on his most desired goals and "is willing to compromise everything and anything on the way to achieving this goal if he feels that these tactical compromises, zigzags, retreats ... do not interfere with his achievement of that goal and sometimes help him to achieve it."[119] He remains defiant, while still making some of the concessions necessary to avoid a deeper rift with the United States that would harm Israeli interests and hamper his political viability.

---

[117] Haaretz Service, "Prime Minister Benjamin Netanyahu's Speech to AIPAC Conference," *Haaretz*, March 23, 2010.

[118] Thomas L. Friedman, "The Accidental Peacenik," *The New York Times*, May 14, 1999, A27.

[119] Interview with David Bar Ilan, communications director in the Netanyahu government, June 9, 1998, Jerusalem. Bar Ilan first started working with Netanyahu in 1983 and was one of Netanyahu's closest advisors.

Netanyahu has increasingly understood that Israel may have to separate from the Palestinians and that deeper territorial concessions may be necessary. In a weekly cabinet meeting in June 2011, Netanyahu discussed a Jewish People Policy Institute report on demographics which showed that in a number of years, the demographic trends will result in a Palestinian majority between the Jordan River and the Mediterranean Sea. Netanyahu surprised many of the participants by saying, in contradiction to his earlier convictions, that "it does not matter to me whether there are half a million more Palestinians or less because I have no wish to annex them into Israel. I want to separate from them so that they will not be Israeli citizens. I am interested that there be a solid Jewish majority inside the State of Israel. Inside its borders, as these will be defined."[120] This recognition was also reflected in occasional initiatives such as President Shimon Peres and former Labor leader and Defense Minister Ehud Barak's attempt in 2010 to convince Abu Mazen to accept Israel's recognition of a Palestinian state in temporary borders equivalent to 60 percent of the West Bank – a recognition which then would lead to negotiations over permanent borders, security, Jerusalem, and refugees on a state-to-state basis. Netanyahu, under pressure from President Obama to be more forthcoming, apparently approved this initiative, which came to naught when Abu Mazen refused for fear that the temporary borders would become permanent borders.[121]

Given President Obama's demands, Netanyahu looks more favorably on a 2004 letter from then-President George W. Bush to Prime Minister Ariel Sharon, which laid out in broad strokes that, while Israel will have to concede territory on the West Bank for a Palestinian state, Jewish West Bank settlement blocs would need to remain under Israeli sovereignty and Palestinian refugees would be resettled in a future Palestinian state. At the time, Netanyahu rejected the letter's suggestion of territorial concessions, but he turned to it as a favorable alternative during Obama's first term. Netanyahu has indicated that he will agree to base talks on the 1967 borders with land swaps if Obama ratifies Bush's letter to Sharon. In his May 2011 speech to Congress, Netanyahu conceded that Israel would not be able to retain all settlements. To his advisors Netanyahu has said that there is a growing threat of a binational state – a "trend [that] will intensify and become stronger" – and that one state would be a disaster.[122] Together, these statements and gestures indicate that Netanyahu may, under the right conditions, be willing to withdraw from most of the West Bank.

[120] Barak Ravid, "Netanyahu: Israel Needs to Separate From the Palestinians," *Haaretz*, June 21, 2011.

[121] Leslie Susser, "Wrapping a Peace Package," *The Jerusalem Report*, May 2, 2010, 9.

[122] Netanyahu: Binational State Would Be Disastrous for Israel," *Haaretz*, March 4, 2011; Barak Ravid, "Netanyahu Fears 'Surprise' for Israel in Quartet's Latest Peace Push," *Haaretz*, July 11, 2011.

Although on one hand Netanyahu has made significant shifts regarding his professed willingness to accept a Palestinian state in the majority of the West Bank and Gaza, it is unlikely that the concessions he is willing to make will match those offered by his predecessor Ehud Olmert in 2008, or Palestinian demands that East Jerusalem be their capital. At the same time, in his speech to the joint congressional session in May 2011, Netanyahu left some potential flexibility on Jerusalem. Although he claimed that Jerusalem must remain the united capital of Israel, he said that "with creativity and with goodwill a solution can be found."[123]

Netanyahu learned from his first term how to survive politically. Thus, there have been times when, even though Netanyahu was willing to make more significant concessions for peace, his party would constrain him.[124] But this same survival instinct might serve as a seed for change under the right conditions. If he was under tremendous pressure from Obama, the Quartet (the UN, the United States, the Russian Federation, and the EU), and Israeli society, Netanyahu could make significant concessions for peace. The January 22, 2013, elections strengthened the centrist parties, and that, combined with President Obama's planned visit in March 2013, influenced Netanyahu to form a coalition with those centrist parties. This new coalition dynamic opens the door for further leverage on the ultra-orthodox parties to shift their stance on the peace process.[125] In addition, the Labor Party has repeatedly said that if Netanyahu were close to reaching a peace agreement, they would support the effort. Netanyahu also may have signified that he is willing to freeze settlements outside of East Jerusalem and the main settlement blocs, at least temporarily, due to these internal and external pressures.[126] If his political future were on the line, he might stop treading water and take this dive.

However, Netanyahu probably cannot depart from his ideology so much as to grant most of the Old City of Jerusalem to a Palestinian state, as Prime Ministers Barak and Olmert were willing to do. Unlike Prime Ministers Rabin and Olmert, who had families who were more dovish than themselves and who contributed to the changes in their positions over time, Netanyahu's family – including his parents, wife, children, and brother-in-law – are more right-wing than he is. In anticipation of his March 3, 2014 meeting with

---

[123] Herb Keinon, Diplomacy: Netanyahu and 'The Book of Why,'" *The Jerusalem Post*, May 20, 2011.

[124] Interview with Nahum Barnea, August 5, 2010, Jerusalem; interview with Dov Weisglass, August 6, 2010, Ramat Hasharon.

[125] Yair Ettinger, "Shas Official Tells Haaretz: We're Ready to Evacuate Settlements, Back Mideast Talks," March 3, 2013; Jeremy Sharon, "UTJ Weighs Backing Aggressive Peace Agenda," *The Jerusalem Post*, February 17, 2013.

[126] Barak Ravid, "New Israeli Coalition Will Have to Freeze Construction Outside Settlement Blocs, Netanyahu's Aides Say," *Haaretz*, March 3, 2013.

President Obama, Netanyahu claimed that Israelis expect him to stand strong against pressure. Given his ideological, cognitive, and familial barriers to conceding what will be necessary to reach a peace agreement, it seems that only pressure that threatens his tenure as prime minister will induce him to take risks that are ideologically difficult for him.

4

Ariel Sharon: From Warfare to Withdrawal

You mean that we should hand our security over to somebody other than Jews?
Never! I emphasize, never! I say it again, never![1]

– Ariel Sharon, 1989

We would like you to govern yourselves in your own country. A democratic
Palestinian state with territorial contiguity in Judea and Samaria.[2]

– Ariel Sharon, 2003

In January 2006, Israeli Prime Minister Ariel Sharon was struck down by a
stroke, which left him in a coma until his death eight years later. His fall left a
question that will forever haunt political scientists and those interested in
Middle East peace. Sharon started out as a hawk who opposed the creation
of a Palestinian state, had a high threat perception, a low sense of urgency to
resolve the dispute, a high predilection to use force, and believed that the
probability of peace was low.[3] He was afraid that accommodations would be
interpreted as weakness, and viewed the opponent as monolithic, and as
having unlimited aims.[4] But by the time he was struck down, Sharon had
overseen the withdrawal of Israeli troops and settlers from the Gaza Strip,
and was setting the stage for the potential unilateral withdrawal of Israeli
troops from much of the West Bank.[5] Did Sharon dramatically change his
position about Israel's occupation of the territories, or did he remain so hard-
line that he would need to be replaced in order to reach an agreement? Would
he have followed through with his plan and withdrawn from most of the West

[1] Murray J. Gart, "Never! Never! Never!" *Time*, April 17, 1989.
[2] Uri Dan, *Ariel Sharon: An Intimate Portrait* (New York: Palgrave, 2006), 221, 227.
[3] Efraim Inbar, *War and Peace in Israeli Politics: Labor Party Positions on National Security*
(Boulder: Lynee Reiner Publishers, 1991), 15.
[4] Snyder Glenn, H.and Paul Diesing, *Conflict Among Nation: Bargaining, Decision Making, and*
System Structure in International Crises (Princeton: Princeton University Press, 1977), 297–310.
[5] Interview with Naomi Chazan, July 17, 2007, Jerusalem; Freddy Eytan, *Sharon: A Life in Times of*
Turmoil (Paris: Studio 9 Books, 2006), 215. Eytan cites a recorded interview of one of Sharon's
advisors, Kalman Gayer.

Bank – thereby marking a dramatic shift in policy by a hard-liner toward an adversary that some commentators were already comparing to Richard Nixon's trip to China? Or was Sharon's Gaza withdrawal a cynical ploy to hang on to the West Bank by a hard-liner who had not undergone any real change? What explains the decision of one of the architects and strongest supporters of settlements in the West Bank and Gaza to unilaterally withdraw from the Gaza Strip and four West Bank settlements, and pursue a new strategy of unilateral disengagement?

In this chapter, I argue that a change in the opponent was necessary to precipitate Sharon's policy shifts. However, it was Sharon's weak commitment to any one ideology, his present time orientation, his high risk propensity, his moderate cognitive flexibility, and his wealth of emotional intelligence that enabled the significant changes that he underwent. His agreement with some components of Labor Party ideology enabled change, while the influence of other Likud ideological tenants restricted the extent of those changes. I examine key elements in Sharon's biography and construct a profile of Sharon based on ideology, time orientation, cognitive flexibility, emotional intelligence, and risk propensity. I then test the explanatory power of this profile by analyzing Sharon's perceptions of the first intifada, the Gulf War, and previous efforts to pursue peace. Sharon's ideological beliefs and personality traits acted as permissive variables that enabled him to listen to advisors – who warned of the demographic problem and the costs of occupation – and react to changing circumstances – to the Road Map and the Geneva Initiative by initiating disengagement. Having thereby tested my hypotheses, I offer conclusions, expanding on the implications of this research for the analysis of Israeli foreign policy.

SHARON: MILITARY AND POLITICAL BACKGROUND

Ariel Sharon was born in Moshav Kfar Malal in 1928. He joined the Haganah, the precursor of the Israeli Defense Forces, in 1942 at age fourteen. Over the course of his military career, Sharon fought in all of Israel's wars, beginning with the War of Independence. In 1971, Sharon was instrumental in encouraging the establishment of Jewish settlements in the occupied territories. He achieved his most famous victories during the 1973 War, when he led the Israeli forces in a daring counterattack, crossing the Suez Canal and surrounding the Egyptian forces.

Sharon initiated the establishment of the Likud Party in 1973 and was first elected to the Knesset in 1974. He resigned to work with Rabin and left him to head a party of his own – Shlomzion, with a moderate platform – and won two seats. The morning after the 1977 elections, he joined Herut and was appointed to the Begin cabinet as Agriculture Minister. As Chairman of the Ministerial Settlement Committee, he initiated a large-scale plan to settle the West Bank and Gaza. He was minister of defense from 1981 to 1983 during the Lebanon War, and was forced to resign after an investigation found him indirectly responsible for failing to prevent the massacre of Palestinians by the Lebanese Christian phalange in the Palestinian refugee camps of Sabra and Shatilla. As minister of construction and housing from 1990 to 1992, Sharon was responsible for establishing additional settlements in the West Bank and in Gaza. In 1998, he was appointed minister of foreign affairs and head of the Permanent Status Negotiations with the Palestinians; in 1999, he was elected chairman of the Likud Party after Netanyahu's electoral defeat and his subsequent departure from the leadership of the Likud. He became prime minister in February 2001 and remained in office until January 4, 2006, when Ehud Olmert became acting prime minister after Sharon suffered a severe hemorrhagic stroke.

Throughout his life, whenever he was asked if Israel would withdraw from the West Bank and Gaza, Sharon would answer, "You mean that we should hand our security over to somebody other than Jews? Never! I emphasize, never! I say it again, never!"[6] He claimed that Jordan was the Palestinian state and opposed the creation of a state on the West Bank and Gaza. Given this history, what can explain Sharon's decision to pull out of Gaza and a few settlements in the West Bank and accept the inevitability of a Palestinian state? According to Uzi Landau, who had supported Sharon for three decades and had been appointed by Sharon to be his minister of internal security in 2001 and minister in the Prime Minister's Office in 2003, Sharon started talking about a Palestinian state in August 2002 – at which point Landau withdrew his support of Sharon within Likud.[7] In his address at the Fourth Herzliya Conference, on December 18, 2003, Prime Minister Sharon claimed, "We would like you [the Palestinians] to govern yourselves in your own country. A democratic Palestinian state with territorial contiguity in Judea and Samaria."[8] This clearly signified that he no longer insisted that Jordan be the Palestinian state. In his speech to the United Nations Assembly on September 15, 2005, he reiterated that the Palestinians "are also entitled to freedom and to a national, sovereign existence in a state of their own." Sharon argued that the creation of a Palestinian state is inevitable and that such a state "is the best solution for both us and the Palestinians. We should not continue to dominate another people. It's bad for us and for the Palestinians."[9]

In the next sections, I will analyze the ideological and cognitive factors that made it more likely for Sharon to undergo such a shift, as well as the factors that make it likely that he would not have been able to make concessions deep enough to meet Palestinian demands.

---

[6] Gart, "Never! Never! Never!"
[7] Interview with Uzi Landau, July 5, 2007, Raanana.
[8] Uri Dan, *Ariel Sharon: An Intimate Portrait* (New York: Palgrave, 2006), 221, 227.
[9] Ibid.

DETERMINANTS OF CONVERSION

Ideology

As I have argued in the preceding chapters, an important factor in determining the likelihood of a hard-liner changing position is ideology – both the specific beliefs of a particular ideology, and the strength of the leader's commitment to that ideology. Ariel Sharon was influenced by Likud ideology, but he grew up in a Labor household and *moshav*, and joined the Labor Youth Movement. His parents were strong individualists and his father disliked rigidly ideological people. Sharon followed his father's repeated advice to not toe any particular line. Sharon helped create the Likud Party but claimed, "I was not eager to put myself in the position of having to accept party discipline and a party line."[10] Therefore, some prominent Likud activists refer to Sharon as having been tied to the roots of Labor, as "a Ben Gurionist who despises revisionism."[11] After vigorously opposing Labor, Sharon joined Rabin's first government as his national security advisor. Eight months later he resigned and formed a new political party, arguing that for him a political party was a means, not an end in itself. He formed the party Shlomzion and attempted to recruit a wide variety of politicians to join, and offered to merge with another new party, The Democratic Movement for Change. When he failed to get important people from the left and center to join, he shifted course again and ended up back in Likud.[12] He left Likud for good in 2005, when fellow members resisted his unilateral disengagement plan and he established a new, centrist Kadima party.

While Sharon's weak commitment to any one ideology is crucial to understanding his shifts in position, the specific components of the ideologies he manuevered between are also important. Labor ideology enables a shift from a hard-line position more easily than does Likud ideology because of the two ideologies' perspectives on time, their central goals, their perception of world opinion concerning Israel, and their beliefs concerning what peace with the Palestinians will entail. As outlined in the previous chapters, I argue that the ideological components thwarting change in attitude toward an enemy are (1) specific, rigid goals contradicting those of the enemy; (2) a long, optimistic time horizon preventing adherents from recognizing policy failure or the urgency of change; (3) the perception that the world is permanently hostile; and (4) that security can be achieved without peace and that peace with the Palestinians will not require significant territorial concessions. Sharon's straddling between Labor and Likud perspectives acted as both a permissive variable to some of his change, but also a restraint on others, such as giving up the entire West Bank and dividing Jerusalem. In the first two ideological components he resembled Labor Party adherents, but in the latter two he resembled Likud Party members.

---

[10] Ariel Sharon, *Warrior* (New York: Simon & Schuster, 2001), 11, 224, 279, 285.
[11] Leslie Susser, "Why Ruby Lost His Sparkle," *The Jerusalem Report*, March 8, 2004; interview with Eyal Arad, June 29, 2004, Ramat Aviv.
[12] Uzi Benziman, *Sharon: An Israeli Caesar* (New York: Adama Books, 1985), 190–99.

1. Is Time on Israel's Side?

Likud ideology emphasizes that "time is on our side" with respect to Israel's conflict with the Palestinians and, therefore, its adherents are less likely to perceive a particular policy as a failure in the "short run." Since they believe that the enemy will be defeated in the long run, there is no perceived urgency to negotiate with the enemy today.

Sharon was influenced by this aspect of Likud ideology. Uri Dan, Sharon's lifelong friend and spokesman in the Defense Ministry from 1981 to 1983, writes that Sharon believed that time is working in Israel's favor, that the relative Arab military power will diminish over time, and that an influx of one million immigrants will arrive.[13] Sharon argued that it may be possible to reach an agreement on an interim phase of nonbelligerency, which would provide for Israel "the necessary time to examine and see that conditions for a true and lasting peace have materialized."[14]

2. Ideological Goals: General and Adaptable, or Specific and Rigid?

The more general the ideological goals, the more flexible they are to support differing strategies to respond to changed circumstances. Therefore, because Labor ideology emphasized the general goal of security, after the Six-Day War, the Labor-led government professed Israel's willingness to trade newly acquired territory, including most of the West Bank, for peace. By contrast, the Greater Land of Israel is central to Likud ideology. Jabotinsky was adamant that Israel keep the two banks of the Jordan River and the Revisionists opposed partitioning the land in 1948. The occupation of the West Bank, then, was an end in itself, rather than the means to another end, such as security. As Israel Eldad put it, "[T]he 'security' of our ownership of Eretz Yisrael is beyond all questions of security."[15]

On this issue, Sharon's thinking resembled Labor ideology. When Israel attained the territories in 1967, Sharon wanted to establish footholds to secure it and insisted that Israel retain the high controlling terrain and strategic junctions and roads for security reasons rather than from ideological dogma.[16] Knesset Speaker Reuven Rivlin, who was close to Sharon for many years, says, "[A]ll Sharon cares about is whether settlements serve Israeli security" and that Sharon did not regard Judea, Samaria, and Gaza as holy. He did not "see concessions as sacrilege, the way we (born and bred rightists) do."[17]

---

[13] Sharon, *Warrior*, 8.

[14] Ariel Sharon, "Security and Coexistence: An Alternative Approach to Breaking the Deadlock Between Israel and the Palestinians," October 1999, Likud Archives, 12/372, Jabotinksy House, Tel Aviv.

[15] Interview with Shamir, July 5, 1998; Rael Jean Isaac, *Israel Divided: Ideological Politics in the Jewish State* (Baltimore: The Johns Hopkins University Press, 1976), 12–13, 36, 44, 64.

[16] Sharon, *Warrior*, 209.

[17] Leslie Susser, "Why Ruby Lost His Sparkle."

3. Is the World With Us or Against Us?

Central to Likud ideology is the view that the world is eternally hostile and is "actively involved in efforts to destroy Israel and the Jewish people."[18] Likud's battles against enemies take place outside history, with each battle seen as merely the latest iteration of an eternal battle against the same enemy, appearing in different guises. Ariel Sharon described Yasser Arafat as just a step below Hitler and repeatedly claimed, "I don't know anyone [besides Arafat] who has so much civilian Jewish blood on his hands since Hitler."[19] He also emphasized that "nowhere else do four million people carry on their lives in the midst of a hundred million hostile people."[20] Sharon thought that 25 percent of the world wanted to see Israel dead, there were those that did not care, and then there was the United States. He believed that no other nation on earth had so many enemies.[21]

Since Likud ideology emphasized Israel's isolation and the world's hostility, Sharon was proud of Begin's defiant reply to the U.S. government's urging of Israel to use restraint in its 1982 war with Lebanon: "[T]he man has not been born who will ever obtain from me consent to let Jews be killed by a bloodthirsty enemy."[22] Ariel Sharon, who was defense minister during the Lebanon War, did not request a green light from the United States for the Lebanon War in 1982 and flouted its opinions during the war.[23] Ronald Reagan wanted Sharon to move ten miles from the Damascus Road so that the United States could bring in its Sixth Fleet, but Sharon would not budge an inch.[24] According to Uzi Landau – who fought under Sharon in 1973, backed Sharon in forming the Likud, and served as minister in Sharon's governments – Sharon told him that he would have been willing to fire on U.S. troops during the Lebanon War.[25] Sharon also described Henry Kissinger, the American secretary of state, as Israel's greatest enemy.[26] Consequently, Americans ostracized Sharon. As prime minister, he learned to be more sensitive to U.S. opinion, and this sensitivity eventually prompted some of his changes.[27]

---

[18] Ilan Peleg, *Begin's Foreign Policy, 1977–1983* (New York: Greenwood Press, 1987), 53; Ilan Peleg, "Israeli Foreign Policy Under Right-Wing Governments: A Constructivist Interpretation," *Israel Studies Forum* 19, no. 3 (2004), 111.

[19] Serge Schmemann, "Hawkish Talons as Sharp as Ever," *The New York Times*, May 25, 1996.

[20] Sharon, *Warrior*, 531.

[21] Interview with Dov Weisglass, August 6, 2010, Ramat Hasharon. Director of Sharon's Bureau 2001–2005, previously his lawyer for twenty-four years.

[22] Sharon, *Warrior*, 451.

[23] Uri Dan, *Blood Libel* (New York: Simon and Schuster, 1987), 12.

[24] Interview with Uri Dan, July 1, 2004, Yaffo, Israel.

[25] Interview with Uzi Landau, July 5, 2007, Raanana, Israel.

[26] Benziman, *Sharon*, 189.

[27] Interview with Eli Landau, June 2004, Herziliyah, Israel. Landau has known Ariel Sharon for almost forty years. He worked with him when Sharon was defense minister and minister of agriculture.

4. How Much Will Peace Contribute to Security? Does Peace Require Territorial Compromise?

Integrated with the belief that time is on Israel's side and the desire to keep the West Bank as an article of faith, is the notion that peace with the Palestinians does not require territorial compromise and that security can be provided without this compromise. Likud ideology has traditionally called for an iron wall of military defense that would eventually force the Arabs to accept Israel's existence in the Greater Land of Israel.

Shaped by these ideological conceptions of when and what peace would mean with the Palestinians, Sharon thought that security could be achieved through an actual security barrier. He thought that he could withdraw unilaterally, without any need for real negotiation with a partner considered to be untrustworthy, incapable of assuring security, and also likely to demand more compromise than Sharon was willing to make.[28]

Thus, Sharon's thinking could be described as drawing on elements of both Labor and Likud ideology. Given his more general goals of security, without an attachment to Judea and Samaria as an article of faith – an idea more characteristic of Labor ideology – Sharon had the flexibility to be able to conceive of security without the West Bank and Gaza. At the same time, his sense that "time is on Israel's side," and his belief that much of the world – and certainly the Palestinians – were set against Israel, limited the degree to which Sharon would shift from his original hard-line positions. In the next section, I will argue that these ideological factors are inflected by the specifics of Sharon's individual cognitive style.

Cognitive Style

1. Time Orientation

This study suggests that those leaders who are emotionally attached to and focus on a violent, conflict-ridden past – who see history as repeating itself, and view this past as a living reality – are less able to forge a new image of a past opponent as a potential partner in peace. For example, I have argued that Itzhak Shamir was and Benjamin Netanyahu is immersed in a past of perennial persecution toward Jews and believe that this persecution will continue to repeat itself. Filtering this perception of the present through the lens of a violent past, each was unlikely to perceive change in the regional environment, much less in an enemy with prior aspirations to destroy Israel.

While a focus on the past inhibits change, a present or future orientation makes it easier for a leader to change. Leaders who focus primarily on the present change relatively slowly as they take note of information about ongoing changes in small increments. Sharon was not immersed in the past and did not make as many analogies to the past as have other Likud leaders such as Yitzhak

---

[28] Interview with Eli Landau, June 2004, Herzliya, Israel.

Shamir, Menachem Begin, or Benjamin Netanyahu. He used history in terms of his more recent military experience, but he often also thought two steps ahead.[29] Sharon made plans for the immediate time frame. He realized that day-to-day changes influence how one attempts to achieve a goal.[30] Therefore, in this regard as well, Sharon was amenable to changing his perceptions of whether all settlements actually strengthen rather than weaken Israeli security.

2. Risk Propensity

Sharon was widely known for risk taking. Militarily, he always believed in taking risks to seize the initiative. For instance, in the 1973 war, Major General Sharon planned a risky initiative to place his armored division on the west side of the Suez, even though he would not be able to reinforce or support those troops, who would have to fight alone behind enemy lines.[31] Similarly, Sharon deceived Menachem Begin during the Lebanon War, going beyond the authorized 40 kilometers into Lebanon.[32] He applied this faith in seizing the initiative to, first, establishing settlements, and then years later in planning to tear some down. This same propensity for risk taking also explains his withdrawal from Gaza. Similarly, Sharon's move to leave Likud and form Kadima was a real risk: as Dov Weisglass has said, Sharon "jeopardized everything" at a time when he could have "rested comfortably in his chair" with great public support, and with forty Likud members in the coalition, in the middle of an intifada.[33]

3. Cognitive Flexibility

In the spectrum from cognitive rigidity on one end and cognitive flexibility on the other, Sharon fell in the middle. On the one hand, he was a creative tactician who thought out of the box. Even as a twenty-five-year-old major, he encouraged his officers to take initiative and think originally.[34] He repeatedly got into trouble for questioning and even disobeying orders. He demonstrated cognitive flexibility as early as 1979, when he advocated dismantling settlements that he himself had created: although responsible for building settlements in the Sinai, Sharon played a crucial role in the success of the Camp David Accords between Egypt and Israel by convincing Begin on the twelfth day of the negotiations that Israel should evacuate those settlements.[35]

---

[29] Interview with Naomi Chazan, July 17, 2007, Jerusalem.

[30] Sharon, *Warrior*, 554.

[31] Benziman, *Sharon*, 156.

[32] Zvi Harel, "Sharon Deceived Begin on Lebanon, Judge Rules; Throws Out Libel Suit Against Ha'aretz," *Haaretz*, May 11, 1997.

[33] Interview with Dov Weisglass, August 6, 2010, Ramat Hasharon.

[34] Benziman, *Sharon*, 45, 56.

[35] Shlomo Ben-Ami, *Scars of War, Wounds of Peace: The Israeli-Arab Tragedy* (New York: Oxford University Press, 2006), 262.

On the other hand, Sharon never entertained the thought that Arafat could change. He had pigeonholed him permanently in the category of "enemy," had tried to kill him, and never deigned to shake his hand. Therefore, Sharon was capable of thinking creatively, but was not open-minded about the ability of leaders who use terrorist tactics to change their stripes. He also was capable of being contemptuous toward others, whether it was his military superiors or fellow parliamentarians. He often walked out of meetings.[36] Therefore, he could think creatively, but could also hold rigid, categorical opinions of other people.

4. Emotional Intelligence

Politicians across the Israeli political spectrum agree that Prime Minister Sharon had emotional intelligence. Naomi Chazan, who disagreed vehemently with his policies, argues that he was very personable and much more considerate than most politicians. She sat with him on the Secret Services subcommittee, which met for hours every week. Chazan claims that he would always notice the little things about people, whether they looked pale and he asked how they were feeling, or whether they looked hungry and he suggested that they go out to eat and not talk about politics. He would know when somebody's spouse was sick or when someone's baby had a stomachache and he would ask about it. He would offer to go with Chazan to meet someone else to change her mind about an issue. She claims that partially because he was so personable and such a good politician who could implement his preferences, that to her he was the most dangerous politically. This also accounts for the immense loyalty that advisors – often with very different political views – felt toward him. For instance, Leo Horeb, who was from Labor, talked about him as a mixture of a father and a hero. His ability to be personable also contributed to his chemistry with President George W. Bush – a chemistry that Prime Minister Olmert and Bush did not share. Bush empathized with Sharon's efforts to counter terror and complimented his bold move of evacuating Gaza.[37]

Dov Weisglass, his close advisor, argues that in terms of emotional intelligence, Sharon was unparalleled. He had an incredible knack for sensing people, understanding people, and communicating with them. He had an exceptional ability to detect the undercurrent, and this influenced the team around him. This contributed to his flexibility in several ways. It enabled him to forge relationships with politicians who were more dovish than himself (such as Shimon Peres) and thus opened him to receiving multiple points of view; it also allowed him to forge long-lasting relationships with experienced advisors (some of whom, like Dov Weisglass, were more dovish than himself) because he did not feel threatened by them. Not only did his emotional intelligence contribute to his

---

[36] Benziman, *Sharon*, 178–79.
[37] Interview with Naomi Chazan, July 17, 2007, Jerusalem. See also George W. Bush, *Decision Points* (New York: Crown Publishers, 2010), 145, 406.

exposure to a wider spectrum of views, but it also enabled him to more effectively implement his preferred policies.

Advisors

Sharon's emotional intelligence enabled him to establish an inner circle of experienced and loyal advisors that was the envy of his political opponents. For instance, Gidi Greenstein, a former advisor to Barak, claimed that Sharon was a much better politician than Barak, and that he had a strong, loyal team with whom he would meet at his home in a more relaxed atmosphere – which in turn induced more loyalty from his advisors. Each one of Sharon's team was extremely powerful, and together they were even more powerful.[38] As opposed to leaders like Benjamin Netanyahu, who tend to be threatened by potential rivals, Sharon sought out experienced advisors. Yoram Peri argues that when Shimon Peres was Sharon's foreign minister, he had greater power than preceding foreign ministers and was equal in age and stature to Sharon. They disagreed publicly, but were perceived by Israelis as "two forces with equal status."[39] Dov Weisglass argues that Sharon would not hire anyone to work for him unless he or she had twenty-five years of experience, was not arrogant, and had no professional ego. He was not convinced that he was the smartest and he was open to listening and to taking advice. His emotional intelligence positively influenced his team. Unlike Netanyahu, he was not suspicious of his advisors and had the confidence to delegate important tasks to experienced people. For instance, two weeks after Sharon took office, Secretary of State Colin Powell called him. Sharon, whose English was not excellent and who also had full faith in his advisors, asked Dov Weisglass to take the call and to inquire as to what it was about.[40] Sharon's kitchen cabinet of powerful advisors not only exposed him to diverse views, but also improved his ability to successfully implement his policies.

IMAGE OF THE ENEMY

Sharon had an entrenched view of the Palestinian Liberation Organization as a terrorist organization bent on Israel's destruction; that view was difficult for him to reevaluate. When Sharon was defense minister, he would have tried to kill Yasser Arafat in Lebanon in 1982 were it not for American opposition, and he might have tried to kill him again when he was prime minister in 2002 in the midst of the second intifada were it not once more for American demands for restraint. Sharon's defense minister, Shaul Mofaz, echoed Sharon's desire to

---

[38] Interview with Gidi Grinstein, August 4, 2010, Tel Aviv.
[39] Y. Peri, *Generals in the Cabinet Room: How the Military Shapes Israeli Policy* (Washington, DC: United Institute of Peace Press), 115.
[40] Interview with Dov Weisglass, August 6, 2010, Ramat Hasharon.

either expel Arafat or target him in a military strike.[41] If he could not literally eliminate Arafat, he successfully did so politically, by refusing to negotiate with him, and by influencing President George W. Bush's decision also to treat him as an irrelevant leader who had to be replaced. During the negotiations leading up to the Wye Agreement, Sharon refused to shake Arafat's hand, and Secretary of State Madeleine Albright reflects that she thought it odd that "Sharon talked about Palestinians in the third person with Arafat and his delegation sitting there at the table."[42] Dov Weisglass admits that it "did not even cross our minds" to coordinate the withdrawal from Gaza with Arafat or to negotiate with him.[43]

Sharon's view of Abu Mazen, president of the Palestinian Authority, however, was less hostile. Sharon had much more faith in Abu Mazen's good intentions and honesty, and maintained contact with him, but ultimately thought that he was too weak to be a partner to peace negotiations. Sharon never demonized Abu Mazen as he had Arafat.[44] Even during Abu Mazen's first term as prime minister in 2003, there were indications that Sharon did not view Abu Mazen in the same category as Arafat: by the end of the summer 2003, according to Dov Weisglass, Sharon had agreed to freeze settlements, remove illegal settlements, and withdraw from all Palestinian areas to the pre-intifada lines, leaving almost 100 percent of the population under Palestinian control. On the morning the cabinet was ready to approve the deal, there was a suicide bombing in Jerusalem, killing twenty-two people, carried out by Hamas. Sharon did not think that the Palestinian Authority was trying to trace those responsible. Abu Mazen resigned and put the blame on Arafat. Sharon always demonized Arafat, but lost any ray of hope for reform under Arafat when Abu Mazen was not empowered to crack down on terror.[45] Scholars such as Alan Dowty have argued that Sharon's assessment of Arafat was probably correct: as someone whose worldview was rooted in the refugee camps outside Palestine, he was, Dowty argues, unlikely to have internalized a two-state solution.[46] At the same time, however, Sharon's military officers thought that Sharon had not done enough during Abu Mazen's first term to support the Palestinian leader against those within the Palestinian Authority who sought to undercut him, first and foremost Arafat himself.[47] So while Sharon did show some cognitive flexibility in differentiating Abu Mazen from Arafat, he did not seem flexible enough in his refusal to entertain the notion that Palestinians would ever agree to live in peace with Israel. After Arafat died and Abu Mazen returned to the

---

[41] Peri, *Generals in the Cabinet Room*, 113.

[42] Albright, *Madam Secretary*, 310.

[43] Interview with Dov Weisglass, August 6, 2010, Ramat Hasharon.

[44] Robert Freedman, "George W. Bush, Barack Obama, and the Arab-Israeli Conflict from 2001–2011," in Robert O. Freedman, ed. *Israel and the United States: Six Decades of US-Israeli Relations* (Boulder: Westview Press, 2012).

[45] Interview with Dov Weisglass, July 4, 2004, Jerusalem.

[46] Alan Dowty, *Israel/Palestine* 2nd ed. (Cambridge: Polity Press, 2008), 217.

[47] Peri, *Generals in the Cabinet Room*, 146.

prime ministership, according to Weisglass, Sharon slowly gained confidence in the leader: Sharon had met him several times by the summer of 2004, had warned Abu Mazen of plots against him, and reached a cease fire with him on February 8, 2005.

REACTIONS TO THE FIRST INTIFADA AND THE GULF WAR

Sharon's decision to withdraw from Gaza and to begin withdrawing from the West Bank were not, as was the case with Rabin, influenced by lessons learned form the first intifada and the Gulf War. In contrast, when Sharon was asked how he would have responded to the first intifada had he been defense minister, he said that he would have rounded up the terrorists and expelled them.[48] He believed that time was on Israel's side and did not perceive the strategy of forceful suppression as having failed. The lesson for him was not that a political solution was necessary, but that the military could have done a better job of stopping the intifada.

Like the intifada, the Gulf War, beginning in January 1991 after the invasion of Kuwait by Saddam Hussein, also did not alter Sharon's vision of what was needed for Israel's security, as it did, I will argue, for Rabin. Sharon maintained that, "due largely to the combined threat of large scale ground forces coupled with long-range ballistic missiles" being amassed by Arab countries, and particularly the threat of weapons of mass destruction emanating from Iran and Iraq, territory and strategic depth were vital for Israel's security.[49] Although he shared Rabin's preoccupation with security, in the immediate aftermath of the Gulf War, he did not alter his view that the West Bank and Gaza were needed for strategic depth.

INITIAL POLICY PREFERENCES

Opposition to the Madrid and Oslo Negotiations, and to Withdrawal

After the Gulf War, the United States exerted great pressure on Israel and its neighbors to attend a Middle East peace conference in Madrid. While even Shamir reluctantly agreed to attend, Sharon was one of the few to oppose Israel's participation, believing that it legitimized dialogue over Israeli withdrawal from the West Bank and Gaza. Although Sharon had been ready to talk to the PLO in the 1970s, it was only over Jordan as a Palestinian state. By signing the Oslo Accords, Rabin agreed to compromises that he had previously rejected, perceiving a window of opportunity created by the intifada and the Gulf War, both of

---

[48] Gart, "Never! Never! Never!"
[49] Ariel Sharon, "Security and Coexistence: An Alternative Approach to Breaking the Deadlock Between Israel and the Palestinians," October 1999, Likud Party Archives, 12/1372, Jabotinsky House, Tel Aviv.

which weakened the PLO in relation to Hamas.[50] In contrast, Sharon vehemently opposed the "terrible and dangerous" Oslo Accords and had complete disdain for Arafat, whom he regarded as a war criminal.[51] Sharon argued that there was a Palestinian state in Jordan and that a second Palestinian state would only be a front for terrorists. He voted against his government's decision to withdraw from most of Hebron.

In the aftermath of the September 11, 2001, terrorist attacks on the World Trade Center and the Pentagon, President George W. Bush announced his support for a Palestinian state, partially in order to garner support among Muslim majority states for his efforts to combat al-Qaeda. He also pressured Sharon to have foreign minister Shimon Peres meet with Arafat to establish a cease fire, even though Sharon had argued that violence must stop before his government talks to Arafat. Sharon compared this request to the 1938 Munich Conference when Czechoslovakia was granted to Hitler.[52] Finally, Sharon's support for settlements seemed firm: in Sharon's election campaign in January 2003, he responded to his Labor opponent's call for evacuating the Gaza settlements by arguing that it would only "bring the terrorism centers closer to [Israel's] population centers"; the settlements in Gaza, he argued, were equal to Tel Aviv in his eyes.[53] He brought visitors to settlements to show their importance due to their proximity to potential strategic targets in Israel.[54]

CONSEQUENT POLICY PREFERENCES

Unilateral Withdrawal from Gaza and Parts of the West Bank

Yet surprisingly, in Sharon's Herzlya speech in December 18, 2003, he announced his disengagement plan to unilaterally pull out the 7,500 settlers from Gaza and 400 settlers from the West Bank. What can explain Sharon's evacuations from these settlements, which previously he had thought so necessary for Israel's security?

1. Context of Pressure from the Road Map and Geneva Initiative

In April 2003, the Quartet – the United States, the Russian Federation, the EU, and the UN – officially announced President Bush's "Road Map" for a staged

[50] Interview with Rahel Rabin, Rabin's sister, July 7, 1998, Kibbutz Menarah; interview with Eitan Haber, July 27, 1997, Tel Aviv.

[51] Serge Schmemann, "Hawkish Talons as Sharp as Ever," *The New York Times*, May 25, 1996.

[52] Freedman, "George W. Bush, Barack Obama, and the Arab-Israeli Conflict."

[53] David Makovsky, "Assessing Sharon's Gaza Settlement Evacuation Proposal," The Washington Institute for Near East Policy, February 9, 2004; Daniel Pipes, "Jerusalem Syndrome," *The Jerusalem Post*, June 30, 2004.

[54] Alan Cowell, "Among West Bank Settlers, Resignation and Resentment," *The New York Times*, February 27, 2005.

process toward a two-state solution. Sharon's cabinet accepted the Road Map with reservations, but Sharon's true feelings about the Road Map are echoed by Uri Dan, who said that Sharon tried to go along with the "Road Map Shmord Map."[55] Although he thought the Road Map was futile, Sharon did not dismiss it out of hand, stating, "I will not harm the deep strategic understandings with the United States, and the special relationship formed with the American administration."[56] He understood that the influence of the "new Roman Empire is something that you cannot ignore."[57] Knesset Speaker Reuven Rivlin echoes this sentiment: "Sharon is a pragmatist who understands that America is the global sheriff and that he needs American help."[58] The Americans in private channels had been saying for weeks that Israel had not been living up to its promises.[59]

Sharon's relative cognitive flexibility and his emotional intelligence enabled him to realize that the settlement issue was perceived by the United States as a major issue – one that could threaten his excellent relationship with President Bush and therefore the vital U.S.-Israeli relationship. As prime minister, he was fully aware of the massive scale of the Israeli relationship with the United States, that not only included $3.2 billion in aid, but military and technological support, intelligence sharing, and diplomatic maneuvering, such as blocking attempts by Egypt and others to pressure Israel to sign the nuclear nonproliferation treaty. He understood that Bush – who had affection for and was exceptionally friendly to Israel, shared an animosity to terrorism, and was very supportive of Israel's counterterror measures – strongly objected to settlements, in a stronger way than even had the Clinton administration. He also understood the importance of retaining President Bush's support for his counterterror measures during the second intifada, such as targeted killings and reoccupying parts of the West Bank that had been evacuated under Rabin – measures that were unpopular around the world.

According to Weisglass, the primary reason for Sharon's change was his recognition that he would have to freeze settlements, and that his dream about everlasting presence in Greater Israel was over. In late 2002, Sharon would get angry phone calls from the Bush administration at 3 AM about apartments being built in the settlement of Kedumim. After every high-level meeting between Israel and the U.S., the American representatives would issue a public statement against any actions – such as settlements – that would pre-judge the final status talks. The recognition that the world, and even the United States, would not accept Israel's continued settlement and occupation of the West Bank was made clear to Sharon when a very pro-Israeli U.S. senator, flying in a helicopter with him in late 2002, refused to fly over the West Bank

[55] Interview with Uri Dan, July 1, 2004, Yaffo, Israel.
[56] Joel Greenberg, "Peace Plan by U.S. Splits Netanyahu and Sharon," *The New York Times*, November 8, 2002.
[57] Interview with Eli Landau, June 2004, Herzliya, Israel.
[58] Leslie Susser, "Why Ruby Lost His Sparkle."
[59] Leslie Susser, "Administration Angst," *The Jerusalem Report*, December 1, 2003.

despite Sharon's encouragement. When driving back in the car with Weisglass immediately following this incident, Sharon told him that "the war is over," meaning that the dream of Greater Israel was over. Weisglass agreed with Elliot Abrams and Steven Hadley that Israel would not create any new settlements. Significantly, it was around this time that Sharon started to use the term *occupation* in describing Israel's presence in the West Bank.[60]

Sharon's military strategy during war was to "gain the initiative and attack," and he translated this into taking the political initiative rather than following the U.S. plan.[61] Sharon initiated his own unilateral disengagement plan, gambling that this initiative would result in a shift in U.S. policy and fewer Israeli concessions. For the first time, the U.S. government asserted in a letter that in a final agreement between Israel and the Palestinians, Israel would hold on to certain West Bank settlements near Jerusalem, and that the Palestinians did not have a right of return to Israel proper. Sharon explained that he was pursuing his plan because "a situation has been created in which it is possible to do the things I want and to get an American commitment."[62] As Uri Dan has put it, Sharon thought, "I can make painful concessions to consolidate lines which I can hold for many years to come with U.S. backing."[63] When the United States pressured Israel to change the route of the security barrier for humanitarian reasons, Sharon likewise wanted to accommodate their wishes, despite opposition from the Likud; he thus welcomed the Israeli Supreme Court decision requiring that the security barrier be moved.[64]

The pressures exerted on Sharon to accept the Road Map led him to come up with his own alternative so that he could control the process under the best terms and conditions. Only a few months after the announcement of the Road Map initiative, the Geneva Accord, sponsored by Yossi Beilin and Abu Mazen and which offered a detailed draft Israeli-Palestinian peace treaty, was publicly announced in October 2003. This compounded Sharon's desire to come up with his own initiative to abort pressures to seriously consider the treaty negotiated by some Palestinians and Israelis on an unofficial basis.[65] According to Naomi Chazan, "the straw that broke the camel's back was Geneva" in that it showed that there was somebody to talk to and something to talk about – a position that makes inaction unjustifiable.[66] Therefore, just one month after the announcement of the Geneva Plan, and only seven months after the announcement of the Road

[60] Interview with Dov Weisglass, August 6, 2010, Ramat Hasharon.
[61] Sharon, *Warrior*, 309.
[62] "Ariel Sharon's Double Win: Undercutting the Palestinians," *The New York Times*, April 15, 2003.
[63] Interview with Uri Dan, July 1, 2004, Yaffo, Israel.
[64] Interview with Dov Weisglass, July 4, 2004, Jerusalem.
[65] Robert O. Freedman, "The Bush Administration and the Arab-Israeli Conflict," in David W. Lesch, ed. *The Middle East and the United States: A Historical and Political Reassessment* (Boulder, CO: Westview Press, 2007).
[66] Interview with Naomi Chazan, July 17, 2007, Jerusalem.

Map peace plan, Sharon announced his own plan to unilaterally disengage from Gaza. Sharon argued that Israel would receive domestic and international pressure to impose the Geneva agreement on Israel if his own disengagement program was not accepted.[67] Ra'anan Gissin, Sharon's spokesperson, said in an interview with CNN Radio that "the Prime Minister believes that in order to move forward we need to shake things up, shuffle the cards, plunge ahead like he did in his days in the army, not looking back, not waiting, but just going on ahead courageously.[68]" Sharon's risk propensity prompted him to seize the initiative even though he had previously articulated the risks of withdrawal.

2. Military and Intelligence Assessments of the Need for Withdrawal

Sharon was also influenced by retired military officers who believed in the need to evacuate settlements; at the same time, however, he defied the advice of the military leadership and the Chief of General Staff, Moshe Ya'alon, in deciding to withdraw unilaterally from Gaza. He did not consult the General Staff who, in April 2002, thought that unilateral withdrawal would turn Gaza into a haven for terrorism and therefore should only take place as a product of negotiations with the Palestinian Authority. Sharon had been moved by the call from senior Israeli army officers to uproot several dozen isolated Jewish settlements in the West Bank and the Gaza Strip because of the military burden of protecting them. A group of reserve officers who had just finished serving in Netzarim, a settlement in Gaza, publicly demanded that Israel evacuate the settlement.[69] The same year, Labor representatives such as former military intelligence chief Uri Saguy, former prime minister Ehud Barak's ex-bureau chief, Gilead Sher, as well as Haifa Mayor Amram Mitzna, who headed the army's Central Command during the first intifada, argued for a unilateral Israeli plan that would entail redeployment of Israeli troops to a line close to the 1967 border, a physical barrier on the temporary line, a small number of settlements, and reform of Palestinian Authority institutions. They intended that, a year and a half later, sixty-eight settlements would be dismantled and an international force would control areas evacuated. Negotiations would ensue after the separation.[70] Sharon, who had served as intelligence officer of the northern and southern command, gave significant weight to intelligence assessments. Even though he had initially opposed a security barrier, he was eventually convinced by these former heads of the security services.[71]

[67] Menachem Klein, *A Possible Peace Between Israel & Palestine: An Insider's Account of the Geneva Initiative* (New York: Columbia University Press, 2007), 15.

[68] Gregory Levey, *"Shut Up, I'm Talking," And Other Diplomacy Lessons I Learned in the Israeli Government* (New York: Free Press, 2008), 196.

[69] Peri, *Generals in the Cabinet Room*, 195, 202–3; "Israel's Historic Miscalculation," *The New York Times*, Editorial Page, April 26, 2002.

[70] "The Privatization of Peacemaking," *The Jerusalem Report*, August 26, 2002.

[71] Ephraim Halevy, "Understanding the Middle East: A View from Inside the Mossad," *Washington Institute for Near East Policy*, May 2006.

In addition to these intelligence assessments, Sharon was also persuaded by advisors that Israeli occupation of Gaza was a military burden rather than an asset. Eli Landau had tried to persuade Sharon for many years to leave Gaza, and Sharon was beginning to realize that the situation of 7,500 settlers facing 1.1 million Palestinians in Gaza was not viable. According to Dov Weisglass, the argument that Israel needed strategic depth was undermined by the international community's recognition of Palestinian national claims and that the formation of a Palestinian state could not be stopped. Now, Weisglass argues, "I don't think anyone sees settlements as a security asset."[72] Because Sharon was not cognitively rigid, he was open to influence by advisors such as Weisglass and Landau. Since he was not immersed in a past orientation, as was Shamir, he was amenable to recognizing that the context had changed due to American support for a Palestinian state.

3. Demography

Although the Road Map and the Geneva Initiative were catalysts for Sharon's decision to withdraw from Gaza and start withdrawing from the West Bank, he also became convinced that demographic trends made occupation untenable in the long run.[73] Sharon finally recognized that Israel could not retain the West Bank and Gaza and have a democracy with a Jewish majority while the Palestinian population was rising in comparison to the Jewish one. Reuven Rivlin says that Sharon started talking about disengagement in October 2000. In talks with then-Prime Minister Ehud Barak on a unity government, Sharon said that he would be ready to evacuate some settlements in order to reduce contact with the Palestinians. He was considering the evacuation of seventeen relatively isolated West Bank settlements.[74] Naomi Chazan claims that Sharon "replaced geography with demography."[75] This is in contrast to Shamir, who, despite statistics, believed that only despairing defeatists say that there are far more Palestinians than Jews in the West Bank.[76]

Ehud Olmert, Sharon's deputy and successor as prime minister, had himself undergone deep changes in position, and in turn influenced Sharon's shift. Olmert's father was a member of the Irgun, a militant underground militia that fought the British. Olmert was mayor of Jerusalem from 1993 to 2003. In mid-November 2003, Olmert said that if the Road Map negotiations failed as he anticipated, "Israel will have the right to take unilateral actions to separate from the Palestinians."[77] He proposed a unilateral withdrawal from a large part of the West Bank, including outlying Arab neighborhoods of Jerusalem, in order to

---

[72] Interview with Dov Weisglass, July 4, 2004, Jerusalem.
[73] Interview with Yossi Beilin, July 26, 2007, Tel Aviv.
[74] Leslie Susser, "Why Ruby Lost His Sparkle."
[75] Interview with Naomi Chazan, July 17, 2007, Jerusalem.
[76] Itzhak Shamir, *For the Sake of Zion, Vision and Faith: Addresses and Speeches* (Hebrew), (Tel Aviv: Beit Yair-Stern House, 1993), 274; interview with Shamir.
[77] Leslie Susser, "Preventing the Unthinkable," *The Jerusalem Report*, December 15, 2003.

guarantee an 80 percent Jewish majority in Israel. Olmert made this dramatic shift because he recognized the demographic problem posed by future Jewish and Palestinian population trends, was disillusioned by Abu Mazen's failure to attain sufficient power under Arafat, and was influenced by his wife and children who are supporters of the left-wing Meretz Party.[78] Olmert quoted David Ben-Gurion's words about the War of Independence: "When we faced the choice of the complete land without a Jewish state, or a Jewish state without the complete land, we chose a Jewish state."[79] Olmert was also influenced by Labor Party member Haim Ramon, who joined Kadima and as a cabinet member advised both Olmert and Sharon. For years Ramon had been talking about separation and the demographic problem. He floated the idea of the security barrier in 2001.[80] As his own position shifted, Olmert, as an advisor to Sharon, was in a position to influence Sharon's own thinking on withdrawal.

Sharon could propose evacuation of land and settlements, while most of his Likud compatriots voted against disengagement, because he was never rigidly tied to the Greater Land of Israel as an article of faith. In fact, he took the risk of establishing a completely new party, with only four months to build the infrastructure and logistics for a campaign, in order to pursue his agenda, given opposition to it within the Likud. He "declared himself ready to plunge forward like a tightrope walker on a high wire act with no safety net below him."[81]

4. *Popular Domestic Support*

A contributing, although not primary, factor in Sharon's disengagement plan, was growing public support for the idea. Alan Dowty perceptively argues that "the Sharon government was significantly more hawkish than the Israeli public as a whole, which helped explain why Ariel Sharon moved verbally in a moderate direction."[82] Sharon's approval rating reached a low of 33 percent the week before his withdrawal remarks. Days after the remarks, his rating was up to 39 percent. Sharon had some of the best pollsters around him on a regular basis; he also had an incentive to divert attention from the ongoing investigation into his involvement in a bribery scandal.[83] However, even some of his political opponents admit that Sharon was capable of advocating unpopular positions and that winning greater public support was not his prime motivation for unilateral disengagement.[84]

---

[78] Joseph Berger, "How a Zionist Hawk Grew His New Dovish Feathers," *The New York Times*, August 13, 2004.

[79] Gershom Gorenberg, "The Cracking of the Israeli Right," *The Jerusalem Report*, December 29, 2003.

[80] Interview with Naomi Chazan, July 17, 2007, Jerusalem.

[81] Eytan, *Sharon*, 206.

[82] Dowty, *Israel/Palestine*, 167.

[83] David Makovsky, "Assessing Sharon's Gaza Settlement Evacuation Proposal," *The Washington Institute for Near East Policy*, February 9, 2004.

[84] Interview with Naomi Chazan, July 17, 2007, Jerusalem.

Sharon's significant shift in policy can be explained by ideological and personality factors that enabled the change, in combination with more proximate, sufficient causes. Sharon's weak ideological commitment to the Likud enabled him to think of the territories in terms of security rather than as an article of faith. His moderate cognitive flexibility enabled him to listen to advisors who were pushing the withdrawals, and – as opposed to his earlier stance during the Lebanon War, when he was willing to defy U.S. demands – to conclude that he could not completely disregard American influence. Sharon was influenced by Ehud Olmert, his advisor Eli Landau, and his Chief of Staff Dov Weisglass, among others.[85] These advisors helped Sharon to recognize the demographic trend, to see the necessity of preempting greater American pressure, and to attend to the military's assessment of the detrimental cost of providing security for the settlers in Gaza.[86] His propensity to take risks also enabled him to take a leap that he had previously thought too dangerous. Sharon's present time orientation also enabled him to make the determination that the present context was different from the past and that the United States could not be ignored.

EXPLAINING THE LIMITS TO SHARON'S CHANGES

Although Sharon withdrew Israeli forces and settlements from Gaza and probably would have evacuated many more West Bank settlements had he not suffered the stroke, it is likely that he would not have been able to make the concessions that are necessary for a permanent agreement on a two-state solution. He would have been, I would argue, unlikely to compromise on Jerusalem. He went to the Temple Mount in 1985 as minister of infrastructure to make the statement that it belonged to Israel, as he did in 2000.[87] Sharon built a house for himself in the middle of the Palestinian part of the old city in Jerusalem, from which an enormous Israeli flag hangs, guarded by Israeli soldiers. Sharon also maintained, up to the time of his stroke, his belief that it is essential for Israel to keep a significant part of the West Bank for strategic depth (unlike, for instance, Shimon Peres, who as I argue later no longer thinks that territory is vital in the age of missiles). Sharon wanted to keep the strip of the West Bank along the Jordan River (25 kilometers for three divisions to fight a tank battle) and a 12-kilometer strip along the Dead Sea. He would have been willing to withdraw from at least 60 percent of the West Bank, and when felled by his stroke was working for an interim solution that would put off final status talks for up to twenty years. Dov Weisglass believes that because Sharon was so happy with the letter he received from President Bush supporting the Israeli claim to keep the major settlement blocs, that by implication this meant that he

[85] Interview with Dov Weisglass, July 4, 2004, Jerusalem.
[86] Interview with Uri Dan, July 1, 2004, Yaffo, Israel.
[87] Interview with Uri Dan, July 1, 2004, Yaffo, Israel.

was happy to concede the other 93 percent of the West Bank that the letter implies Israel would not keep.[88]

Sharon believed that Israel would always face hostility, and moving to a permanent agreement would always entail security risks.[89] In March 2005, one month before the Gaza withdrawal, Yossi Beilin met with Sharon to persuade him to negotiate with the Palestinian Authority over the withdrawal so that they could get the credit rather than Hamas; Sharon responded that, unlike Beilin, he did not think it was possible to make peace or have an agreement implemented with the Palestinians. He did not believe that if he signed something with Abu Mazen that he could or would cement it. He did not trust him and never invited him to his home.[90] Setting Beilin's account of this conversation next to Dov Weisglass's account of Sharon's growing trust in Abu Mazen, we see the way in which Sharon's moderate cognitive flexibility allowed him to differentiate among Palestinian leaders – but only to a limited degree. While Sharon might have trusted Abu Mazen more than Arafat, this is only a relative shift. Saeb Erekat claims that in his last conversation with Sharon on June 21, 2005, Sharon told him, "I don't trust any Arabs." Sharon's final conversations with Erekat also illustrate the limits of Sharon's willingness to accept outside advice. As already suggested, Sharon's military recommended against a unilateral withdrawal from Gaza; that advice was echoed by Erekat, who said that by not negotiating the withdrawal, "[y]ou're shooting me in the head and you're shooting yourself in the foot, don't do that."[91] Sharon was a master tactician, and perhaps did not assess the overall strategy.[92] Sharon was not sufficiently cognitively flexible to change his old opinions of Palestinian leaders. Although Sharon was not able to concede what will be necessary to achieve a two-state solution, his concessions have laid the groundwork, precedent, and legitimacy for future, more extensive withdrawals.

CONCLUSIONS AND IMPLICATIONS

In this project I am arguing that, in examining Israeli foreign policy decision making, especially in regard to dramatic shifts in policy toward the Palestinians, it is crucial to examine the perceptions of Israeli prime ministers that are shaped by both ideology and personality traits. Israel is preoccupied with security in its formation of foreign policy, as would be predicted by realists. However, given that the Israeli public is often divided over how best to provide for its security, the individual beliefs and traits of prime ministers are crucial to understanding

---

[88] Interview with Dov Weisglass, August 6, 2010, Ramat Hasharon.
[89] Interview with Dov Weisglass, July 4, 2004, Jerusalem.
[90] Interview with Yossi Beilin, July 26, 2007, Tel Aviv.
[91] Interview with Saeb Erekat, July 20, 2007, Jericho.
[92] Interview with Efraim Halevy, August 6, 2013, Ramat Aviv. Halevy was director of the Mossad and then the National Security Council when Sharon was prime minister.

Israeli decision making. In the many crises that characterize the Israeli conflict with the Palestinians, as well as domestic and external pressures for cooperation, the prime minister plays a crucial role in obstructing or initiating cooperation. While hard-liners in enduring rivalries vary in their ability to reach accommodation, not all hard-liners must necessarily be replaced before concessions can be made. The case of Ariel Sharon's dramatic initiative to withdraw from Gaza and to start to evacuate settlements from the West Bank, yet his refusal to withdraw from all of the West Bank or divide Jerusalem, can only be fully understood when one understands his cognitive style and ideological influences.

Sharon was able to change because he did not adhere to all the components of Likud ideology, which make change less possible. Sharon was not cognitively rigid and was therefore also open to the contrasting views of advisors. His emotional intelligence gave him the confidence and the relationships that enabled him also to seek the advice of experienced advisors, some of whom were more dovish than himself. He did not focus on the past and therefore was not resistant to expecting or recognizing change. Sharon was more likely to compromise than, for example, Itzhak Shamir, for whom ideology was central. Unlike Shamir, Sharon did not grow up steeped in Revisionist ideology, did not rigidly toe the Likud line, left the Likud to create the Kadima Party, and ultimately publicly accepted the idea of a Palestinian state. He proposed unilateral Israeli withdrawal from the Gaza Strip, while most members of his Likud Party voted against withdrawal in a referendum, forcing the formation of a unity government with Labor. Given the comparatively more rigid adherence to Likud ideology of most of its members, having Labor in their government was a necessity.[93] Many Likud members did not approve of Sharon's plan precisely because of their ideological commitment to the Greater Land of Israel and their recognition that, once a precedent is set for evacuating settlements in the West Bank and Gaza, the ideological rationale for keeping them is eroded.[94] Because Sharon did not share the traditional Likud centrality given to the Greater Land of Israel, he was able to make withdrawals he had claimed he would never make.

At the same time, Sharon's sense that "time is on Israel's side," which is rooted in Likud ideology, limited the extent of his changes. Although he ultimately was willing to concede the majority of the West Bank, Sharon believed that the Arabs' relative military strength will diminish, and that peacemaking can be put off for another twenty years while Israel builds other settlements and increases immigration.[95] He also endorsed the notion that peace would only be possible some day when Palestinians give up on East Jerusalem.

[93] Interview with Dov Weisglass, July 4, 2004, Jerusalem.
[94] Jonathan Rynhold and Dov Waxman argue that not all Likud members voted against disengagement due to ideology; see their "Ideological Change and Israel's Disengagement from Gaza," *Political Science Quarterly* (2008), 15
[95] Uri Dan, "Foreword," to Ariel Sharon's *Warrior*, 8.

Sharon's propensity to take risks and seize the military initiative also facilitated his plans to forge ahead with his own unilateral withdrawal, preempting peace plans that would require greater concessions than he was willing to make. He left his secure coalition, which included forty Likud members, in order to form a new political party to implement further withdrawals. U.S. pressure on Sharon to follow the Road Map led him to placate the United States with his own initiative. Finally, Sharon's emotional intelligence – which garnered public support, effective management, and the building of political alliances – contributed to his being able to effectively execute his desired policies, even when they contradicted the ideology of his strongest political allies. He had a stroke at the height of his popularity: polls in December 2005 showed that in an election Sharon would have secured up to fifty-five seats for Kadima. Dov Weisglass points to the different conditions that exist today, rather than the period of extreme violence during Sharon's term. Now, Weisglass argues, the Palestinian Authority is doing incredible work: Fayyad has accomplished miracles, it has well-organized and well-equipped security forces who struggle against terrorism and control the West Bank, and there is unprecedented security coordination with Israel. Sharon, Weisglass predicts, would be engaged today in final status talks under present conditions.[96] While this is only one (interested) observer's opinion, scholars are left only to wonder, what if?

---

[96] Interview with Dov Weisglass, August 6, 2010, Ramat Hasharon.

5

Yitzhak Rabin: From Hawk to Nobel Prize Peacemaker

Those who believe that the Palestinian issue is the obstacle to peace are mistaken . . .
those that claim that it is the key to peace, the formula for peace, the means to
achieve peace . . . are simply misreading reality.[1]

– Yitzhak Rabin, 1976

We need to sober up and to recognize the reality that there is a Palestinian entity in
the territories. An entity that stands on its own, which the Egyptians don't speak for,
which the Syrians don't speak for, and maybe not even the Jordanians. With that
entity, that sits in the territories, who we confront every day in the intifada, with them
we are ready to sit. We see in them a partner. We are willing to talk with them.[2]

– Yitzhak Rabin, 1991

Yitzhak Rabin, chief of staff of the Israeli Defense Force (IDF) during the Six-Day War and prime minister from 1974 to 1977 and from 1992 until his assassination in 1995 at age seventy-three, is one of the most dramatic and well-known examples of a hard-liner changing his stance toward a long-standing enemy. In 1988, he was a hawkish defense minister who was known for cracking down on the intifada through force.[3] Thousands of Peace Now activists demonstrated to demand Rabin's resignation because of his responsibility for the administrative detention of hundreds of Palestinians. Yet only five years later, this same man reluctantly shook the hand of his mortal enemy, Yasser Arafat, after signing the Oslo Accords, which provided for mutual recognition between the PLO and Israel. Only two years from that moment, he stood on a stage singing the song of peace in front of tens of thousands of Peace Now supporters, who were now cheering him on. On that same night, an

---

[1] As quoted from Efraim Inbar, *Rabin and Israel's National Security* (Baltimore: The Johns Hopkins University Press, 1999), referring to "interview with Yitzhak Rabin," *Bamahane*, February 4, 1976, 4.

[2] Labor Party Central Committee, March 27, 1991, Document #1053, 18, 19.

[3] Most experts define Rabin as a lifelong hawk. For example, see Efraim Inbar, *War and Peace in Israeli Politics: Labor Party Positions on National Security* (Boulder, CO: Lynne Rienner Publishers, 1991), 17. Rabin was defense minister from 1984 to 1990.

assassin's bullet tore through the words of the song that he had placed in his breast pocket and pierced his heart.

What can explain Rabin's dramatic shift? I argue that Rabin's ideology and cognitive style, as well as his advisors, influenced his perception of events and his image of the PLO, which in turn influenced his policies. Labor's ideology is a permissive one that enables its adherents to perceive change in the opponent and in the regional environment. Virtually all Labor Party members changed their perception of the PLO and voted for the Oslo agreement, whereas many Likud members voted against it. Rabin's sister claims that he "paid attention to the changes around him and realized the changes happening in the world were giving us a once-in-a-lifetime opportunity. He thought we would need to change our previous opinions."[4]

A significant component of Labor ideology that enabled party members to adopt more soft-line positions over time is that it, in contrast to Likud ideology, did not have an extended, optimistic time frame in regard to winning the conflict with the Palestinians. Therefore, Rabin, like many other Labor members, increasingly believed that time was not on Israel's side and that peace had to be promoted with urgency. Labor ideology also did not hold that hostility toward Israel in the world was permanent, and this enabled Rabin to be open to changes on the part of the Palestinians and to be influenced by world opinion. Labor ideology also focused on a general conception of security that was not necessarily tied to territory; thus, Labor leaders had always been willing to compromise territory for peace. Finally, Labor leaders were more likely to risk political solutions because they did not view absolute security as possible without peace, as did adherents of Likud ideology. Rabin's ideological beliefs largely remained constant, yet they enabled shifts in his perception of the PLO.

Although Labor Party members underwent a softening of their positions toward the Palestinians, as did Rabin, not all members changed at the same rate or through the same mechanisms. Rabin's cognitive rigidity and focus on the present influenced him to do so in a slower manner than Shimon Peres, to learn from events as opposed to trends, and to react to daily events as opposed to initiating dramatic changes such as the Oslo negotiations. His formal advisory system influenced the change. Although the deputy foreign minister pushed the Oslo process forward without Rabin's knowledge, Rabin's respect for the foreign minister's position led him to take the Oslo negotiations seriously once they came to his attention, and to subsequently sign the Oslo Accords.

Although changes in the PLO and in the region were necessary conditions for Rabin's adaptations, his ideology, present time orientation, and exposure to advisors holding differing views were sufficient to change his image of the PLO.

---

[4] Interview with Rahel Rabin, July 7, 1998, Kibbutz Menarah, Israel.

DETERMINANTS OF CONVERSION

Ideology

Born in Jerusalem in 1922 to Russian parents, Rabin was the first Israeli prime minister to be born in Israel, and he was steeped in an ideology that greatly shaped his worldview and enabled him to change his perceptions of the PLO. The Labor Party had a universalistic social-democratic ideology that emphasized pioneering, settlement of the land, and egalitarianism.[5] Not only was he a party leader for more than twenty years, but Rabin in his youth was strongly influenced by the precursors of the Labor Party's ideology. Rabin's parents were committed socialists, he joined a socialist youth group, and he graduated from the Kadoorie Agricultural School, which was heavily influenced by the precursors of Labor ideology. Rabin's sister relates, "[O]ur school reflected the worldview of my parents, a special school for the young workers. Our home, our school, and our youth group, the Working Youth, were circles of the same thing, expressing the values of pioneers."[6] At age nineteen, in 1941, Rabin enlisted in the Palmach, an underground Labor Zionist commando unit, and in 1947 became its deputy commander.

Labor ideology has no one blueprint that contains Labor doctrine. The Labor Party was an outgrowth of many socialist groups and factions that were first established in 1906 and eventually merged into three political parties (Mapai, Achdut Haavoda, and Rafi). These three parties merged to form the Labor Party in 1968. In contrast to Vladimir Jabotinsky's predominant influence on Revisionist Zionism, which is the basis for Likud ideology, Labor ideology has no single founder. Therefore, the components of Labor ideology that influenced Yitzhak Rabin, Shimon Peres, and Ehud Barak are gathered from different sources, including Berl Katznelson and David Ben-Gurion, who formed the leadership of Achdut Haavoda, the faction that most heavily influenced Rabin before the formation of the Labor Party. They transformed the utopian movement into a reformist party that sought to attract other factions.

In order to explore the party's ideology, I examine the values and goals that were articulated through Labor Party platforms over the span of several decades, and the observations of scholars who have studied the Labor Party and its ideas over time. The Labor Party's ideology is often perceived as a flexible one, perhaps because it represented a compromise among factions holding different views. Berl Katznelson argued for general values and the avoidance of any definite program in order to be open to all factions and workers. Ezer Weizman argued that Labor Party members adhered to the principles of realpolitik.[7]

---

[5] David Ben-Gurion, *Israel: A Personal History* (New York: Funk & Wagnalls, 1971), 434.
[6] Interview with Rahel Rabin, July 7, 1998, Kibbutz Menarah, Israel.
[7] Peretz Merhav, *The Israeli Left: History, Problems, Documents* (New York: A. S. Barnes & Company, 1980), 39, 49; Ezer Weizman, *The Battle for Peace* (Jerusalem: Edanim Publishers, 1982), 163.

Ideology had a greater influence on Rabin than did public opinion or the desire to stay in power. He resigned as prime minister in 1977 as a consequence of the revelation that his wife had kept an illegal bank account in the United States containing $2,000 – a violation which many politicians would have regarded as minor, not warranting resignation. In his second term, he was willing to step ahead of public opinion in recognizing the PLO.[8] Between 1986 and 1993, it was a crime for an Israeli citizen to knowingly have contact with a member of the PLO, which was considered a terrorist organization. Both the Labor and Likud parties formally rejected negotiations with the PLO.[9] Rabin knew that the Oslo negotiations would have to be conducted in extreme secrecy since talking directly with PLO officials was a strong taboo in Israel.

Even if Rabin had been influenced by public opinion, it would have been hard to please the majority of the Israeli population, which had been highly polarized, producing close elections between 1984 and 1996. Fewer than 30,000 votes brought Netanyahu to power in 1996. Polls were inconclusive on the question of dealing with the PLO. Some polls conducted during the Oslo talks showed that the public would support Rabin if he reached a deal with Arafat. However, other polls showed that the majority of citizens were against recognizing the PLO.[10] Rabin thought that leaders could mold public opinion and defied the advice of most of his advisors not to go to the signing of the Oslo Declaration of Principles with the PLO in Washington because they did not think Israelis were ready to accept his meeting with Arafat.[11]

Rabin was clearly more influenced by ideology than by public opinion. Labor's flexibility on the issue of time in regard to the Palestinians, amenability to territorial compromise, view of the world, and acknowledgment that absolute security was not possible were, I argue, enabling factors in Rabin's dramatic change from opposing recognition of the PLO and the establishment of a Palestinian state to accepting both. In the following section, I show that Rabin's views emanated from the ideology that he grew up with and believed in throughout his life, and are shared by other adherents of the ideology.

1. Is Time on Israel's Side?

Whereas Likud ideology influenced its leaders to think time was on Israel's side in regard to the Israeli-Palestinian conflict, David Ben-Gurion, Israel's first prime minister and a strong influence on Labor ideology, argued that time could work

---

[8] Interview with Amos Eiran, June 23, 1998, Tel Aviv. Amos Eiran spent five years with Rabin in the United States when Rabin was Israeli Ambassador to the United States; he was the director general of the Prime Minister's Office from 1974 to 1977 and was a close friend of Rabin's. He played tennis with him every Saturday for twenty years.

[9] Leah Rabin, *Rabin: Our Life, His Legacy* (New York: Putnam's Sons, 1997), 247; Inbar, *War and Peace in Israeli Politics*, 151.

[10] Asher Arian, *Security Threatened: Surveying Israeli Opinion on Peace and War* (Cambridge: Cambridge University Press, 1995), 106, 107.

[11] Interview with Yossi Sarid, July 5, 1998, Tel Aviv; interview with Shimon Sheves, July 1, 1998, Tel Aviv.

for or against Israel.[12] Rabin was thus free to adapt his view on this issue to changing circumstances. Soon after the Six-Day War, Rabin suggested that "much water would flow through the Jordan" before the resolution of the Palestinian crisis would be achieved.[13] Having been a longtime believer in the "ripeness" of the moment, Rabin complimented President Jimmy Carter on exhausting other means before hosting the Camp David summit, "for it is necessary to reach a certain stage in the development of a crisis or a stalemate before both sides realize that now – at a given moment, at a given level, in a given set of negotiations – they are in a 'make it or break it' situation, once and for all."[14]

But with changing circumstances, Rabin and other Labor Party members increasingly came to believe that time was working against Israel. The 1988 elections kit for party activists emphasized the economic and military burden of the occupation.[15] Rabin argued in 1991, "[I]n my eyes, the window of opportunity for the advancement of peace at the end of 1989, beginning of 1990, was wider and bigger than today."[16] This sense of time growing short prompted him to initiate peace with urgency, and to learn from policies that seemed to be failing.

2. Ideological Goals: General and Adaptable, or Specific and Rigid?

The more general the ideological goals, the more flexible they are to support differing strategies to respond to changed circumstances. Therefore, because Labor ideology emphasized the general goal of security, as opposed to the specific retention of a particular territory, it was amenable to changing interpretations as to whether the West Bank was needed to maintain security. Thus the land acquired after the Six-Day War was significant only insofar as it enhanced Israel's security. The Labor Party had long advocated territorial compromise, and after the Six-Day War, Rabin, along with the Labor-led government, professed Israel's willingness to trade newly acquired territory, including most of the West Bank, for peace. The historical roots of the land did not interest

---

[12] Shimon Peres, *From These Men: Seven Founders of the State of Israel* (New York: Wyndham Books, 1979), 45.

[13] Meeting of the Lishkah [Labor Party Leadership Bureau], September 4, 1974, 51. All documents pertaining to Labor Party meetings were gathered from the Labor Party Archives in Beit Berl, Israel. I translated these documents from Hebrew into English. The meetings from the 1970s do not have document numbers, only dates and page numbers. Meetings from the 1990s do have document numbers.

[14] Yitzhak Rabin, *The Rabin Memoirs*, expanded ed. (Berkeley: University of California Press, 1996), 255.

[15] Merhav, *The Israeli Left*, 285; Inbar, *War and Peace in Israeli Politics*, 111.

[16] Yitzhak Rabin, "Remarks by Prime Minister Yitzhak Rabin to a Joint Session of the United States Congress on the Occasion of the Rabin-Hussein Meeting," Washington, July 26, 1994, published in Yitzhak Rabin, *Rodef Shalom: Neumey Hashalom Shel Rosh Hamimshala Yitzhak Rabin* [Pursuing Peace: The Peace Speeches of Prime Minister Yitzhak Rabin] (Tel Aviv: Zmorah-Beitan, 1995), 35–39; Meeting of the Merkaz [Labor Party Central Committee], May 13, 1991, Document #1111, 11.

Rabin, who was, in the words of close aides, "willing to give up the land of Abraham's grave if it was unnecessary for security."[17]

A good example of Rabin's evolving stance is his reaction to the 1974 Rogers Plan. In 1974, Rabin reiterated that Israel, although willing to make territorial concessions for peace, was not willing to return to the 1967 borders in response to Arab intransigence, even in any final agreement.[18] Although Israel was in a strong position, Rabin was against the Rogers Plan, which entailed Israel's returning the occupied territories, except for minor border adjustments, because he thought it would take Israel's negotiating cards away, precluding the need for negotiations. Twenty years later, with the Oslo Accords, Rabin agreed to a framework very similar to the Rogers Plan.[19]

Yigal Allon (1918–1981), a Labor leader and Rabin's commander and mentor in the Palmach, had considerable influence on Rabin. In 1977, the Allon Plan was explicitly incorporated into the Labor Party's platform. At that time, it was considered preferable to give densely populated areas in the mountains south and north of Jerusalem to Jordan and keep them demilitarized. The compromises Rabin made at Oslo went further than had the Allon Plan but were based on this model for territorial compromise, which entailed keeping land needed for a security zone. By April 1986, the Labor Party had removed the southern Gaza Strip from the party's list of security zones.[20]

In 1988, the Labor Party's Platform on Foreign Affairs and Security for the Twelfth Knesset stated, "[T]he withdrawal from territories which are inhabited by a large Arab population within the framework of peace agreements, would be a significant contribution to the security of the State of Israel."[21] Rabin claimed that the desire to absorb 1.6 million Palestinians and the Whole Land of Israel was an ideological failure on the part of Likud.[22] Labor Knesset Member Haim Ramon concurred, "[F]rom the moment you accept that you can't absorb two million Palestinians, you have to divide the country. That's the ideological point

[17] Interview with Eitan Haber, July 27, 1997, Tel Aviv. Eitan Haber was close to Rabin for thirty-eight years; he was director of Rabin's bureau, his speech writer, and his right-hand man from 1984 until his assassination in 1995.
[18] Meetings of the Labor Party Leadership Bureau, September 29, 1974, and August 27, 1975, 5.
[19] Interview with Amos Eiran, June 23, 1998, Tel Aviv.
[20] Interview with Dan Pattir, May 28, 1998, Ramat Aviv. Dan Pattir was Counselor for Press and Information in the Israeli Embassy in the United States during the time that Rabin was Ambassador to the United States. He was his press secretary when Rabin became Prime Minister in 1974, and worked with him on a daily basis in his first administration until May 1977. Pattir covered military affairs for the paper *Davar* when Rabin was chief of staff. He remained in contact with him after he stopped working for him as they were neighbors; Inbar, *War and Peace in Israeli Politics*, 88, 92.
[21] As quoted in Inbar, *War and Peace in Israeli Politics*, 85, 161.
[22] Central Committee of the Labor Party, March 27, 1991. Document #1053, 20.

that determines everything."[23] Rabin's shift in attitude did not significantly concern the *amount* of land to be ceded, but rather who would receive it, in this case, the PLO rather than Jordan – and how urgently this needed to be accomplished.

3. Is the World with Us or Against Us?

Since the Labor Party ideology did not view the world as permanently hostile as did the Likud Party ideology, its members were more receptive to perceiving change in an opponent. Labor ideology allows its adherents to recognize when hostility is diminishing. Rather than providing a bulwark against an eternal enemy, Jews who had their own state would become part of a "normal" nation, no longer despised by other nations as a stateless people. Early Labor leaders, such as Israel's first foreign minister Moshe Sharrett, believed in Israel's eventual acceptance by the world. He reported to the Knesset that Israel's admission into the United Nations brought Israel back into the community of nations and closed the dark chapter of persecution.[24] In this tradition, Rabin stated in 1964 that Arab "hostility is not an eternal factor. Even today when the situation looks hopeless, we have to remember that nations, hostile to each other for tens of years, found avenues to each other's heart, when the political circumstances changed."[25] In a meeting of the Labor Party after the UN resolution equating Zionism with racism, Rabin did not say anything accusatory about countries that voted for the resolution, even though he disagreed with its allegations.[26]

Given this belief, adherents of the Labor ideology were more likely to recognize changes in the environment. The leadership of the Labor Party perceived an overall decrease in Arab hostility toward Israel after the 1978 Camp David Accords and Egypt's subsequent adherence to the peace agreement despite Israel's 1981 air raid on the Iraqi nuclear reactor and the 1982 Israeli invasion of Lebanon. Labor leaders, including Rabin, also continued to differentiate between the perceived threats emanating from different Arab actors, which led to a philosophy of aligning with relatively weaker enemies to face stronger ones. This differentiation led Rabin to conclude that peace with the PLO was urgent, so that Israel could diminish the influence of Hamas and form alliances with its immediate neighbors in the face of Iraqi hostility. Rabin's policies engendered a more friendly response to Israel. Two weeks before Rabin's assassination, 160 countries had recognized Israel, compared to 91 before he came to power.

---

[23] Interview with Labor Party Knesset Member Haim Ramon, June 23, 1998, Jerusalem.
[24] Aaron S. Klieman, *Israel & the World After 40 Years* (Washington, DC: Pergamon-Brassey's International Defense Publishers, 1990), 30, 87.
[25] As quoted by Inbar, *Rabin and Israel's National Security*, from *Bamahane*, January 9, 1964, 4.
[26] Meeting of the Labor Party Leadership Bureau, November 27, 1975, 10–17.

The Labor Party, over the span of two decades, reacted to changes in the environment by giving an increasing role to the Palestinians in any future settlement. The 1973 platform mentioned Palestinian identity and a Jordanian-Palestinian state; in 1977, it allowed for inhabitants of the West Bank and Gaza to be represented by a Jordanian-Palestinian delegation; in 1981, it stated that talks were allowed with Palestinian individuals and bodies that recognized Israel and denounced terrorism; and in 1988, it stated that Israel was willing to negotiate with representatives of the West Bank and Gaza.[27]

Since not all international actors were perceived as adversaries by Labor leaders, the party's increasing dovishness was motivated by putting great value on a good relationship with the United States. Rabin was an Americanophile who had served as ambassador to Washington from 1968 to 1973 and was sensitive to U.S. wishes. When he wanted to become ambassador to the United States, he gave a memo to the prime minister describing why Israel needed an American orientation and how to build proximity of interests.[28] He cited U.S. objections as one reason for his opposition to the Israeli bombing of the Iraqi nuclear reactor. By 1990, Rabin began to worry that the deadlock in reaching peace would lead to problems with the United States.[29] Although deference to America was not the prime reason for the negotiations, it was a factor in the urgency with which Rabin sought reconciliation with the Palestinians in his second term as prime minister.

4. How Much Will Peace Contribute to Security? Does Peace Require Territorial Compromise?

Labor ideology recognizes that peace can contribute to security and requires territorial compromise. Ben-Gurion argued that Israel could not have a policy of no peace and no war: either the heavy price of peace had to be paid or the country had to take the terrible risk of war. When he was helping to construct the interim agreement between Israel and Egypt in the 1970s, Rabin said that Israel would be getting something that has a *chance* to change the relationship and that the agreement entailed limited risks. As defense minister in 1985, Rabin said that the IDF could not prevent all terrorist attacks.[30] Therefore, even without peace negotiations, there would be no absolute security. Rabin claimed that the signing of the Israeli-Palestinian Declaration of Principles would perhaps end violence and wars. Rabin's sister, Rahel, claims that Rabin knew that the Oslo Accords

---

[27] Inbar, *Rabin and Israel's National Security*, 34, 73, 79.

[28] Interview with Dan Pattir, May 28, 1998, Ramat Aviv.

[29] Mark Segal, "Post Political Reporter Mark Segal Talks to Former Premier Yitzhak Rabin," *The Jerusalem Post*, July 31, 1981, 16; Labor Party Central Committee, July 26, 1990, Document #177, 5.

[30] Peres, *From These Men*, 45; Labor Party Leadership Bureau, August 27, 1975, 9–11, 37–38; Rabin, *The Rabin Memoirs*, 256; Inbar, *Rabin and Israel's National Security*, 86.

entailed dangers, but that he was willing to take a chance with peace after Israel had taken many risks with wars.[31]

Cognitive Style

Rabin stated in 1976 that Israel had reached a military might that allowed it to seek peace.[32] However, there was a lag of seventeen years between his perception of Israeli strength and his entering negotiations with the Palestinians, partially due to his cognitive style. Although Labor ideology enabled Rabin to change his image of the Palestinians, recognize the PLO, and accept a future Palestinian state, it did not determine the rate and mechanisms for this change. His personal time orientation and the relative rigidity of his mind determined the slow pace of change, the fact that he seemed to learn most from dramatic events, and his acceptance of an Oslo process that he himself did not initiate.

1. Time Orientation

Unlike Yitzhak Shamir who thought the Middle East would always be the same, and Shimon Peres who thought there would be a new Middle East, Rabin emphasized how the present was different from the past and refused to make predictions. According to Rabin, two days before the Yom Kippur War, nobody would have predicted it, and even he did not know one day before. He claimed that he could not even predict his own political future. Unlike Shimon Peres, Rabin did not look to the future as a visionary engaged in long-term planning.[33] When he was told that Nixon would be bad for Israel in the long run, Rabin responded, "Israel lives in the short run."[34]

Because he did not dwell on the past, Rabin could more easily change his image of the PLO and acknowledge that it was not condemned to repeat its use of terrorism or continue to try to destroy Israel. Rabin rarely referred in speeches or correspondence to past instances of Jewish persecution. He thought scholars

---

[31] Interview with Rahel Rabin, July 7, 1998, Kibbutz Menarah; Remarks by Prime Minister Yitzhak Rabin on the Occasion of the Signing of the Israeli-Palestinian Declaration of Principles, Washington, September 13, 1993, printed in Rabin, *Pursuing Peace*, 24–25.

[32] Rabin, *The Rabin Memoirs*, 104, 192; *Ha'aretz*, "Rabin: Otsma Hamarchiva Et Halev" [Rabin: Power That Broadens the Heart], *Ha'aretz*, December 19, 1976.

[33] Labor Party Leadership Bureau, September 4, 1974, 8, 49–50, 58–60; January 1, 1991, Document #278, 11; February 14, 1991, Document #288, 21. Yehudit Auerbach, "Yitzhak Rabin: Portrait of a Leader," in *Israel at the Polls 1992*, eds. Daniel J. Elazar and Shmuel Sandler (Lanham: Rowman & Littlefield Publishers, 1995), 292, 308; interview with Dan Pattir, May 28, 1998, Ramat Aviv, Israel; interview with Aliza Goren, June 26, 1998, Mevasseret, Israel. Goren worked in the Prime Minister's Office in Rabin's first term and was his spokesperson during his second term.

[34] David Philip Horovitz, *Yitzhak Rabin: Soldier of Peace* (London: Peter Halban, 1996), 57; Labor Party Leadership Bureau, September, 4, 1974, 6, 52.

were not useful because they could only analyze history.[35] Although Rabin's present orientation enabled change, coupled with a relatively rigid mind it slowed the pace of change and explains why he accepted, but did not initiate the Oslo process. Rabin was a guarded analyst of the present, obsessed by details and therefore viewed new information concerning the Palestinians on a daily basis, making the Palestinians' incremental changes seem less significant.[36] The focus on the present influenced Rabin to take a decade longer to change his perception of the PLO than Peres. Immersed in the present, Rabin suppressed any thoughts about the final status issues with the Palestinians.[37]

2. Risk Propensity

Unlike Ariel Sharon, Rabin did not have a strong propensity for risk; instead, he often moved with great deliberation and caution. This trait influenced his slower path to change and accounts for the fact that he did not initiate the Oslo negotiations with the PLO. He had been more cautious than Sharon with military operations – for example, he voted against the Israeli military strike against a nuclear weapons development facility in Iraq, and he had a nervous breakdown preceding the preemptive military strike in the Six-Day War in 1967 – and likewise was hesitant to deal with the PLO.

3. Cognitive Flexibility

Rabin's ideology and orientation toward the present enabled changes despite his cognitive rigidity. Although Rabin was rigid by nature, he did not have a closed mind as evidenced by his changes over the years on various issues. He grew to view environmental issues as important, whereas previously he had no sympathy for them, and he also changed his views on economics. He grew up with socialist parents who refused to have a phone or comfortable couch because that was too materialistic; as an adult, Rabin believed more strongly in capitalism.[38] In addition, although he was initially against closing the border with the occupied territories as a response to acts of terrorism, in March 1993 he changed his

---

[35] Klieman, *Israel & the World After 40 Years*, 54; Peri, "Afterword," *The Rabin Memoirs*, 360; Dan Kurzman, *Soldier of Peace: The Life of Yitzhak Rabin 1922–1995* (New York: HarperCollins, 1998), 30.

[36] Interview with Elyakim Rubinstein, July 9, 1998, Jerusalem. Rubinstein led the Israeli negotiating team for the Washington talks during the Rabin Administration and was Attorney General in the Netanyahu government. He has been a Justice of the Israeli Supreme Court since 2004. He confirms that Rabin did not initiate the negotiations. Uri Savir, *The Process: 1,100 Days That Changed the Middle East* (New York: Random House, 1998), p. 25; interview with Itamar Rabinovitch, May 25, 1997, Ramat Gan; Peri, "Afterword," *The Rabin Memoirs*, 361.

[37] Inbar, *Rabin and Israel's National Security*, 153.

[38] Interview with Rahel Rabin, July 7, 1998, Kibbutz Menarah; interview with Yossi Sarid, July 5, 1998, Tel Aviv. Sarid was formerly a Knesset member of the Labor Party and then the Meretz Party who was the minister of environment in the Rabin's second term as prime minister and became close to Rabin in the last few years of Rabin's life.

mind.[39] Rabin had also shown an earlier capacity for changing his perception of an enemy because of Anwar Sadat's visit to Jerusalem. Rabin claimed that by coming to Israel, Sadat created a "true revolution in our attitude toward him and toward Egypt"; his understanding "of our need for security ... was absolutely revolutionary," and his visit "forced Israel's government, as well as its citizens, to reassess what they had formerly considered to be their minimal demands for peace."[40]

Although Rabin was capable of changing his mind, on a spectrum from flexibility to rigidity, he tended toward rigidity. According to family members, close friends, and advisors he was unusually stubborn and rigid and had a very difficult time changing his mind.[41] Shimon Sheves, Director General of Rabin's Office, claims that this stubbornness was a factor in his taking longer than Peres to reach a decision to recognize the PLO.[42]

Rabin hated ambiguity and tended to view both the internal and external environments in simplistic, two-dimensional ways and differentiated between "good guys" and "bad guys." Rabin disliked intellectuals, the "leftist" media, and human rights organizations that he perceived to be naive and weakening the nation. Advisors describe him as having strong likes and dislikes, never in between. Rabin was frequently dismissive of others' opinions, at times leaving the room when he disagreed, or saying "you're talking stupidities" and giving a backhanded wave to let the person know a discussion was over.[43] In one Labor Party meeting about the Gulf War, he typically dismissed the opinions of others claiming that they did not know what they were talking about.[44] Because Rabin was dismissive of others' opinions, he took much longer to change his perception of the PLO than did Peres, and these perceptions did not fully change until a couple of years after the initial Oslo Accords were signed.

4. *Emotional Intelligence*
Rabin did not only tend toward cognitive rigidity, but he also did not have a strong emotional intelligence (although he was not as deficient in this respect as Netanyahu or Barak). Rabin himself claimed that, partially because he was a lonely child who suffered from his parents' frequent absences, "I was a closed,

---

[39] Interview with Haim Ramon, June 23, 1998, Jerusalem.

[40] Rabin, *The Rabin Memoirs*, 253–54.

[41] Interview with Rahel Rabin, July 7, 1998, Kibbutz Menarah; interview with Amos Eiran, June 23, 1998, Tel Aviv; Inbar, *Rabin and Israel's National Security*, 5.

[42] Interview with Shimon Sheves, July 1, 1998, Tel Aviv. Sheves knew Rabin from 1974 and worked for him from 1984 until Rabin's assassination. He was his personal assistant from 1985 to 1992 and the director general of the Prime Minister's Office from 1992 to 1995.

[43] Interviews with Yossi Sarid, July 5, 1998, Tel Aviv, and with Dan Pattir, May 28, 1998, Ramat Aviv; Y. Auerbach, "Yitzhak Rabin: Portrait of a Leader," in *Israel at the Polls 1992*, eds. D. J. Elazar and S. Sandler (Lanham, MD: Rowman & Littlefield Publishers, Inc.) 304–5; Horovitz, *Yitzhak Rabin*, x; Kurzman, *Soldier of Peace*, 20.

[44] Labor Party Leadership Bureau, February 14, 1991, Document #288, 11–15, 21.

introverted child with a tendency to shyness. I am accused of still having those traits today."[45] Rabin's sister uses the identical words to describe her brother.[46] He did not put much emphasis on the importance of sensitivities to others' feelings and emotions, or even to his own. As scholars have shown, self-perception theory applies particularly well to those who lack sensitivity: thus, as I will discuss, self-perception theory seems, to some extent, to describe Rabin's evolving image of the PLO after he signed the Oslo agreement.

Rabin's mistrust toward the immediate environment contributed to his emphasis on loyalty and to his choice of advisors, even from rival parties, over political partners who were also potential rivals. He picked Elyakim Rubinstein to head the Washington negotiations with the Palestinians because he perceived him to have no political ambitions.[47] Eitan Haber was an experienced, loyal advisor who came from a Likud family. Rabin was less suspicious and was able to nurture long-lasting loyalty from Haber. Therefore, unlike Netanyahu, Rabin did not feel compelled to surround himself with like-minded young yes-men – as long as they were not in direct competition for his position.

Advisors

Rabin's personality made it difficult for him to be receptive to a rich stream of advice, even from his own advisors. He did not share his feelings or want feedback from people, was a loner, and kept all his deliberations to himself. Rabin's experience as chief of staff, ambassador, defense minister, and prime minister often led him to act independently of advisors.[48] He admitted to his strategic advisor, Haim Assa, "I do not know what to do with advisors," and some of his closest advisors did not know where he was heading.[49]

Although Rabin did not rely heavily on advisors, he preferred the formalistic approach to managing them, possibly because of his thirty years in the military. Alexander George describes the formalistic model as "characterized by an orderly policymaking structure, one that provides well-defined procedures, hierarchical lines of communication, and a structured staff system."[50] Rabin had no "kitchen" cabinet and no close friends with whom he would confide (he had learned his lesson from consulting with Ezer Weizman right before the Six-Day War; Weizman subsequently circulated reports to the press

[45] Yitzhak Rabin with Dov Goldstein, *Pinkas Sherut* [The Rabin Memoirs] (Tel Aviv: Ma'ariv, 1979), 17.

[46] Interview with Rahel Rabin, July 7, 1998, Kibbutz Menarah.

[47] Auerbach, "Yitzhak Rabin: Portrait of a Leader," 294–95.

[48] Moshe Arens, *Broken Covenant* (New York: Simon & Schuster, 1995), 25; interview with Amos Eiran, June 23, 1998, Tel Aviv.

[49] Inbar, *Rabin and Israel's National Security*, 146, 148, 152.

[50] Alexander George, *Presidential Decisionmaking in Foreign Policy: The Effective Use of Information and Advice* (Boulder, CO: Westview Press, 1980), 129.

that Rabin had suffered a breakdown just before the war). He relied almost exclusively on the people in the official chain of command, behavior consistent with his rigorous military background. He acted as both prime minister and defense minister.[51]

In addition to some of the overlooked benefits of formal advisory arrangements analyzed by John Burke and Fred Greenstein, the formal arrangement Rabin followed could allow for the influence of more dovish ministers, even if he was both personally and intellectually skeptical of their position.[52] Although Rabin did not rely heavily on advisors, he respected his ministers because of his respect for hierarchical subordinates in the formal system. He therefore did not immediately dismiss the Oslo initiative brought to him by Foreign Minister Peres (and more indirectly by Deputy Foreign Minister Yossi Beilin), despite his personal dislike of Peres. Beilin initially presented Peres, and then Rabin, with the successful Oslo negotiations that he had initiated without their knowledge. Beilin argues that Rabin and Peres probably would not have supported the Oslo negotiations at the beginning when Beilin initiated them, but that Rabin was tempted to accept the agreement since it was successful in gaining commitments from the Palestinians that they had never previously made.[53] Nevertheless, had Rabin not had a formalistic approach that gave due respect to ministries, he might have scolded Peres and brought an abrupt halt to the Oslo process, as Peres feared he might.

The formalistic approach to managing advisors also led Rabin to be indirectly influenced by other, more dovish ministers, such as Yossi Sarid, leader of the Meretz Party. Although Rabin had not talked to Sarid for years after Sarid stopped supporting him in 1977, claiming that Rabin had not accomplished anything in his first term as prime minister, Rabin appointed him to be minister of the environment because of the number of votes Sarid received. Rabin's respect for the role of his ministers enabled him to form a closer relationship with Sarid, whom he later included in negotiations with the Palestinians. The changes in his relationship with Sarid reflected his changing perspectives regarding solutions to the Israeli-Palestinian conflict. Sarid relates that previously, "There was nobody in Israel he hated more than me ... I do not think there was a person I criticized more harshly. We had huge differences of opinion on everything: PLO or not, negotiations or not, right to self-determination or not, Golan or not, any issue that one can remember, we differed."[54] In addition to the influence of more dovish actors in various ministries, Rabin was influenced by his more dovish wife and children.[55]

---

[51] Leah Rabin, *Rabin*, 171, 222.

[52] John P. Burke, Fred I. Greenstein, Larry Berman, and Richard Immerman, *How Presidents Test Reality: Decisions on Vietnam, 1954 and 1965* (New York: Russell Sage Foundation, 1989) 276–77.

[53] Interview with Yossi Beilin, August 12, 1997, Tel Aviv. Beilin was the deputy foreign minister under Peres and initiated the Oslo process.

[54] Interview with Yossi Sarid, July 5, 1998, Tel Aviv.

[55] Labor Party Secretariat, January 31, 1991, Document #278, 14.

IMAGE OF THE ENEMY

Rabin ignored the Palestinian issue for many years. In Rabin's discussions in Labor Party meetings during his first term as prime minister, as well as with his advisors, he barely mentioned the Palestinians and infrequently talked to Palestinians in the territories. Rabin said that the key to the advancement of peace was with the Arab states, not the Palestinians.[56]

Until presented with the fait accompli of the successful Oslo negotiations, which had been conducted without his knowledge, Rabin had vehemently opposed negotiating with and recognizing the PLO. In fact, before the Oslo talks, Abu Mazen wrote Rabin asking if he would agree to establish a "back channel" for secret peace talks and Rabin answered no. In response to U.S. Speaker of the House of Representatives Tip O'Neill's questions as to why Israel could not negotiate with the PLO when the United States talked with the Vietcong, the French with the Algerian FLN, and the British with former Israeli underground movements, Rabin claimed that the PLO sought the destruction of Israel, whereas all these other groups did not seek to destroy the country with which they were negotiating.[57] When Peres first showed him the kernel of a peace agreement from Oslo, Rabin found it unacceptable but later gave it a reluctant and skeptical green light. He said hundreds of times that Israel would not talk to the PLO since it was a terrorist organization, and he was "allergic" to Arafat. He remained vehemently opposed to negotiating with the PLO until the Oslo negotiations.[58]

Jordanian Solution

Until 1988, when King Hussein of Jordan abdicated any control over the West Bank, the Israeli Labor Party, including Rabin, claimed that a solution to the conflict with the Palestinians could be found only within an agreement between Jordan and Israel, placing the Jordanians in charge of the Arab civil administration and Israel in charge of security.[59] Rabin believed that a Jordanian solution would be less hostile to Israel than an independent Palestinian entity. As a military person, he associated the degree of threat with the degree of military capability and never perceived the Palestinians to be

---

[56] Labor Party Leadership Bureau meetings, August 27, 1975, 36, and September 29, 1974, 8, 11, 12; interview with Amos Eiran, August 12, 1997, Tel Aviv, Rabin's "chief of staff" during his first term as prime minister; interview with Aliza Goren, June 26, 1998, Mevasseret, Israel.

[57] Interview with Rahel Rabin; Rabin, *The Rabin Memoirs*, 230–32, 260, 262.

[58] Interview with Yossi Sarid, July 5, 1998, Tel Aviv; Central Committee of the Labor Party, March 27, 1991, Document #1053, 18.

[59] "Palestinian Representation in Geneva," *Ha'aretz*, December 14, 1976; Labor Party Leadership Bureau, September 29, 1974, 23; Rabin, *The Rabin Memoirs*, 230–32.

a threat to Israel's existence. However, Rabin could no longer ignore the Palestinians after the intifada.

REACTIONS TO THE INTIFADA, 1988 PLO PROCLAMATION, AND THE GULF WAR

Rabin's ideology and individual characteristics shaped his perspectives on events and enabled him to learn from perceived policy failure, which had a profound influence on eventual Israeli agreements with the Palestinians. Rabin (describing his failure in a mathematics exam) claimed that failure was an impetus to success; this idea was enacted in Rabin's increased motivation in his second term as prime minister, as he believed (along with many others) that his first term as prime minister was disappointing.[60] In particular, the intifada and the Gulf War emphasized for Rabin the urgent need for a political solution to the Israeli-Palestinian conflict.

The first intifada convinced the then-Minister of Defense Rabin of the necessity for a political settlement with the Palestinians. Rabin's initial expectation was that the Palestinian uprising would be a passing phase, and he did not even cut short his visit to the United States when it started. When the intifada continued, Rabin attempted to quell it by force, "through the use of live ammunition, then after many deaths and international outcry, the shift to rubber bullets, and after that to billy clubs and the policy of 'breaking their bones.'"[61] His wife described him as having a predilection to use force: "Yitzhak's philosophy was simple: If a reliable military option existed, that was the preferred course of action. If not, one must negotiate, at least until other options suggested a more positive outcome."[62]

Because Labor ideology does not promote the appraisal of policy in messianic terms, and because Rabin was not consumed by the notion that history was bound to repeat itself, he was able to eventually learn from his own failure to stop the intifada through force. His generals told him they could do no more. Rabin came to realize that Israel could not do anything against children throwing stones, and he saw the negative influence this had on soldiers, as well as the suffering of the Palestinians; these factors combined to influence him to seek peace urgently and with greater concessions than he was once willing to make.[63] However, his rigidity and individual focus on the present prompted him to reach

---

[60] Rabin, *Pinkas Sherut*, 217; Arens, *Broken Covenant*, 23; Inbar, *Rabin and Israel's National Security*, 3; Karen Rasler, "Shocks, Expectancy Revision and the De-Escalation of Protracted Conflicts: The Israeli-Palestinian Case," *Journal of Peace Research* 37, no. 6 (November 2000), 699–720.

[61] Peri, "Afterword," *The Rabin Memoirs*, 354.

[62] L. Rabin, *Rabin*, 141.

[63] Interview with Eitan Haber, July 27, 1997, Tel Aviv.

this conclusion in a slow, gradual manner, and not until 1991 did Rabin recognize the importance of reaching an agreement with the Palestinians.[64]

As a military person, Rabin had previously ignored the Palestinians partly because he perceived them to be weak. The intifada led Rabin to respect Palestinian determination and aspirations. He believed that the intifada had led to increased power for the local leadership in the occupied territories as opposed to the outside leadership of Arafat's PLO in Tunis. The intifada "had turned the Palestinian people into a proper enemy. And as such, they had earned the right in Rabin's eyes to a proper peace."[65] Over time, Rabin perceived the intifada as a civil uprising of a politically aware population and distinguished it from previous acts of terrorism. The intifada had greater influence on Rabin than statements made by the PLO because he had been personally involved in trying to crack down on it and he was more willing to receive information regarding changes on the part of the PLO from trusted sources such as his generals and lawyer, Joel Singer.[66]

In contrast to Rabin's changes in response to the intifada, he ignored PLO proclamations that hinted at growing moderation. At its November 1988 Palestinian National Council meeting, the PLO approved United Nations Resolutions 242 and 338 and made an ambiguous public statement that could be read as recognizing Israel and abrogating terrorism. Rabin did not give any attention to these signals and considered them to be a publicity stunt. However, the declarations did have an indirect effect on Rabin. The changes on the part of the PLO led some party doves, including Beilin, to establish the Labor Forum for the Promotion of Peace in December 1988 in order to encourage a party debate on their platform's exclusion of the PLO from the political process.[67] The 1988 declaration gave Yair Hirschfeld and Yossi Beilin the legitimacy to talk with Palestinians in the territories who were supporters of the PLO, which they had not done previously. They were able to make connections with important leaders from the West Bank who ultimately encouraged them to talk to PLO officials in Oslo.[68]

For Rabin, the Gulf War also highlighted the need for peace, and presented the opportunity to pursue it with a weakened PLO. He was horrified that for the first time tens of thousands of Israelis fled Tel Aviv because of a few Scud missiles, which killed only one person, and that they dared to say on TV that they

---

[64] Labor Party Central Committee, March 27, 1991, Document #1053, 18, 20; interview with Shimon Sheves, July 1, 1998, Tel Aviv; L. Rabin, *Rabin*, 246.

[65] Horovitz, *Yitzhak Rabin*, 100; Peri, "Afterword," *The Rabin Memoirs*, 353, 356.

[66] H. Ben-Yehuda, "Attitude Change and Policy Transformation: Yitzhak Rabin and the Palestinian Question, 1967–95," *Israeli Affairs* 3, no. 3 (1997), 209; Chaim D. Kaufmann, "Out of the Lab and into the Archives: A Method for Testing Psychological Explanations of Political Decision Making," *International Studies Quarterly* 38 (1994), information delivered in a vivid, emotionally interesting way will receive greater weight.

[67] Peri, "Afterword," *The Rabin Memoirs*, 360; Inbar, *War and Peace*, 77.

[68] Interview with Ron Pundak, March 30, 1997, Jerusalem.

were going abroad. In 1948, thirty civilian casualties left no imprint on daily life in Tel Aviv. Rabin realized that the Israeli population had no stomach to incur more losses and its ability to support wars was much weaker: "We have changed," he concluded.[69] His sense that Israel's staying power for continued conflict was diminishing reinforced his view that time was not on Israel's side.[70]

Rabin's Labor ideology not only enabled his realization that time was working against Israel, but also allowed him to differentiate among the relative threats of various actors because that ideology did not view Israel's neighbors as equally or permanently hostile. The Gulf War substantiated for Rabin that Iraq and Iran were Israel's worst enemies, and in comparison the perceived gravity of the PLO threat receded. Rabin said that if Israel did not make peace with the Palestinians, "the alternative will be a hostile Arab posture led by Iraq, instead of Egypt.... We have already seen the movement due to the deadlock [in the peace process] to the direction of Iraq from Egypt."[71] The Gulf War emphasized for Rabin that there was a window of opportunity to reach an agreement with the Palestinians, for several reasons: first, Iraqi hostility required reconciliation with Israel's immediate neighbors; second, peace would diminish the influence of Iraq; and third, the Palestinians were weakened in the aftermath of the war and had therefore lowered their expectations, from replacing Israel with a Palestinian state to establishing a state alongside Israel.[72]

CONSEQUENT POLICY PREFERENCES

Cultivating an Internal Palestinian Leadership on the West Bank

After the intifada, Rabin grew to view the Palestinians as an independent body and believed that time was working against Israel, so he needed to pursue peace with greater urgency. These shifts in view, in combination with Jordan's abdication of its role in the West Bank in 1988, led Rabin to support cultivating an internal non-PLO Palestinian leadership in the West Bank with whom Israel would negotiate an interim agreement on self-rule, which would later lead to a final agreement.[73]

On July 12, 1992, the day before he presented his new government, Rabin stated that his government would be tested on its ability to proceed with the peace process, first and foremost with the Palestinians in the occupied territories, but not with the PLO.[74] Rabin repeatedly rejected pleas by Yair Hirschfeld and

---

[69] Interview with Eitan Haber, July 27, 1997, Tel Aviv; Inbar, *Rabin*, 162.

[70] Peri, "Afterword," *The Rabin Memoirs*, 367.

[71] Labor Party Central Committee, July 26, 1990, Document #177, 6.

[72] Interview with Dan Pattir, May 28, 1998, Ramat Aviv; Kurzman, 426.

[73] Interview with Leah Rabin, July 2, 1997, Ramat Aviv; Meeting of the Labor Party Central Committee, July 26, 1990, Document #291, 5.

[74] Labor Party Central Committee Meetings, July 12, 1992, Document #4076, 7, and March 27, 1991, Document #1053, 20.

Yossi Beilin, who urged Rabin to talk with Faisal Husseini, a Palestinian leader who had both a Jerusalem and West Bank address. As they continually advised Rabin to talk to the PLO, he finally said he would talk to Husseini, as he preferred talking to him over negotiating with the PLO. Rabin was disappointed when he realized that Husseini would not move without Arafat. Rabin failed in his attempt to develop an independent, internal leadership.[75]

Recognizing the PLO Through the Oslo Accords

In the last few years of his life, Rabin's image of the PLO changed as a result of a combination of factors: the lessons he drew from the intifada and the Gulf War, the growing competition between the PLO and Hamas, and the changes in the PLO that became apparent through the Oslo negotiations.[76] However, Rabin's rigidity and present time orientation contributed to his reacting to rather than initiating an agreement.

The Oslo negotiations started with two Israeli academics, Yair Hirschfeld and Ron Pundak, speaking to PLO officials in Norway with the knowledge and support of Israel's Deputy Foreign Minister Yossi Beilin. The talks started on January 21, 1993, while the Washington talks (held with Palestinians from the West Bank who were not PLO officials) had been on hold since the end of December, when Rabin had expelled 450 Hamas members. Leah Rabin claims that Yossi Beilin, Shimon Peres, Ron Pundak, and Yair Hirschfeld deserve credit for taking the initiative and playing an important role. Rabin did not know about the process for several weeks and was then skeptical about it for a long time.[77] Had it not been for the successful Oslo negotiations carried out by others, Rabin may have never reached the decision to talk to the PLO. Rabin saw that the PLO was making many more concessions in Oslo than Israel had ever thought possible from the talks in Washington.[78] The Foreign Ministry, under Peres's leadership, desperate to keep the Oslo process going, involved Joel Singer, a lawyer trusted by Rabin. Singer encouraged Rabin to recognize the PLO on certain conditions because the talks with the PLO would eventually leak, because negotiations virtually imply recognition, and because it was in Israel's interests to have an agreement.[79] Although Rabin had undergone a heightened urgency to pursue peace with the Palestinians over the span of several years, his ultimate decision to negotiate with the PLO during the successful Oslo process came relatively quickly.[80]

---

[75] Interviews with Yair Hirschfeld, Haim Ramon, and Rahel Rabin.
[76] Interview with Hemi Shelev, May 24, 1998, Jerusalem.
[77] Interview with Leah Rabin, July 2, 1997, Ramat Gan.
[78] Interview with Ron Pundak, March 30, 1997, Jerusalem.
[79] "The 50 Years War: Israel & the Arabs," PBS Video, directed by Dai Richards and Norma Percy (2000).
[80] Ben-Yehuda, "Attitude Change and Policy Transformation," 201–24.

Although Rabin had portrayed Arafat as a murderer and terrorist for decades, he understood with his teeth closed there was no alternative but to face the reality of Arafat. Rabin realized that there was no alternative leadership to the PLO and thought that by supporting the PLO, he could weaken Hamas. He had promised that within nine months Israel would get an agreement (with non-PLO Palestinians) and that date had passed. Rabin gave the go-ahead to Oslo after his efforts to pursue peace with Syria, which he had preferred, fell through. Rabin was ready to make only one big change, either on the Syrian front or on the Palestinian one, but not both. Rabin agreed to compromises that he previously rejected because of his perception of a window of opportunity created by the intifada and Gulf War, which left the Palestinians weak.[81]

Settlements

Unlike members of the Likud Party, Rabin saw many religious settlers as hampering rather than strengthening Israel's security and almost immediately upon coming to office in 1992, put a halt to all construction of new settlements in the territories. Rabin told Dennis Ross to tell U.S. Secretary of State Baker that this was "a new Yitzhak," who would not compromise on this issue by allowing settlements to be built, as he had during his first term as prime minister in the 1970s.[82] At that time he had made concessions that he later thought were tactical mistakes.[83] Rabin's wife relates, "[T]he settlers demand protection, complain, and have too much money allocated to their settlements by the Israeli Government."[84] Rabin's sister adds that Rabin "mentioned that the most extreme populations of the Palestinians and ours were living in the same place in Hebron. The Arabs in Hebron are known to be fundamentalists and about ours I don't have to tell you. It is the closest physical contact with the least amount of tolerance. With people like that it is a source of explosions."[85] In the spring of 1994, when Hebron was under curfew after Baruch Goldstein had massacred Muslim worshipers in the Tomb of the Patriarchs in Hebron, Rabin told Israeli journalists, "I feel very uncomfortable over the fact that 100,000 Palestinians are shut up in their houses for the sake of 400 Jews" and called the Jewish settlement program in Hebron totally insane, promising that the future peace treaty would deal with political settlements.[86]

---

[81] Interviews with Leah Rabin, July 2, 1997, Ramat Gan; Rahel Rabin, July 7, 1998, Kibbutz Menarah; Dan Pattir, May 28, 1998, Ramat Aviv; Ron Pundak, March 30, 1997, Jerusalem; Haim Ramon, June 23, 1998, Jerusalem; Itamar Rabinovitch, May 25, 1997, Ramat Gan; Eitan Haber, July 27, 1997, Tel Aviv.

[82] Kurzman, *Soldier of Peace*, 441.

[83] Labor Party Leadership Bureau, July 29, 1974; interview with Eitan Haber, July 27, 1997, Tel Aviv.

[84] Interview with Leah Rabin, July 2, 1997, Ramat Aviv.

[85] Interview with Rahel Rabin, July 7,1998, Kibbutz Menarah.

[86] Akiva Eldar, "Where Is Barak – and Where Is Rabin?" *Ha'aretz*, November 3, 2000.

Leaning Toward Favoring a Palestinian State

Rabin not only changed regarding recognition of the PLO and ended construction of new settlements, but also changed his stance toward a Palestinian state. In 1977, Rabin wrote that Labor opposed "in the strongest terms" a Palestinian state in the West Bank and the Gaza Strip because he believed those leaders of the PLO who claimed that such a state would merely be the first phase in the eventual destruction of Israel.[87] Whereas Yossi Beilin began advocating for a Palestinian state in 1981, when he was political secretary of the Young Guard of the Labor Party, Rabin only began moving in the direction of accepting the establishment of a Palestinian state *during* the Oslo negotiations because he came to understand that it was inevitable. The Oslo agreements set up the infrastructure of a state by calling for the establishment of a government with legislative, executive, and judicial branches and for popular elections. Rabin had earlier viewed a potential Palestinian state as a security threat that could ally with Iran or Iraq. Rabin's perception of moderation on the part of the PLO in regard to recognition of Israel and abrogation of terrorism, in addition to a growing relationship with Arafat, influenced him to regard a Palestinian state as less threatening than he had in the past. Rabin thought a strong Hamas was more likely than a strong PLO to make alliances with Iran.[88] Rabin would say "I am against a Palestinian state *now*," as he envisioned it as the last concession of negotiations.[89]

Questioning the Taboo of Dividing Jerusalem

It is unclear whether Rabin would have made any concessions on Jerusalem. On one hand, he was chief of staff of the Israel Defense Forces that united Jerusalem in 1967 and claimed that the unification of Jerusalem was the greatest victory of the Jewish people.[90] On the other hand, Yossi Beilin believes that Rabin probably would have approved the compromise plan that he and Abu Mazen drew up, conceding Arab villages that were part of municipal Jerusalem to a future Palestinian state. Yair Hirschfeld, one of the architects of Oslo, worked on a draft of the Beilin–Abu Mazen plan, with another Israeli academic and two Palestinian professors in Stockholm. The four academics agreed on a blueprint in September 1995, and Beilin and Abu Mazen put their stamp on it on October 31,

[87] Rabin, *The Rabin Memoirs*, 262.
[88] Interviews with Eitan Haber, July 27, 1997, Tel Aviv; Amos Eiran, June 23, 1998, Tel Aviv; Yossi Sarid, July 5, 1998, Tel Aviv; Yossi Beilin, August 12, 1997, Tel Aviv. Donald Sylvan finds that in his 1994 and 1995 speeches, Rabin refers to Hamas as central to his image of the conflict. Donald A. Sylvan, "Assessing the Impact of Problem Representation upon Israeli-Palestinian Conflict and Cooperation," 21st Annual Scientific Meeting of the International Society of Political Psychology, Montreal, July 12–15, 1998.
[89] Interview with Haim Ramon, June 23, 1998, Jerusalem.
[90] Labor Party Central Committee, May 13, 1991, Document #1111, 10.

five days before Rabin's assassination. According to Yair Hirschfeld, the plan had been masterminded for Rabin.[91]

Continued Change in Image Following Two Years of the Oslo Peace Process

Although Rabin had intellectually changed his view of the PLO because of its increased moderation as shown in Oslo, and its diminished threat as compared to Hamas, Iraq and Iran, he did not fully change his image of the PLO until two years after the signing of the Oslo Accords. It was emotionally difficult for him to deal with yesterday's terrorists. This process took longer for him than for Peres. According to his sister, Rabin involved both his heart and his head with Hussein of Jordan, but only his head with Arafat. Rabin did not believe the PLO had fully changed when he initially signed the 1993 Oslo Accords and was unsure if Arafat would want to or be able to fulfill his commitments. Only when Arafat took action against terrorism did Rabin begin to respect him. At the signing of the 1995 interim agreement, Rabin acknowledged that it had taken him the past two years to more fully consider Arafat as a partner to peace and said, "[W]e began to get used to each other, we are like old acquaintances."[92]

Rabin moved from viewing the conflict in zero-sum terms to viewing it in mutually beneficial terms. He acknowledged that gaining too many concessions at Arafat's expense would weaken the Palestinian leader and therefore ultimately be disadvantageous for Israel. Arthur Stein and Rupen Cetinyan stress that the recognition that "neither party is aided by extracting more than the other can deliver or demanding so much as to delegitimate the other" is what characterizes those leaders who are partners to peace negotiations.[93]

Rabin also focused on the necessity of reaching an agreement with the Palestinians and the spirit of the overall framework, as opposed to individual violations. Because Rabin emphasized deeds over words, he was a strong believer in staged agreements whereby the opponent could be tested. In the past, Rabin had also examined the general tone of the response rather than singling out infractions as indicating a failure of an agreement. In describing the Separation of Forces Agreements with Syria in 1974, Rabin said that although Syria had some infractions they had not significantly disturbed the agreement.[94] Although Rabin wanted to test the Palestinian Authority and have

---

[91] Interview with Yair Hirschfeld, May 11, 1997, Ramat Yishai.

[92] Interview with Rahel Rabin, July 7, 1998, Kibbutz Menarah. Peri, "Afterword," *The Rabin Memoirs*, 364; interview with Leah Rabin, July 2, 1997, Ramat Gan; signing ceremony of the Israeli Palestinian Interim Agreement, September 28, 1995, Israel Foreign Office Website.

[93] Rupen Cetinyan and Arthur Stein, "Extremists and Peace Agreements in the Middle East." Presented at the Annual Meeting of the American Political Science Association, September 2–5, 1999, Atlanta, Georgia, 26.

[94] Labor Party Leadership Bureau, September 29, 1974, 3, 7.

staged agreements, he gained confidence in the Palestinian Authority and began to trust Arafat, within limits.[95] Rabin perceived halting the peace process as playing into the hands of Hamas because he thought the terrorism was emanating from Hamas rather than Arafat. Also, as tragic as the terrorist acts were, he did not perceive them to be a threat to the country, but isolated acts of cowards who represented a minority of the Palestinian population. Therefore, Rabin complained that the media made too much of Palestinian terrorist attacks aimed at stopping the peace process. In March 1993, he stated on Israeli television that the headlines about the stabbing of several youths had been three times the size of the headlines in the papers at the outbreak of the Six-Day War.[96]

The fact that Rabin's image of the PLO did not fully change until two years after his recognition of the PLO supports the predictions of self-perception theory. According to this theory, individuals realize what their attitudes are in part by observing their own behavior. This implies that behaviors can induce changes in attitude, as well as the other way around. This was partially true for Rabin in that he had to decide whether to go along with the Oslo agreement presented to him before his image of the PLO had fully changed. Furthermore, Bem and Funder suggest self-perception theory may particularly apply to people who are not sensitive to their feelings. This might apply to Rabin, since he did not analyze his feelings. However, Rabin's case provides only limited support for self-perception theory. Rabin's changed image was not wholly spurred by his Oslo decision, but also by a changing attitude toward the Palestinians. Also, self-perception theory is generally believed to apply to people who have no stable or well-defined beliefs.[97] In contrast, Rabin had a life-long, well-established image of the PLO. Therefore, even though he may not have been an especially introspective person, he was well aware of his initial negative perceptions of the PLO.

CONCLUSIONS AND IMPLICATIONS

Despite the end of the Cold War and the Gulf War, the Oslo Accords came as a surprise to many Middle East experts.[98] Although changes within the PLO and in the regional and international context are necessary elements in explaining the Oslo Accords between Israel and the PLO, they are

---

[95] Interview with Yossi Sarid, May 1998, Jerusalem.

[96] Peri, "Afterword," *The Rabin Memoirs*, 368.

[97] Daryl J. Bem, "Self-Perception Theory," in *Advances in Experimental Social Psychology*, ed. Leonard Berkowitz (New York: Academic Press, 1972), 6: 1–61; Daryl J. Bem and David C. Funder, "Predicting More of the People More of the Time: Assessing the Personality of Situations." *Psychological Review* 85 (November 1978), 485–501; Deborah Larson found that self-perception theory explained the shift in U.S. policymakers' attitudes toward the Soviet Union following the inauguration of the Truman Doctrine. Larson, *Origins of Containment: A Psychological Explanation* (Princeton, NJ: Princeton University Press, 1985), 47, 346.

[98] Joel Migdal, lecture at Columbia University, April 13, 1998.

not sufficient: individual leaders can make a significant difference in reaching agreements such as Oslo. Yitzhak Rabin was able to adapt to changing circumstances and to reach the Oslo Accords with the PLO, something that Likud Party prime ministers Yitzhak Shamir and Benjamin Netanyahu did not do. Since Rabin's Labor Party ideology did not prohibit him from making territorial concessions and did not dictate that time was on Israel's side, Rabin was also able to learn from policy failures, such as the failed attempt to cultivate non-PLO leadership and the failed attempt to quell the intifada by force, since Labor ideology assessed policies in a relatively short-term time horizon in comparison with Likud ideology. Finally, since his ideology held that peace can contribute to security and that absolute security was not possible, Rabin was able to recognize and adapt to changes in the PLO and in the environment by taking the *risk* of the Oslo process. Rabin was also able to acknowledge Arafat's efforts at curtailing terrorism on the part of Hamas, since he did not expect that Arafat could put an absolute halt to terrorism.

Rabin's image of the enemy was in the process of change when he decided to negotiate with the PLO, and the results of his Oslo policies in turn effected a continued change in his image of the PLO. Rabin learned from the intifada that he could no longer ignore the Palestinians, that a political solution was becoming increasingly urgent, and that Hamas posed a greater danger than did the PLO. His perception of a moderating PLO through the successful Oslo negotiations led to his decision to recognize the PLO. But signing the Oslo agreement in turn eventually led to a fuller change in Rabin's perception of the PLO. His "behavior" in opting for peace preceded a fully changed view of the enemy. Rabin's process of change suggests that cognitive change may precede affective change in reconciliation with an enemy. Although one may intellectually find reasons for recognizing a long-standing enemy, the process may be slowed down by emotional barriers. A full change in one's image may not be necessary for the initial stages of reconciliation, but only to successfully implement a full peace agreement.

Although ideology plays a key role in understanding the reasons for Rabin's capacity for change, the structure of his thinking and focus on the present also influenced how and the rate at which he changed. Rabin's present orientation enabled him to learn from events such as the Gulf War and the intifada that the Palestinians were demanding to speak for themselves, that force would not quell the Palestinian uprising, that a political solution was necessary, and that it was also urgent as time was working against Israel. Israelis were less willing to withstand the costs of war, Iraq was becoming more of a threat, and Hamas was more likely to ally with Iran or Iraq than with the PLO. In contrast, as will be discussed in the next chapter, the future-oriented Shimon Peres learned much less from these events, and much more from his perception of future trends that would redefine security and minimize the importance of territory and borders.

Because Rabin was rigid in his thinking, and because he emphasized incremental decision making based on a focus on the present, he was slow to alter perceptions and policy preferences. Other members of the Labor Party, such as Yossi Beilin and Shimon Peres, recognized the need to talk to the PLO and the necessity of establishing a Palestinian state years before Rabin did. Had it not been for their Oslo initiative, Rabin would have taken much longer to recognize the PLO – and perhaps never would have done so. Although Rabin had difficulty making use of advisors, his respect for key ministers who were more dovish than himself – primarily Peres – influenced him to change his preferences earlier than he otherwise would have. Under Peres's influence, Rabin shifted his views of managing the conflict from emphasizing deterrence to emphasizing reconciliation. The specific government coalitions, growing domestic support, and his own prominence in turn allowed Rabin's preferences, as expressed through the Oslo negotiations, to become policy as the Israeli Parliament voted to sign the Oslo Accords.[99] Leah Rabin describes Rabin's handshake with Arafat at the signing of the Oslo Peace Accord as follows: "[Yitzhak Rabin] was shaking the hand of a man he said he would never dignify with direct contact [Yasser Arafat] . . . I imagine he was thinking, The whole world has heard me say *never*, and now I *am*."[100]

---

[99] It is possible that had the coalition that Rabin originally envisioned formed, the Oslo Accords would not have received the necessary Knesset votes. Rabin ended up with a narrow liberal left coalition including Meretz as the right-wing Tsomet refrained from joining.

[100] L. Rabin, *Rabin*, 254.

6

Ehud Barak: All or Nothing

Arguably, no Israeli leader better illustrates the importance to negotiation of an individual's personality and psychology than Barak.[1]

– Aharon Klieman, 2005

I compared our government to the people listening to the orchestra on the Titanic. We are sailing into an iceberg.[2]

– Ehud Barak, 2004

We are facing a diplomatic-political tsunami that the majority of the public is unaware of that will peak in September.[3]

– Ehud Barak, 2011

Many Israelis cried for joy, thinking Yitzhak Rabin had come back to life, when in July 1999, Rabin's protégé Ehud Barak defeated Benjamin Netanyahu in a landslide to become Israel's tenth prime minister. Madeleine Albright writes that "Barak entered office like a rooster at dawn," and expectations that Barak could reach a peace agreement with the Palestinian Authority were high.[4] Barak not only pledged to follow in the footsteps of his mentor, Yitzhak Rabin, but he had the faith of the majority of the Israeli population behind him. After all, he was the most decorated soldier in Israel's history, having served thirty-five years in the military, including as IDF chief of staff; he was known to have a very high IQ and great analytic capabilities, and he even masterfully played the piano. Moshe Dayan had commented that Barak was too good to be true.

Frustrated by Netanyahu's slow approach to carrying out the Wye Agreements, U.S. President Bill Clinton loaned three close political consultants to Barak to

---

[1] Aharon Klieman, "Israeli Negotiating Culture," in *How Israelis and Palestinians Negotiate: Cross-Cultural Analysis of the Oslo Peace Process*, ed. Tamara Cofman Wittes (Washington, DC: United States Institute of Peace Press, 2005), 111.

[2] Interview with Ehud Barak, June 28, 2004, Tel Aviv.

[3] Ethan Bronner, "In Israel, Time for Peace Offer May Run Out," *The New York Times*, April 2, 2011.

[4] Madeleine Albright, *Madam Secretary: A Memoir of Madeleine Albright* (New York: Miramax Books, 2003) 474.

advise him in his campaign, and the celebration and high hopes were not just in the Israeli camp: when Netanyahu lost the election in May 1999, there were open celebrations in the office of Yasser Arafat. The late Faisal Husseini, PLO official in charge of Jerusalem affairs, explained that Palestinians favored Barak in the elections since they thought he would be more prepared to compromise on land. A Jordanian columnist wrote that only the "mentally lazy" would say there was no difference between Labor and Likud.[5]

Yet, Barak had not always been celebrated as the best prospect for achieving peace. He had started out as a hard-liner who was against a Palestinian state, and, like the other prime ministers, against dialogue with the PLO, and he had also opposed the Oslo Accords as chief of staff in 1993. He even abstained from the vote on Oslo II as a member of the cabinet in 1995 – despite the fact that this hurt one of his main political backers, Yitzhak Rabin.

What motivated Barak's newly found commitment as prime minister to close the deal with the Palestinian Authority, and to make more concessions in order to reach a peace deal than any previous prime minister, including dividing Jerusalem? And why were the hopes of his supporters dashed when he failed to do so, having lasted only eighteen months as prime minister before losing the next election to Ariel Sharon by a two-to-one margin? Adding to the mystery is Barak's subsequent political career trajectory. He made a comeback in June 2007 by winning the Labor Party leadership election and was appointed minister of defense in Prime Minister Ehud Olmert's Kadima government, and subsequently in the second Netanyahu Likud-led government. Did he become disillusioned by his failure to make peace, thus leaving him skeptical about the prospects for peace? Or is he still dedicated to the process for which he broke new ground in 2000?

I argue in this chapter that Ehud Barak was – as he proved at the Camp David and Taba negotiations – open ideologically to compromise and that his willingness to compromise was facilitated by moderate cognitive flexibility, a present time orientation, and risk propensity. However, his lack of emotional intelligence contributed to the negotiations' ultimate failure, and the subsequent weakening of the Labor Party and the political left more generally. In the 2009 elections, 80 percent of former Labor supporters voted for Kadima.[6] Shimon Peres claims that "Barak's most catastrophic mistake was to declare that there was no partner, which led to the downfall of Labor and Sharon's election."[7] Although believing in the urgency of peace, he then ultimately put his own

---

[5] John M. Broder, "White House Is Quietly Pro-Barak," *The New York Times,* May 17, 1999; Deborah Sontag, "A Swing to Center," *The New York Times,* May 18, 1999, A1; Jeff Berak, "Husseini: Barak/ One Israel Preferable to Likud," *The Jerusalem Post,* May 14, 1999; Douglas Jehl, "In Israeli Vote, Arabs Hold Their Breath and Their Tongues," *The New York Times,* May 16, 1999, 4.

[6] Leslie Susser, "The Barak Bombshell," *The Jerusalem Report,* February 6, 2011, 8.

[7] Interview with Shimon Peres, June 27, 2004, Tel Aviv.

personal ambitions first in continuing to serve in the Netanyahu government, which did not share that sense of urgency and largely rejected Barak's advice.

DETERMINANTS OF CONVERSION

Ideology

From an early age, Ehud Barak was exposed to Labor Party ideology, and it had a great influence on his ability to change his perceptions of the PLO, the desirability of a Palestinian state, and the urgency of reaching a peace agreement with the PLO. Barak was born in 1942 in Kibbutz Mishmar HaSharon, where he lived throughout his youth. Mishmar HaSharon represented the left-wing of the socialist parties that formed the precursors of the Labor Party. His parents came to Israel in the 1930s from Russia and Poland and were part of a group called Hapoel Hatsair, which represented the left faction of the Shomer Hatsair; they were two of the founding members of the kibbutz in 1933. At age sixteen, Barak joined the youth group of the Shomer Hatsair.[8]

Although Barak was heavily influenced by Labor ideology, he also represented a younger generation than did Rabin, Shamir, and Peres. For example, public opinion was a relatively greater motivating force for Barak than for the prime ministers who represented the founding fathers of the country. Barak reads polls for breakfast and – as a number cruncher himself – appreciates working with statistics.[9] This concern with poll numbers and public opinion manifested itself, for example, in Barak's negotiations with Syrian President Haez Assad. Although he seriously pursued peace negotiations with Assad, his concerns about domestic opposition to conceding the Golan Heights kept him from committing upfront to withdrawal to the 1967 borders in return for peace and security – a commitment Rabin had made as a basis for the peace process with Syria.[10]

Although strongly influenced by Labor ideology through his lifelong membership in the Labor Party, Barak was open to joining or creating other parties to benefit his own political prospects and influence as long as the ideology of the parties was similar. For instance, he begged Sharon to take him to Kadima, believing that he might have greater political opportunities in this new party since Labor had weakened and Kadima headed the government. This did not, however, represent any ideological change that had any deep principled relevance. Sharon declined because he did not want Kadima to be too left-wing, and he had

---

[8] I. Kfir. *Barak: Bibliography* (Israel: Alfah Communications, 1999), 19, 20.
[9] Interview with Yossi Beilin, July 26, 2007, Tel Aviv; interview with Naomi Chazan, July 17, 2007, Jerusalem.
[10] Martin Indyk, *Innocent Abroad: An Intimate Account of American Peace Diplomacy in the Middle East* (New York: Simon' & Schuster, 2009).

already included Peres in its ranks.[11] When Barak subsequently became defense minister in Netanyahu's government and stayed despite lack of progress in the peace process with the Palestinians, Member of Knesset Daniel Ben-Simon quit the Labor Party in protest, and in reaction to this and subsequent calls by Labor Party leaders to quit the government, Barak eventually broke away from Labor. With four fellow party members, he formed his new party, Atzmaut or "Independence" Party, which he claimed was centrist, Zionist, and democratic.[12] Despite his political opportunism, his changes were facilitated by his adherence to important tenets of the Labor ideology.

1. Is Time on Israel's Side?

By the time Barak became prime minister, he believed that time was working against Israel. "I compared our government," he has said, "to the people listening to the orchestra on the *Titanic*. We are sailing into an iceberg" unless Israel makes peace with the Palestinians.[13] Dennis Ross depicts Barak as "a man in a hurry," who thought that unless Israel urgently reached a peace agreement with the Palestinians, violence would erupt.[14] Gilead Sher, Barak's right-hand man who was the chief negotiator for Barak at Camp David and who became Barak's bureau chief and policy coordinator, stated that the goal of ending the conflict and all claims was based precisely on the calculation that time was working against Israel.[15] This continues to be Barak's position into the present. He continues to argue that it is impossible to leave the situation in a state of paralysis with no peace agreement because the world will lose interest in Israel or support a one-state solution, which will leave Israel with three equally undesirable options: a Bosnian-Belfast situation in which communities are bleeding for centuries, an apartheid situation, or the threat of a binational state.[16] Although Israel is strong, he continues to argue that "the reality will not change for the better if we will sink into inaction. We have to move forward all the time with the peace process."[17] In

---

[11] Interview with Nahum Barnea, August 5, 2010, Jerusalem. Barnea is a staff writer for the leading Israeli newspaper, *Yedioth Achronot*, who has extensively covered and interviewed all the prime ministers and won the Israel Prize in 2007 for his journalism.

[12] Jonathan Lis, "Ehud Barak Quits Labor to Form 'Centrist, Zionist and Democratic' Party," *Haaretz*, January 17, 2011; Barak Ravid, "Netanyahu Helped Barak Leave Labor," *Haaretz*, January 17, 2011.

[13] Interview with Ehud Barak, June 28, 2004, Tel Aviv; Shlomo Ben-Ami, *Scars of War, Wounds of Peace: The Israeli-Arab Tragedy* (New York: Oxford University Press, 2006), 255.

[14] Dennis Ross, *The Missing Peace: The Inside Story of the Fight for Middle East Peace* (New York: Farrar, Straus, and Giroux, 2004), 622.

[15] Interview with Gilead Sher, June 20 2004, Jerusalem.

[16] Gidi Weitz, "Barak: Israel Can and Must Make Peace Within Three Years," April 28, 2009; Etgar Keret, "Barak to *Haaretz*: Netanyahu's Government Will Surprise People Yet," *Haaretz*, June 10, 2009; Ehud Barak, "Special Policy Forum Report," July 24, 2001.

[17] "Barak: Israel Must Move Ahead Toward Peace," *The Jerusalem Post*, February 11, 2011.

the aftermath of the tragic tsunami in Japan, Barak argued, "We are facing a diplomatic-political tsunami that the majority of the public is unaware of that will peak in September" with the Palestinian plan to ask for recognition of a Palestinian state at the United Nations.[18]

2. Ideological Goals: General and Adaptable, or Specific and Rigid?

Like Rabin and Peres, Barak believed in Labor's general goal of attaining security for Israel, rather than any more rigid or concrete goal regarding territory. Therefore, he did not oppose the territorial concessions demanded by the Oslo peace process. He thought that strategic depth was no longer as important to provide security and that a peace agreement would likely enhance security. In 2010, Barak argued that Israel's failure to reach a peace deal with the Palestinians was a greater threat to the country than a nuclear Iran.[19] Like Rabin, Barak thought it important to reach peace with its immediate neighbors in order to be better able to face the greater threats from Iran and Iraq.[20] Therefore, like Peres and Rabin, Barak thought that in the past twenty years peace with the Palestinians would contribute to Israel's security.

3. Is the World with Us or Against Us?

Like his fellow Labor Party members, Barak did not think that hostility toward Israel and war with its neighbors was permanent. In fact, after more than six years in the military, he quit because he thought that Israel would soon be at peace with its neighbors. The PLO had just been formed, but Barak did not foresee a significant danger to Israel's existence from it. He thought that in another thirteen years, he would take his son to tour Lebanon, and Israel would not be as dependent on its military.[21] In 2010, he recognized a real shift in the region in its stance toward Israel. He argues that, whereas the region used to reject Israel in no uncertain terms, "today Arab state[s] are competing amongst themselves in arguing over which peace initiative will be adopted by the international community."[22]

Closely connected with this belief that the world is not inherently hostile to Israel is Barak's sensitivity to Israel's international image, and how Israel's behavior could influence its relationships with other countries. In the summer of 2010, Israeli-Turkish relations reached an all-time low when a flotilla of ships, with passengers that included several Turkish citizens, attempted to breach the Israeli naval blockade of the Gaza Strip. When Israeli naval commandos boarded the ships, flotilla participants attacked the commandoes on one of the ships, and in defending

---

[18] Bronner, "In Israel, Time for Peace Offer May Run Out."

[19] "Barak: Peace Process Failures Greater Threat Than Iran Nukes," *Haaretz*, January 26, 2010.

[20] Albright, *Madam Secretary*, 474.

[21] Kfir, *Barak*, 60.

[22] Ari Shavit, "Barak to Haaretz: Israel Ready to Cede Parts of Jerusalem in Peace Deal," *Haaretz*, September 1, 2010.

themselves the commandoes killed nine activists, including eight Turkish citizens. In the wake of this incident, Barak strongly advocated reducing tensions with Turkey and possibly apologizing if that was what would be needed. He also opposed Israel's deportation of migrant children, partially on moral grounds but also because it would severely damage Israel's image.[23]

Barak does perceive Iran as a significant threat to Israel, but not as an existential threat in the way that Netanyahu does. He claims that part of Iran's desire for nuclear weapons has nothing to do with Israel, but with its place in the world. He also argues that there is no comparison between the ease with which Israel could bomb the Iraq reactor in 1981 and how difficult it would be in the case of Iran.[24] At the same time, despite this threat assessment and caution about military strikes, Barak criticized those (such as Israel's ex-Mossad chief, Meir Dagan) who dismiss military strikes on Iran as stupid, saying that military options must be left on the table for the sake of deterrence, and so that international efforts to stop Iran from developing nuclear weapons are effective.[25]

Barak does not perceive hostile relationships with Israel, such as those with Syria, to be permanent. Barak argued, along with others in the defense system, that negotiations were positive for Israel and that Assad was prepared to consider a peace agreement.[26]

Not only did Barak think that Israel would face diminished threats in the future, but he also valued a strong relationship with the United States, which he believed was necessary to be able to fight guerrilla warfare and weapons of mass destruction. According to Barak, Israel required American support, intelligence, and advanced military technology, which would be possible only if Israel were a partner to America's interests for peace in the region. Even before he became prime minister, as chief of staff of the military, Barak emphasized the erosion of Israeli-U.S. relations and that an understanding with the United States was vital to protecting Israel's interests.[27] Barak formed a close relationship with President Clinton. According to Dennis Ross, "Clinton probably spoke on the phone with Barak more than any other leader in the world."[28] Clinton would meet with Barak for fifteen hours after having given the visiting Australian prime minister twenty minutes.[29]

[23] "Barak: Israel Must Reduce Tensions with Turkey," *Haaretz*, December 27, 2010; Barak Ravid, "Barak: Deportation of Migrant Children Could Severely Damage Israel's Image," *Haaretz*, October 4, 2010.

[24] Weitz, "Barak: Israel Can and Must Make Peace Within Three Years."

[25] "Barak: Dagan's Comments on Iran Hurt Israel's Ability of Deterrence," *Haaretz*, June 6, 2011.

[26] "Barak: Assad Ready to Consider Israel-Syria Peace Deal," *Haaretz*, February 28, 2011; "Barak: Dagan's Comments on Iran Hurt Israel's Ability of Deterrence."

[27] Yoram Peri, *Generals in the Cabinet Room: How the Military Shapes Israeli Policy* (Washington D.: United Institute of Peace Press, 2006), 225; Emmanuel Sivan, "What's An Ex-Chief of Staff to Do?" *Haaretz*, May 31, 2010.

[28] Clyde Haberman, "Dennis Ross's Exit Interview," *New York Times Magazine*, March 25, 2001.

[29] Kfir, *Barak*, 416.

Barak's emphasis on the importance of the Israel-U.S. alliance continues through the present. While defense minister in the Netanyahu government, Barak conducted negotiations on the settlement issues with the Obama administration. He claimed that Israel's main priority should be negotiating an agreement with the Palestinians, but that Israel's relationship with the United States and fighting the campaign of delegitimization against Israel are also extremely important. He has repeatedly told Netanyahu that close relations with the United States are the cornerstone of Israel's existence, and Israel must act in a way that coincides with U.S. interests. He also continually implored Netanyahu to present the United States with a peace initiative to save the relations between the two countries, to end attempts to isolate Israel internationally, and to strengthen the moderate camp in the Arab world.[30]

4. How Much Will Peace Contribute to Security? Does Peace Require Territorial Compromise?

Barak's strong ties to Labor ideology also enabled him to change his initial opposition to negotiating with the PLO and to the creation of a Palestinian state because he did not think that keeping the West Bank and Gaza would ensure total security and that Israel was sufficiently strong to make concessions for peace since he sees Israel as the strongest country for 1,000 miles around Jerusalem. Therefore, Israel should have the confidence to negotiate from a position of greater military and economic strength as well as a sounder, democratic system. He says that peace agreements must be reached before conditions are perfect and argues that the alternatives to the peace process are more complicated and more dangerous.[31]

Cognitive Style

1. Time Orientation

In addition to Barak's ideology being conducive to his changing perceptions of the PLO, his time orientation also enabled these shifts. Like Rabin was, Barak is immersed in the present and has great analytical skills in interpreting the present international, regional, and domestic situation and the policy initiatives that are warranted. This orientation includes an understanding of the importance of a political agreement with the Palestinians. However, he does not dwell on history,

---

[30] Herb Keinon, "FM Explains Why Barak Heads Talks," *The Jerusalem Post,* July 6, 2009; "Barak: 2010 Was Israel's Quietest Year in Many, but IDF Is Prepared," *Haaretz,* January 4, 2011; Jerrold Kessel and Pierre Klochendler, "A Grand Initiative for Netanyahu," *The Jerusalem Report,* May 10, 2010; Rebecca Anna Stoil, "Barak: We Must Give US Clear Initiative," *Haaretz,* July 6, 2010; Hilary Leila Krieger, "Barak: US Wants Israel to Risk 'Assertive Peace Process,'" *The Jerusalem Post,* June 27, 2010.

[31] Sontag, "A Swing to Center," A12; "Barak: Israel Must Move Ahead Toward Peace," *The Jerusalem Post,* February 11, 2011; "Barak: Israel Is Strong Enough to Make Mideast Peace Concessions," *Haaretz,* May 19, 2011.

nor does he think in terms of long-range future trends.[32] In his farewell party from the military, Barak commented that he always had the feeling that time was short.[33] Political scientist Orit Galili-Zucker, who worked with Barak as a political consultant, argues that Barak does not have patience for long-term processes.[34] For example, Barak often said that he preferred not to speculate as to whether Iran might be an existential threat to Israel in the future, and rather to focus on his assessment that it is not such a threat at the present.[35]

2. Risk Propensity

Not only was Barak's time orientation conducive to change, but so was his propensity for risk. He is confident in his ability to quickly overcome any challenge and tackle the most difficult tasks. When he was told that the hardest discipline for admission at the Technion, the Israeli equivalent of the Massachusetts Institute of Technology, was electrical engineering, he had to prove to himself that he could tackle it. Once he did get in, he decided to attend the Hebrew University instead. Barak dared one of his friends to go out in stormy weather on the sea and see if they could cross the waves. Likewise, his propensity for risk often led him to put his life on the line as a military commander. In the military, he joined the elite forces and wanted to participate in the most dangerous missions. In his special operations missions, he proved that he could succeed at dangerous actions that were considered impossible. When he learned that a Lebanese police station was close to where he and his men were going to assassinate some PLO terrorists, this extra risk did not stop him. When he was told to stop a mission in Syria because it was too risky, he closed the radio and did it anyway.[36] A former army commander of Barak's claimed that as a soldier he often risked either commendation or demotion in the risky operations he undertook.[37]

Just as Barak took academic, personal, and military risks, he also was willing to take the risks of negotiating a peace agreement with the Palestinian Authority. Barak repeatedly states that he took risks in entering negotiations and took great calculated risks during them.[38] In my three-hour interview with Barak, he directly referred ten times to his taking "political risks," "severe risks," and "gambles." He related that a year before Camp David, and a half year after he

---

[32] Interview with Yitzhak Frankenthal, August 5, 2010, Jerusalem, chairman of the Israeli-Palestinian Parents Circle and executive director and founder of Fund for Reconciliation, Tolerance and Peace; interview with Yossi Beilin, July 26, 2007, Tel Aviv.

[33] Kfir, *Barak*, 11, 191.

[34] Susser, "The Barak Bombshell," 8.

[35] Mike Mullen, "Barak: Iran Poses No Immediate Existential Threat to Israel," *Haaretz*, April 19, 2010.

[36] Interview with Shlomo Gazit, June 14, 2004, Israel. Gazit is former head of military intelligence, senior research fellow at the Jafee Center at Tel Aviv University; Kfir, *Barak*, 117, 133.

[37] Jonathan Tepperman, "Barak's Last Battle," *Foreign Affairs*, 92, no. 1 (Jan./Feb. 2013), 91–104.

[38] Ehud Barak, "Special Policy Forum Report: Israel's Search for Peace and Security: Lessons of the Past, Options for the Future," *The Washington Institute for Near East Policy*, Peace Watch #338, July 24, 2001.

came to power, he went to Oslo to celebrate the sixth anniversary of the Oslo agreement. There he met with Arafat and told him that they had the most complicated conflict on earth to solve, and that each of them would have to make the most painful decision vis-à-vis his own people and their beliefs and dream wishes. They were meeting on the fifth floor of a building, and Barak said,

> [W]e have, both of us to jump, to step outside the window and jump out of the window into the unknown. We both have parachutes, we have to jump together . . . but, I have your hand on the handle of my parachute, and you have my hand on the handle of your parachute. If we are ready to do this we can change history. If not we will be responsible.[39]

In March 2011, Barak urgently pleaded for Israel to take more timely initiatives toward negotiating a peace agreement with the Palestinians, claiming that "nothing of value was ever achieved without taking risks."[40]

3. Cognitive Flexibility

Barak's cognitive flexibility is moderate. He is creative and analytic; he listens to advice at times and is capable of changing his mind on important issues. However, he also is stubborn and convinced of his superior logic. Barak earned his B.A. in physics and mathematics from Hebrew University and his master's in engineering-economic systems from Stanford University. Accordingly, he has an unusually logical mind and thinks mathematically.[41] This analytic frame of mind is an unusual talent he cultivated since his youth, when he would take clocks and watches apart, fix them, and put them back together. His abilities were so legendary that while he was growing up, people said he could take apart 100 clocks in an hour blindfolded.[42]

Although as an officer he was nicknamed Napoleon, Barak can go out of his way to get input from his subordinates and to give them a chance to brainstorm. For instance, when Barak was head of military intelligence, his chief of staff, Amos Gilad, commented that Barak was open and creative and encouraged active and sometimes fierce debate among those who worked for him in order to get people to think freely and creatively, and to look at the military through the eyes of the enemy. When he headed military intelligence, he established a new department to check the intelligence. Members of the department did not work together on their research so that they would not be susceptible to "group think." He always advised his staff to look at intelligence skeptically. Yoni

---

[39] Interview with Ehud Barak, June 28, 2004, Tel Aviv.

[40] "Barak: Mideast Peace Does Not Go Against Israel's Security Interests," *Haaretz*, March 7, 2011.

[41] Interview with Nahum Barnea, August 5, 2010, Jerusalem; interview with Roby Nathanson, May 30, 2006, Banff, Alberta, Canada. Nathanson met Barak in 1997 and advised him on economic and social issues during Barak's 1999 campaign. He now directs the Israeli Institute for Economic and Social Research. After having proved to himself that he was able to get into the highly competitive Technion, he decided instead to study at the Hebrew University, Kfir, *Barak*, 60.

[42] Kfir, *Barak*, 28, 32.

Netanyahu, Benjamin Netanyahu's younger brother, wrote Barak a letter of appreciation, thanking Barak for looking at things in a new fashion and commenting that as a commander he showed flexibility, but was also stubborn when that was necessary.[43] Barak received the letter in the mail after Yoni's death during the mission to free the hijacked passengers at Entebbe.

Barak's cognitive flexibility is demonstrated by the interest he often shows in learning from others. For instance, he wanted to learn how Tony Blair, a member of the British Labour Party, was able to win the prime ministership of England after twenty years of Conservative Party dominance. A month after the Labour Party primaries in 1997, he went to London to meet Blair. Barak was amazed by the "war room" where they had prepared the campaign. Computers showed lists of voters from different districts, internal communications that allowed several people to communicate simultaneously, divisions of strategy, and research. Blair also recommended that Barak use the American advisor Stanley Greenberg, who in turn recommended James Carville, who also agreed to help Barak.[44]

However, Barak was very stubborn from a young age. From first grade on, his parents noticed this trait and his refusal to concede to other children. At times this caused him to prefer to be alone to build his constructions and do his logic games.[45] Naomi Chazan worked with Barak in the finance and defense Knesset committees and found him to be a poor listener. As chief of staff, he was arrogant and knew all the answers to all the questions but did not have questions of his own. When Chazan talked to him about sexual harassment in the army, he would lecture her for a half hour on feminism, rather than tackle her specific questions. She described him as "very clever, but not very smart." His choice of advisors, with one or two exceptions, were from the "old boys' network." There were some people he would listen to, and others he would dismiss with a motion of his hand if he was not interested. As Chazan noted, "It was basically a movement of dismissal, that forget it, you got one of those hands, you were erased ... he spent so much time putting down the people that might be a threat to him that he got none of their knowledge or expertise. . . . Barak is very binary, in the sense that he kept using the terms *all or nothing.*"[46]

An example of both these traits – his "binary thinking" and his ability to change his mind – might be Barak's positions on the Lebanon War. Barak was initially completely against pulling troops out of Lebanon and then totally changed his mind. Yossi Beilin had been advocating a pullout for years; this, in combination with soldier casualties, eventually led the public support for this position to rise from 18 percent to 72 percent. In February 1999, Netanyahu was leading Barak in the polls by 7 percent, so Barak decided to make withdrawal

[43] Ibid., 11, 44, 94, 125, 176–191, 345.
[44] Ibid., 392–394.
[45] Ibid., 26–27.
[46] Interview with Naomi Chazan, July 17, 2007, Jerusalem.

from Lebanon the main issue of the election. Beilin and President Clinton tried to convince Barak to put the Beilin–Abu Mazen Agreement of 1995 on the agenda, but he thought that would become the minimum Israeli position and would be a bad negotiating tactic.[47]

Overall, Barak demonstrates contradictory characteristics. He exhibits a moderately flexible mind – analytic and precise – yet he is often stubborn in his views or dismissive of the opinions of others. At times Barak could learn from other's experiences and enjoyed thinking through unconventional or unorthodox approaches. Consequently, he shifted his position on key issues – adhering to the new position as stubbornly as he had held to the previous one.

4. Emotional Intelligence

Despite Barak's ideological pragmatism and dedication to reaching a peace agreement, his present time orientation, moderate cognitive flexibility, and risk propensity, his Achilles heel – which contributed to his inability to conclude a peace agreement with the Palestinian Authority, and his downfall after eighteen months as prime minister – was his lack of emotional intelligence. In a chapter entitled "When Smart Is Dumb," Daniel Goleman concludes that IQ contributes about 20 percent in determining life success, but emotional intelligence is a large contributing factor. Barak is not attuned to the emotional signals of others and therefore lacks "people skills." He lacks the ability to nurture relationships and keep friends, the ability to resolve conflicts, and to analyze a social situation. Barak is "emotionally tone deaf" and lacks empathy, the ability to take another person's perspective, or to be sensitive to others' feelings. He lacks interpersonal intelligence or the "ability to understand other people: what motivates them, how they work, how to work cooperatively with them" – skills that are common for many politicians. He therefore often cannot respond appropriately to the moods of others.[48]

Barak's lack of emotional intelligence has been noted by those close to him throughout his career. In the military, some opposed his promotions because they thought that although he was brilliant, he was hard to get along with and lacked patience. Every argument became an intellectual battle in which he could be sarcastic, impatient, and patronizing to others. As early as 1986, journalists such as Amnon Abromowitz opined that his only criticism of Barak did not concern his intelligence – Barak, he noted, can do in five minutes what it takes others an hour to do – but his personality.[49]

---

[47] Interview with Yitzhak Frankenthal, August 5, 2010, Jerusalem, Franthenthal has known Barak for many years and met with him six weeks before the rally to request Barak's help; interview with Yossi Beilin, July 26, 2007, Tel Aviv; Zeev Maoz, *Defending the Holy Land: Critical Analysis of Israel's Security and Foreign Policy* (Ann Arbor: The University of Michigan Press, 2006), 215.

[48] Daniel Goleman, *Emotional Intelligence: Why It Can Matter More Than IQ* (New York: Bantam Books, 1995), 39, 96, 284.

[49] Kfir, *Barak*, 199–200.

Even Barak's closest advisors, and Barak himself, are willing to admit that he lacks sensitivity. Barak thinks very logically: as a person who knows how to quickly fix watches, he believes that everyone's thinking is merely made up of logical steps that he can anticipate based on his own logic. Shlomo Brom claimed that Barak is a "perfect rationalist, if A leads to B and B leads to C then A must lead to C, but with people it does not work that way."[50] Barak fully admits that he lacks sensitivity to others' emotions; after his first term, he decided he needed to improve in this area. Barak admitted to Charlie Rose, "I made many mistakes in many aspects according to people's sensitivities. I didn't realize how important gestures of sensitivity were."[51] The secretary general of the Labor Party, Wizmann Shiri, is close to Ehud Barak and says that his main problem is that he does not understand politics.[52] Former Labor Party Trade and Labor Minister Binyamin Ben-Eliezer, who was Barak's loyal ally when he was Labor chairman, claimed that Barak "has a problem with emotional intelligence" and "does not know how to get close to people."[53] Gilead Sher agrees that "Ehud is brilliant, but has zero social intelligence."[54] Ron Pundak argues that "the contradiction between his emotions and his rationality ... created a dissonance that amplified his natural inability to market almost any policy."[55] Similarly, Efraim Halevy, Director of the Mossad during Barak's term, says that Barak has a brilliant mind, but a warped personality."[56]

For instance, the Labor Party scheduled primaries in June 1997. Shimon Peres and Ehud Barak haggled over how long the transition period would be if Barak were to win as predicted. After Barak was able to shorten the transition period by months, they haggled over days. Barak wanted it to be September 15 before the Jewish holidays, and Peres wanted to be able to enjoy the holidays. Barak refused to concede and deeply hurt Peres. When Giorah Eini mentioned to Barak that he made a mistake, Barak responded that he had behaved logically.[57]

Barak's political insensitivity seemed to plague his time as deputy and chief of staff of the military, prime minister, and defense minister. A former high Israeli official who advised several prime ministers explained that Barak had always been told that he was the brightest guy, and so "[h]e thinks so highly of himself that he cannot have a real conversation with anybody."[58] He is arrogant, and

[50] Interview with Shlomo Brom, June 21, 2004; Brom served as Deputy to the National Security Advisor in the Barak government.

[51] Interview of Ehud Barak by Charlie Rose, January 25, 2005.

[52] "Labor Party Secretary General Wizmann Shiri, "Why Is Barak So Isolated Within His Own Party?" interview by Mazal Mualem, *Haaretz*, July 6, 2010.

[53] Gil Hoffman, "Ben-Eliezer: Only the Right Can Make Peace," *The Jerusalem Post*, November 23, 2009.

[54] Interview with Gilead Sher, June 20, 2004, Jerusalem.

[55] Ron Pundak, "From Oslo to Taba: What Went Wrong?" *Survival* 43, no. 3 (2001), 37.

[56] Interview with Efraim Halevy, Director of the Mossad when Barak was prime minister, August 6, 2013, Ramat Aviv, Israel.

[57] Kfir, *Barak*, 384–85.

[58] As quoted in Tepperman, "Barak's Last Battle."

as deputy chief of staff he called General Norman Schwarzkopf, the U.S. commander of the invasion of Iraq in 1991, *kleinkopf* ("small head"). When he was appointed chief of staff, he explained to then Defense Minister Moshe Arens that he (Barak) was much more important as chief of staff, and said that former Prime Minister Ehud Olmert was a Churchillian parody of a leader.[59] After the 1996 election, Barak excluded the Labor Party leadership from the process of negotiating a government coalition, and when it was assembled, the process left everyone angry. He destroyed his relations with Uzi Baram and Ra'anan Cohen of the Labor Party and attempted to keep Shimon Peres out of the government, finally allowing him to be minister of regional cooperation.[60] He also was condescending toward the 95 percent of Palestinian Israelis who had voted for him.[61] As defense minister in Netanyahu's second government, Barak denounced his own IDF chief of staff, Gabi Ashkenazi, and refused to extend his term because of what he considered Ashkenazi's serious ethical and professional defects. He refused to attend committee meetings if Ashkenazi was also there.[62]

Barak is confident in his own perceptions and logic. Barak was the head of Peres's 1996 campaign against Netanyahu. At one function he introduced himself for forty-five minutes by going from one person to the next of the six or seven people there, guessed what each was going to say, and answered.[63] This trait was also demonstrated in the three-hour interview this author conducted with Barak, in which he anticipated the questions he thought I *should* have been asking and then proceeded to answer them: the interview became something more like a three-hour monologue. He repeatedly used the phrase "it was clear to us" and "we had a clear perception." He said, "[W]hatever seems to me, kind of, seems to others as very stable judgment." When asked whether he could have significantly increased the chances of reaching an agreement had he communicated more with Arafat at Camp David, as others have argued, Barak protested that such a question made no sense. He seemed to be somewhat cognizant that he operates logically and expects others to operate by his logic, by going out of his way to say that politics is not like running an experiment in your lab: "I had almost no doubt it will not end up with anything, but I realized that if I will try to impose my judgment on the world, because it is the world, not dealing with nature or the sciences ..." Then when asked why he went to negotiate if he thought it such a gamble, he replied, "Because we're not living in the world of mathematics."[64]

[59] Yoel Marcus, "Ehud Barak Is a Parody of a Leader," *Haaretz*, January 7, 2011.

[60] Pundak, "From Oslo to Taba," 38.

[61] Ibid.

[62] Bradley Burston, "Ehud MuBarak Must Go. Now," *Haaretz*, February 3, 2011; Lahav Harkov, "Hasson: Barak and Askenazi Refuse to Testify Together," *The Jerusalem Post*, October 13, 2010.

[63] Interview with Avi Gil, June 16, 2004, Jerusalem.

[64] Interview with Ehud Barak, June 28, 2004, Tel Aviv.

Advisors

Barak can be a suspicious person, often thinking that those who are trying to influence him have a hidden agenda.[65] On the one hand, as chief of staff he encouraged others who were experienced to speak their minds before he made decisions.[66] But because Barak was suspicious, by the time he was prime minister, he had a team of close advisors made up mostly of people from the military who he trusted. In addition to his role as prime minister, he also took on the defense minister's portfolio in order to increase his own control and to get around potential opposition to peace agreements from within the military.[67]

However, one of Barak's advisors during his term as prime minister described it as the worst working atmosphere that he had ever encountered. Barak did not trust anyone, so he would meet with advisors one at a time; advisors' responsibilities were blurred and often they were unsure of what was going on. These turf battles at times led to yelling matches among the advisors. He created a permanent sense of instability among his staff – never giving them the confidence that comes from knowing their positions were secure. Because Barak was not sensitive to people's emotions, he treated bickering among his staff members as nonsense. Many of them publicly criticized Barak when his term was over, and few if any stuck with him. As a consequence, he lacked a strong, loyal inner circle such as the one Sharon gathered around himself.[68]

According to Dennis Ross, Barak "alienated everybody around him, basically because he didn't trust anybody. He is someone who felt he knew best, that if he thought something was reasonable, ipso facto it was."[69] While he was defense minister in the Netanyahu government, his former advisors organized to bolt the government if no progress on peace was made. These advisors included Gilead Sher, former bureau chief when Barak was prime minister, and Dedi Suissa, a former Barak aide.[70]

IMAGE OF THE ENEMY

Barak's image of the PLO and its leaders has undergone continual change. His perception of the PLO changed after the PLO recognized Israel in 1993, but he still distrusted Arafat. Barak's self-confidence and belief in the possibility of achieving a peace agreement led him to reject the assessment of several senior advisors – the head of military intelligence, Amos Gilead; the Israel Security Agency; the Planning and Policy Directorate; and the head of the Military

[65] Interview with Yossi Beilin, July 26, 2007, Tel Aviv.
[66] Interview with Assa Kasher, August 4, 2010, Ramat Gan.
[67] Peri, *Generals in the Cabinet Room* 60, 89.
[68] Off the record part of interview with former Barak advisor, August 4, 2010, Tel Aviv.
[69] Haberman, "Dennis Ross's Exit Interview," 39.
[70] Gil Hoffman, "Labor Activists Start Campaign to Get Ministers to Quit Government," *The Jerusalem Post*, July 22, 2010.

Intelligence Directorate, Major General Amos Malka – who argued that Arafat was not ready to accept a Jewish state since he wanted full refugee return to Israel and he would not compromise on his basic demands.[71] Barak first met Arafat in Barcelona, when he was foreign minister after Rabin's assassination. He said to Arafat, "I also heard a lot about you before you were welcomed in the castles of Europe. I followed you as a military person and as head of intelligence. I am happy that we meet with everything behind us, even though I know we'll have many divisions of opinion and difficult times."[72] Barak claims that he was unsure about Arafat, but that he treated him as a sophisticated and devoted national leader and did not demonize him. However, he claims that at Camp David, he learned the "painful . . . truth," that "probably":

> Arafat does not recognize the right of the Jewish people to have a Jewish, demo-
> cratic, Zionist state. . . . If it were about occupation we could be well into the
> solution of the whole issue. Arafat does not only want to correct for the occupation
> of the West Bank and Gaza.[73]

Barak claims that had Arafat been interested in a solution, he would have taken the Clinton parameters or Barak's offers "as a basic starting point, and try to negotiate for more, and probably would have gotten a lot more." He then relates a story told to him by the former president of Indonesia, who asked a visiting Arafat why he did not take the Clinton and Barak offers as a basis for negotiation. Arafat is said to have answered, "I'm not sure whether they [the Israelis] will be there in fifty years." Barak concluded that Arafat was not a partner for the present.[74]

Even after the disappointments at Camp David, when Barak publicly said that Arafat had failed the test and was not a partner, he privately had not completely given up on Arafat and invited him to his house on September 25, 2000. He believes that Abu Mazen and Salam Fayyad (the Palestinian Authority finance minister from June 2002 to November 2006, and the prime minister from June 2007 to June 2013) are sincere and that Israel was closer to reaching an agreement in 2011 than it was at Camp David in 2000 because Abu Mazen and Fayyad are willing to sign an end of conflict and claims for refugee return to Israel, which Arafat was not. He also argued that Israel should not reject all contacts with an upcoming Fatah-Hamas unity cabinet but should expect the government to be ready to recognize Israel and previous agreements and to denounce terror.[75] Barak is not sure there will be a peace agreement in the foreseeable future, but he firmly believes that the negotiating

---

[71] Peri, *Generals in the Cabinet Room*, 97–98.
[72] Kfir, *Barak*, 344.
[73] Interview with Ehud Barak, June 28, 2004, Tel Aviv.
[74] Interview with Ehud Barak, June 28, 2004, Tel Aviv.
[75] "Barak: Israel Is Strong Enough to Make Mideast Peace Concessions," *Haaretz*, May 19, 2011.

process must be pursued.[76] He also helped obtain many permits for Palestinians from the West Bank to come to Rabin Square for a peace rally.[77]

The Oslo Accords

Barak was one of only two cabinet ministers who abstained from the vote on Oslo II when he was minister of the interior in the government led by Rabin. He did not oppose the principle of conceding land for peace, but he thought it represented a tactical mistake and wanted to keep more cards in Israel's hands before the tough negotiations over borders, Jerusalem, and refugees. Barak wanted to extend the deadlines for the planned Israeli withdrawals from 25 percent of the territories, so that the withdrawals would not happen before the final negotiations started. In his first vote in the government, Barak deeply hurt, disappointed, and angered Rabin, his lifelong supporter, by not voting with him. Barak defended his position by saying that he backed the Oslo process with all his heart, but that the devil is in the details.[78] He does not understand the importance of trust in relationships and in peace processes, which is why he was initially against the Oslo process, arguing that it gave 90 percent of the land before the larger issues would be negotiated.[79] Barak resented the military's exclusion from the Oslo negotiations, believing that this resulted in security loopholes. He also thought it was preferable to negotiate with Syria first, since it was a greater military threat and would decrease the bargaining power of Palestinians.[80]

Public opinion was not the main motivator for Barak's participation in peace negotiations with the Palestinians and Syrians, but the timing of elections limited his concessions. He was on the verge of signing an agreement with Syria but got cold feet about being able to convince the people to make the necessary concessions, even though polls showed that whatever agreement Barak would have signed, either with Syria or with the Palestinian Authority, he would have a huge amount of support.[81] Efraim Halevy, director of the Mossad during this time, laments Barak getting cold feet; according to Halevy, a peace with Syria would have changed history.[82] As the elections neared, Barak began saying that he did not intend to return the Syrians to the Kineret (Sea of Galilee) and would not let Syrian terrorists make use of the

---

[76] Interview with Nahum Barnea, August 5, 2010, Jerusalem.

[77] Interview with Yitzhak Frankenthal, August 5, 2010, Jerusalem.

[78] Kfir, *Barak*, 318–20.

[79] Interview with Ami Ayalon, August 4, 2010, Herzliya, Israel. Ayalon was director of the Shin Bet 1996–2000, Minister Without Portfolio September 2007–March 2009, and part of Blue White Future Organization for promoting two-state solution.

[80] Peri, *Generals in the Cabinet Room*, 64–65.

[81] Interview with Yossi Beilin, July 26, 2007, Tel Aviv.

[82] Interview with Efraim Halevy, August 6, 2013, Ramat Aviv.

lake.[83] His own foreign minister, Shlomo Ben-Ami, claims that Barak grew hesitant and tried to maneuver to get an even better deal. According to Ben-Ami, Barak was concerned about public opinion polls in Israel that showed distrust of the Syrians and therefore little enthusiasm for withdrawal to the border of Lake Kineret. His own cabinet and chief of staff advised focusing on the Palestinian front. When in February 2000 Barak showed willingness to reach peace with Syria based on the 1967 lines, Assad, who was terminally ill, was no longer interested.[84]

The Camp David Negotiations

Although Barak had initially opposed the staged process of Oslo because he believed it would decrease Israel's bargaining power, the failures of a staged process were only confirmed for him when it gave time to spoilers such as Hamas to try to breed distrust and end the process through its suicide bombings within Israel. Therefore, when he became prime minister, Barak thought there was no point in implementing further partial withdrawals required at Oslo; instead, he wanted to reach a comprehensive agreement that would achieve peace and end all further claims against Israel. The timing of Camp David was determined by Barak's conviction that time was working against Israel, and that there was a short window of opportunity to reach an agreement since Clinton was committed to Israel and the peace process and needed to strike a deal. His strategy took into account a sense that Israelis were fatigued from attempts at interim agreements and that there was a need for the Palestinians to agree to the end of conflict and the finality of claims. Eleven days into Camp David, the Palestinian negotiators demanded for the first time that compensation to the Palestinian people for occupation be negotiated: "This is exactly what concerned him [Barak]: that he would say, 'here's the final agreement,' but Arafat would say, 'no, here's something new out of nowhere, let's come back to this in two years' ... that would totally undermine agreements."[85]

There are multiple narratives among and within different negotiating teams as to what exactly happened during the Camp David negotiations in 2000, and who was to blame for the failure to reach a peace agreement, but Barak's lack of emotional intelligence is widely perceived as a contributing factor.[86] Shlomo Ben-Ami writes:

---

[83] Kfir, *Barak*, 348.

[84] Shlomo Ben-Ami, *Scars of War, Wounds of Peace: The Israeli-Arab Tragedy* (Oxford: Oxford University Press, 2006), 244–45.

[85] Interview with Gidi Grinstein, secretary of Barak's delegation at Camp David, August 4, 2010, Tel Aviv.

[86] For a comprehensive analysis of the varied narratives of the Camp David negotiations, see Myron J. Aronoff, "Camp David Rashomon: Contested Interpretations of the Israel/Palestine Peace Process," *Political Science Quarterly*, 124, no. 1 (2009), 143–67.

It is difficult to imagine a greater incompatibility than that which existed between the Israeli Prime Minister, an intellectually arrogant and undoubtedly brilliant general who was totally blind and deaf to cultural nuances and always convinced that he possessed the powerful Cartesian logic that would surely persuade his interlocutor of the invalidity of his own arguments on the one hand, and Arafat, a mythological leader who to his last day continued to embody the general will of his people, but at the same time was full of personal complexes and was incapable, or pretended to be so, of conducting a fluid dialogue on the other.[87]

Minister of Foreign Affairs Shlomo Ben-Ami also said that Barak "doesn't understand cultures and doesn't understand people ... He failed to engage Arafat."[88] He not only lost Arafat's trust by not implementing the third redeployment envisioned by the Framework Agreement that was scheduled to be concluded by February 2000, but he also undermined confidence by failing to take steps such as prisoner releases, and by putting the Palestinian track on the back burner while he first pursued the Syrian track. During the almost two weeks at Camp David, he refused to hold one-on-one meetings with Arafat.[89] He did not understand the implications of his losing Arafat's trust. The Palestinian Authority initially had high expectations of Barak and thought of him as the reincarnation of Rabin. Ami Ayalon warned Barak that he would lose Arafat's trust by going to Syria first, as did the intelligence bodies, but Barak did not listen.[90] Shlomo Ben-Ami writes in his diary that in June he had asked Barak "to develop a more personal and empathetic approach to Arafat" to no avail and declares that "Barak really did have severe personality defects, which led to his downfall in the end."[91] Madeleine Albright agrees that Barak lacked people skills, that he let others know that he thought he was smarter, and that he had his own logic. He was not only patronizing to the Palestinians, but even to Clinton himself. Barak produced a script for Clinton's meeting with Syrian president Assad and said it would be fine for the president to improvise the opening generalities, but not the description of Israel's needs.[92]

Barak also thought that he knew how Palestinians bargain and that low initial bids would make Arafat feel better about gaining more land concessions from Israel later in the negotiations. He thought that one should bargain in peace negotiations the way one would haggle in a Middle Eastern bazaar. A good illustration of this occurred when Israelis and Tunisians were close to exchanging consulates in 1996. U.S. Secretary of State Warren Christopher invited Barak, who was Israel's foreign minister, and Tunisian Foreign Minister Habib Ben Yahia to a formal lunch to sign the prepared documents and shake

[87] Ben-Ami, *Scars of War, Wounds of Peace*, 253.
[88] Interview with Shlomo Ben-Ami, July 12, 2007, Ramat Aviv.
[89] Pundak, "From Oslo to Taba," 37.
[90] Interview with Ami Ayalon, August 4, 2010, Herzliya.
[91] Peri, *General in the Cabinet Room*, 238, citing Shlomo Ben-Ami, *A Front With No Rear* [in Hebrew] (Tel Aviv: Miskal-Yedioth Ahronoth Books, 2004), 473, 144.
[92] Albright, *Madam Secretary*, 480, 488.

hands in front of the cameras. When Ben Yahia balked, Barak explained to the Americans that "this is the Middle East. He is behaving like in a Turkish bazaar, he is pretending to break the deal in the last moment in order to make an additional gain." After some delays, a Tunisian office was established in Israel.[93] Therefore, believing in the analogy of the bazaar, Barak initially offered Arafat far fewer concessions than he was actually willing to give, which only angered Arafat rather than making him feel better about gradually gaining more during negotiations.

Barak admits that "we probably made a hundred mistakes" but that none of his mistakes were as significant as Arafat's. Barak met with Arafat for only thirty minutes during the fourteen days at Camp David, and Avi Gil claims that had Peres been the prime minister, he would have spent much more time with him.[94] When asked why he did not meet with Arafat more often at Camp David, Barak said that meetings with leaders before substantial groundwork is made between advisors could do more damage than good:

> I never raised my voice. I kept it soft. I never insulted. It is ridiculous to think that Arafat would have acted differently with such a momentous decision if he was treated like a child. If he were given some meal, given some jellybeans. Treat him well, flatter him, and he will change his position about the basic issues of the Palestinian people for which he fights.[95]

Saeb Erekat agrees that Barak was not the main obstacle to reaching a peace agreement and said that "Barak made mistakes, we make mistakes, it's not Barak."[96] Barak was infuriated and frustrated that Arafat would not give an inch in negotiations. He explains, "Probably we would go a mile and they would go an inch, doesn't matter; because that would have shown readiness, substantive reciprocity, quality rather than quantity. We would be ready to go much further ... we have to see them moving. However infinitesimal. Ultimately at the moment of truth they rejected it."[97]

Barak also determined:

> Arafat does not recognize the right of the Jewish people to have a Jewish democratic state ... What we found in Camp David is that Arafat did not want to correct 1967, I mean the occupation, but he wants to correct 1948 ... I found that when we talked for ten years about two states for two nations, we meant something totally different. When we speak about two states for two nations we think about a Palestinian Palestine that reflects a Palestinian identity, history, side by side with a Jewish democratic, Zionist Israel that reflects ours ... Arafat thinks about a Palestinian Palestine, the same one that I mentioned earlier, side by side with a democratic tolerant entity called Israel that through the political right of the return, even if

[93] Kfir, *Barak*, 351.
[94] Interview with Avi Gil, June 16, 2004, Jerusalem.
[95] Interview with Ehud Barak, June 28, 2004, Tel Aviv.
[96] Interview with Saeb Erekat, July 20, 2007, Jericho.
[97] Interview with Ehud Barak, June 28, 2004, Tel Aviv.

executed by the return of 200,000 refugees from Lebanon they will become within ten years a bi-national state and within another generation or two another state with a Jewish minority. Then they will want one state for two nations.[98]

Taba Negotiations

Despite the fact that Barak had said publicly after Camp David that Arafat had failed the test and was not interested in a two-state solution, he pursued negotiations in January 2001 at Taba because he did not think there was *no* chance of ever reaching a deal with Arafat and that even a 10 percent chance was worth pursuing. Barak said, "[T]he logic is very clear. You will not get anything by turning to terror. At the same time we are still confident enough and generous enough not to pretend to be able to punish the whole Palestinian people for the failure of leadership of Mr. Arafat."[99] Barak also continued negotiations after Camp David because he was attuned to international public opinion and wanted to make sure everyone knew of the concessions that he was ready to make. He was skeptical that one could have serious negotiations three or four weeks before the Israeli elections, but he pursued negotiations "to explore what could be done after the election if we win."[100]

At Taba, gaps were narrowed on territorial borders, security matters, refugees, and the narratives about the source of the refugee problem. There was still no agreement on the symbolic number of refugees to be allowed to return to Israel, but creative ideas were discussed. Yossi Beilin, one of the main Israeli negotiators at Taba, believes that had Arafat agreed to it, Barak would have signed the agreement.[101] Saeb Erekat agrees that the parties were close to reaching an agreement and has repeatedly said, "[W]e don't need negotiations any more. It's time for decisions. We know that there'll be an Israel, next to the state of Palestine, on the Israel border, minus/plus swaps of land, certain security arrangements, a Palestinian state for Palestinians and an Israeli state for Israelis. We know that. We came a long way and the negotiations are over."[102] The joint Israeli-Palestinian statement of January 27, 2001, that concluded the Taba Conference stated, "The sides declare that they have never been closer to reaching an agreement and it is thus our shared belief that the remaining gaps could be bridged with the resumption of negotiations following the Israeli elections."[103]

After Taba, Barak canceled a proposed meeting with Arafat in Sweden after Arafat falsely accused Israel of using depleted uranium against Palestinians during the intifada. Foreign Minister Shlomo Ben-Ami, Justice Minister Yossi

---

[98] Ibid.
[99] Ibid.
[100] Ibid.
[101] Interview with Yossi Beilin, July 26, 2007, Tel Aviv.
[102] Interview with Saeb Erekat, July 20, 2007, Jericho.
[103] Joint Israeli-Palestinian statement, January 27, 2001, available at http://www.mfa.gov.il/mfa/go. asp?MFAH0j700

Beilin, and Director-General of the Prime Minister's Office Gilead Sher all favored holding the meeting.[104] Barak was convinced that Arafat had deliberately turned to violence in the second intifada. He compared his experience with Arafat – the initial attempt to negotiate only to discover that he was not a negotiating partner – to the international community's similar experiences with other leaders such as Serbian leader Slobodan Milosevic, Iraq's Saddam Hussein, Libyan leader Muammar al-Qaddafi, and North Korea's President Kim Il-Sung.[105]

REACTION TO EVENTS SINCE THE END OF BARAK'S TERM AS PRIME MINISTER: 2001–2013

As defense minister and deputy prime minister under the government of Ehud Olmert (2007–2009) and the second Netanyahu government (2009–2013), Barak continued to believe in the urgency of peace with the Palestinian Authority. He failed, however, to significantly influence Netanyahu to move more urgently toward peace, and ultimately put his own personal ambitions to remain defense minister above his concern with government stalling on the peace process. Although Barak supported Olmert's serious negotiations with Abu Mazen, the leaders did not reach an agreement. Abu Mazen questioned Olmert's ability to deliver because Olmert was a lame duck prime minister facing potential corruption charges. Olmert also was skeptical of Abu Mazen's ability to implement a deal when Hamas controlled the Gaza Strip and opposed any peace agreements.

When Arab foreign ministers re-endorsed the Saudi 2002 peace proposal at an Arab League summit in Riyadh in March 2007, Barak proposed that Israel use the peace initiative as a basis for negotiation. This may partially be attributed to the influence of Peres, who had been speaking enthusiastically about the initiative.[106] It was also a function of Barak's belief that relationships in the region could become more positive as well as his concern for international legitimacy. This concern also played a role in his push for a shorter campaign during Operation Cast Lead in December 2008–January 2009. The operation was intended to put a halt to the several thousand rockets that had been fired from Gaza at Israel; Barak called to end the campaign in a few days, but he failed and it continued for three weeks.

Barak criticized some of the rhetoric emanating from Fatah's Sixth General Assembly of August 2009 as grave and unacceptable, but he nevertheless reiterated that there is no other solution but a comprehensive peace deal between

[104] Aluf Benn and Ora Coren, "PM Halts Talks After Angry Arafat Speech," *Ha'aretz*, January 29, 2001.
[105] Barak, "Special Policy Forum Report," July 24, 2001.
[106] Aluf Benn and Barak Ravid, "Arab Peace Initiative Has Barak Backing, But Livni Still Cautious," *Haaretz*, October 28, 2008.

Israel and the Palestinians. In contrast, some Israeli ministers, such as Transportation Minister Yisrael Katz, emphasized that it signalled greater hostility and intransigence on the part of Fatah: Fatah, they claimed, was falsely accusing Israel of murdering Arafat, committing itself to violent resistance, demanding West Jerusalem, and upping the ante for preconditions for negotiations to include release of prisoners and settlement freezes. However, Barak's determination to reach an agreement was not shaken.[107]

What has mystified observers is why, given Barak's emphasis on the importance and urgency of reaching an agreement, he agreed to join Netanyahu's right-wing coalition and remain in it. Barak justified this controversial decision by saying that he could influence Netanyahu from within the government to pursue peace. However, his attempts had limited effect. Although Barak succeeded in influencing Netanyahu to support a two-state solution (which Netanyahu did with conditions), and to freeze settlements in the West Bank for ten months, he ultimately failed to push Netanyahu to pursue peace with greater urgency, to solidify rather than weaken Israel's ties with the United States, to renew a freeze of settlements past the ten months, or to agree to dividing Jerusalem. Barak reiterated Israel's willingness to divide Jerusalem in Washington, and this was retracted by Netanyahu as not representing the government's view. Barak often bemoaned the coalition as constraining the ability to make serious peace initiatives, but his repeated calls for Netanyahu to work harder to include Kadima in the government coalition fell on deaf ears.[108]

Barak's and Netanyahu's divergent perception as to whether or not time is working in Israel's favor and, therefore, the extent to which peace must be reached urgently, was highlighted by their different reactions to the uprisings in the Middle East beginning in 2010. The changes in the region solidified Barak's opinion that Israel's response should be to pursue a peace process.[109] His interpretation is echoed by many Israelis. Three out of four Israelis polled felt that the uncertainty generated by demonstrations in the Middle East and the pending Palestinian appeal to the UN in a bid to gain statehood made it more urgent for Israel to agree on a final status accord with the Palestinians.[110] Netanyahu, on the other hand, agreed with the 15 percent of Israelis whose reaction to the Arab Spring was that Israel should be even more cautious as a result of the uncertainty in the region, and who interpreted the lessons to be that long-standing peace treaties can no longer be taken for

---

[107] "Fatah: Return J'lem Before Talks Go On," *The Jerusalem Post*, August 8, 2009; "Barak: Fatah's Rhetoric Is Unacceptable," *The Jerusalem Post*, August 9, 2009.

[108] "Labor Must Throw Out Barak and Join the Opposition," *Haaretz*, January 3, 2011; "Barak: Make-up of Government Is Problematic for Advancing Peace," *Haaretz*, March 3, 2011.

[109] "Barak: IDF Needs to Deal with Changing Mideast," *The Jerusalem Post*, February 15, 2011; "Barak: Israel Must Move Ahead Toward Peace," *The Jerusalem Post*, February 11, 2011.

[110] Dahlia Scheindlin, "Stuck in the Status Quo," *The Jerusalem Report*, April 25, 2011, 10. Results of a New Wave Research survey conducted on March 22, 2011.

granted. While acknowledging these concerns, Barak claimed that "I still believe despite all uncertainty Israel should make a real attempt to enter negotiations."[111]

Just as Barak, as prime minister, expressed his urgency to reach peace in a dramatic fashion by comparing Israel to the *Titanic* when it was about to hit an iceberg, in the wake of the tragic tsunami in Japan in March 2011, Barak argued that Israel could face a diplomatic tsunami if the standstill in Mideast peace talks continued and the UN recognized a Palestinian state in September. He argued that for the past two years (the same two years that he had served as defense minister in the Netanyahu government), Israel had not put the core issues on the negotiating table, and that now Israelis must take diplomatic initiatives and be willing to discuss security, borders, refugees, and Jerusalem. He also expressed that sense of immediacy in March 2011 by rebuking Netanyahu that his intended speech to the U.S. Congress in May 2011 was much too late. He had been advocating that Israel be the first to accept President Obama's frameworks for peace for the entire two years since he thought that the leaders were not far apart in reaching substantive agreements.[112] Barak was concerned by the reconciliation agreement between Hamas and Fatah in April 2011, arguing that "Hamas is a terrorist organization that fires rockets at Israeli towns and recently used an anti-tank missile against a school bus." He reiterated to UN Secretary General Ban Ki-Moon that Israel expects the UN and world leaders to make cooperation with a joint Palestinian government conditional on that government's accepting the conditions put forth by the Quartet (the UN, the United States, the Russian Federation, and the EU): the recognition of Israel, the abandonment of terror, and the acceptance of all previous agreements with Israel.[113] However, Barak continued to advocate negotiations with Abu Mazen. He told Israel Radio that Israel should seriously consider the French initiative to hold peace negotiations in July 2011 based on 1967 lines with swaps.[114]

Despite Barak's public disagreements and even rebukes of Netanyahu's policies, as well as his fear of an impending diplomatic tsunami, Barak refused to heed the calls of many of his Labor Party Knesset members to withdraw from the coalition and end the Labor Party's participation. Labor Party member Daniel Ben Simon, for instance, had originally opposed Labor's joining the Netanyahu government; he resigned as Labor Knesset chairman in October 2009 to protest the government's lack of progress on the peace track. In September 2010, when despite significant carrots offered by the American administration, Netanyahu

[111] "Barak: Israel Should Push Forward with Negotiations," *Haaretz*, June 21, 2011.

[112] Barak Ravid, "Barak: Israel Must Advance Peace or Face a 'Diplomatic Tsunami,'" *Haaretz*, March 13, 2011; "Barak: Mideast Peace Does Not Go Against Israel's Security Interests," *Haaretz*, March 7, 2011; "Barak: Israel Should Accept U.S. Peace Plan," *Ha'aretz*, August 4, 2009.

[113] "Barak to UN Chief: Hamas Must Recognize Israel," *Haaretz*, April 30, 2011.

[114] Barak Ravid, "White House Trying to Restart Mideast Peace Talks Based on Obama Guidelines," *Haaretz*, June 7, 2011.

did not renew the settlement freeze demanded by the Palestinian Authority as a precondition to peace negotiations, many of Barak's fellow Labor Knesset members demanded that Labor withdraw from the coalition. Calls for Barak to withdraw from the government grew even louder in January 2011, when the U.S. administration itself seemed to be furious with Barak for not following through on his promises to influence Netanyahu to do more to get to the negotiating table.[115] That was the last straw for many disaffected Labor members and ministers, and several withdrew from the coalition. Ben Simon even threatened to leave the Labor Party entirely in protest before Barak himself left the Labor Party, but remained defense minister. Consequently, Barak formed a new party with four remaining Labor legislators on January 17, 2001, called Atzmaut or "Independence." The Atzmaut Party was not ideologically differentiated from the Labor Party, but by allowing Barak and his new party to remain in the coalition, Netanyahu was able to stay in power his full second term. Ben Simon argues that despite his many discussions with Barak in which he expressed his concerns, ultimately Barak is loathe to give up on being defense minister because of his own personal ambitions, which supersede his party loyalty and dire predictions for Israel.[116]

CONCLUSIONS AND IMPLICATIONS

Ehud Barak started his term as prime minister with seemingly everything going for him. He had been the most decorated soldier in Israel's history, entered office with an unprecedented majority, formed a broad coalition, had dozens of academics advising him, and had a close relationship with President Clinton. His ideology and many of his cognitive traits (moderate cognitive flexibility, present time orientation, and risk propensity) enabled him to change earlier views of Arafat as merely a terrorist bent on Israel's destruction. He began to think that Arafat might be capable of reaching a peace deal, for which Barak was willing to be the first Israeli prime minister to concede much of East Jerusalem. In the end, though, partially as a result of his lack of emotional intelligence and political skills, he only lasted eighteen months and was unable to reach his hoped-for peace with the Palestinians and Syrians, despite making more far-reaching concessions than any previous prime minister.[117] Barak's ideology and cognitive style enabled him to maintain his new conviction after Oslo that peace was urgent and that it was in Israel's security interests. It enabled him to take the risk of negotiating with Arafat even though he was not convinced that Arafat was a true partner for peace, and to continue to negotiate with him when he concluded that there was only a minimal chance for peace after Camp David. It

---

[115] Barak Ravid, "Despite Public Denial, U.S. Officials Tell *Haaretz*: We' re Angry at Barak," *Haaretz*, January 2, 2011.
[116] Interview with Knesset member Daniel Ben Simon, August 3, 2010, Yaffo, Israel.
[117] Hirsh Goodman, "Barak's Downfall," *The Jerusalem Report*, December 18, 2000.

also prompted him to continually reassess his image of the leadership of the Palestinian Authority and to have greater faith in Abu Mazen and Salam Fayyad as partners for peace. Therefore, Barak's changes were sustained. Although it is unclear whether Arafat was capable of alienating a portion of his public to reach a deal, Barak undermined Arafat's trust through his lack of sensitivity, his demands that others operate according to his own logic, and his diminution of the importance of trust itself in relationships. By claiming that there was no Palestinian partner after Camp David, Barak also contributed to his own political demise as prime minister and to the election of Ariel Sharon. After Barak was elected, an Israeli Democracy Institute poll showed that 67 percent of Israelis believed that real peace was possible. A year and a half later, only 20 percent thought that a peace agreement would solve the conflict and thought of themselves as "suckers." If there was no partner to peace, there was no perceived need to vote for the Labor Party, which had had a political platform based on the urgency of peace negotiations for almost two decades.[118]

While Barak's ideology and personality largely made him amenable to change, recounting his experiences also points to the importance of assessing both emotional intelligence and political ambition in analyzing the extent to which a leader is able to successfully implement his or her changed policy preferences. Barak, by not perceiving the value of cultivating relationships and trust, played a role in undermining his own peace agenda and ultimately the support within his own staff and his own party. Ultimately, his own interest in retaining his position as defense minister prevented him from effectively challenging Netanyahu's coalition policies that stymied President Obama's efforts to reach an agreement during Obama's first term. The once daring and courageous military and political leader had become a cog in legitimizing his opponent's policies for fear of losing even this minimal political stature. In so doing, he sacrificed what he publically defined as Israel's vital interest for retention of his political office. Knowing that he would fair poorly, he did not run in the January 2013 elections.

[118] Deborah Sontag, "As Israelis Vote, Dreams of Peace Seem to Be Fading," *The New York Times*, February 6, 2001.

7

Shimon Peres: From Dimona to Oslo

I'm willing to go by air, land, sea, even to swim, to achieve peace.[1]
— Shimon Peres, August 24, 2009

Peres has done more for the cause of peace in the Middle East than just about anybody alive.[2]
— U.S. President Barack Obama, June 14, 2012

Shimon Peres's change from a hard-liner to a peacemaker is often captured by the phrase, "from Dimona to Oslo."[3] Peres was one of the initiators of Israel's nuclear military facility in Dimona in the 1950s, but he ultimately received a Nobel peace prize for signing the Oslo Accords with Yasser Arafat in 1993. Peres moved from relying on deterrence alone, to believing that creating mutual, shared economic interests were as important as deterrence, and he has established the Peres Center for Peace to foster that vision of peace through economic cooperation. Peres's changes in attitude are reflected in the titles of his books: in 1970 he wrote *David's Sling*, in which he emphasized his primary role in Israel's defense buildup. He wrote that Israeli declarations of a desire for peace are perceived as a sign of weakness by the Arabs, who want to destroy Israel.[4] In contrast, in the late 1980s and early 1990s, he wrote books with the titles *Battling for Peace* and *The New Middle East*, emphasizing Israel's need to take the initiative in making peace with its neighbors. Peres believed that the

---

[1] Avi Issacharoff, "Lebanon Will Never Negotiate with Israel – Directly or Indirectly," *Ha'aretz*, August 24, 2009. Quote from interview published in Kuwaiti Daily *Al Rai*.
[2] Kate Andersen Brower and Matt Bok, "Obama Awards Peres Medal of Freedom at White House Dinner," *Bloomberg Businessweek*, June 14, 2012.
[3] Interview with Avi Gil, June 2, 1998, Tel Aviv. Gil worked for Peres from 1988 and was his close advisor. He is deputy director of the Peres Center for Peace.
[4] Shimon Peres, *David's Sling* (London: Weidenfeld and Nicolson, 1970), 10, 258; Shimon Peres, *The Next Step* (Hebrew) (Tel Aviv: Am Hasefer, 1965), 11.

world had changed and that territory was no longer as important for strategic depth.[5] Whereas previously more land would afford more time for preparation and lessen risks to main cities during a tank attack, he concluded that land no longer fully protects one from nuclear weapons, missiles, and terrorism and that therefore diplomacy was the best way to achieve national security.

Until the early 1980s, Peres had largely ignored the Palestinians and had adamantly opposed negotiating with the PLO for the establishment of a Palestinian state. After serving in the Ministry of Defense for many years, Peres was nominated its director general in 1953, at the age of twenty-nine. He also served as deputy minister of defense from his first year as a Knesset member in 1959 until 1965. After Israel's withdrawal from Lebanon in 1982, he perceived Israel to be sufficiently strong to negotiate Palestinian issues, and he thought that the war had shown the futility of armed conflict.

How was Peres able to both participate in and adapt to changing circumstances, such that his views toward the Israeli-Palestinian conflict could alter so radically? Both ideological and psychological factors played a role in enabling these changes. Labor ideology allowed for change as indicated by the fact that many members of the Labor Party, including Peres, adopted a more dovish position over time.[6] An important aspect of Labor ideology that enabled this shift is that it did not have an extended, optimistic time frame with regard to winning the conflict with the Palestinians, as did Likud ideology. Therefore, Peres perceived that time was working against Israel and recognized that certain options were closing off, and that new ones would have to be considered. Labor ideology's notion of security was not necessarily tied to territory and therefore was more amenable to territorial compromise. In addition, this view of security did not argue that absolute security was possible, which reinforced the willingness of Labor leaders to risk political solutions. Labor ideology also did not focus on world hostility, which enabled Peres to think both that neighbors' perceptions of Israel were open to change and that Israel needed to be more sensitive to world and U.S. opinion.

Whereas Peres's flexible ideology enabled change, his cognitive style influenced the rate, mechanisms for, and breadth of his changes. Peres's future orientation led him to contextualize the history of conflict and to perceive and adapt to regional change, as well as to recognize change in an opponent. His focus on future trends led him to be influenced more by a perception of what changes *could* occur – such as changes in the relative importance of territory and economic cooperation in fostering peace – than by actual, specific events such as the intifada.

---

[5] Interview with Shimon Peres, June 19, 1998, Tel Aviv; Labor Party Central Committee, March 27, 1991, Document #1053, p. 14; Shimon Peres with Arye Naor, *The New Middle East* (New York: Henry Holt and Company, 1993), 200.

[6] Efraim Inbar, *War and Peace in Israeli Politics: Labor Party Positions on National Security* (Boulder, CO: Lynne Rienner Publishers, 1991), 16.

Peres's cognitive flexibility allowed him to listen to a variety of opinions and to think creatively with staff about possible solutions to the Israeli-Palestinian conflict. This in turn enabled him to alter his image of the PLO more quickly than Yitzak Rabin, who was relatively less open and whose ideas were less differentiated. Therefore, Peres changed his view of the Palestinians and the PLO a decade before Rabin, and through different mechanisms (perceived trends as opposed to events), and his changes were more extensive than were Rabin's, encompassing a new focus on regional economic development and cooperation.

After discussing the ideological and individual characteristics that enabled Peres to change his perceptions of and policies toward the Palestinians, this chapter goes on to specify the changes that actually occurred in Peres's image of the PLO and the Palestinian conflict as reflected in his policies over time. It also analyzes the extent to which he learned from perceived regional and international trends, as opposed to particular events, as well as how this learning led to changed perceptions of and policies toward the PLO.

DETERMINANTS OF CONVERSION

Ideology

Israel's first prime minister and Labor Party leader, David Ben-Gurion, was Peres's ideological mentor; according to Peres, Ben-Gurion knew that "circumstances change" and that therefore "decisions must change too."[7] Peres acknowledges that ideology has a strong influence on him; unlike historical events that do not repeat themselves, he says, values remain constant. However, these values allow for changing strategies.[8] Peres was deeply exposed to Labor ideology from an early age. Peres immigrated to Palestine from Poland (a part that is now Belarus) at age eleven in 1934 and grew up in Tel Aviv. He joined the No'ar Oved (Working Youth) youth movement, which was affiliated with the Workers' Party (Mapai). At age fifteen, Peres was sworn into the Haganah, the defense organization under the control of the Labor-dominated Jewish Agency. When he was seventeen, he became secretary general of his youth movement and a member of the Party Central Committee, and he joined Kibbutz Alumot. Peres spent a day each week discussing ideology with Berl Katznelson, a major philosopher of the Labor Party, and was deeply impacted by Katznelson's lectures, which focused on a practical and flexible socialist philosophy. Although he grew up steeped in ideology (even courting his wife by reading to her pages of

---

[7] Shimon Peres, *The Imaginary Voyage with Theodor Herzl in Israel* (New York: Arcade Publishing, 1998), 106; interview with Shimon Peres, June 19, 1998, Tel Aviv; interview with Yisrael Peleg, June 28, 1998, Tel Aviv. Peleg has known Peres since 1945 and was a former advisor to Peres who worked for him for many years; Shimon Peres, *From These Men: Seven Founders of the State of Israel* (New York: Wyndham Books, 1979), 45.

[8] Interview with Shimon Peres, June 19, 1998, Tel Aviv.

Marx's *Das Kapital*), he also admires Theodor Herzl, the founder of Zionism, for his pragmatism, saying that "reality does not always conform to the demands of ideology."[9]

Ben-Gurion, Peres, and Moshe Dayan (Rafi Knesset member who became defense minister in 1967) represented the most pragmatic, yet the most hawkish, faction in Mapai and they consequently split off to form Rafi in 1965. As secretary general of Rafi, Peres led the move toward its reunification with Mapai and Achdut Haavoda to form the Labor Party in 1968. Labor ideology rested on humanistic and universalist values of equality and justice, combined with a style stressing compromise and adaptability. Peres believed that Israel should be a "model society, righteous and peace-loving, which will be a light unto itself and unto the nations of the world."[10] Like Ben-Gurion, Peres argued that socialism could adapt to new circumstances. He realized that capitalism was needed to spur growth, but that government revenues could be distributed in a relatively equal manner.[11]

Peres has held various cabinet posts in Labor governments and has been the Labor Party chairperson and leader since 1977. Peres was foreign minister from 1986 to 1988 and from 1992 to 1995, as well as finance minister from 1988 to 1990. He was prime minister from 1984 to 1986 and from 1995 to 1996. He was minister for regional development in the Ehud Barak government. Yet, Peres is not an ideologue and in his eighties, he changed his lifelong party affiliation from Labor to Kadima, a centrist party that had advocated unilateral withdrawal from most of the West Bank. Peres agreed to be Ariel Sharon's foreign minister and support his unilateral plan, believing it was preferable to doing nothing, even though he thought that to work unilaterally was a mistake. Peres has been president of Israel since 2007 when he was elected by the Knesset for a seven-year term.[12]

Peres differentiated Labor's more dovish realism from Likud's nationalism and argued, "[I]deological considerations play a central role in even the most practical of our decisions."[13] Public opinion did not play a significant role in influencing Peres's changed image of the PLO and policy preferences regarding the Palestinians because he changed before the majority of Israelis did. Peres gave an indication of his own view of public opinion when he wrote that for David Ben-Gurion, public relations "were conducted not with a view to the pages of newspapers, but with a view to the pages of history."[14]

[9] Peres, *From These Men*, 140, 148, 164; *The Imaginary Voyage*, 100.
[10] Rael Jean Isaac, *Party and Politics in Israel: Three Visions of a Jewish State* (New York: Longman, 1981), 6, 112; Peres, *David's Sling*, 257.
[11] Mitchell Cohen, *Zion and State: Nation, Class and the Shaping of Modern Israel* (New York: Basil Blackwell, 1987); interview with Shimon Peres, June 19, 1998, Tel Aviv; interview with Avi Gil, June 2, 1998, Tel Aviv.
[12] Interview with Shimon Peres, June 27, 2004, Tel Aviv.
[13] Labor Party Leadership Bureau, July 4, 1991, Document #1156, p. 14; Peres, *David's Sling*, 154.
[14] Peres, *From These Men*, 38.

1. Is Time on Israel's Side?

The Labor Party's time horizon regarding security issues fosters flexibility. Peres claimed that Ben-Gurion "insisted that time could work either for us or against us, it all depended on how it was used."[15] Along the same lines, Peres argued that in the Middle East conflict, time was on nobody's side, and that actors should take the initiative rather than be passive. During the 1970s, Peres believed that Israel had the time to absorb immigrants rather than reach a settlement with its Arab neighbors, including the Palestinians. Peres argued for a gradual process that would give time to both Israel and Egypt to move away from being enemies.[16] However, when he voted for the Camp David Accords in 1978, Peres argued that voting against them would endanger peace not only in this generation, but also in those to come. In 1985, Peres argued that "peace can come when rare constellations occur in the history of the two sides of the conflict ... At times they happened and sometimes they can be created."[17]

By the late 1980s, Peres perceived that time was working *against* Israel in terms of its conflict with its neighbors, and this influenced him to work with urgency toward peace. With the strengthening of Hamas in relation to the PLO, Peres perceived a greater need to resolve the dispute. He said in 1998 that if you slowed down the peace process, the anti-peace forces accelerated. Claiming that Israel had to combat dangers from Iran immediately, he urged President Hafez Assad of Syria to proceed with quick negotiations because the ambiguous status quo harbored in itself the seeds of calamity. Peres asserted, "We have neither the time nor the patience to learn slowly and prepare for the new era that is arriving rapidly."[18]

In 1991, Peres argued that there was only one year left for negotiations because in 1992 there would be elections in both the United States and Israel and it would be many years before negotiations could take place. He claimed that in ten years everything would be harder, there would be more missiles and more nonconventional weapons, and Israel's world support would not be as great as if it had led the peace process.[19] When Peres was foreign minister under Ariel Sharon, he disagreed with Sharon about time being on Israel's side. Peres argued, "It's like having a sickness and saying that time will heal it. You need doctors, medicines and operations. You also need to understand ... the future."[20] According to Peres, "Every day we wait our situation only worsens and the terms we will get in the future will be only more difficult"; thus, he

---

[15] Ibid., 29.

[16] Peres, *David's Sling*, 258; Labor Party Leadership Bureau, May 20, 1975, 72, 75.

[17] *Knesset Records*, September 25, 1978, 4067–71; Inbar, *War and Peace*, 37.

[18] Shimon Peres, *For the Future of Israel* (Baltimore, MD: The Johns Hopkins University Press, 1998), 89, 163; *The New Middle East*, 53, 83, 159.

[19] Labor Party Central Committee Meetings, March 27, 1991, Document #1053, 12–13, and May 13, 1991, Document #1111, 22, 27.

[20] Leslie Susser, "Ever the Peacenik: Shimon Peres Still Believes He Can Create a New Middle East," *The Jerusalem Report*, May 7, 2001, 24.

disagreed with Sharon and thought that political negotiations should be conducted with the Palestinians immediately because time was running out for the peacemakers.[21] In July 2012, Peres reiterated that without serious political negotiations with the Palestinian Authority that lead to a peace agreement, things will not remain stagnant, but they will get worse for Israel:

> If there is no diplomatic decision, the Palestinians will go back to terror. Knives, mines, suicide attacks. The silence that Israel has been enjoying over the last few years will not continue, because even if the local inhabitants do not want to resume the violence, they will be under the pressure of the Arab world. Money will be transferred to them, and weapons will be smuggled to them, and there will be no one who will stop this flow."[22]

On his nineteenth birthday in August 2013, Peres reiterated that the two-state solution has a short window of opportunity "that could close, maybe forever."[23]

2. Ideological Goals: General and Adaptable, or Specific and Rigid?

The Labor Party's amenability to territorial compromise made it easier for Peres to change his image of the Palestinians. He asserted that Ben-Gurion's aim was for more Jews, not more territory, and that he understood that partition based on compromise was inevitable. The prime minister of the Labor Party, Levi Eshkol, was willing to give back the Sinai, the Golan, and most of the West Bank in 1977. Although Peres supported this Labor Party platform that rested on territorial compromise for peace, he thought there was no Palestinian partner with whom to talk since Yasser Arafat was not considered a legitimate option at that time.[24]

3. Is the World with Us or Against Us?

Labor ideology does not emphasize Israel's permanent isolation. This enabled Peres to perceive changes in the PLO and pursue cooperation with the Palestinians, which brought dozens of additional countries to officially recognize and establish relations with Israel. As a result of increased cooperation between Israel and the Palestinians in the 1990s, which Peres played a significant role in fostering, Israel maintained political and economic ties with thirteen out of twenty-one members of the Arab League. Peres, like his mentor Ben-Gurion, used forums of international socialist organizations to cultivate relations with other countries.[25]

[21] Yossi Verter, "Peres Says: Further Suicide Attacks May Mean the End of PA," *Ha'aretz*, July 27, 2001; "Peres at 80: Peace Can Be Grasped," *The Observer*, September 28, 2003.

[22] Ronen Bergman, "Shimon Peres on Obama, Iran, and the Path to Peace, *New York Times Magazine*, January 9, 2013.

[23] "Peres Awards Clinton the Presidential Medial of Freedom," *The Jerusalem Post*, June 21–27, 2013, 8.

[24] Peres, *For the Future of Israel*, 32, 61; *From These Men*, 63; *The New Middle East*, 166; Labor Party Leadership Bureau, May 13, 1976, 12; *The New Middle East*, 20.

[25] Peres, *David's Sling*, 155.

Although the European-born Peres claimed earlier in his life that the world hated the Jews, by the early 1990s he no longer thought that was true. He claimed that isolation was characteristic of Jewish history, but that it could be overcome. Peres was embittered by the early refusal of most countries to sell Israel arms during the War of Independence, but he attributed these policies to inertia and the lack of Soviet involvement in the region at the time, as opposed to hostility toward Israel. Peres's own initiatives helped Israel attain arms and jets from France in the late 1950s and early 1960s. Peres believed that it was particularly important for a small state to be accepted in an interdependent world.[26]

Labor members have also tended to differentiate among various Arab actors. For instance, unlike Shamir and Netanyahu, who rarely had anything positive to say of Egyptian President Hosni Mubarak, Peres claims that Mubarak should receive recognition for his efforts to advance the peace process.[27] In 2012, Peres was understanding of, rather than bitter, when the newly elected President Morsi of Egypt denied having sent President Peres a letter reaffirming the peace between Egypt and Israel. Peres said, "President Morsi has to answer a great many questions inside his own party. I was surprised not by his denial but rather by the fact that he sent me the letter. The whole matter shows me that Morsi, like any leader taking office, faces tough dilemmas."[28] Peres grew to believe that Arab countries were not universally hostile toward Israel, and those that still were, were not all equally so. Consequently, he was more amenable to perceive moderation in the PLO and to differentiate it from Hamas.

Because Peres's distrust of other states was not as great as Netanyahu's and Shamir's, he was more concerned with maintaining good relations with the United States. His sensitivity to the American administration's position reinforced this shift in policy toward the PLO. Peres attributed America's practical embargo on arms to Israel in the early 1950s to geopolitical realities, rather than hostility toward Israel – realities that shifted with the increased Soviet penetration into the Middle East by the 1960s, leading the United States to supply tanks and planes to Israel. By 1975, he believed that America was firmly invested in Israel's well-being for moral, historical, and strategic reasons and was willing to pay an unprecedented price, both financially and diplomatically, to help Israel achieve peace with Egypt.[29] Peres argued that the United States has a right to pressure Israel, and that Israel should be sensitive to this pressure, because Israel needs the United States for weapons and for support. Whether an action would enhance or harm relations with the United States became a frequent reference

---

[26] Peres, *For the Future of Israel*, 10; Labor Party Central Committee, March 27, 1991, Document #1053, 10; Peres, *David's Sling*, 32–44, 64, 120, 149, 257; Labor Party Leadership Bureau, April 22, 1976, 8.

[27] Inbar, *War and Peace in Israeli Politics*, 34; Peres, *The New Middle East*, 22.

[28] Bergman, "Shimon Peres on Obama, Iran, and the Path to Peace."

[29] Peres, *David's Sling*, 89; Labor Party Leadership Bureau, March 29, 1976, 72.

point for Peres – during the vote on the Camp David Accords, at Labor Party meetings, and in arguments over negotiations with the Palestinians. In 2010, a time of friction between Prime Minister Benjamin Netanyahu and President Barack Obama, Peres reiterated that Israel needed to forge good relations with the United States to guarantee political support in times of need.[30] In 2012, he cautiously criticized Netanyahu for contributing to great friction with the United Stated and claimed, "We must not lose the support of the United States. What gives Israel bargaining power in the international arena is the support of the United States. Even if the Americans do not take part in the negotiations, they are present at them. If Israel were to stand alone, its enemies would swallow it up. Without U.S. support, it would be very difficult for us. We would be like a lone tree in the desert."[31] In awarding Peres the Presidential Medal of Freedom, America's highest civilian honor, in June 2012, Obama said that Peres "has done more for the cause of peace in the Middle East than just about anybody alive" and added that Peres has been "strengthening the bonds between our nations for some 65 years, the entire life of the state of Israel."[32]

4. How Much Will Peace Contribute to Security? Does Peace Require Territorial Compromise?

For Peres, diplomacy, and ultimately peace, is essential to security. War, he argues, can never be a solution in itself: total wars are not feasible, and wars with limited operative goals will not end with the decisive defeat of one of the warring parties. More importantly, war itself, Peres claims, is futile in that there are no military solutions to, and no absolute protection against, the present dangers emanating from nuclear weapons, missiles, fundamentalism, and terrorism. Peres perceives the risks in all policies and, therefore, accepts the risks of peace.[33] Ben-Gurion thought that a policy of no peace and no war was not possible – one either had to pay the heavy price for peace or take the terrible risk of war. Peres agrees that political solutions are necessary because "a decision not to act may be as disastrous as a decision to strike."[34] Peres admits that Israeli strength is important to deterrence, and that Israel's nuclear capability convinced others that war was no longer an option. However, Peres believes that Israel has been sufficiently strong to negotiate the Palestinian issues since 1982,

[30] Yaacov Bar-Siman-Tov, *Israel and the Peace Process 1977–1982* (Albany: State University of New York Press, 1994), 149; Labor Party Central Committee, May 13, 1991, Document #1111, 25; Labor Party Leadership Bureau, September 6, 1990, Document #1262, 12; Greer Fay Cashman, "We Must Work to Form Good Ties, Especially with the U.S.," *Jerusalem Post*, March 16, 2010.

[31] Bergman, "Shimon Peres on Obama, Iran, and the Path to Peace."

[32] Kate Andersen Brower and Matt Bok, "Obama Awards Peres Medal of Freedom at White House Dinner," *Bloomberg Businessweek*, June 14, 2012.

[33] Interview with Shimon Peres, June 27, 2004, Tel Aviv; Labor Party Leadership Bureau, September 6, 1990, Document #1262, p. 1262; Peres, *The New Middle East*, 51, 81–83.

[34] Peres, *From These Men*, 45; *For the Future of Israel*, 103, 148; *David's Sling*, 166.

more than a decade before Oslo. He believes that rather than motivating nations to negotiate, a position of strength can make the strong country lose its appetite for negotiation: to combat this complacency, Peres recalls, "I told myself be careful, don't forget the moment, you may lose the train."[35] Thus, for Peres, a peace agreement with Israel's neighbors is more important for security than territory as such, and thus territorial compromise is a necessary and acceptable sacrifice to bring about that peace.

Cognitive Style

1. Time Orientation

Whereas Labor's ideology facilitated Peres's changes, his individual propensity to focus on the future also enabled him to perceive change in a relatively quick manner, and to be more influenced by perceived world trends than by specific events. Peres asserts that he has always emphasized the future over the present and the past and that what distinguishes humans from animals is that they can imagine rather than only remember. He declared, "I fell in love with the future, all the time my dreams were not about the past and I did not write about the past, but rather what does the future offer, what are the wings of the future? That fascinated me all my life."[36] Peres agrees with Nietzsche's recommendation that the future always rules your present. According to Peres, life is a stream, and you have to see things dynamically as opposed to statically.[37] Peres wrote:

> Life is not made of repetitions, but of mutations of progress ... You cannot go backward ... the Lord gave us eyes in our foreheads so that we could go forward ... Life is moving faster than our intellectual capacities. We are always late. You know, intellectually we are not in a car, we are in a boat. When you drive a car the driver sits in the front, when you drive a boat the driver sits in the rear. So all the time the boat is way ahead of where the driver is.[38]

Peres is a creative visionary who recognizes change and is obsessed by the future.[39] In his books, Peres spends more time talking about the future than the past. This is even shown in the titles of his books – *For the Future of Israel* and *The New Middle East*. In them, he praises Theodor Herzl as "a visionary genius who knew ... how to project himself into the future" and claims that

---

[35] Interviews with Shimon Peres, June 19, 1998, Tel Aviv, and August 5, 1997, Tel Aviv.

[36] Interview with Shimon Peres, June 19, 1998, Tel Aviv, and June 27, 2004, Tel Aviv.

[37] Peres, *The Imaginary Voyage*, 120; interview with Shimon Peres, June 19, 1998, Tel Aviv.

[38] Peres, *For the Future of Israel*, 178.

[39] Interview with Aliza Goren, June 26, 1998, Mevasseret. Goren has known Peres since 1974, was his spokesperson while he was prime minister in 1995, and works in the Peres Center for Peace; interview with Avi Gil, June 2, 1998, Tel Aviv; Uri Savir, *The Process: 1,100 Days That Changed the Middle East* (New York: Random House, Inc., 1998), 25; interview with Naomi Chazan, July 17, 2007, Jerusalem; Susser, "Ever the Peacenik."

"Ben-Gurion always used to say that ... our vocation is to see things that may happen and not to analyze things that have already happened."[40] Peres sees himself in this mold.

Peres's tendency to look to the distant future was already evident in his efforts to develop Israel's nuclear program in the 1950s. The explosion of the first nuclear bomb brought home to Peres the great changes that were coming, and he fought for an Israeli nuclear weapons program long before many of his contemporaries thought it was feasible. He and Ernst David Bergmann, an Israeli scientist Peres described as a visionary who represented the future, were heavily criticized by members of the government and the Defense Ministry, since atomic energy was widely seen as a hope for the distant future, whereas the present was filled with more urgent needs. Peres insisted that the development of a nuclear program should be a priority.[41] Israel's nuclear deterrent, of course, ultimately has played a decisive role in Israel's foreign policy (and even, some might argue, in its survival) – and this is largely due to Peres's foresight.

Coupled with Peres's emphasis on the future is a willingness to break with the past – to consciously decide that past events are not predictors of future developments. What some might regard as the extremity of Peres's forward-looking optimism is perhaps most starkly illustrated in the way he maintains that optimistic view of the future, even in light of the very personal, as well as national, trauma of the Holocaust. Nearly all of Peres's family were killed in the Holocaust, including his grandparents, who were burned alive in a synagogue in Poland after he left them to go to Israel at age eleven. Yet Peres addressed the German parliament on Holocaust Day in 2010 and implored that "while we can't forget, we can look forward to a new future."[42]

Peres's belief that the future is more important than the past, and that time is a process of constant change, is born out in his stance toward negotiations with the Palestinians since the mid-seventies. Already in 1976, he was promoting the idea within the Labor Party that the future with the Arabs would be different and better. Peres argued that Palestinians and Israelis should leave the historical polemics to the historians, while the politicians work on molding the future.[43] As Jacob Lassner and Ilan Troen suggest, Peres "called on Jews to make a conscious decision to ignore history."[44] This stance, of course, lies behind Peres's acceptance and encouragement of the Oslo process. Peres wrote that the period of the Oslo negotiations was "not a time for memories, but a time to look forward" and build a Middle East with a new, long-range agenda;

---

[40] Peres, *The Imaginary Voyage*, 160; *For the Future of Israel*, 9, 81; *The New Middle East*, 71.

[41] Interview with Shimon Peres, June 19, 1998, Tel Aviv; Peres, *From These Men*, 189–93, 212.

[42] "Peres to Address German Parliament in Hebrew on Holocaust Day," *Haaretz*, January 25, 2010.

[43] Peres, *David's Sling*, 166, 250; *The New Middle East*, 3, 76, 188.

[44] Jacob Lassner and S. Ilan Troen, *Jews and Muslims in the Arab World: Haunted by Pasts Real and Imagined* (New York, NY: Rowman & Littlefield, 2007), 336.

Palestinian autonomy severed the past from the present and was a passageway to a new future for all.[45]

Future trends influence Peres more than do particular events.[46] He admires the French historian Bernard Robel, who claimed that it was better to judge history by developments than by events. Peres recognized in the 1980s that, in the nuclear age, geographic size became less important and he was the first Israeli prime minister to recognize the demographic trends in the West Bank.[47] Thus, he argued, political, defense, and economic patterns, as well as thought patterns, were destined to change.

The European Common Market also influenced Peres to conclude that, while the past might be characterized by a chain of military conflicts, today's international relationships were mainly based on the trend toward regional economic organization. He first met Jean Monnet, chief architect of the Common Market, in 1957, and Monnet emphasized to Peres that the goal of economic integration was political. In 1970, Peres wrote that the Common Market – starting to deal with a political subject from the economic end – could apply to the Middle East. Peres believed that a regional economic system would enable a gradual long-term process of reciprocal disarmament and regional security from which Israel and the Palestinians could mutually gain.[48] At Peres's ninetieth birthday celebration, Bill Clinton asserted that "[o]ne of the reasons [Peres] has lived this long is that he always lives in the future. He is always thinking about tomorrow."[49]

2. Risk Propensity

Peres is known for his multiple statements over many years that risks must be taken for peace. This attribute also induced him to take risks in war and with his political career. As Defense Ministry Director General, he encouraged Ben-Gurion to go to war with Egypt in 1956. As Yoram Peri writes, "A war initiated by Israel, they estimated, would enhance Israel's geostrategic position in advance of a peace agreement" that might establish the 1949 borders as permanent.[50] The 1956 war also served to infuriate the United States, who made Israel retreat after the war. Rather than running for election shortly after Rabin's assassination in order to maximize his chances of getting elected by capitalizing on the mood in the country in support of Rabin's policies, he took the risk of postponing the elections precisely so that he could feel that he was getting elected on his

---

[45] Peres, *The New Middle East*, 32, 66; remarks by Foreign Minister Shimon Peres on the Occasion of the Signing of the Israeli-Palestinian Declaration of Principles, Washington, September 13, 1993.

[46] Interview with Joel Singer, August 6, 1999, Washington, DC. Singer worked in the Israeli Defense Ministry under Rabin and Peres and negotiated on behalf of Israel in Oslo.

[47] Interview with Saeb Erekat, July 20, 2007, Jericho.

[48] Shimon Peres, "Vision and Reality," *The Brown Journal of World Affairs* 3, no. 2 (Summer/Fall 1996), 58; Peres, *The New Middle East*, 34–35, 67–69, 77, 96–99, 111, 156.

[49] "President Peres," *The Jerusalem Post*, June 21–27, 2013, 7.

[50] Peri, *Generals in the Cabinet Room*, 161.

own merit rather than on Rabin's coattails.[51] Peres has reiterated the connection between risks and peace so often that President Obama's ambassador to the United Nations during his first term, Susan Rice, could refer to it as his mantra: at a conference hosted by President Peres, she began with "As President Peres always reminds us, being serious about peace means taking risks for peace."[52] At his ninetieth birthday celebration, Peres claimed that Ben-Gurion "taught me that there is nothing more responsible than to take risks today for the sake of tomorrow's chance."[53]

3. Cognitive Flexibility

Peres's open and flexible cognitive system also enabled him to change his mind often and helps explain his changing image of the Palestinians. Peres changed his views on religious settlements on the West Bank, socialism, the question of functional or territorial autonomy, the definition of security and the best means for attaining it, and the PLO. He did not categorize people only in black-and-white terms, as did Rabin. Peres viewed almost all problems as solvable and underwent more dramatic and more numerous changes than did Rabin.[54] He also did not think that talking with an enemy was taboo, and used to play with the idea of speaking with Libyan leader Muammar al-Gaddafi when Gaddafi was "considered to be a criminal, the Bin-Ladin of these days."[55]

Peres prides himself on his reputation in Israel for being a visionary. He put a great emphasis on knowing how to learn, from both intellectuals and leaders from around the world and books. He has written more than fourteen books of his own.[56] Even as a young man, Peres was adept at borrowing ideas from others and using his lively imagination to make them his own. For instance, he proudly wrote that as a youth working in an agricultural kibbutz, he urged its members to consider industry. This, he recalls, "was like talking in the synagogue about eating pigs' feet."[57] Amnon Noybach, an advisor to Peres, claims that he was always coming up with new ideas, some of which were "forty-five feet above the ground."[58] Peres always had one genius or another who would be around him.

---

[51] Interview with Nahum Barnea, August 5, 2010, Jerusalem.

[52] Avi Issacharoff, "American UN Envoy to Israel: Relaunch Mideast Talks Now," *Haaretz*, October 21, 2009.

[53] Transcript of Shimon Peres Speech, on the occasion of his 90th birthday, June 19, 2013.

[54] Interview with Yossi Sarid, May 1998, Jerusalem. Sarid was a prominent Knesset Party member, then leader of the Meretz Party; Scott Crichlow, "Idealism or Pragmatism? An Operational Code Analysis of Yitzhak Rabin and Shimon Peres," *Political Psychology* 19, no. 4 (December 1998), 684.

[55] Interview with Avi Gil, June 16, 2004, Tel Aviv.

[56] Interview with Avi Gil, June 2, 1998, Tel Aviv; Peres, *From These Men*; interview with Shimon Peres, June 19, 1998, Tel Aviv; Peres, *David's Sling*, 72; interview with Yisrael Peleg, June 28, 1998, Tel Aviv.

[57] Interview with Yisrael Peleg, June 28, 1998, Tel Aviv; Peres, *For the Future of Israel*, 186.

[58] Interview with Amnon Noybach, June 14, 1998, Jerusalem. Noybach was one of Peres's economic advisors and a member of the team of nine that advised Peres.

As compared with Rabin and Netanyahu, Peres had the most complex representations of the Palestinian conflict between 1995 and 1997.[59]

4. Emotional Intelligence

Peres has a strong emotional intelligence that leads him to highly value trust and personal relationships in his interactions with leaders from around the world. In addition to the fact that many Arab leaders in the region, U.S. presidential administrations, and European leaders often prefer his policies to those of Likud leaders, they also value his sensitivity and consider him to be a statesman. Because Peres has formed long-lasting relationships with the Palestinian leadership, during Netanyahu's second term, when negotiations were almost nonexistent, Peres held regular meetings with senior officials of the Palestinian Authority and refers to Abu Mazen as his friend.[60]

Advisors

Peres's cognitive flexibility and his emotional intelligence contributed to his seeking diverse, creative, views from a collegial, large team of advisors. Openness to creative problem solving and willingness to listen to a variety of views led him to organize a collegial advisory system.[61] He involved academically trained aides and government professionals, consulted with scientists, founded policymaking forums, and formed a network of informal contacts between his office and academia.[62] He would challenge intelligence reports based on the variety and extent of information he received. According to Yoram Peri, he became even more critical of intelligence assessments after the start of the second intifada, and thought the assessments were exaggerated and too one-sided.[63] He claimed, when he worked for Ben-Gurion, "We never took a decision on any serious matter" without consulting Nathan Alterman, a national poet and friend of his.[64] Peres continues to consult a friend and novelist, Amos Oz.

---

[59] Donald A. Sylvan, "Assessing the Impact of Problem Representation upon Israeli-Palestinian Conflict and Cooperation," the 21st Annual Scientific Meeting of the International Society of Political Psychology, Montreal, July 12–15, 1998, 12–13.

[60] Yossi Verter, "As Netanyahu's Coalition Struggles, Peres May Need to Step In," *Haaretz*, December 31, 2010; Barak Ravid, "Peres to Abbas: Resume Talks or Face New Intifada," *Haaretz*, January 21, 2010.

[61] Alexander George, *Presidential Decisionmaking in Foreign Policy: The Effective Use of Information and Advice* (Boulder, CO: Westview Press, 1980), 157.

[62] Michael Keren, *Professionals Against Populism: The Peres Government and Democracy* (New York: State University of New York Press, 1995), 8.

[63] Peri, *Generals in the Cabinet Room*, 55, 116; also confirmed by my interview with Aliza Goren, June 26, 1998, Mevasseret.

[64] Peres, *From These Men*, 177.

During his first term as prime minister, Peres had a team of nine advisors, all under the age of forty, and actively encouraged them to brainstorm together. He was willing to hear opposing views and did not seek out yes-men. He encouraged discussions over future withdrawal from Gaza and the West Bank in 1985 and did not rule out any suggestions. Peres was particularly influenced by his deputy foreign minister and most trusted protégé, Yossi Beilin. Beilin initiated the Oslo talks on his own, telling Peres about them only when they bore fruit. Beilin believed in the urgency of an agreement with the Palestinians: the 1973 war, he says, changed his view from one of waiting for an Arab phone call and believing there was no one to talk to, to taking the initiative and taking advantage of opportunities. He became much more attentive to the idea of talking to the PLO and favored the establishment of a Palestinian state as early as 1974. Beilin was one of Peres's closest advisors and had a significant influence on Peres's thinking about negotiations with the PLO.[65]

IMAGE OF THE ENEMY

The Jordanian Solution

Unlike prime ministers such as Shamir, Peres did not see all Arab leaders as alike. Like Rabin, Peres initially focused on the Arab states, not on the Palestinians, and supported a Jordanian-Palestinian confederation for more than twenty years, in which the West Bank would be demilitarized. He also thought that no political solution was possible as long as there were no West Bank Arab leaders prepared to publicly declare their readiness to reach one. Peres reached an unofficial secret agreement with King Hussein of Jordan, without the PLO, in 1987 in which Israel would have returned the West Bank to Jordan in exchange for peace. Peres expressed his fury with Israel having missed this opportunity in his books, meetings, and interviews; he repeatedly claimed that if Shamir had not torpedoed the agreement, the intifada, negotiations with the PLO, and the establishment of a Palestinian state could have been avoided. Even in 1991, Peres continued to state that his preference was the Jordanian-Palestinian solution as he thought that one nation existed on both sides of the Jordan.[66]

Despite his preference for a Jordanian option, Peres realized it was no longer possible when King Hussein surrendered claims of Jordanian sovereignty over the West Bank and called on the PLO to take responsibility for it on July 31, 1988.[67] These Jordanian actions made Peres look toward the

---

[65] Interview with Naomi Chazan, July 17, 2007, Jerusalem; interview with Yossi Beilin, July 26, 2007, Tel Aviv; interview with Amnon Noybach, June 14, 1998, Jerusalem.

[66] Interview with Shimon Peres, June 19, 1998, Tel Aviv; Labor Party Central Committee Meetings, May 13, 1991, Document #1111, 22, and March 27, 1991, Document #1053, 14. Peres, *The New Middle East*, 174, 175; *David's Sling*, 261, 278, 280.

[67] Interview with Shimon Peres, August 5, 1997, Tel Aviv; interview with Avi Gil, June 16, 2004, Tel Aviv.

Palestinians for a solution to the Palestinian-Israeli conflict. He still refused to talk to the PLO because of its terrorist activities and demand for the entire territory including Israel, but unlike his Likud colleagues at the time, he agreed to elections in the West Bank. He still preferred a Jordanian-Palestinian delegation because he thought that the establishment of a solely Palestinian delegation would lead to a Palestinian state in which demilitarization might not be assured.[68] But his ideological time frame, through which he perceived time as working against Israel, led him to recognize the closing of the Jordanian option, whereas Shamir, Netanyahu, and Sharon continued to hope for it.

Peres's ideology, cognitive style, and advisory system combined to enable him to change his image of the PLO, even before many of the events analyzed herein – events which only confirmed to him that his vision of future trends was correct. Peres claimed that opportunities were missed because Israelis and Arabs "were blinded, making us incapable of changing our images of either 'them' or ourselves."[69] Despite Peres's preference for the Jordanian option, his advisors and colleagues confirm that he was ready to talk to the PLO as early as 1981, but especially by the mid-1980s after Peres's Jordanian plan was rejected by Shamir. He did not express this change publicly because he wanted to first build a constituency that would be receptive to the idea. In Labor Party forums, he couched his public opposition in equivocal language, saying that we do not *necessarily* have to talk to the PLO.[70]

Peres changed his image of the PLO partially in response to the relatively greater threat of Hamas. Peres claimed that negotiating with the PLO in the 1990s was no longer a zero-sum game since negotiations had made the PLO rethink the utility of terror and Hamas posed a worse threat because it was under the thumb of Iran. According to Peres, "I definitely decided to pursue the peace process when I reached the conclusion – I was warned also by my friend Amos Oz – that Yasser Arafat had become so weak that he might fall." He claimed that Arafat's "disappearance was in my opinion a greater danger than his existence."[71] On an Israeli televised interview with Shamir and Peres, Shamir claimed that all the Palestinians want to destroy Israel. Peres answered, "There are those [who do] and there are others [who do not]."[72] Peres's increasing

---

[68] Interview with Shimon Peres, August 5, 1997, Tel Aviv; Labor Party Leadership Bureau, February 14, 1991, Document #1015, 30; Labor Party Central Committee, March 27, 1991, Document #1053, 12, 13.

[69] Peres, *The New Middle East*, 2; interview with Shimon Peres, August 5, 1997, Tel Aviv.

[70] Interviews with Yossi Beilin, August 12, 1997, Tel Aviv; Avi Gil, June 16, 2004, Tel Aviv; Haim Ramon, June 23, 1998, Jerusalem; Labor Party Leadership Bureau, September 6, 1990, Document #1262, 12, 16, 18; Labor Party Central Committee Meeting, March 27, 1991, Document #1053, 10, 12.

[71] Peres, *For the Future of Israel*, 74–75; *The New Middle East*, 19.

[72] Interview of Shimon Peres on Israeli Television, Israeli Broadcasting Authority, Channel One, "Popolitika," interviewer Nissim Mishaal, December 7, 1997.

distinction between Hamas and the PLO was facilitated by the fact that his ideology differentiated degrees of hostility.

REACTIONS TO THE 1973 WAR, THE FIRST INTIFADA, THE 1988 PLO PROCLAMATION, AND THE GULF WAR

1973 War and Its Aftermath

The 1973 war convinced Peres that military victories do not result in political victories and that the limbo that is neither war nor peace must end one way or another. In 1975, looking back on the failed negotiations with Egypt in 1970, Peres questioned the Israeli demand that it withdraw only 8 kilometers from the Suez, as opposed to the Egyptian request for a 20–30 kilometer withdrawal, as well as the Israeli refusal to agree to specific dates.[73] By 1975, Peres was open enough to question missed opportunities that led to the 1973 war while people were still in the midst of mourning their losses. Peres claims that the venture into Lebanon in 1982 was tragic and unnecessary, and only substantiated the lesson from the 1973 war: that war is futile and there are no total victories. In the immediate aftermath of the 1973 war, Peres believed that some settlements were needed for strategic depth to enhance security, and he was a strong supporter of such settlements from 1974 to 1975; he later became concerned as they kept expanding. By 1990, he vehemently opposed the settlements.[74] The more Peres realized that an agreement with the Palestinians was necessary and urgent, the more he realized that Israeli settlements on the West Bank were an obstacle to peace.

Intifada

The intifada did not have as large an impact on Peres's changing attitudes as it did on Rabin's because Peres was more influenced by perceived broad developments than by particular events. Peres barely mentions the intifada in his books. When asked specifically about its influence on him, Peres offered no suggestions.[75] He argued that the Israeli Defense Forces were not meant for quelling a civil uprising. In the spring of 1989, an Israeli intelligence report was leaked that suggested the need to talk with the PLO in order to end the intifada. Peres agreed that the peace process was key to ending the uprising.[76]

---

[73] Interview with Shimon Peres, August 5, 1997, Tel Aviv; Peres, *The New Middle East*, 50, 53; Labor Party Leadership Bureau Meeting, August 27, 1975, 14.

[74] Peres, *The Next Step*, 15; interview with Avi Gil, June 2, 1998, Tel Aviv; Labor Party Central Committee Meeting, May 13, 1991, Document #1111, 26, 27.

[75] Interview with Avi Gil, June 2, 1998, Tel Aviv; interview with Shimon Peres, August 5, 1997, Tel Aviv.

[76] Peres, *The New Middle East*, 55, 58, 60; Myron Joel Aronoff, *Power and Ritual in the Israel Labor Party: A Study in Political Anthropology* (Amsterdam: Van Gorcum, 1977), 210; Party Central Committee Meeting, March 27, 1991, Document #1053, 10.

1988 PLO Proclamation

In the 1970s, Peres said in the Knesset that the moment the leopard PLO began to behave like a cat, then Israel would pet it.[77] Peres's ideology and open mind led him to be the only one of six Israeli prime ministers discussed here to have believed that the leopard was shedding its spots following the PLO's 1988 proclamation that it might recognize Israel and renounce terrorism (although he did not believe it was giving up terrorism).[78] His advisor, Uri Savir, did not take the PLO proclamation seriously. Foreign Minister Peres claimed he would negotiate with any Palestinian who recognized Israel's right to exist and renounced terrorism, regardless of his biography. Peres was ready to talk to the PLO, but he knew that the public would not accept breaking this taboo until the PLO renounced terrorism.[79]

Gulf War

The Gulf War did not so much change Peres's beliefs as it confirmed his perception of regional trends that countries such as Iran were a greater threat to Israel than its immediate neighbors, and that in the age of missiles, territory was not as vital to security. As early as 1979, Peres wrote that missiles undermined the concept of space. He argued that if a missile hit Israel from 700 kilometers away, one could not say that Israel's interests were within 30 kilometers.

Peres was also able to quickly perceive the new realities the war was shaping. He noted the rising influence of Egypt as opposed to Iraq, now relegated to the status of rogue state. Peres also predicted that the Palestinians would become more moderate as a consequence of being cut off from sources of significant financial support after the Gulf War.[80] He realized how weakened the PLO had become when he participated in a meeting with the Socialist International and, for the first time, the PLO was warned that it would not be invited in the future unless it changed its position regarding Saddam Hussein. Israel needed to seize the opportunity to be included in postwar regional plans to resolve the conflict with the Palestinians. The Gulf War also confirmed to Peres that power interests continue to play a fundamental role in the stability of the region, and neither Israel nor its enemies would be given the chance to undermine them.[81]

[77] Interview with Avi Gil, June 16, 2004, Tel Aviv.

[78] Interview with Shimon Peres, August 5, 1997, Tel Aviv; interview with Avi Gil, June 16, 2004, Tel Aviv.

[79] Interviews with Uri Savir, July 15, 1998, Tel Aviv, and Avi Gil, June 2, 1998, Tel Aviv.

[80] Interview with Shimon Peres, August 5, 1997, Tel Aviv.

[81] Peres, "Vision and Reality," 63; *From These Men*, 69; Labor Party Central Committee Meetings, May 13, 1991, Document #1111, 22, and March 27, 1991, Document #1053, 14; Labor Party Leadership Bureau, September 6, 1990, Document #1262, 11, and February 7, 1991, Document #1009, 4, 7; Peres, *The New Middle East*, 51.

CONSEQUENT POLICY PREFERENCES

Peres's assessment of present and future regional trends, as influenced by his future orientation, led him to believe that the threat had shifted from Israel's most immediate neighbors to countries on the periphery, as evidenced by Scud missiles hitting Israel during the Gulf War.[82] Peres wanted to foster cooperation so that Palestinian territories would not be used by other more hostile neighbors. In 1993, Peres also concluded that terrorist activity and missile attacks, which make strategic depth less significant, were more imminent dangers than an Arab military incursion from the east. Spurred by Labor's understanding that time was not necessarily on Israel's side in its relations with its neighbors, Peres grew to believe that the heart of the Arab-Israeli conflict was the Palestinian issue.[83] His perception of world economic trends also led him to conclude that Arabs and Israelis must face dangers posed by the global economy together. Peres acknowledges that his acceptance of the PLO as a partner was a significant change that was also prompted by European friends in the Socialist International.[84]

Signing the Oslo Agreement

Although public opinion did not determine Peres's changes toward the PLO, it explains the lag between his changed attitudes and his public advocacy of consequent policy changes. Peres claimed, "Nothing is more powerful than an idea which reaches its time": he could have met with Arafat in Senegal in the 1970s, he claims, but "if it were to become known that I had seen Arafat, how could I go back home? And if there were to be an act of terror, what would I say?"[85] Although public support for negotiating with the PLO had risen from 13 percent to 22 percent in 1978 and to 43 percent in 1992, those willing to negotiate with the PLO still represented a minority of the population.[86] Peres knew that negotiating with Arafat would be anathema to most Israeli citizens. Even during Oslo, Yossi Beilin urged Joel Singer to white out the word PLO from a draft of a mutual recognition document just in case it leaked. The acceptance of the PLO in light of the taboo just a few years back was revolutionary.[87]

Leah Rabin has said that Peres, Beilin, Ron Pundak, and Yair Hirschfeld deserved credit for Oslo.[88] Yossi Beilin reached the basis of an agreement

---

[82] Peres, "Vision and Reality," 63.

[83] Peres, *The New Middle East*, 15, 20, 42, 169, 196.

[84] Interviews with Shimon Peres, August 5, 1997, Tel Aviv, and June 19, 1998, Tel Aviv.

[85] Peres, *For the Future of Israel*, 85, 106; interview with Shimon Peres, June 19, 1998, Tel Aviv.

[86] Labor Party Central Committee Meeting, March 27, 1991, Document #1053, 16; Asher Arian, *Security Threatened: Surveying Israeli Opinion on Peace and War* (Cambridge: Cambridge University Press, 1995), 106, 107.

[87] Interview with Joel Singer, August 6, 1999, Washington, DC. Peres, *For the Future of Israel*, 85.

[88] Interview with Leah Rabin, July 7, 1998, Ramat Gan.

alone, without Peres's knowledge, so that if word leaked, Peres and Rabin had deniability. Once the negotiations were reaping success, the temptation to accept the agreement was great. Peres acknowledged to Beilin that if he raised the Oslo option from the beginning, the chances for his accepting the initiative would have been low. His concerns over public acceptance would have led him to say, "It's a good idea, but just not now."[89] During Hirschfeld and Pundak's first meeting in Oslo in January, Abu Ala, a senior PLO official, made two proposals that were tailored for Peres. He proposed "Gaza first," which Peres had advocated for many years, and a Marshall plan for economic development in the West Bank and Gaza. Only in the beginning of February, after the second meeting in Oslo – which produced the principles to an agreement – did Beilin tell Peres about the negotiations.[90]

Peres thought that despite Arafat's occasional anti-Israel rhetoric, he took historic and courageous steps and that Arafat had an interest in combating terror, since those responsible were a greater internal threat to him than to Israel. Peres argued in 1998 that the Palestinian police had killed twenty Hamas organizers, and that putting peace on hold until all the bombs disappeared merely encouraged the 100 to 300 remaining terrorists to continue. He believed that since Hamas was not involved in the negotiations, its demagogic language was not relevant. Peres did not take the PLO Covenant calling for Israel's destruction seriously because the Palestinians saw Israel as stronger than even Israelis did.[91]

Beilin started advocating for a Palestinian state in 1981; even a decade later, Peres voiced his opposition because of fears of future militarization and the operation of foreign troops in Palestine. He also opposed advocating Palestinian independence before the start of negotiations because Israel was not ready for such a change. By 1991, Peres was willing to give up Gaza because he did not think Israel could absorb 700,000 Palestinian residents, and he had no interest in governing Gaza. Peres dramatically changed his opinion regarding a Palestinian state because he believed that its potential threat could be minimized through cooperative economic and security arrangements modeled on those of Europe and he understood that the Oslo process would lead to the establishment of a Palestinian state.[92] Support for this had increased from 20 percent in 1987 to 48 percent in 1996, when Peres publicly

[89] Interview with Leah Rabin, July 2, 1997, Ramat Aviv; interview with Yossi Beilin, August 12, 1997, Jerusalem; interview with Ron Pundak, March 30, 1997, Jerusalem.

[90] Interview with Yair Hirschfeld, May 11, 1997, Ramat Yishai.

[91] Interviews with Uri Savir, July 15, 1998, Tel Aviv; Avi Gil, June 2, 1998, Tel Aviv. Peres, *The New Middle East*, 14, 177; Labor Party Leadership Bureau, April 22, 1976, 7; Peres, *For the Future of Israel*, 97, 115, 118.

[92] Interviews with Yossi Beilin, August 12, 1997, Tel Aviv; Avi Gil, June 2, 1998, Tel Aviv; Avraham Shochat, July 1, 1998, Jerusalem; Labor Party Central Committee Meetings, May 13, 1991, Document #1111, 22, 26, and March 27, 1991, Document #1053, 12; Peres, *For the Future of Israel*, 76, and *The New Middle East*, 171.

advocated a Palestinian state. Although he did not want to be too far ahead of public opinion, he publicly changed his preferences before the majority of the population had.[93]

Jerusalem

After the initial Oslo negotiations, Peres was willing to consider creative solutions concerning Jerusalem because of the flexibility in Labor ideology regarding territorial compromise, his open and future-oriented cognitive style, and Yossi Beilin's influence. Another example of Peres's sensitivity to the "ripeness" of an idea occurred after Beilin's decision to publicize the Beilin–Abu Mazen plan concerning the division of municipal Jerusalem. Peres did not say that he opposed the plan, but that he was against Beilin publicizing it, because the premature publicity defeated its chances for success. Peres believed in keeping the element of surprise in order to combat unnecessary opposition and to keep a fallback position for negotiations.[94] Upon becoming acting prime minister after Rabin's assassination, Peres did not think that he had the political mandate to accept and follow through with the plan. He was not willing to *say* whether he had in mind a creative solution concerning Jerusalem because "if I say it people will think that I'm ready to divide Jerusalem. I'm not ready to say it."[95]

CONCLUSION AND IMPLICATIONS

Shimon Peres underwent the greatest and most rapid changes of all the six prime ministers analyzed in this book. He not only changed his image of the PLO at the quickest rate, but also changed his whole concept of security. Peres moved from focusing on military security – largely based on military deterrence and the need for strategic depth – to focusing on political and economic cooperation as the source of security. He came to believe that territory no longer provided a significant defense in the age of missiles. Peres was the first prime minister to publicly advocate for the establishment of a Palestinian state and to be open to creative solutions regarding the sharing of Jerusalem. Peres's ideology and some of his individual personal characteristics gave him the freedom and flexibility to learn from perceived changes in the region and in the world, and to do so more quickly than the other prime ministers.

Labor ideology centered on a notion of security that was able to adapt to changing circumstances by not hinging on specific territorial goals. This eliminated a significant obstacle to revising the image of the PLO. By not having an extended time frame that was considered to be on Israel's side in its conflict with the Palestinians, this ideology allowed for a growing sense of urgency, starting in

---

[93] Arian, *Security Threatened*, 105; Alan Arian, *Israeli Public Opinion and the War in Lebanon* (Tel Aviv: Tel Aviv University, Jaffee Center for Strategic Studies, 1985), 20.

[94] Interviews with Shimon Peres, June 27, 2004, and August 5, 1997, Tel Aviv.

[95] Peres, *For the Future of Israel*, 77, 82–83, 121; *The New Middle East*, 4.

the late 1980s, about reaching an agreement with the Palestinians; it also enabled Peres to judge some policies as failures, as opposed to believing they would eventually be successful "in the long run." Labor ideology also made Peres more likely to differentiate among degrees of hostility toward Israel, including an increasing differentiation between Hamas and the PLO. Peres was willing to pursue the risks of political solutions.

Peres's future time orientation, combined with his open cognitive system, explains his more rapid changes in comparison with Rabin and his mechanisms for change. Peres was more apt to look at future trends, rather than specific events – perceiving, for example, the strengthening of Hamas and that in the age of missiles, security would become less dependent on territory, whereas increased regional economic cooperation would enhance security. Peres was intellectually ready to negotiate with the PLO more than a decade before Rabin, and before the intifada and the Gulf War (although he dared not voice this readiness in public for political reasons).[96] Peres was also quicker to make these changes because he actively searches for new ideas through the many diverse books that he reads, through his contact with intellectuals and leaders from around the world, and through encouraging his advisors to brainstorm creatively.

Peres's changes have proven to be constant and deep. During the violent years of the second intifada from 2000–2005, there had been a hardening of positions and partial return to monolithic views of the other among both Israelis and Palestinians. Yet Peres's sense of the urgency of resolving the long-standing dispute, his changed conception of security, and his determination to negotiate with Arafat in order to reach an agreement remained constant despite his disapproval of Arafat's role in inciting the violence. He still emphasized forging ahead with the peace process, which was "as necessary as air was to breathe."[97] Whereas Barak held the Palestinian government responsible for the Jerusalem car bombing on November 2, 2000, Peres claimed that this accusation was counterproductive and negotiations needed to continue. In 2003, in the midst of the second intifada, Peres criticized Sharon's policy of no negotiations, claiming that it gave terrorists the veto on peace.[98] According to Peres, each leader has to negotiate with the other as they are, since there is no guarantee that the next generation will be more forthcoming: "The Israelis would like to wake up one morning, and see instead of Palestinians, Swiss, and the Palestinians would like to wake up one morning and see, instead of us, Norwegians. We need to negotiate with each other as we are."[99]

---

[96] Interview with Uri Savir, July 15, 1998, Tel Aviv.

[97] Peres, *The New Middle East*, 24; interview with Shimon Peres on *Face the Nation*, October 8, 2000.

[98] Deborah Sontag, "Gunfire Erupts After Blast in Jerusalem," *The New York Times*, November 3, 2000; "Peres at 80."

[99] Interview with Shimon Peres, June 27, 2004, Tel Aviv.

Peres's cognitive flexibility made him refrain from thinking that Arafat, after the second intifada, was an implacable enemy with whom one could not negotiate, as both Prime Minister Sharon and U.S. President George W. Bush had determined. In July 2001, Peres defended his meetings with Arafat, which were under attack from right-wing Knesset members, and retorted, "In my eyes, Arafat is a Palestinian serving Palestinian interests. He's not our representative and he is not a Zionist. He represents the suffering of the Palestinian people."[100] He still gives credit to Arafat for agreeing to 22 percent of the land included in the Oslo Accords and recognizing Israel:

> I wouldn't judge him in *absolute terms*, he is like all of us, quite complicated.... This is like love, we have to do it with a little bit of closed eyes, if you want to see everything you will never fall in love, you'll never make peace. So my concept *is not so absolute* as theirs [Prime Minister Sharon]. That doesn't relieve the tremendous mistakes he [Arafat] committed, but you cannot invite for a party just a perfect guest. I wonder if there are perfect guests.[101]

Even after the second intifada, Peres said that he remained an independent thinker and did not rely wholly on intelligence assessments: "I read books they don't read, because I meet people they don't meet, because I have a different view about the world.... [W]hen you drink a glass of water and you bring experts on microbes they say be careful the water is full of microbes. Somebody specialized to see enemies does not see the water." He did not agree with military intelligence that Arafat had 100 percent control over every Palestinian.[102]

Just as Peres had been the only Israeli leader to take the 1988 PLO Proclamation seriously, he also was the only one to argue that the Saudi Arabian Peace Proposal of 2002, which was ratified by Arab foreign ministers in 2007, represented a serious opening for real progress. The initiative would offer pan-Arab recognition of Israel in exchange for Israel's withdrawal from lands captured after 1967. In his remarks at an interfaith dialogue about the Saudi initiative, he said, "We cannot change the past. However, we can shape our future."[103]

After recognizing what he believed to be future trends, Shimon Peres passionately pursued peace and only supported war with great reluctance. When he was vice premier, he testified before the Winograd Commission investigating Israeli decisions before and during the 2006 Lebanon War, saying that if the decision had been his, he would not have gone to war. The fact that he opposed the war from the beginning is also reflected in cabinet meeting minutes. He claimed, "A war is a competition of making mistakes, with the biggest mistake the war itself."[104]

[100] Gideon Alon, "Peres Defends Arafat Meeting," *Haaretz*, July 17, 2001.
[101] Interview with Shimon Peres, June 27, 2004, Tel Aviv.
[102] Alon, "Peres Defends Arafat Meeting."
[103] Shlomo Shamir, "Peres: Arab Peace Plan – A Serious Opening for Real Progress," *Haaretz*, November 13, 2008.
[104] Aviram Zino, "'I Wouldn't Have Gone to War,' Peres Tells Winograd Commission," ynetnews. com, March 22, 2007.

However, despite his opposition, Peres voted for the war because as the deputy prime minister he did not think that he could vote against the prime minister.[105] As president, he also marked the occasion of his eighty-ninth birthday, on August 2, 2012, to publicly declare his opposition at that time to an Israeli strike against Iran. Despite Peres's reluctance to go to war, he is no pacifist. Peres forcefully defended Israel's actions in the Cast Lead Operation in January 2009. He blamed Hamas for intentionally trying to spoil the peace process from the Oslo Accords in 1993 to the present. Peres argued that Israel was defending children, while Hamas was hiding rockets in children's rooms, hospitals, and universities; no European countries, he argued, would tolerate rocket fire on their citizens.[106] Likewise, he defended Operation Pillar of Defense in November 2012 aimed at stopping the firing of rockets from Gaza. "We acted in order to explain to Hamas that it has to decide on one or the other. You want to build houses? No problem. You want to build missile bases inside those houses? Then we'll relate to those houses as targets for our aircraft."[107] Although he defended these strikes, he simultaneously wanted to urgently pursue peace with the Palestinian Authority.

Peres remains determined to reach a peace agreement. In 2008, the tenth anniversary of the Peres Center for Peace took place in what could have been seen as cause for pessimism about the center's main goal: the second intifada had caused scars of mistrust on both sides, and the Palestinian leadership was in disarray after the violent Hamas coup in Gaza. Yet Peres – as is his wont – remained optimistic: "Never in the past 100 years," he intoned, "have we been closer to peace than we are today. We will not cease to negotiate with the Palestinians and help them with all our might in order to establish an independent Palestinian state with a real economy."[108] The uprisings in the Middle East, which started in December 2010, also, according to Peres, made it even more urgent to pursue peace negotiations immediately. He expressed disappointment concerning Netanyahu's demand that Israeli forces would retain control of the Jordan Valley, and concern that the stalemate would negatively affect Israel's standing in the world and its relations with Jordan and Egypt.[109] *Haaretz* reporter Yossi Verter, in a June 2011 interview with Peres, reports that Peres expressed grave concern over the stalemate leading the Palestinians to seek UN recognition as a state. Netanyahu has reminded him that he has no mandate to negotiate the 1967 borders and territorial exchanges. Peres reportedly said, "We're about to crash into the wall. We're galloping at full speed toward a situation where we will lose the State of Israel as a Jewish State."[110] Perhaps because of his incessant persistence and even criticisms – of Netanyahu for his

---

[105] Meeting with MK Yossi Beilin, March 26, 2007, *Meretz USA Weblog.*
[106] "Peres: Europe Needs to Open Its Eyes," *The Jerusalem Post,* January 6, 2009.
[107] Bergman, "Shimon Peres on Obama, Iran, and the Path to Peace."
[108] Tovah Lazaroff, "Peres and Guests Debate Peace Prospects," *Haaretz,* October 28, 2008.
[109] Akiva Eldar, "Peres Seeks Meeting with Obama to Kick-Start Peace Process," *Haaretz,* March 10, 2011.
[110] Akiva Eldar, "Why Are We Not Hearing from President Peres?" *Haaretz,* August 8, 2011.

intransigence, as well as of the Palestinian Authority for reconciling with Hamas without demanding any changes to Hamas's stance against Israel – he contributed through his steadfast belief in peace negotiations, to their resumption in July 2013. Despite all setbacks, Peres keeps looking to his vision of the future, and, while his final goal has not yet been reached, in the process he has gradually made his one-time radical assumption – that there will be a Palestinian state – the accepted, conventional wisdom even among many conservative Israelis. He remains eternally hopeful about the prospects of peace, claims that Abu Mazen is an excellent partner, and says, "If I have another 10 years to live, I am sure that I will have the privilege of seeing peace come even to this dismal and wonderful and amazing part of the world."[111]

[111] Bergman, "Shimon Peres on Obama, Iran, and the Path to Peace."

8

The Psychology of Political Conversion

[Yitzhak Rabin] was shaking the hand of a man he said he would never dignify with direct contact ... I imagine he was thinking, "The whole world has heard me say never, and now I am."
– Leah Rabin, describing Yitzhak Rabin's handshake with Yasser Arafat at the signing of the Oslo Peace Accord, Sept. 13, 1993.[1]

Dramatic changes in the world are often initiated or obstructed by political leaders. The past half century has witnessed Richard Nixon's transformation from a hard-line anti-communist to the first U.S. president to visit China, Jimmy Carter's conversion from a lamb to a lion in regard to the Soviet Union, Ronald Reagan's switch from characterizing the Soviet Union as "the evil empire" to embracing Mikhail Gorbachev, and Gorbachev's own dramatic initiatives transforming Soviet foreign policy and ending the Cold War. An individual leader's personality and preoccupations have become even more central, as witnessed by the importance attributed to assessing leaders in the WikiLeaks scandal. George W. Bush ousted Saddam Hussein, and would not deal with Yasser Arafat; Barack Obama eliminated Osama Bin Laden and hopes to conclude a peace agreement between Israel and the Palestinian Authority; and NATO bombings helped the rebels overthrow Muammar al-Qaddafi's forces and kill Qaddafi in order to take power in Libya. During uprisings in the Middle East in December 2010–2014, President Obama carefully weighed which leaders merited continued support and could adapt to popular demands, and which needed to leave office. The ultimate question facing a president, or any political leader, is, given a desired foreign policy transformation, what types of leaders are more likely to change, and who actually needs to be replaced?

[1] Leah Rabin, *Rabin: Our Life, His Legacy* (New York: Putnam, 1997), 254.

This study refutes the generalization that, because cognitive tendencies make leaders resistant to changing their beliefs, hard-liners necessarily have to be replaced for change to occur. It goes beyond arguing that "leaders matter" by analyzing more specifically what it is about their belief systems and personalities that can ultimately make a difference in their country's foreign policy, especially toward a long-standing enemy. It finds that although most hard-liners cannot stand completely still in the face of important changes, only hard-liners who adhere to ideologies that have specific components that act as obstacles to change, and who have an orientation toward the past, may need to be replaced for dramatic, genuine transformations to take place. Even leaders who fit this category can be pressured into making tactical changes that help clear the path toward peace and help legitimize future, deeper concessions by another leader who is capable of signing an agreement that will end decades of war.

The Israeli-Palestinian conflict and the six Israeli prime ministers examined here reveal a great deal about the dynamics involved in the conversion of hard-liners, for two main reasons. First, the conflict is highly relevant, given its nature, its place in the daily news headlines, and the prime importance that U.S. President Barack Obama has placed on reaching a peace agreement. Second, methodologically, the cases lend themselves well to the question under investigation, since all six leaders operated under similar regional conditions and were responding to similar changes on the part of the opponent, which began officially in 1988.

DETERMINANTS OF CONVERSION: IDEOLOGY AND COGNITIVE STYLE

This study examined both the content and the structure of beliefs, as well as individuals' time orientations, emotional intelligence, and risk propensity, to assess why some hard-liners dramatically shift foreign policy in order to pursue peace, whereas others do not. The case studies indicate that leaders' ideology and the strength of their commitment to that ideology have a profound influence on the likelihood that they will change their image of the enemy, given changing regional conditions and at least ambiguous signals on the part of the opponent. This study thus builds on the work of Gordon Craig and Alexander George, who argue that ideology may increase a leader's tendency to view the enemy as evil and prolong a war, and who delineate which types of ideologies are more likely to do so.[2] The factors that are included in ideologies that decrease the chances for changes in the enemy image are (1) the ideology contains specific goals that contradict those of the enemy; (2) it has a long, optimistic time horizon that prevents adherents from believing that peace is urgent or from perceiving policy

---

[2] G. A. Craig and A. L. George, *Force and Statecraft: Diplomatic Problems of Our Time*, 2nd ed. (New York: Oxford University Press, 1990), 233.

failure; (3) it perceives the world in a hostile manner; and (4) it holds that security is possible without peace.

The differences in ideology among the six Israeli prime ministers had a significant impact on their images of the enemy, as well as their perception of and reaction to the intifadas, the Oslo Accords, the first Gulf War, the Saudi 2002 plan, the uprisings in the Middle East of December 2011–2014 and ultimately on their ability to reach an agreement with the Palestinians. Of the factors discussed – ideology, time orientation, cognitive rigidity, emotional intelligence, and risk propensity – ideology and time orientation seem most influential in determining the capacity for changing one's image of the enemy. These variables distinguished the prime ministers who changed their image of the Palestine Liberation Organization (PLO) from those who did not. The case studies in this study reveal that while a change in image makes a change in policy more likely and can lead to more significant and long-lasting policy shifts, as evidenced by Shimon Peres, changes in perception of the adversary are not necessary for changes in policy. The latter is especially the case for leaders who are not ideologues and who are motivated by internal and external pressures, such as Benjamin Netanyahu. This study also suggests that the particular ideologies and personalities discussed help to differentiate which hard-liners are more likely to change their image of the enemy, and the rates and mechanisms for this change.

Yitzhak Shamir, Benjamin Netanyahu, and Ariel Sharon did not significantly revise their perceptions of the Palestinians. The long-term, optimistic time horizon built into their Likud ideology influenced them to hope for increased Jewish immigration and for the Palestinians to give up on statehood. While Sharon and Netanyahu eventually started to be persuaded by demographic trend projections indicating Israel would not be able to retain the territories while preserving its democratic or Jewish character (twenty years after Labor party colleagues began making this argument), they still held the idea that eventually they would be victorious in extinguishing Palestinian expectations regarding dividing Jerusalem. Because they believed that time was on their side, they did not perceive policies that were not bringing about resolution to the conflict as "failures." For instance, they did not see Israel's military response to the first intifada as a failure, as did Yitzhak Rabin and Shimon Peres, who realized the need for a political solution.

This element of ideology allows one to better see how a group's worldview might or might not be able to adapt to or accommodate an adversary. Hamas, whose ideology differs from Likud's in many obvious ways, does resemble the historical roots of Likud ideology in the sense that it also shares the conviction that victory is assured in the long term because time is on its side. Alan Dowty characterizes the fourth stage of the Israeli-Palestinian conflict, following the second intifada, as including more religious frames of reference induced by Hamas's growing power; although he allows for the possibility of ideological change here too, he perceives these elements as complicating the achievement of peace.[3] This study seeks to further explain how certain ideologies, with an extended time frame in which time is perceived to be on one's side, are so optimistic about winning in the future that those committed to these types of ideologies will find it more difficult to reassess strategy. Scholars have suggested that war terminations depend on perceptions of future trends and the rational utility of continuing a war. Roy Licklider, Paul Pillar, and William Zartman emphasize the role of expectations and perceptions of the future in bringing warring parties to the negotiating table: Licklider asserts, "[A] government which expects to win has no incentive to negotiate."[4]

Likud ideology's emphasis on the territorial Greater Land of Israel inhibited Shamir and Netanyahu from perceiving change in the Palestinians, since to do so would lead to a conflict of goals. The Gulf War and the intifadas only emphasized to them the hostility of the Palestinians and did not lead them to think that a solution was urgent. Likewise, Likud's perception of a hostile world magnified Shamir's and Netanyahu's view that the Palestinians would always be hostile to Israel. Identified with enemies such as Hitler, the Palestinians were considered incapable of change. This distrust of others applied as well to the United States. Shamir and Netanyahu, therefore, were less influenced by U.S. pressure.

Labor Party ideology, unlike Likud ideology, posits that real security can be attained only through peace with one's neighbors. This enabled Prime Ministers Rabin, Peres, and Barak to knowingly take risks for peace, since they believed that the status quo also failed to ensure security and risked war. In contrast, the Likud leaders were all more skeptical that peace agreements with the Palestinian Authority would enhance security. Labor's notion of security did not hinge on specific territorial goals and, therefore, was able to adapt to changing circumstances. Its short-term time horizon regarding the Palestinian conflict led its leaders to believe that time was not on Israel's side. It also did not stress the image of Israel standing alone among nations. These factors allowed Rabin, Peres, and Barak to revise their representation of the Palestinians. The leaders' originally monolithic approach to the Palestinians evolved into a perception that Hamas posed a greater threat than the PLO. Rabin, Peres, and Barak were able to learn from and react to new circumstances such as the intifadas and the Gulf War (albeit in different ways). In addition, both Peres and Barak thought that changes in the wake of uprisings across the region in December 2010–2014 made peace with the Palestinian more urgent.

---

[3] Alan Dowty, *Israel/Palestine*, 2nd ed. (Malden, MA: Polity, 2008), 178–86.
[4] Roy Licklider, "What Have We Learned and Where Do We Go from Here?" in *Stopping the Killing*, ed. R. Licklider (New York: New York University Press, 1993), 309–320; Paul R. Pillar, *Negotiating Peace: War Termination as a Bargaining Process* (Princeton: Princeton University Press, 1983), 49–51; I. William Zartman, "The Unfinished Agenda: Negotiating Internal Conflicts," in *Stopping the Killing*, 20–34; Licklider, "How Civil Wars End: Questions and Methods," in *Stopping the Killing*, 10; D. Wittman, "How a War Ends: A Rational Model Approach," *Journal of Conflict Resolution* 23, no.4 (1979), 743–63.

In addition to analyzing the impact of ideology on a leader's ability to change his or her image of an opponent, this project considered personality factors – individual time orientation, cognitive style, emotional intelligence, and risk propensity – in order to ascertain whether these factors had an impact on the rate and mechanisms for change of those leaders holding the same ideology. The analysis focused on individual time orientation, both because it is understudied in international relations and political psychology, and because field research indicated that it played a significant explanatory role. I conclude that those leaders who are emotionally attached to and focus on a violent, conflict-ridden past, who see history as repeating itself, and who view this past as a living reality are less likely to be able to reach durable peace settlements because they are less likely to be able to forge a new image of a past opponent as a partner in peace. Both Shamir and Netanyahu thought of present events most readily in terms of the past and thus viewed the enemy as unchangeable. Both failed to reassess their images of the PLO as a consequence of the first intifada, the Gulf War, or the Oslo Accords. Netanyahu also did not significantly reassess his image when Abu Mazen largely turned to nonviolence in the aftermath of the second intifada. My analysis of the leaders' individual time orientations supports Vertzberger's findings that individuals who focus to a greater extent on the past are less likely to reevaluate a hostile image of an enemy.[5] It also confirms the detrimental effects for peace negotiations of focusing on the past, bolstering the analysis of Charles W. Kegley, Jr. and Gregory A. Raymond that a peace settlement must look forward rather than backward, and Roy Licklider's findings that a certain amount of forgetting may be necessary for reconciliation after civil wars.[6]

These findings are relevant for the current debate over how groups move toward reconciliation in the face of past injustices, suggesting that a certain amount of forgetting of the past may be necessary in order to establish a cold peace, although an engagement with past injustices might be necessary in the future to establish a warmer peace. When parties begin negotiations after a violent conflict, both often believe themselves to have been the victim and may be emotionally unready to admit their own contribution to the other's suffering. One of the reasons for the initial success of the Oslo negotiations was that they specifically prohibited talking about the past. Tzipi Livni, the head of the Israeli peace negotiating team for the negotiations that started in July 2013, claimed, "In these negotiations, it's not our intention to argue about the past but to create solutions and make decisions for the future."[7] In the same way, countries such as

[5] Yaacov Y. I. Vertzberger, *The World in Their Minds: Information Processing, Cognition, and Perception in Foreign Policy Decision-making* (Stanford: Stanford University Press, 1990), 145, 203, 331.

[6] Charles W. Kegley, Jr. and Gregory A. Raymond, *How Nations Make Peace* (New York: St. Martin's Press, 1999), 230–39; and Roy Licklider, "Memory and Reconciliation After Civil Wars: The U.S. and Nigerian Cases," Paper published by Rutgers Center for Historical Analysis, February 14, 1995.

[7] "Kerry: Parties Aim for Agreement in 9 Months," *The Jerusalem Post*, August 8, 2013.

South Africa and El Salvador turned to truth commissions rather than putting all perpetrators of past atrocities on trial. When parties are not ready to deal with their own guilt and are emotionally involved in the conflict, it may be more conducive to move forward by forgetting in order to establish relations and then to look back in order to strengthen trust and understanding between groups.

The fact that countries often take generations to deal with their own past and their role in the suffering of others, both inside their own country and in other countries, suggests that apologies are important for establishing warmer relations, but they often take time. It took decades before the emperor of Japan apologized to China for aggression in World War II, more than two hundred years for an American president to apologize to African Americans for slavery, and fifty years for countries such as the Netherlands to make films about the German occupation during World War II and the dynamics of collaboration, resistance, and post-war recriminations that followed. Although it is difficult for leaders to intellectually change their view of an opponent, emotional changes that would facilitate a warmer relationship lag behind cognitive ones.

In contrast to those leaders with past orientations, both present and future time orientations enabled a change in perception of the opponent and helped explain differing rates and mechanisms of change for those leaders holding the same ideology. Leaders who focus most on the present, receiving information about ongoing changes in small increments, are more able to change than those immersed in the past. On the other hand, they are slower to perceive overall shifts and to implement changes than those who hold a future orientation. This builds on Jervis's notion that information arriving gradually is more likely to be dismissed by arguing that the *perception* of information arriving gradually may have the same consequences.[8] Therefore, Rabin, Barak, and Sharon were able to change their views concerning withdrawal from the territories, but Rabin took ten years longer than Peres to shift his attitudes.

Rabin's and Peres's different time orientations also influenced the mechanisms for their learning. Peres was more apt to look at future trends – believing that, for example, in the age of missiles, security would become less dependent on territory, whereas increased regional economic cooperation would enhance security. Therefore, Peres was intellectually ready to negotiate with the PLO before the intifada and the Gulf War (although he dared not voice this readiness in public for political reasons). He was also less influenced by the first intifada. Rabin, whose orientation toward the present deemphasized the importance of future trends, learned to a greater extent from trial and error throughout the intifada that military force failed to produce a solution. In addition, whereas the Gulf War merely confirmed Peres's view of future trends, Rabin was shocked that Israelis fled Tel Aviv in fear of a possible Scud attack, and thus the war underscored for him the urgency of making peace.

---

[8] Jervis, *Perception and Misperception in International Politics* (Princeton, NJ: Princeton University Press, 1976), 308–9.

This analysis has generated hypotheses for further research. For instance, dramatic events may serve as a greater learning vehicle for leaders who either have a weak link to ideology or follow an ideology without components that act as obstacles to change. Leaders like Rabin, who have an ingrained image of the enemy and are present-oriented but whose ideology does not pose any specific impediments to perceiving change, may be more likely to learn from dramatic events precisely because they are more influenced by current events than by perceived future trends. Likewise, leaders who have a less rigid image of an enemy may be more apt to learn from events, even if they are future oriented. The mere fact that an image is less ingrained means that a leader will be more open to interpret each behavior of the opponent in multiple ways.

Another hypothesis emanating from this research is that leaders are more likely to question their perceptions and policies as a result of dramatic events when it is their own perceived policy failure that seems to have precipitated the events. Rabin, for whom events caused the greatest reevaluation, perceived his previous policies as having been unsuccessful (e.g., failing to stop the intifada using military measures). This study qualifies Deborah Larson's finding that beliefs change all at once, as in a religious conversion.[9] My findings suggest that there are a variety of rates and mechanisms for learning that are influenced by time orientation and cognitive style. Significantly, none of the six leaders analyzed – not even Peres, who underwent relatively rapid changes in relation to other officials or leaders – had an instantaneous conversion. Peres did not perceive alterations in future trends all at once, but did so over several years through his readings and talks with close advisors, academics, and officials from all over the world.

The structure of individual cognitive systems, on their own, was not able to explain why some hard-liners changed their image of the opponent and others did not; thus, this analysis qualifies theories that propose a high correlation among openness, cognitive complexity, and change.[10] Rabin was moderately rigid, yet he eventually changed his image of and policy preferences toward the PLO. However, it was the flexibility of Rabin's ideology, combined with his orientation toward the present, that enabled him to change despite his rigidity. In the spectrum from cognitive rigidity to flexibility, Sharon was in the middle. He was a creative tactician who could make significant changes but also thought that Yasser Arafat would never change and could not be a partner in peace. Netanyahu's and Shamir's rigidity led them to dismiss information that contradicted their images and thus reinforced the influence of their ideology and individual focus on the past. Peres changed earlier than Rabin because of his

---

[9] Deborah Welch Larson, *Anatomy of Mistrust: U.S.-Soviet Relations During the Cold War* (Ithaca, NY: Cornell University Press, 1997), 14.

[10] For instance, Holsti hypothesizes that images of enemies are likely to be varied by whether one has an open or closed belief system. David J. Finlay, Ole R. Holsti, and Richard R. Fagen, *Enemies in Politics* (Chicago: Rand McNally & Company, 1967), 23.

future orientation and his relative cognitive flexibility. Although cognitive rigidity did not separate leaders who changed their perception of the enemy from those who did not, it, like time orientation, had a greater influence on the rate and extent of change for those who did change. Peres's open mind may have facilitated wider, more complex changes in his image of the enemy.

In addition to cognitive flexibility, emotional intelligence also was a factor in enabling change. A leader's emotional intelligence influences the amount of challenging information a leader is exposed to, the trust he or she places in the source of discrepant information, as well as his or her ability to effectively implement policy preferences. The field of political psychology is increasingly examining the role of emotions in addition to its traditional focus on cognition in the formation of frames of reference and decision making.[11] Having sensitivity to and empathy for others' feelings enables one to maintain relationships with advisors and government ministers with contrasting views and, consequently, to be more likely to listen to them. It also contributes to the creation of a collegial advisory system where a variety of viewpoints can be discussed. Even a leader who does not have strong emotional intelligence (e.g., Rabin) can change, but that change in attitude might – as self-perception theory would predict – follow a shift in policies. Although Rabin started changing his image of the PLO before he signed the Oslo Accords, his image continued to evolve over the following two years. Likewise, Netanyahu, who is challenged in terms of emotional intelligence, made some policy changes that were not preceded by a changed image of the enemy. Finally, emotional intelligence creates the kinds of political relationships and alliances, in addition to experienced and loyal advisory teams, that are more likely to lead to effective policy implementation. In contrast, a lack of emotional intelligence can lead one to be overly suspicious of other ministers and even advisors, so that one surrounds oneself with yes-men and fires ministers with opposing views. It can lead to fraught and dysfunctional advisory teams and to decreased political influence.

Cognitive style and emotional intelligence also influenced the leaders' choice of advisors and whether and how they listened to advice, which in turn affected the probability of changing their image of the enemy. In the cases analyzed, the leaders who listened to opposing opinions, and especially those exposed to an advisor who suggested a different image of the enemy, were more likely to change their own perception of the opponent. Conversely, change is impeded when the advisors share the same opinions as those of the leader and debate is discouraged. The change of image on the part of Rabin and Peres was facilitated by exposure to advisors who had differing perceptions of the Palestinians than their own. Because of the particular government coalition, Rabin was influenced by key ministers who had already changed their image of the PLO, such as Peres. Peres's more collegial advisory system also contributed to analyzing policy

---

[11] McDermott, *Political Psychology in International Relations* (Ann Arbor: The University of Michigan Press, 2004), 267.

alternatives. Peres was particularly influenced by his main advisor, Yossi Beilin, who had long advocated dialogue with the PLO. For both Peres and Rabin, their nominations of dovish protégés in the foreign ministry, especially Beilin, enabled a select group to forge ahead of the leaders in advocating a redirection in foreign policy. Beilin initiated successful negotiations with the PLO at Oslo, without the knowledge of Rabin and Peres, thus creating a reality that was hard for Rabin and Peres to reject. In addition, Rabin and Peres had wives and children who were more dovish than they were and who over time influenced them.

Sharon's limited cognitive flexibility and immense emotional intelligence allowed him to be influenced by more dovish advisors such as his Deputy Prime Minister Ehud Olmert and Chief of Staff Dov Weisglass. He was not suspicious of advisors, had the confidence to pick experienced people, and engendered their loyalty. His sensitivity to personal relationships also enabled him to work well with ministers and Knesset members with opposing views, including Shimon Peres, his foreign minister. Barak was able to think creatively and listen to those whom he respected, but his emphasis on explaining things through his own logic alone and his lack of emotional sensitivity to others at times inhibited him from receiving needed advice, such as that of his advisors to meet more with Arafat at Camp David. He was able to show cognitive flexibility by breaking the previous Israeli taboo against negotiating the division of Jerusalem at the Camp David negotiations, but his own insensitivity and difficulty understanding how others work according to a different logic than his own contributed to the ultimate failure of these negotiations.

In contrast, Shamir's and Netanyahu's advisors, as well as their immediate family members, largely shared their hostile image of the PLO, and they were not open to listening to the opinions of others outside their advisory circle. Shamir's rigidity made him reluctant to accept advice from advisors, which allowed his image of the PLO to remain unchallenged. To the small extent that he depended on advisors, Shamir relied on Likud ministers who were mostly more pragmatic and less dogmatically wedded to their ideologies than he was. Some eventually influenced Shamir's tactics, but not his strategy or his ultimate image of the PLO. At the time, none of his advisors had changed his own image of the PLO. Even though Shamir was more directly exposed to the views of Peres and Rabin in the unity government, he was not influenced by them to change his image. Netanyahu's cognitive rigidity and extreme suspicion prevented him from relying on advice, except from loyal yes-men who were not ministers. All the more moderate ministers were fired or resigned during his first term. He, therefore, was not privy to information from a trusted source that might contradict his image of the Palestinians. He dismissed the information that he did receive from the military that contradicted his views. Concerns over maintaining his coalition ultimately influenced some of his policy preferences but did not fundamentally alter his image of the PLO.

The evidence in this book suggests that risk-tolerant leaders may also be more likely to make peace, qualifying Daniel Byman and Kenneth M. Pollack's hypothesis that risk-tolerant leaders are necessarily more likely to cause wars.[12] Shimon Peres, Ehud Barak, and Ariel Sharon all shared a propensity for risk that facilitated their significant changes toward the Palestinian territories. A propensity to take risks may facilitate territorial withdrawal as well as military action. In order to determine which direction risk taking will lead, it is necessary to analyze the relationship between a leader's ideology and his or her personality. Peres, Barak, and Sharon did not accept the component of Likud ideology that treated the retention of Greater Israel as an article of faith. In addition, risk propensity may make it more likely that a leader will initiate change, rather than merely accept it. Sharon and Barak both initiated risky, radical moves – either peace negotiations toward a final agreement or unilateral withdrawal. On the other hand, Netanyahu and Rabin, who were comparatively more risk averse, did not initiate such innovative negotiations or withdrawals (although they still starkly disagreed as to whether to go along with the Oslo agreement after it had largely already been negotiated).

In sum, the study confirms that leaders with a weak commitment to an ideology or who adhere to a certain type of ideology are amenable to changing their image of the enemy in either direction. Those with personalities that are cognitively open, are emotionally intelligent, and do not focus on the past, in concert with the ideology characteristics just described, are more likely to become either more hard-line or opt for peace in the face of changes on the part of an opponent or in regional circumstances. In addition, the influence of an advisor who has a contrasting image of an enemy can be highly influential, and even serve to combat a leader's natural rigidity.

While I treat ideology and personality traits as largely independent from one another in order to evaluate their respective influences in this study, some scholars have suggested that certain personality traits might be correlated with particular types of ideologies. It may be the case that certain personalities are more attracted to particular ideologies, or that certain ideologies might strengthen some personality traits. But one might also argue that other extenuating circumstances are more influential in determining the ideology a future leader adheres to. One could, for instance, argue that, since many of the prime ministers were exposed to particular political ideologies at a very young age, not only through their families, but through schools and youth groups as well, that personality traits would play less of a role in an individual choosing a particular ideology. This ideological choice is even more constrained than for perhaps other politicians living in societies where the early education and youth groups were not tied to a political ideology. Likewise, one might hypothesize that for the older generation of prime ministers in Israel, these early ideological exposures may have reinforced or shaped individual personality traits.

---

[12] Daniel L. Byman and Kenneth M. Pollack, "Let Us Now Praise Great Men: Bringing the Statesman Back In," *International Security* 25, no. 4 (Spring 2001), 137.

However, it is not my intent here to explore what causes individuals to have certain traits or to pick particular ideologies, or to investigate the causal relationship between the two. At the same time, the findings of this book seem to call into question, or at least qualify, any categorical correlation between personality and ideology. I have shown that Israeli prime ministers of the same ideology differed greatly in terms of their individual traits. I might add that the existence of such a correlation is debated in the scholarly literature. For instance, Fred Greenstein, in his comparison of modern U.S. presidents, also does not find a strict correlation between particular ideologies and personality traits. He finds that there is variety among presidents holding the same ideology in terms of their emotional intelligence and cognitive style.[13] While scholars such as Philip Tetlock have argued that conservative U.S. senators had less integrative complexity than liberal senators, and categorized ideas and people into dichotomous good and bad categories to a greater degree, this study did not consistently bare this out.[14] Leaving aside the complications of transferring conservative/liberal American categories to the Israeli context and the ideological issues discussed, Yitzchak Rabin was cognitively rigid, while his fellow ideological compatriots in the Labor party were less rigid. The personality traits examined in this study (cognitive rigidity, time orientation, emotional intelligence, and risk propensity) were not aligned with one ideology or another. Some Labor and Likud prime ministers were risk averse (such as Rabin and Netanyahu), while others were more prone to take risks (such as Peres, Barak, and Sharon). The two prime ministers who were most challenged in regard to emotional intelligence – Ehud Barak and Benjamin Netanyahu – came from different ideological perspectives.

Perhaps one possible correlation to explore coming out of this particular study is that all the prime ministers who had a past individual time orientation came from the Likud party, while no Labor prime minister analyzed had a past individual orientation. Psychologists have shown that a past orientation leads an individual to be excessively conservative, avoid change, and continue the status quo.[15] This study may lead to the hypothesis that ideology can shape personality at an early age, and that personality can shape ideology. Perhaps an ideology that stressed a permanent hostility toward Jews and Israel helped shape, in prime ministers brought up within that ideology, an orientation toward the idea that the past repeats itself. This study then seems to call into question correlations between cognitive rigidity and other personality traits shaping ideological choice in the cases examined, but could hypothesize that in the Israeli case, at least for prime ministers

---

[13] Fred I. Greenstein, *The Presidential Difference: Leadership Style from FDR to Barack Obama*, 3rd ed. (Princeton, NJ: Princeton University Press, 2009).

[14] Philip E. Tetlock, "Cognitive Style and Political Ideology," *Journal of Personality and Social Psychology* 45, no. 1 (1983), 118–26.

[15] I. Boniwell and P. Zimbardo, "Balancing Time Perspective in Pursuit of Optimal Functioning," in *Positive Psychology in Practice*, ed. P. Linley and S. Joseph (Hoboken, NJ: John Wiley & Sons, Inc., 2004) 169.

who had grown up steeped in ideology, this ideology may have shaped individual time orientation.[16] Some studies show that younger voters today, and especially those in developed economies, are likely to show less group loyalty in their orientation toward politics. As Israel has joined the Organization for Economic Co-operation and Development (OECD), has become relatively more individualized, as ideology plays a relatively lesser role in early childhood, and public opinion polls for leaders play a relatively larger role, one could argue that in the future, any such a correlation between ideology and individual time orientation may weaken.[17]

PERCEPTIONS AND POLICY PREFERENCES

All the leaders who changed their images of the enemy – Rabin, Peres, and Barak – also significantly changed their policy preferences toward that opponent in a corresponding manner. Netanyahu and Shamir, who did not alter their perception of the PLO, did not dramatically change Israeli foreign policy to the extent of being able to divide the Old City of Jerusalem and reach a peace agreement; however, despite their resistance to American and international pressure, they did ultimately make changes. Although it is clear that Shamir would not have been able to make the concessions necessary to reach an agreement with the Palestinians, he did negotiate in Madrid with Palestinians receiving instructions from the PLO.

Similarly, Netanyahu ultimately made territorial compromises in Hebron, agreed to more extensive concessions in the Wye Accords (although implementing only one of the three phases), and in his second term agreed to pursue negotiations leading to the establishment of a Palestinian state under certain conditions and to freeze settlements in the West Bank for ten months. In his third term he agreed to release 104 Palestinian prisoners in order to pave the way for direct peace negotiations, which resumed in July 2013. Although acting to varying degrees as spoilers to the Oslo Accords, Shamir and Netanyahu made shifts that, while not producing foreign policy changes nearly as significant as those produced by Peres, Rabin, and Barak, kept them from standing completely still in the face of changes. Netanyahu's greater sensitivity to public opinion made his shifts more significant than Shamir's. He abandoned his previous ideological purity by signing the Hebron and Wye Accords, which gave up small parts of the Greater Land of Israel, negotiated with the PLO, and acceded

---

[16] Some scholars have suggested that religion plays a greater role in Israeli society than some others, which, they argue, explains why some Israelis are aligned with right-wing ideologies. However, none of the prime ministers analyzed were particularly religious and they did not differ along these lines. This is also why religiosity was not a variable analyzed in the book. See Yuval Plurko, Shalom H. Schwartz, and Eldad Davidov, "Basic Personal Values and the Meaning of Left-Right Political Orientations in 20 Countries," *Political Psychology* 32, no. 4 (August 2011), 537–62.

[17] R. Inglehard, *Modernization and Post-Modernization: Cultural, Economic, and Political Change in 43 Societies* (Princeton: Princeton University Press, 1997).

to conditional statehood for the Palestinians. These findings indicate that a change in enemy image is not always necessary for changes in policy preference, which can be shaped by internal and external pressures. However, a change in image creates sharper and deeper changes in policy preferences.

The cases of Netanyahu and Sharon indicate that it is important to analyze change from a leader's starting point, and not only in terms of what action a leader does or does not take. For instance, before Oslo, Netanyahu on his own would never have recognized the PLO because doing so would fly in the face of his ideology and image of the enemy. In addition, his sensitivity to public opinion would not have motivated him to do so, because immediately before Oslo the majority of Israelis were unwilling to recognize the PLO. Thus, although Netanyahu did not undergo the changes in belief and image that transformed Rabin, Peres, and Barak – and although one might claim he was put in a position not of his own making – he did make significant policy changes relative to his initial stance for the Greater Land of Israel. Likewise, Ariel Sharon was considered by many to be the father of the settlements, but was the prime minister who dismantled the most settlements. Also, according to his trusted advisor Dov Weisglass, Sharon would have been willing to negotiate an agreement under today's environment in which Abu Mazen has control over the West Bank and has taken major efforts to stop terror, as opposed to the second intifada which was in full swing during his time as prime minister.

Thus, it is important not only to look at whether a leader crosses the threshold between a hard-line and one willing to make the concessions necessary to reach a peace agreement, but also the comparative change given the initial starting point.[18] Whereas Rabin's change in image led to Oslo, and subsequent policy revisions in turn solidified and strengthened his new perception, Netanyahu and Sharon's adapted policy preferences did not in turn lead them to alter their view of the PLO, as self-perception theory would suggest. This also suggests further hypotheses for research: hard-liners whose images of the enemy do not change will be motivated only by foreign and domestic pressure to make tactical foreign policy changes. Hard-liners whose views of the opponent do change are more likely to make significant foreign policy revisions that are less motivated by international pressure.

These cases also suggest that the leader's altered view of the enemy will often have a direct influence on policy preferences in both presidential and parliamentary systems. To the extent that a prime minister may have less flexibility in choosing cabinet members than a president, this can work both for and against changes in foreign policy. Because Rabin's ministers, largely dictated by coalition needs, were more dovish than he was and because, to the extent that he

---

[18] This supports Jervis's hypothesis that the presence of uniform movement in one direction may be as significant as the absence of shifts over the midpoint or threshold one is investigating. Jervis, *Perception and Misperception in International Politics*, 289.

sought advice, he relied on ministers, he received and was influenced by information and arguments that contradicted his former beliefs. However, for a
leader such as Netanyahu, who had a weak coalition and who clashed with
and fired many of his ministers in his first term, a presidential system may have
been more conducive to reassessing beliefs, since he would not have to worry
about the premature termination of his government or about his ministers
running against him in the next election. His great suspicion of their political
agendas was exacerbated by his lack of emotional intelligence. Most of a
president's principal advisors, unlike in a parliamentary regime, are not themselves competitors for his office.[19] Therefore, for a leader with Netanyahu's
ideology and personality, a presidential system might be more conducive for
shifts in position.

ALTERNATIVE EXPLANATIONS

Three alternative hypotheses concerning the effect of ideology and personality
on a leader's ability to change enemy images and policy preferences are discussed
in this book. One was that sensitivity to public opinion can constrain or prompt
changed policy toward an opponent. Of the leaders analyzed here, Netanyahu
most closely reflected this political approach. Netanyahu is of a younger generation than Shamir, Rabin, and Peres and was forty-seven years old when he
first became prime minister in 1996. He and Barak were not founding members
of their political parties and did not think of themselves as solely leading public
opinion, but as also being shaped by it. Rabin and Peres stepped ahead of public
opinion in recognizing the PLO, and public opinion was too polarized to be a
necessary or sufficient cause for their dramatic changes. Peres was willing to step
ahead of public opinion, but only so far. He delayed public proclamations of the
changes in his beliefs by several years. Barak was also willing to step ahead of a
clear majority of Israelis by offering to discuss the division of Jerusalem at the
Camp David talks. Thus, one cannot generalize from these cases that public
opinion plays a necessary or sufficient role in prompting changes in policy.
However, if a leader's ideology is an obstacle to change, he or she may still
alter a policy preference if that leader is sensitive to public opinion.

   A second alternative explanation posits that there will not be accommodation
toward an enemy until a leader perceives that the country is in a sufficiently
powerful position to ensure that the risks of negotiation will not be too great,
and that the bargaining power he or she has in negotiations will be significant.
These conditions were necessary, but not sufficient, for the changes on the part of
the leaders analyzed here. Rabin, Peres, and Barak thought that Israel had
reached sufficient strength two decades before any changes in policy preferences
toward the PLO. Shamir's and Netanyahu's perceptions of the strength

---

[19] Morton H. Halperin, *Bureaucratic Politics & Foreign Policy* (Washington, DC: The Brookings
    Institution, 1974), 93.

necessary for territorial concessions may have been a permanent obstacle to making peace. First, it was ideology, not power balance that significantly shaped their views on territorial concessions. Second, they believed that even though Israel's capabilities were superior at present, this could easily change. Third, both believed that the perception of strength was as important as actual capabilities – and to maintain a perception of strength, concessions had to be resisted. Like Netanyahu and Shamir, Sharon did not believe that Israel would reach a point at which it no longer faced hostility, and security would not be imperiled by moving to a permanent agreement.[20]

Another explanation offered for major policy shifts is that as leaders grow older, and are faced with their own mortality, they may seek accommodation with an enemy so as to be remembered for a dramatic change and to leave their mark on history. This is correlated with Rose McDermott's findings that "leaders who believe that their time is limited, and yet retain strong agendas for the work they would like to complete before they lose power or die, often push harder to accomplish things faster than their healthy counterparts."[21] This may have played a role in Ronald Reagan's increased accommodation with the Soviet Union along with the most important factor of the concessions made by Gorbachev, and Menachem Begin's signing of the Camp David Accords. In authoritarian regimes, this may play a role as the aging leader tries to secure his or her successor's reign. It has been suggested that this occurred in Syria's Haez Assad's relative flexibility in negotiations with Israel at Shepherdstown in December 1999, whereas others suggested that Egypt's Hosni Mubarak, in his eighties, wanted to facilitate peace between Israel and the Palestinians to help secure the succession of his son.[22]

Advancing age was a factor for Rabin's policy changes. Rabin was in his early seventies and saw the Oslo Accords as his last chance to do something big and enter history.[23] Peres's age during the Oslo process was a contributing factor in explaining his urgency for resolving the dispute. Peres wanted to be remembered as a prominent statesman who made history.[24] He claimed that both he and Rabin "felt that we were at the last stage of our lives and that our task should be to make all the hard decisions in order to save the younger generation from living with dilemmas."[25] Having turned ninety in August 2013, Peres is the oldest

---

[20] Interview with Dov Weisglass, July 4, 2004, Jerusalem.
[21] Rose McDermott, *Presidential Leadership, Illness, and Decision Making* (Cambridge: Cambridge University Press, 2008), 240.
[22] As suggested by Robert Jervis in regard to Ronald Reagan; Arye Naor in regard to Menachem Begin, "Greater Israel in Likud Governments: Begin, Shamir and Netanyahu,"15th Annual Meeting of the Association for Israel Studies, Washington, DC, May 23–25, 1999; Martin Indyk in regard to Assad in his book *Innocent Abroad: An Intimate Account of American Peace Diplomacy in the Middle East* (New York: Simon & Schuster, 2009).
[23] Interview with Eitan Haber, July 27, 1997, Tel Aviv.
[24] Interview with Efraim Halevy, August 6, 2013, Ramat Aviv.
[25] Shimon Peres, *For the Future of Israel* (Baltimore, MD: Johns Hopkins University Press, 1998), 140.

statesmen in the world, and he may feel an even greater urgency to leave his mark. Defense Minister Barak had stated that he would act with all his might to achieve peace in the next two years, before he turned seventy.[26]

Although advancing age was a contributing factor to Rabin's and Peres's changes, it is not as powerful an explanation as ideology and cognitive style, since advanced age did not differentiate those prime ministers who changed their image of the PLO from those who did not. Shamir was even older than Peres at the time of Peres's major changes, yet his advanced age seemed to solidify his preexisting beliefs as opposed to calling them into question. Similarly, some argue that now that Netanyahu turned sixty-four in October 2013, he is more cognizant of leaving a legacy, and this might make him more interested in making painful concessions for peace than he had been in the past. Yet it remains uncertain what legacy he would like to leave. Since Shamir's ideology acted as an obstacle to change, whereas Rabin's did not, one might hypothesize that age may work as a factor for change only in combination with an ideology that permits change.

POLICY PREFERENCES INTO ACTION

While ideological and personality factors will facilitate or act as obstacles to dramatic foreign policy change, eventual policies cannot be determined by those factors alone. However, the policy preferences of all six leaders analyzed largely became the foreign policy of their respective governments. The specific government coalitions and growing domestic support allowed Rabin's and Peres's preferences, as expressed through the secret Oslo negotiations, to become policy as the Israeli Parliament voted to sign the Oslo Accords. Not all of Rabin's preferences became Israeli policy, however, since he was assassinated before he could implement them. Likewise, Shamir's coalition enabled him to translate his preferences into policy.

Although Netanyahu and Barak succeeded in pursuing many of their policy preferences, their lack of emotional intelligence could be seen as contributing to the premature collapse of their governments (for Netanyahu, his first government). This, of course, limited their ability to further pursue their policies: Netanyahu's fall allowed Barak to become prime minister in the first place, thereby setting the stage for an Israeli leader to offer historic concessions – putting Jerusalem on the table – and in turn setting a benchmark against which all subsequent leaders would be measured; Barak never had a second, post-Taba chance to negotiate a successful peace deal. One might argue that Peres's propensity for risk taking ultimately limited the degree to which he could implement his policy preferences: if Peres had not insisted on postponing elections to avoid the charge of riding Rabin's coattails, he might have won and been able to sign the Beilin–Abu Mazen agreement. Certainly, Israel's type of

[26] Gidi Weitz, "Barak: Israel Can and Must Make Peace Within Three Years," *Haaretz*, April 28, 2009.

parliamentary democracy, which has one of the lowest thresholds in the world for creating a political party, and therefore rests on multiple parties in coalitions, makes it much more likely for governments to fall before they reach their term.[27]

Sharon and Rabin implemented their preferences most effectively. Rabin had a coalition that was able to endorse his policies. Sharon had the emotional intelligence that enabled a strong, effective team of advisors to effectively implement his ideas; it also enabled him to forge political alliances that even induced politicians to reject their former parties to join his new party, Kadima – a party that he created explicitly to implement his policy preference for further withdrawals in the West Bank. Both Rabin and Sharon, in his second prime ministerial election, were elected under the same system, in which voters chose both the prime minister and the candidate's party together. In Sharon's first term as prime minister in 2001, his first move was to cancel the system that allowed direct election of the prime minister and return to the old system before the larger parties had been weakened. It reasserted the control of the prime minister over portions of the list as people were beholden to the person rather than to the party.[28] Sharon ended up having five years to implement his policies before being felled by a stroke – as opposed to Rabin's three years, Barak's eighteen months, and Peres's seven months in his second term.

In addition to opposition from parliament, opposition from one's coalition, domestic and international pressures, assassination, and debilitating strokes, a host of other factors can intervene between a leader's beliefs and eventual policy. Nevertheless, all six leaders significantly shaped their country's foreign policy. Even Shamir's and Netanyahu's tactical changes ultimately had significant, if unintentional, political consequences, since they paved the way for broader public support for negotiating with the Palestinians, accepting the Oslo Accords, and providing greater legitimacy in Israel for a Palestinian state.

RELEVANCE TO THE STUDY OF ISRAELI-PALESTINIAN RELATIONS

There are formidable international and regional structural conditions that favor reaching a peace agreement between the Palestinian Authority and Israel – perhaps most importantly Israel's, the United States', and the Arab League's (most members) common desire to balance Iran. However, these structural forces can be in place for years, but in themselves are necessary yet not sufficient for determining if and when such an agreement will occur. Just as in the past, the particular ideology and individual traits of leaders can make a crucial difference.

---

[27] For an elaborate exploration of ways in which Israel's parliamentary system can contribute to complicating the peace process, see *Democracy and Conflict Resolution, The Dilemmas of Israel's Peacemaking*, eds. Miriam F. Elman, Oded Haklai, and Hendrik Spruyt (New York: Syracuse University Press, 2013).

[28] Interview with Naomi Chazan, July 17, 2007. Chazan pointed out the influence of the changing electoral system on the leaders' ability to implement policy. While a Knesset member, she helped lay the groundwork for Sharon's changing the electoral system back to what it had been.

One could argue that there was a strong possibility for reaching agreements in the past with certain leaders, or at least making more progress toward reaching an agreement had they been able to stay in power longer before another leader, less amenable to change toward accommodation, replaced them. Had Yitzhak Rabin not been assassinated in 1995, it is possible that we would already have had a peace agreement over a decade ago. Rabin and Arafat had been forming a more trusting partnership, Rabin had the legitimacy among most Israelis as someone who deeply cared about Israeli security to make concessions, and the Beilin–Abu Mazen plan had been carefully crafted for him, days before his assassination. When Shimon Peres became prime minister after the assassination, there is a strong possibility that he would have been able to reach a peace agreement had he won the next election. This could have been possible had he been willing to use the nation's mourning of Rabin to pledge to carry his mantle, rather than erroneously try to prove to himself that he could be elected on solely his own without resting on the prestige of his former rival. Peres could have gone with the Beilin–Abu Mazen plan while he was acting prime minister. In addition, had he not ventured into Lebanon to go after Hezbollah, and had Israel not mistakenly hit civilians at Qana, Palestinian Israelis might not have boycotted the elections, and it is likely that he would have won against Netanyahu and would have had the motivation and time to reach an agreement. Instead, Netanyahu, who had vehemently opposed Oslo, came to power and attempted to diminish and delay withdrawals and did not believe, as Rabin and Peres had, that Arafat could be a partner to peace.

Similarly, had Ehud Barak lasted as prime minister for more than eighteen months, he may have been able to achieve an agreement as negotiations right before the elections at Taba were closing gaps between the two sides; some participants of those negotiations claimed that had they had just six additional weeks, a peace agreement could have been concluded. Barak incorrectly gambled that early elections would strengthen his position. After losing the election, he retained his belief that Israel should pursue serious peace negotiations throughout his government service as defense minister, proclaiming toward the end of his term in March 2013 that Israel should initiate a daring peace initiative that could attain a peace agreement with the Palestinians.[29] This book shows that the changes that Rabin, Peres, and Barak underwent could have made an agreement possible had each of them been able to stay in office.

Ariel Sharon's changes might have paved the way toward resolving the conflict had he been able to remain in office during his full term. George W. Bush also reflects in his memoirs, "I've always wondered what might have been possible if Ariel had continued to serve. He had established his credibility on security, he had the trust of the Israeli people, and I believe he could have been

---

[29] Chemi Shelev, "Barak Calls for U.S.-led Regional Security Alliance in Mideast to Combat Terror, Iran," *Haaretz*, March 4, 2013.

part of a historic peace."[30] Had Sharon not had a debilitating stroke, he probably would have withdrawn unilaterally from most of the West Bank, thereby paving the way for decreased tension between the two sides and a greater probability of successful negotiations under Ehud Olmert. Predicting whether an agreement not only can, but will be reached by the end of President Obama's second term forces one to rely on political psychology for the analysis of leaders. Will leaders and stable coalitions that are capable of reaching an agreement emerge? Will the inclusion of center parties in Netanyahu's third term create opportunities to make significant concessions in the peace negotiations that were rekindled in July 2013 if the internal and external pressures create an environment in which such negotiations are again on the world agenda?

Before the Oslo Accords, no one would have predicted that such an agreement would come to pass; afterwards, everyone pointed to the reasons why it did. Before President Anwar Sadat's visit to Jerusalem, many Israelis objected to conceding the Sinai; after his visit, the vast majority supported the land-for-peace deal. Before the Oslo Accords were signed in 1993, many Israelis objected to negotiations with the PLO; afterward, most supported its recognition. Likewise, although many Israelis are reluctant to cede much of East Jerusalem or the Golan Heights, evidence of an agreement is likely to change minds.

Success primarily depends on active mediation and dedication on the part of U.S. leaders to overcome the institutional obstacles in the Israeli and Palestinian political systems, the reluctance of Benjamin Netanyahu to divide Jerusalem, and the even greater reluctance of Hamas to recognize Israel or accept a two-state solution that is not merely a transitional stage. Although it is unlikely that Netanyahu would sign a final, comprehensive agreement, given his ideology and personality, he could make significant concessions to close the gaps. Defense Minister Ehud Barak proclaimed in February 2009 – contrary to Benjamin Netanyahu's view, that the lack of a resolution to the Israeli-Palestinian conflict poses a greater threat to Israel than does Iran. President Obama's visit to Israel and to Ramallah in March 2013, along with Netanyahu's coalition formed in January 2013, which includes center parties, may enable the peace negotiations started in July 2013 with the active involvement of Secretary of State John Kerry, to make significant progress.

Although this book concludes that ideological differences, as well as individual time orientations, played a dominant role in determining the likelihood that a hard-liner would become more accommodating, a sense of deep ideological commitment may be receding as the next generation of leaders in both Palestine and Israel gain greater political power and the founding fathers of the nations age. Therefore, ideologies with aspects that act as obstacles become lesser deterrents to change, as the next generation pays more attention to public opinion. The members of this next generation, represented by both Barak and Netanyahu, are

---

[30] George W. Bush, *Decision Points* (New York: Crown Publishers) 407.

not ideologues (as was Shamir) and are willing to compromise (although to significantly different degrees since they are still influenced by ideology). The Fatah Convention of 2009, in which the first party elections were held in twenty years, also signaled the growing power of the next generation of Palestinian leaders, who have grown up in the occupied territories and are largely pragmatic. This may also point to similar predictions for other younger postcolonial countries, or those that have been formed in the past half century as a result of the disintegration of the Soviet Union.

Although ideology will remain an important but receding factor in future analyses of Israeli-Palestinian relations, the personalities of the leaders may become more dominant features in explanations of the likelihood of compromise and change. Therefore, issues of cognitive rigidity, individual time orientation, risk propensity, and emotional intelligence will play a greater role in differentiating those leaders who are able to listen to and solicit advice, take risks for peace, and negotiate in a sensitive manner with an adversary, from those who succeed only in further alienating an adversary.

As the impact of ideology becomes less dominant, parties will also be even more vulnerable to American and international pressure. Lisa Anderson has suggested that countries dependent on foreign aid and loans can use peace negotiations to attain or retain such aid.[31] They, of course, will also be dependent on security guarantees.

IMPLICATIONS FOR U.S. FOREIGN POLICY

This analysis also has significant implications for U.S. foreign policy. As the world's only superpower, the United States will continue to play a decisive role not only in mediating the conflict between the Israeli government and the Palestinian Authority, but also in engaging in preventive diplomacy to contain conflicts around the world before they erupt into large-scale violence. Analyzing leaders by the criteria used in this book will also help guide policymakers as to the best methods for persuading leaders to end enduring conflicts. President Obama has repeatedly declared his desire to reach an Israeli-Palestinian agreement. Israeli and Palestinian leaders were the first foreign leaders to receive calls from Obama after his first inauguration. Although supporting candidates likely to promote peace can be effective, so can U.S. pressure on even those leaders who seem recalcitrant. In Shamir's case, U.S. pressure on Syria cornered Shamir because Syria agreed to negotiations without preconditions regarding territorial compromise. In Netanyahu's case, in his first term the Unites States would at times challenge specific areas in which Netanyahu maintained that the Palestinians had not met their obligations and tried to use the notion of reciprocity to persuade Netanyahu to implement Israel's obligations. Once a nonideological condition or standard is set,

---

[31] Lisa Anderson, "Peace and Democracy in the Middle East: The Constraints of Soft Budgets," *Journal of International Affairs* (Summer 1995), 25–44.

the United States can pressure even ideologically rigid leaders on that basis. These historical lessons can serve as a guide for the United States in its current dealings with Netanyahu.

However, as has been witnessed during Obama's first term, Netanyahu more readily challenges the United States publicly than did Rabin, Peres, or Barak. He is influenced by the Likud ideology, which emphasizes that Israel faces a hostile world that works against its interests. This part of the ideology has only been reinforced for Netanyahu in the wake of the ousting of President Mubarak and the increasing power of Hezbollah in Lebanon. Netanyahu writes that because the fate of Jews has been entirely determined by others for centuries; people have to learn, he argues, that "you can shape the actions of others to conform to your needs" and not only bend to their will.[32] Therefore, one can expect Netanyahu's resistance to U.S. pressure to continue, although this pressure has resulted in some changes on the part of Netanyahu and will continue to do so. After both Obama and Netanyahu were reelected, their coordination increased, the pressure was more often exerted in private rather than public, they frequently talked on the phone.[33]

It would be fruitful to apply this framework to the foreign policies of other presidents, such as Ronald Reagan's altered position toward the Soviet Union and Richard Nixon's rapprochement with the People's Republic of China. In addition, some similarities might be drawn between George W. Bush and Jimmy Carter, specifically with respect to their common inexperience in foreign policy. Therefore, like Carter, Bush's interpretation of events and policies was more likely to be influenced by the foreign policy advisor who had the most access to him, and ultimately succeeded in persuading him.[34] As President Obama also did not have extensive foreign policy experience, the influence of advisors shaped his strategies in Afghanistan and Pakistan, as well as on the Israeli-Palestinian conflict.

The Middle East is undergoing a dramatic transition. Demonstrations for democracy successfully toppled President Mubarak in Egypt and President Ben Ali of Tunisia after three decades of rule; NATO has successfully helped the rebels topple Muammar al-Qaddafi's regime in Libya; the Palestinian Authority and Hamas have made attempts to reconcile in the wake of popular demands; Jordan has introduced reforms. Other uprisings in the Middle East have been, tragically, less successful: demonstrations in Iran were suppressed, and Yemen and Syria have brutally suppressed the growing uprisings on the part of their citizens, with over 120,000 Syrians killed in these crackdowns. Understanding the political psychology of leaders helps us to understand why some Israeli leaders view these changes as urgent opportunities to pursue peace,

---

[32] Benjamin Netanyahu, *A Place Among the Nations: Israel and the World* (New York: Bantam Books, 1993), 371, 392.

[33] Leslie Susser, "Decision Time," *The Jerusalem Report*, September 23, 2013, 9.

[34] Yael Aronoff, "In Like a Lamb, Out Like a Lion: The Political Conversion of Jimmy Carter," *Political Science Quarterly*, 121, no. 3 (Fall 2006), 425–50.

whereas others question the wisdom of making concessions for peace when peace treaties can be cast away in an instant by a new regime. As the changes in the region remain dramatic yet uncertain, understanding leaders' interpretations of their ambiguous environments is central to how these regional dynamics will continue to be shaped in the future.

This study challenges Realist approaches that generally rely on the more deterministic structural adjustment model of adaptation to environmental change where leaders with the same goals and information are assumed to perceive the environment similarly. Rather, this analysis suggests how a constructivist approach, using political psychology, better captures differences in perceptions of environmental change by explaining how ideology and personal attributes share in the formation of the prism through which the state's interests and position vis-à-vis other players are understood. Changes in the international environment and the balance of power are often ambiguous and not sufficient to explain accommodation with a long-standing enemy. There can be generation-long gaps between these structural changes and cooperation since not all leaders recognize these changes and those who do perceive change at significantly different rates.

In today's world, where asymmetric or civil conflict is becoming increasingly common, violence is more likely to be resolved, not by military victories, but by leaders around the negotiating table. Therefore, it becomes increasingly important to understand the ways in which a leader's perceptions of the enemy can be changed to bring them to the negotiating table. Parties to conflicts are often deeply skeptical about the potential for an "evil" leader to change his or her behavior; this in turn makes targeted assassinations or military interventions aimed at regime change seem like attractive options. These strategies can lead, at best, to temporary respite; at worst, they lead to long, costly wars. At the same time, efforts to engage adversaries are often equally challenging and may not yield higher success rates, if hard-line leaders only perceive engagement as a sign of weakness that can be manipulated. Thus, it is paramount for those interested in resolving a conflict to be able to assess if and how leaders are likely to change. Some types of hard-liners can undergo genuine transformation; others can be pressured to back into at least tactical changes. While the latter process – backing into peace as opposed to pursuing it with born-again zeal – can be drawn out and frustrating, the end result can still begin the momentum for peace. The trick is how to recognize when an enemy begins the transformation from a lion to a lamb, how to recognize the opportunities to coax one's own leaders' changes – and to make sure both sides recognize the transformations in each other at the same time. This study, I hope, will facilitate that process.

APPENDIX A

Summary of Key Factors and Findings

		Ideology					Cognitive Style				
	Adherence	Goals Specific or General?	Is the World With Us, Or Against Us?	Is Time On Israel's Side?	Peace with Palestinians Adds Security?	Time Orientation	Cognitive Flexibility	Risk Propensity	Emotional Intelligence	Advisors	Change
Itzhak Shamir	Very High	Specific	Against	Yes	No	Past	Rigid	Low for Land	Low	Not Diverse	Almost None
Benyamin Netanyahu	High	Specific	Against	Yes	No	Past	Rigid	Low	Low	Not Diverse	Image – No Policy – Some
Ariel Sharon	High to some elements	General	Against, but considered U.S. important	Yes	No	Present	Moderate	High	High	Diverse	Image – No Policy – Some
Ehud Barak	High	General	With, if policies are right	No	Yes	Present	Moderate	High	Low	Diverse	Yes
Itzhak Rabin	High	General	With, if policies are right	No	Yes	Present	Rigid	Low	Moderate	Diverse	Yes
Shimon Peres	High	General	With, if policies are right	No	Yes	Future	Flexible	High	High	Diverse	Yes

APPENDIX B

Interviews Conducted by the Author

Adler, Reuven. August 3, 2010, Tel Aviv, Israel.
Advisor to both Ariel Sharon and Ehud Olmert.

Arad, Eyal. June 29, 2004, Ramat Aviv, Israel.
Political aide to Likud members of Knesset and a minister 1981–1994, former director of Israel's Media Watch 1995–2000, and currently at the Menachem Begin Heritage Center in Jerusalem and unofficial spokesperson for the Jewish Communities in Judea and Samaria.

Ayalon, Ami. August 4, 2010, Herzliya, Israel, and June 24, 2012, Har Carmel, Israel.
Director of the Shin Bet 1996–2000, Minister Without Portfolio September 2007–March 2009. One of the leaders of Blue White Future Organization for promoting two-state solution.

Bar Ilan, David. June 9, 1998, Jerusalem, Israel.
Communications director in the first Netanyahu government. Began working with Netanyahu in 1983.

Barnea, Nahum. August 5, 2010, Jerusalem, Israel.
Staff writer for the leading Israeli newspaper, *Yedioth Achronot*, who has extensively covered and interviewed all the prime ministers and won the Israel Prize in 2007 for his journalism.

Barak, Ehud. June 28, 2004, Tel Aviv, Israel.
Prime minister 1999–2001. See chapter devoted to him.

Beilin, Yossi. PhD. August 12, 1997, June 29, 2004, and July 26, 2007, Tel Aviv, Israel.
Architect of the Oslo peace process while serving as the deputy foreign minister under Shimon Peres in the second government led by Yitzhak

Rabin. He also held ministerial positions in the governments led by Peres and Barak, including minister of justice (1999–2001). Beilin served in the Knesset for eleven years representing Labor and later led the Social Democratic Israel (Yahad, the former Meretz) before retiring from politics.

Ben-Ami, Shlomo. Ph.D. July 4, 2004, and July 12, 2007, Ramat Aviv, Israel.
Former professor of history, Tel Aviv University, Israel ambassador to Spain (1987–1991). Minister of internal security (1991–2001) and minister of foreign affairs (2000–2001). Internal Labor Party rival of Peres who, unlike Barak, refused to serve in the Sharon-led government. Resigned from the Knesset in August 2002 and backed Meretz in the 2009 Knesset election.

Ben Simon, Daniel. August 3, 2010, Yaffo, Israel.
Labor Party Knesset member 2009–2011.

Brom, Shlomo. June 21, 2004, Tel Aviv, and June 11, 2012, Karme Yosef, Israel.
From 1990 to 1998 he was deputy chief and then chief of Strategic Planning Division of the Israeli Defense Forces. In 2000, he was deputy to the national security advisor. On the faculty of Tel Aviv University.

Chazan, Naomi. PhD. July 17, 2007, Jerusalem, Israel.
Professor and former head of the Truman Institute for the Advancement of Peace at the Hebrew University of Jerusalem. Member of the Knesset representing Meretz (1992–2003) and deputy speaker of the Knesset (1996–1999).

Dan, Uri. July 1, 2004, Yaffo, Israel.
Journalist, member of Sharon's staff during the war of 1973. Close friend of Sharon.

Eiland, Giora. June 21, 2012, Ramat Aviv, Israel.
Former general, head of the National Security Council under Prime Minister Ariel Sharon. Took party in Israeli-Palestinian negotiations in 2001. Currently in the Institute for National Security Studies.

Eiran, Amos. June 23, 1998, Tel Aviv, Israel.
Spent five years with Rabin in the United States when Rabin was Israeli ambassador to the United States, was the director general of the Prime Minister's Office under Rabin 1974–1977, and was a close friend of Rabin.

Enderlin, Charles. June 15, 2004, Jerusalem, Israel.
Journalist, Middle East correspondent for France 2 Television, author of *Shattered Dreams* and a documentary film by the same name.

Erekat, Saeb. PhD. July 20, 2007, Jericho, the Palestinian Territories.
Chief of the PLO steering and monitoring committee 1995–2011, chief Palestinian negotiator with Israel from 1993 to the present, including the Oslo Accords.

Fares, Kadura (Qadura). July 3, 2004, East Jerusalem, Israel.
Minister in the Palestinian Authority, member of the Palestinian Legislative Council (Parliament), close friend and advisor to Marwan Barghouti.

Frankenthal, Itzhak. August 5, 2010, Jerusalem, Israel.
Chairman of the Israeli-Palestinian Parents Circle and executive director and founder of Fund for Reconciliation, Tolerance and Peace.

Gazit, Shlomo. June 14, 2004, Israel, and June 16, 2012, Tel Aviv, Israel.
Former head of military intelligence, senior research fellow at the Jafee Center at Tel Aviv University and the Institute of National Security Studies.

Gil, Avi. June 2, 1998, and June 16, 2004, Tel Aviv, Israel.
Deputy director of the Peres Center for Peace and Peres's aide for many years since 1998.

Gissin, Raanan. June 20, 2004, Tel Aviv, Israel.
Senior advisor to Prime Minister Ariel Sharon. He participated in the negotiations that led to the Wye Agreement. He was also senior public affairs and media advisor to Sharon when Sharon was foreign minister.

Gold, Dore. June 2, 1999, New York.
President of the Jerusalem Center for Public Affairs. Worked closely with Netanyahu from 1991 as his main policy advisor until he became ambassador to the United Nations, 1997–1999. He was present at the Wye negotiations.

Goren, Aliza. June 26, 1998, Mevasseret, Israel.
Worked in the Prime Minister's Office in Rabin's first term as prime minister and was his spokesperson during his second term. She was Peres's spokesperson while he was prime minister in 1995 and works in his Peres Center for Peace.

Grinstein, Gidi. July 2, 2004, Tel Aviv, and August 4, 2010, Tel Aviv, Israel.
Secretary for Barak's delegation at Camp David.

Haber, Eitan. July 27, 1997, Tel Aviv, Israel; July 12, 1997 and June 10, 1998, Ramat Gan, Israel.
Chief of staff and speechwriter during Rabin government. He was close to Rabin for thirty-eight years and was his right-hand man from 1984 until Rabin's assassination.

Halevy, Efraim. August 6, 2013, Ramat Aviv, Israel.
Worked in the Mossad for forty years and served as its director 1998–2002. He served as the head of Israel's National Security Council 2002–2003.

Harel, Amos. August 4, 2010, Herzliya, and June 17, 2012, Hod Hasharon, Israel.
Correspondent for *Haaretz*.

Harel, Yehuda. May 26, 1998, Jerusalem, Israel.
Knesset member of the Third Way Party.

Hirschfeld, Yair. May 11, 1997, Ramat Yishai, Israel, and June 20, 2004, Jerusalem, Israel.
Co-director of Economic Cooperation Council, professor of history at Haifa University, and initiator of and participant in Oslo negotiations.

Isaacharov, Avi. June 23, 2004, Jerusalem, and August 3, 2010, Tel Aviv, Israel.
Correspondent for *Haaretz*.

Kasher, Assa. PhD. August 4, 2010, Ramat Gan, and June 11, 2012, Jerusalem, Israel.
Philosopher, linguist, author of Israel Defense Force Code of Conduct, and recipient of the Israel Prize (2000).

Kim, Hannah. May 17, 1998, phone interview.
Journalist for the Israeli newspaper *Ha'aretz*.

Klein-Halevi, Yossi. May 20, 1998, phone interview.
Wrote article on the influence of Benjamin Netanyahu's father on him for the *Jerusalem Report* for which he is a senior writer. Contributes to the *Jerusalem Post*, the *New York Times*, the *Los Angeles Times*, and the *Washington Post*, and is contributing editor of *The New Republic*.

Kleiner, Michael. June 30, 2008, Jerusalem, Israel.
Gesher Knesset member and chair of the Land of Israel Front.

Landau, Eli. June 2004, Herzliya, Israel.
Landau knew Ariel Sharon for almost forty years. He worked with him when Sharon was defense minister and minister of agriculture.

Landau, Uzi. July 5, 2007, Raanana, Israel.
Minister of national infrastructure (Yisrael Beiteinu), former minister of internal security (Likud, 2001–2003).

Meidan-Shani, Pini. June 21, 2004, Tel Aviv, Israel.
Former officer of the Institute for Intelligence and Special Roles (Mossad).

Meridor, Dan. June 18, 1998, Jerusalem, Israel; June 29, 1998, Jerusalem, Israel; and June 30, 2004, Tel Aviv, Israel.
Likud Knesset member. Cabinet secretary 1981–1984, minister of justice 1988–1990 under Yitzhak Shamir, finance minister under Benjamin Netanyahu 1996–1997, deputy prime minister of intelligence and atomic energy 2009–2013.

Mozgovaya, Natasha. January 31, 2013, East Lansing, Michigan.
Chief U.S. correspondent for *Haaretz* 2008–2013. Reporter for *Yedioth Ahronot* 2001–2008.

Nathanson, Roby. May 30, 2006, Banff, AB, Canada, and July 2010, Jerusalem, Israel.

Met Barak in 1997, advised him on his campaign in 1999 on economic and social issues, and now directs the Israeli Institute for Economic and Social Research.

Noybach, Amnon. June 14, 1998, Jerusalem, Israel.

One of Peres's economic advisors and member of the team of nine that advised Peres during his first terms as prime minister.

Nusiebah, Sari. PhD. June 30, 2004, East Jerusalem, Israel.

President of Al-Kuds University. With Ami Ayalon, co-leader of The People's Voice initiative for peace between Israel and Palestine.

Oren, Amir. August 2, 2010. Phone interview.

Correspondent for *Haaretz*.

Pattir, Dan. May 28, 1998, Ramat Aviv, Israel.

Counselor for press and information in the Israeli embassy in the United States 1968–1969 when Rabin was ambassador to the United States. He was his press secretary when Rabin became prime minister in 1974 and worked with him on a daily basis in his first administration until May 1977. Pattir covered military affairs for the paper *Davar* when Rabin was chief of staff. He remained in contact with Rabin after he stopped working for him as they were neighbors.

Peleg, Yisrael. June 28, 1998, Tel Aviv, Israel.

Knew Peres since 1945; was an advisor and employee of Peres for many years.

Peres, Shimon. August 5, 1997; June 19, 1998; and June 27, 2004, Tel Aviv, Israel.

Prime minister 1984–1986, 1995–1996; finance minister 1989–1990; minister for regional co-operation 1999–2000; foreign minister 2001–2002; president 2007–2014.

Pundak, Ron. March 30, 1997, and June 29, 2004, Jerusalem, Israel.

Co-director, Economic Cooperation Council; participant in Oslo negotiations.

Rabin, Leah. July 2, 1997, and July 7, 1998, Ramat Gan, Israel.

Widow of Prime Minister Yitzhak Rabin.

Rabin-Yaacov, Rahel. July 7, 1998, Kibbutz Menarah, Israel.

Yitzhak Rabin's sister and only sibling.

Rabinovitch, Itamar. May 25, 1997, Ramat Gan, Israel.

Israeli ambassador to the United States and chief negotiator with Syria 1992–1996. Professor and former president of Tel Aviv University 1999-2007. He is president of the Israel Institute, professor emeritus of Middle Eastern History of Tel Aviv University, distinguished global professor at NYU, and a distinguished fellow at the Brookings Institution.

Ramon, Haim. June 23, 1998, Jerusalem, Israel.
Knesset member (1983–2009), minister of health (1992–1996), minister of internal affairs (1995–1996, 2000–2001), minister without portfolio (2005); joined Kadima and became minister of justice (2006) and vice premier and minister in Premier Olmert's office (2007–2009).

Rivlin, Reuven July 26, 2007, Jerusalem, Israel.
Knesset member (1988–1992, 1996–present). Speaker of the Knesset (Likud) 2003–2006 and 2009–2013. Minister of communications (2002–2007).

Ross, Dennis. August 6, 1999, Washington, DC.
State Department's special coordinator for the Middle East during the Clinton administration and Netanyahu's tenure as prime minister, and National Security Council member during Netanyahu's second term.

Rubinstein, Elyakim. July 9, 1998, and June 23, 2004, Jerusalem, Israel.
Israeli legal expert at Camp David 1977–1981, cabinet secretary 1991–1993; led the Israeli negotiating team for the Washington Talks under Rabin; attorney general in the Netanyahu, Barak, and Sharon governments 1997–2004. Judge on the Supreme Court.

Sarid, Yossi. May 26, 1998, Jerusalem, Israel, and July 5, 1998, Tel Aviv, Israel.
Member of Knesset, formerly of the Labor Party and then of the Meretz Party. Minister of environment in the Rabin government and minister of education and culture in the Barak government. Became close to Rabin in the last couple years of his life.

Savir, Uri. July 15, 1998, Tel Aviv, Israel.
Former director general of the Foreign Office under Peres; director of the Peres Institute for Peace and negotiator at Oslo.

Shamir, Yitzhak. July 5, 1998, Tel Aviv, Israel.
Prime minister 1983–1984, 1986–1992, foreign minister 1981–1983, 1984–1986.

Shelev, Hemi. May 24, 1998, Jerusalem, Israel.
Journalist for the newspaper *Ma'ariv*.

Sher, Gilead. June 20, 2004, Jerusalem.
Chief of staff and policy coordinator to Prime Minister Ehud Barak and co-chief negotiator (1999–2001), including Camp David and Taba. Sher was a close confidant and advisor to Barak.

Sheves, Shimon. July 1, 1998, Tel Aviv, Israel.
Knew Rabin from 1974 and worked for him from 1984 until Rabin's assassination in 1995. He was Rabin's personal assistant 1985–1992 and director general of the Prime Minister's Office 1991–1995.

Shochat, Avraham. July 1, 1998, Jerusalem, Israel.

Labor Party Knesset member and minister of treasury in the last Rabin and Peres governments, as well as in the Barak government.

Shuval, Zalmon. July 2, 2004, Israel.

Member of the Knesset (1970–1981, 1988–1990), deputy minister of foreign affairs under Moshe Dayan, ambassador to the United States (1990–1993, 1998–2000).

Singer, Joel. August 6, 1999, and August 20, 1999, Washington DC.

Worked in the Israeli Defense Ministry under Rabin and Peres and negotiated on behalf of Israel in Oslo.

Weisglass, Dov. July 4, 2004, Jerusalem, and August 6, 2010, Ramat Hasharon.

Director of Sharon's bureau 2001–2005. Previously Sharon's lawyer for twenty-four years.

Wilf, Einat. June 18, 2012, Jerusalem.

Member of Knesset for the Labor Party 2010–2011 and for the Independence Party 2011–2013.

Interview with Netanyahu family member who wanted to remain anonymous, 1998, Jerusalem.

Interview with senior civil servant in Shamir's government who met with him at least once a week but wanted to remain anonymous, May 5, 2010, Toronto.

Bibliography

Books, Journals, and News Magazines

Abbas, M. (1995). *Through secret channels*. Reading, UK: Garnet Publishing Ltd.

Abudullah II, al Hussein. (2011). *Our last best chance: The pursuit of peace in a time of peril*. New York: Viking.

Aggestam, K. (1996). Two-track diplomacy: Negotiations between Israel and the PLO through open and secret channels. *Davis Papers on Israel's Foreign Policy No. 53*. Jerusalem: The Leonard Davis Institute of International Relations.

Ajzen, I., & Fishbein, M. (1980). *Understanding attitudes and predicting social behavior*. Englewood Cliffs, NJ: Prentice Hall.

Albright, M. (2003). *Madeleine Albright: Madam Secretary*. New York: Miramax Books, 2003.

Allison, G. T. (1971). *Essence of decision: Explaining the Cuban missile crisis*. New York: HarperCollins.

Allison, G. T., & Halperin, M. H. (1972). Bureaucratic politics: A paradigm and some policy implications. *World Politics 24* (Issue Supplement: Theory and Policy in International Relations, spring), 66, 76.

Anderson, L. (1995). Peace and democracy in the Middle East: The constraints of soft budgets. *Journal of International Affairs 49*(1), 25–45.

Arens, M. (1995). *Broken covenant*. New York: Simon & Schuster.

Arian, A. (1995). *Security threatened: Surveying Israeli opinion on peace and war*. Cambridge: Cambridge University Press.

Arian, A. (1999). *Israeli public opinion on national security 1999*. Tel Aviv: Jaffee Center for Strategic Studies.

Arian, A., & Shamir, M. (1995). Two reversals: Why 1992 was not 1977. In A. Arian & M. Shamir (Eds.), *The elections in Israel 1992*. Albany: State University of New York Press.

Aronoff, M. J. (1989). *Israeli visions and divisions: Cultural change and political conflict*. New Brunswick, NJ: Transaction Publishers.

Aronoff, M. J. (1993). *Power and ritual in the Israel Labor Party: A study in political anthropology* (rev. ed.). London: M. E. Sharpe.

Aronoff, M. J. (2001, May). Temporal and spatial dimensions of contested Israeli nationhood. Presented at the Annual Association of Israel Studies Conference, Washington DC.

Aronoff, M. J. (2009). Camp David Rashomon: Contested interpretations of the Israel/ Palestine peace process. *Political Science Quarterly 124*(1), 143–67.

Aronoff, M. J. (2010). The politics of collective identity: Contested Israeli nationalisms. In J. Resefeld (Ed.), *Terrorism, identity, and legitimacy* (pp. 168–87). Oxford: Routledge.

Aronoff, M. J. (2001). Political culture. In *International encyclopedia of the social and behavior sciences.* N. J. Smelser and P. B. Baltes (Eds.), Oxford, UK: Elsevier Science, Ltd.

Aronoff, M. J., & Aronoff, Y. S. (1996). Explaining domestic influences on current Israeli foreign policy: The peace negotiations. *The Brown Journal of World Affairs* 3(Summer/Fall), 83–101.

Aronoff, M. J., & Aronoff, Y. S. (1998). Domestic determinants of Israeli foreign policy: The peace process from the Declaration of Principles to the Oslo II Interim Agreement. In R. O. Freedman (Ed.), *The Middle East and the peace process: The impact of the Oslo Accords.* Gainesville: University Press of Florida.

Aronoff, M. J., & Kubik, J. (2013). *Anthropology & political science: A convergent approach.* New York: Berghahn Books.

Aronoff, Y. S. (2001). When and why do hardliners become soft? An examination of Israeli Prime Ministers Shamir, Rabin, Peres, and Netanyahu. In O. Feldman & L. O. Valenty (Eds.), *Profiling political leaders: Cross-cultural studies of personality and behavior.* London: Praeger.

Aronoff, Y. S. (2006). In like a lamb, out like a lion: The political conversion of Jimmy Carter. *Political Science Quarterly 121*(3), 425–429.

Aronoff, Y. S. (2009). When do hawks become peacemakers? A comparison of two Israeli prime ministers. *Israel Studies Forum 24*(1), 39–61.

Aronoff, Y. S. (2010). From warfare to withdrawal: The legacy of Ariel Sharon. *Israel Studies, 15*(2), 149–72.

Aronoff, Y. S. (2013) Predicting peace: The contingent nature of leadership and domestic politics in Israel. In H. Spruyt, M. F. Elman, & O. Haklai (Eds.), *Democracy and conflict resolution: The dilemmas of Israel's peacemaking.* Syracuse, NY: Syracuse University Press.

Ashrawi, H. (1995). *This side of peace: A personal account.* New York: Simon & Schuster.

Astorino-Courois, A. (1995). The cognitive structure of decision making and the course of Arab-Israeli relations, 1970–1978. *Journal of Conflict Resolution 39*(3), 419–438.

Auerbach, Y. (1986). Turning-point decisions: A cognitive-dissonance analysis of conflict reduction in Israel–West German relations. *Political Psychology 7*, 533–550.

Auerbach, Y. (1995). Yitzhak Rabin: Portrait of a leader. In D. J. Elazar & S. Sandler (Eds.), *Israel at the polls 1992* (pp. 283–320). Lanham, MD: Rowman & Littlefield Publishers, Inc.

Axelrod, R. (Ed.). (1976). *Structure of decision: The cognitive maps of political elites.* Princeton, NJ: Princeton University Press.

Baker, J. A. (1995). *The politics of diplomacy: Revolution, war and peace 1989–1992.* New York: G. P. Putnam's Sons.

Barak, E. (2001). Special policy forum report: Israel's search for peace security: Lessons of the past, options for the future. *The Washington Institute for Near East Policy.* Peace Watch #338, July 24.

Barber, J. D. (1977). *Presidential character: Predicting performance in the white house* (2nd ed.). Englewood Cliffs, NJ: Prentice Hall.

Barnea, N. (1999). *Yemey Netanyahu* [Bibi Time: Political Columns, 1993–1999]. Tel Aviv: Lezmorah-Beitan.

Bar-Siman-Tov, Y. (1994). *Israel and the peace process 1977–1982.* Albany: State University of New York Press.

Beilin, Y. (1997). *Lagaat BeShalom* [Touching Peace]. Tel Aviv: Miskal-Yedioth Ahronoth Books and Chemed Books.

Bell, R. (1994). World War II in a Dalmatian village: Atrocity and memory. Paper presented at the Center for Historical Analysis, at Rutgers University, New Brunswick, NJ.

Bem, D. J. (1972). Self perception theory. In L. Berkowitz (Ed.), *Advances in experimental social psychology* (Vol. 6) (pp. 1–62). New York: Academic Press.

Bem, D. J. (1978). Self perception theory. In L. Berkowitz (Ed.), *Cognitive theories in social psychology.* San Francisco, CA: Academic Press.

Bem, D. J., & Funder, D. C. (1978). Predicting more of the people more of the time: Assessing the personality of situations. *Psychological Review 85,* 485–501.

Ben-Ami, S. (2006). *Scars of war, wounds of peace: The Israeli-Arab tragedy.* New York: Oxford University Press.

Ben-Gurion, D. (1971). *Israel: A personal history* New York: Funk & Wagnalls, Inc.

Bennett, A., & Alexander, G. L. (1997, October). Process tracing in case study research. Paper presented at the MacArthur Foundation Workshop on Case Study Methods, at the Belfer Center for Science and International Affairs (BCSIA), Harvard University, Boston.

Ben-Porat, Y. (1981). *Dialogues.* Jerusalem: Edanim Publishers.

Ben-Yehuda, H. (1997). Attitude change and policy transformation: Yitzhak Rabin and the Palestinian question, 1967–95. *Israel Affairs 3*(3), 201–224.

Benziman, U. (1985). *Sharon: An Israeli Caesar.* New York: Adama Books.

Berger, P. L., & Luckmann, T. (1967). *The social construction of reality.* Garden City, NY: Anchor.

Betts, R. K. (1982). *Surprise attack: Lessons for defense planning.* Washington DC: The Brookings Institution.

Betts, R. K. (1991). *Soldiers, statesmen, and Cold War crises.* New York: Columbia University Press.

Boniwell, I., & Zimbardo, P. (2003). Time to find the right balance. *The Psychologist* 16(3), 129–131.

Boniwell, I., & Zimbardo, P. (2004). Balancing time perspective in pursuit of optimal functioning. In P. Linley & S. Joseph (Eds.), *Positive psychology in practice.* Hoboken, NJ: John Wiley & Sons, Inc.

Breslauer, G. W., & Tetlock, P. (Eds.). (1991). *Learning in U.S. and Soviet foreign policy.* Boulder, CO: Westview Press.

Burke, J. P., & Greenstein, F. I. (1991). *How presidents test reality.* New York: Russell Sage Foundation.

Burton, J. W. (1984). *Global conflict: The domestic sources of international crisis.* College Park, MD: The Center for International Development.

Bush, G. W. (2010). *Decision points.* New York: Crown Publishers.

Byman, D. L., & Pollack, K. M. (2001). Let us now praise great men: Bringing the statesman back in. *International Security 25*(4), 107–146.

Caspit, B., & Kfir, I. (1998). *Netanyahu: The road to power.* Secaucus, NJ: Carol Publishing Group.

Cetinyan, R., & Stein, A. (1999, September). Extremists and peace agreements in the Middle East. Paper presented at the Annual Meeting of the American Political Science Association, Atlanta, GA.

Chaiken, S., & Stangor, C. (1987). Attitudes and attitude change. *Annual Review of Psychology 38*, 944–59.

Checkel, J. T. (1997). *Ideas and international political change: Soviet/Russian behavior and the end of the Cold War.* New Haven, CT: Yale University Press.

Clinton, W. (2004). *My life.* New York: Knopf Publishing Group.

Cohen, M. (1987). *Zion and state: Nation, class and the shaping of modern Israel.* New York: Basil and Blackwell.

Craig, G. A., & George, A. L. (1990). *Force and statecraft: Diplomatic problems of our time* (2nd ed.). New York: Oxford University Press.

Crichlow, S. (1998). Idealism or pragmatism? An operational code analysis of Yitzhak Rabin and Shimon Peres. *Political Psychology 19*(4), 683–706.

Dan, U. (1987). *Blood libel.* New York: Simon & Shuster.

Dan, U. (1989). Foreword. In A. Sharon, *Warrior: An autobiography.* New York: Simon & Schuster.

Dan, U. (2006). *Ariel Sharon: An intimate portrait.* New York: Palgrave.

Dayan, M. (1981). *Breakthrough: A personal account of the Egypt-Israel peace negotiations.* London: Weidenfeld and Nicolson.

Dowty, A. (1998). Zionism's greatest conceit. *Israel Studies 3*, 11–23.

Dowty, A. (2001). *A Jewish state: A century later.* Berkeley, CA: University of California Press.

Dowty, A. (2008). *Israel/Palestine* (2nd ed.). Cambridge: Polity Press.

Druckman, D., & Zechmeister, K. (1970). Conflict of interest and value dissensus. *Human Relations 23*, 449–66.

Eldad, I. (1971). *The Jewish revolution: Jewish statehood.* New York: Shengold Publishers, Inc.

Elman, M. F., O. Haklai, H. Spruyt. (Eds.). (2013). Democracy and Conflict Resolution: the Dilemmas of Israel's Peacemaking. Syracuse, NY: Syracuse University Press.

Elster, J. (Ed.). (1986). *Rational choice.* New York: New York University Press.

Etheredge, S. L. (1985). *Can governments learn? American foreign policy and Central American revolutions.* New York: Pergamon Press.

Evans, P. B., Jacobson, H. K., & Putnam, R. D. (1993). *Double edged diplomacy: International bargaining and domestic politics.* Los Angeles: University of California Press.

Eytan, F. (2006). *Sharon: A life in times of turmoil.* Paris: Studio 9 Books.

Farnham, B. R. (1990). Political cognition and decision-making. *Political Psychology 2*(1), 83–112.

Farnham, B. R. (1997). *Roosevelt and the Munich crisis: A study of political decision-making.* Princeton, NJ: Princeton University Press.

Finlay, D. J., Holsti, O. R., & Fagen, R. R. (1967). *Enemies in politics.* Chicago: Rand McNally & Company.

Flamhaft, Z. (1996). *Israel on the road to peace.* Boulder, CO: Westview Press.

Fox, W. T. R. (1970). The causes of peace and conditions of war. *The Annals of the American Academy of Political and Social Science 392*, 1–13.

Frankel, G. (1996). *Beyond the promised land: Jews and Arabs on the hard road to a new Israel.* New York: Simon & Schuster.

Freedman, R. O. (2007). The Bush Administration and the Arab-Israeli conflict. In David W. Lesch (Ed.), *The Middle East and the United States: A historical and political reassessment.* Boulder, CO: Westview Press.

Freedman, R. O. (2009). Israel and the United States. In Robert O. Freedman (Ed.), *Contemporary Israel: Domestic politics, foreign policy, and security challenges.* Boulder, CO: Westview Press.

Freedman, R. O. (Ed.). (2012). *Israel and the United States: Six decades of US-Israeli relations* Boulder, CO: Westview Press.

Frenkel-Brunswick, E. (1950). Dynamic and cognitive personality organization as seen through the interviews. In T. W. Adorno, et al. (Eds.), *The authoritarian personality.* New York: Harper.

Gart, M. J. (1989, April 17). Never! Never! Never! *Time, 133*(16), 40–4.

Gates, R. M. (1996). *From the shadows.* New York: Simon & Schuster.

Geertz, C. (1964). Ideology as a cultural system. In D. E. Apter (Ed.), *Ideology and discontent* (pp. 47–75). New York: The Free Press of Glencoe.

Geertz, C. (1973). *The interpretation of cultures.* New York: Basic Books.

Gen-Ari, E., & Bilu, Y. (Eds.). (1997). *Space and place in contemporary Israeli discourse and experience.* Albany: State University of New York Press.

George, A. L. (1959). Quantitative and qualitative approaches to content analysis. In I.deS. Pool (Ed.), *Trends in content analysis.* Urbana: University of Illinois Press.

George, A. L. (1967). *The "operational code": A neglected approach to the study of political leaders and decision-making.* Santa Monica: The RAND Corporation.

George, A. L. (1979). The causal nexus between cognitive beliefs and decision making behavior: The "operational code." In L. Falkowski (Ed.), *Psychological models in international politics.* Boulder, CO: Westview Press.

George, A. L. (1980). *Presidential decisionmaking in foreign policy: The effective use of information and advice.* Boulder, CO: Westview Press.

George, A. L. (1991). *Forceful persuasion: Coercive diplomacy as an alternative to war.* Washington DC: United States Institute of Peace Press.

George, A. L. (2000). Strategies for preventative diplomacy and conflict resolution: Scholarship for policymaking. *Political Science & Politics 33*(1), 15–19.

George, A. L. (2002). The need for influence theory and actor-specific behavioral models of adversaries. In B. R. Schneider & J. M. Post (Eds.) *Know thy enemy: Profiles of adversary leaders and their strategic cultures.* Maxwell Air Force Base, AL: United States Air Force Counterproliferation Center.

Goertz, G., & Diehl, P. (1993). Enduring rivalries: Theoretical constructs and empirical patterns. *International Studies Quarterly 37*, 147–71.

Golan, G. (1992). Arab-Israeli peace negotiations: An Israeli view. In S. L. Spiegel (Ed.), *The Arab-Israeli search for peace.* Boulder, CO: Lynne Rienner.

Goleman, D. (1995). *Emotional intelligence: Why it can matter more than IQ.* New York: Bantam Books.

Goodman, H. (2000, December 18). Barak's downfall. *The Jerusalem Report.*

Gorenberg, G. (2003, December 29). The cracking of the Israeli right. *The Jerusalem Report.* LexisNexis Academic. Web. Date accessed: 2013/12/09.

Greenstein, F. I. (1967). The impact of personality on politics: An attempt to clear away underbrush. *The American Political Science Review 61*(3), 634, 639.

Greenstein, F. I. (1975). *Personality & politics: Problems of evidence, inference, and conceptualization.* New York: Norton.

Greenstein, F. I. (1992). Can personality and politics be studied systematically? *Political Psychology 13*(1), 105–128.

Greenstein, F. I. (2001). George W. Bush and the ghosts of presidents past. *PS: Political Science and Politics 34*(1), 77–80.

Greenstein, F. I. (2009). *The presidential difference: Leadership style from FDR to Barack Obama* (3rd ed.). New York: The Free Press.

Greenstein, F. I., & J. P. Bruke. (1989). *How presidents test reality: Decisions on Vietnam, 1954 and 1965.* New York: Russell Sage Foundation.

Greenstein, F. I., & R. H. Immerman. (1991). History as Rashamon: Eisenhower, Kennedy and Vietnam. Unpublished paper.

Greenstein, F. I., & M. Lerner. (1971). *A source book for the study of personality and politics.* Chicago: Markham Publishing Company.

Haber, E., Schiff, Z., & Yaari, E. (1979). *The year of the dove.* New York: Bantam.

Haberman, C. (2001, March 25). Dennis Ross's exit interview. *New York Times Magazine.*

Halevy, E. (2006). *Understanding the Middle East: A view from inside the Mossad.* Washington, DC: Washington Institute for Near East Policy.

Halperin, M. H. (1970). War termination as a problem in civil-military relations. *The Annals of the American Academy of Political and Social Science 392*, 86–95.

Halperin, M. H. (1974). *Bureaucratic politics & foreign policy.* Washington DC: The Brookings Institution.

Halperin, M. H. (1977). The "Operational Code" as an Approach to the Analysis of Belief Systems. Final Report to the National Science Foundation Grant No. SOC75-15368, December.

Handelman, D., & Shamgar-Handelman, L. (1997). The presence of absence: The memorialism of national death in Israel. In E. Gen-Ari & Y. Bilu (Eds.), *Space and place in contemporary Israeli discourse and experience.* Albany: State University of New York Press.

Heller, J. (1995). *The Stern Gang: Ideology, politics and terror, 1940–1949.* London: Frank Cass.

Hermann, M. G. (1987). *Handbook for assessing personal characteristics and foreign policy orientations of political leaders.* Columbus, OH: Mershon Center, Ohio State University.

Hermann, M. G. (1995). Leaders, leadership, and flexibility: Influences on heads of government as negotiators and mediators. *ANNALS AAPSS 542*, 152.

Hermann, M. G., & Milburn, T. W. (1977). *A psychological examination of political leaders.* New York: The Free Press.

Holsti, O. (1970). The "Operational Code" approach to the study of political leaders: John Foster Dulles' philosophical and instrumental beliefs. *Canadian Journal of Political Science 3*, 123–57.

Hornik, J., & Zakay, D. (1996). Psychological time: The case of time and consumer behavior. *Time and Society 5*, 384.

Horovitz, D. (Ed.). (1996). *Yitzhak Rabin: Soldier of peace.* London: Peter Halban Publishers.

Horovitz, D. (1993, November 19). [If you're going to make peace, then now]. *Al Hamishmar.*

Ikle, F. C. (1971). *Every war must end.* New York: Columbia University Press.

Inbar, E. (1991). *War and peace in Israeli politics: Labor Party positions on national security*. Boulder, CO: Lynne Rienner.

Inbar, E. (1999). *Rabin and Israel's national security*. Baltimore, MD: The Johns Hopkins University Press.

Indyk, M. (2009). *Innocent abroad: An intimate account of American peace diplomacy in the Middle East*. New York: Simon & Schuster.

Isaac, R. J. (1976). *Israel divided: Ideological politics in the Jewish state*. Baltimore, MD: The Johns Hopkins University Press.

Isaac, R. J. (1981). *Party and Politics in Israel: Three visions of a Jewish state*. New York: Longman.

Israel Ministry of Foreign Affairs. (1990, June 11). *Basic policy guidelines for Israel's twenty-fourth government*. Jerusalem.

Israel Ministry of Foreign Affairs. (1992, July 13). *Basic policy guidelines for the Rabin government*. Jerusalem.

Israel's future: The time factor: A debate between Efraim Inbar and Ian S. Lustick. *Israel Studies Forum* 23(1), 3–14.

Janis, I. L. (1982). *Groupthink: Psychological studies of policy decisions and fiascoes*. Boston: Houghton Mifflin.

Jervis, R. (1970). *The logic of images in international relations*. Princeton, NJ: Princeton University Press.

Jervis, R. (1976). *Perception and misperception in international politics*. Princeton, NJ: Princeton University Press.

Jervis, R. (1980). Political decision making: Recent contributions. *Political Psychology* 2, 86–101.

Jervis, R. (1986). Cognition and political behavior. In R. R. Lau & D. O. Sears (Eds.), *Political cognition*. Hillsdale, NJ: Lawrence Erlbaum Associates.

Jervis, R. (1994). Ideas and foreign policy. *APSA Roundtable Memo*.

Jervis, R. (1997) *System effects: Complexity in political and social life*. Princeton, NJ: Princeton University Press.

Katzenstein, J. P. (1996). *Cultural norms and national security: Police and military in postwar Japan*. Ithaca, NY: Cornell University Press.

Katzenstein, L. (1997). Change, myth, and the reunification of China. In V. Hudson (Ed.), *Culture and foreign policy*. Boulder, CO: Lynne Rienner.

Kaufman, C. D. (1994). Out of the lab and into the archives: A method for testing psychological explanations of political decision making. *International Studies Quarterly* 38, 557–86.

Kecskemeti, P. (1958). *Strategic surrender: The politics of victory and defeat*. Stanford, CA: Stanford University Press.

Kecskemeti, P. (1970). Political rationality in ending war. *The Annals of the American Academy of Political and Social Science* 392, 105–15.

Kegley, C. W., Jr. & Raymond, G. A. (1999). *How nations make peace*. New York: St. Martin's Press.

Kelman, H. C. (1958). Compliance, identification and internationalization: Three processes of attitude change. *Journal of Conflict Resolution* 2, 51–60.

Keren, M. (1995). *Professionals against populism: The Peres government and democracy*. Albany: State University of New York Press.

Kfir, I. (1999). *Barak: HaBiographie [Barak: The biography]*. Tel Aviv, Israel: Alfah Communications.

Kimhi, S. (2001). Benjamin Netanyahu: A psychological profile. In O. Feldman & L. Valenty (Eds.), *Profiling political leaders: Cross-cultural studies of personality and behavior*. London: Praeger.

King, G., Keohane, R. O., & Verba, S. (1994). *Designing social inquiry: Scientific inference in qualitative research*. Princeton, NJ: Princeton University Press.

Kissinger, H. (1979). *White house years*. Boston: Little, Brown.

Kissinger, H. (1982). *Years of upheaval*. Boston: Little, Brown.

Kissinger, H. (1994). *Diplomacy*. New York: Simon & Schuster.

Klein, M. (2007). *A possible peace between Israel and Palestine: An insider's account of the Geneva Initiative*. New York: Columbia University Press.

Klieman, A. S. (1988). Statecraft in the dark: Israel's practice of quiet diplomacy. *The Jerusalem Post*.

Klieman, A. S. (1990). *Israel & the world after 40 years*. Washington, DC: Pergamon-Brassey's International Defense Publishers, Inc.

Klieman, A. S. (2005). Israeli negotiating culture. In T. C. Wittes (Ed.), *How Israelis and Palestinians negotiate: A cross-cultural analysis of the Oslo peace process*. Washington DC: United States Institute of Peace Press.

Klingberg, F. L. (1966). Predicting the termination of war: Battle casualties and population losses. *Journal of Conflict Resolution 10*(2), 129–71.

Kluckhohn, F. R., & Strodtbeck, F. L. (1961). *Variations in value orientations*. Westport, CT: Greenwood Press Publishers.

Kruglanski, A. W., & Webster, D. M. (1996). Motivated closing of the mind: "Seizing" and "freezing." *Psychological Review 103*(2), 263–83.

Kurtzer, D. (2012). *Pathways to peace: America and the Arab-Israeli conflict*. New York: Palgrave Macmillan.

Kurtzer, D., & Lasensky, S. B. (2008). *Negotiating Arab-Israeli peace: American leadership in the Middle East*. Washington, DC: United States Institute of Peace Press.

Kurtzer, D., Lasensky, Scott B., Quandt, William B., Spiegel, Steven L., & Telhami, Shibley Z. (2012). *The peace puzzle: America's quest for Arab-Israeli peace, 1989–2011*. Ithaca, NY: Cornell University Press.

Kurzman, D. (1998). *Soldier of peace: The life of Yitzhak Rabin 1922–1995*. New York: HarperCollins.

Larson, D. W. (1985). *Origins of containment: A psychological explanation*. Princeton, NJ: Princeton University Press.

Larson, D. W. (1997). *Anatomy of mistrust: U.S.-Soviet relations during the Cold War*. Ithaca, NY: Cornell University Press.

Larson, D. W. (1997). Trust and missed opportunities in international relations. *Political Psychology 18*(3), 701–34.

Lassner, J., & Troen, S. I. (2007). *Jews and Muslims in the Arab world: Haunted by pasts real and imagined*. New York: Rowman & Littlefield Publishers.

Lebow, R. N. (1981). *Between peace and war: The nature of international crisis*. Baltimore, MD: The Johns Hopkins University Press.

Lebow, R. N. (1997). Transitions and transformations: Building international cooperation. *Security Studies 6*, 154–79.

Lebow, R. N. (2010). *Bitter fruit: Counter-factuals and international relations*. Princeton, NJ: Princeton University Press.

Lebow, R. N., & Stein, J. G. (1993). Afghanistan, Carter, and foreign policy change: The limits of cognitive models. In D. Caldwell & T. J. McKeown (Eds.), *Diplomacy, force, and leadership: Essays in honor of Alexander George*. Boulder, CO: Westview Press.

Levey, G. (2008). *Shut up, I'm talking, and other diplomacy lessons I learned in the Israeli government*. New York: Free Press.

Levy, J. S. (1994). Learning and foreign policy: Sweeping a conceptual minefield. *International Organization 48*(2), 279–312.

Levy, J. S. (1997). Prospect theory, rational choice, and international relations. *International Studies Quarterly 41*(1), 87–112.

Licklider, R. (1993). How civil wars end: Questions and methods. In R. Licklider, (Ed.), *Stopping the killing: How civil wars end*. New York: New York University Press.

Licklider, R. (1993). What have we learned and where do we go from here? In R. Licklider, (Ed.), *Stopping the killing: How civil wars end*. New York: New York University Press.

Licklider, R. (1995, February 14). Memory and reconciliation after civil wars: The U.S. and Nigerian cases. Paper published by Rutgers Center for Historical Analysis.

Lochery, N. (1999). *The difficult road to peace: Netanyahu, Israel and the Middle East peace process*. Reading, UK: Garnet Publishing Ltd.

Lochery, N. (2000). The Netanyahu era: From crisis to crisis. *Israel Affairs 6*(3 & 4), 225, 226.

Lustick, I. S. (1993). *Unsettled states, disputed lands: Britain and Ireland, France and Algeria, Israel and the West Bank–Gaza*. Ithaca, NY: Cornell University Press.

Lustick, I. S. (1996). To build and to be built by: Israel and the hidden logic of the Iron Wall. *Israel Studies 1*(1), 196–223.

Lustick, I. S. (1999, August). The Oslo Agreement Used as an Obstacle to Peace. Prepared as a Working Paper for the panel on "The Palestinians and the Peace Process" for the American Political Science Association Annual Meeting, Washington DC.

Makovsky, D. (1996). *Making peace with the PLO: The Rabin government's road to the Oslo Accord*. Boulder, CO: Westview Press.

Makovsky, D. (2004). *Assessing Sharon's Gaza settlement evacuation proposal*. Washington, DC: The Washington Institute for Near East Policy.

Maoz, Z. (2006). *Defending the Holy Land: A critical analysis of Israel's security and foreign policy*. Ann Arbor: The University of Michigan Press.

Maoz, Z., & Astorino, A. (1992). The cognitive structure of peacemaking: Egypt and Israel, 1970–78. *Political Psychology 13* (4), 647–62.

Maoz, Z., & Gat, A. (Eds.). (2001). *War in a changing world*. Ann Arbor: The University of Michigan Press.

Maoz, Z., & Mor, B. D. (1996). Enduring rivalries: The early years. *International Political Science Review 17*, 141–60.

May, E. R. (1973). *"Lessons" of the past: The use and misuse of history in American foreign policy*. New York: Oxford University Press.

McDermott, R. Rose. (1998). *Risk taking in international politics: Prospect theory in American foreign policy*. Ann Arbor, MI: The University of Michigan Press.

McDermott, R. Rose. (2004). *Political psychology in international relations*. Ann Arbor: The University of Michigan Press.

McDermott, R. Rose. (2008). *Presidential leadership, illness, and decision making*. Cambridge: Cambridge University Press.

McGuire, W. J. (1985). Attitudes and attitude change. In G. Lindzey & E. Aronoson (Eds.), *The handbook of social psychology*. New York: Random House.

Mendelson, S. (1987). Internal battle and external wars: Politics, learning, and the Soviet withdrawal from Afghanistan. *International Security 12*.

Mendilow, J. (1999). The Likud's double campaign: Between the devil and the deep blue sea. In A. Arian & M. Shamir (Eds.) *The elections in Israel 1996*. Albany: State University of New York Press.

Merhav, P. (1984). *The Israeli left: History, problems, documents*. New York: A. S. Barnes & Company, Inc.

Miller, G., & M. Rokeach. (1969). Individual differences and tolerance for inconsistency. In R. Abelson, E. Aronoson, W. McGuire, T. Newcomb, M. Rosenberg, & P. Tannenbaum (Eds.), *Theories of cognitive consistency: A sourcebook*. Chicago: Rand McNally.

Mintz, A., & DeRouen, Jr., K. (2010). *Understanding foreign policy decision making*. Cambridge: Cambridge University Press.

Misgav, H. (1997). *Sichot Im Yitzhak Shamir [Conversations with Yitzhak Shamir]*. Tel Aviv: Sifriat Poalim Publishing House, Ltd.

Mitchell, C. R., & Nicholson, M. (1983). Rational models for the ending of wars. *Journal of Conflict Resolution 27*(3), 495–520.

Murray, K. S., & Cowden, J. A. (1999). The role of "enemy images" and ideology in elite belief systems. *International Studies Quarterly 43*, 455–81.

Naor, A. (1999, May). *Greater Israel in Likud Governments: Begin, Shamir, and Netanyahu*. Presented at the 15th Annual Meeting of the Association for Israel Studies, Washington, DC.

Naveh, D. (1999). *Sodot Mimshala [Executive secrets]*. Tel Aviv: Miskal, Yedioth Ahronoth Books and Chemed Books.

Netanyahu, B. (1986). *Terrorism: How the West can win*. New York: Farrar Straus & Giroux.

Netanyahu, B. (1993). *A Place Among the Nations: Israel and the World*. London: Bantam Press.

Netanyahu, B. (1993, September 3). [Only the people (are) entitled to decide]. *Ma'ariv*, Section B2.

Netanyahu, B. (1993, September 5). Peace in our time? *The New York Times*, Section E11.

Netanyahu, B. (1993). Statement to the Knesset on Israeli-Palestinian Declaration of Principles, September 21, 1993. *Journal of Palestine Studies 23*(1).

Netanyahu, B. (1994, February 18). [Autonomy not statehood]. *Yediot Ahronot*.

Netanyahu, B. (1996, July 10). Address of Prime Minister to a Joint Session of the United States Congress, Washington DC.

Netanyahu, B. (1999, April 20). Looking Forward. *The Jerusalem Post*.

Netanyahu, B. (2000). *A durable peace: Israel and its place among the nations*. New York: Warner.

Netanyahu, B., & Netanyahu, I. (1980). Afterword to *Self-Portrait of a Hero: The Letters of Jonathan Netanyahu (1963–1976)*. New York: Random House.

Neustadt, R. E. (1960). *Presidential power: The politics of leadership*. New York: Wiley.

O'Donnell, G., & Schmitter, P. C. (1986). *Transitions from authoritarian rule: Tentative conclusions about uncertain democracies*. Baltimore, MD: The Johns Hopkins University Press.

Olson, J. M., & Zanna, M. P. (1993). Attitudes and attitude change. *Annual Review of Psychology 44*, 117–54.

Peleg, I. (1987). *Begin's foreign policy, 1977–1983*. New York: Greenwood Press.

Peleg, I. (1995). The Likud under Rabin II: Between ideological purity and pragmatic readjustment. In R. O. Freedman (Ed.), *Israel under Rabin*. Boulder, CO: Westview Press.

Peleg, I. (2000). The right in Israeli politics: The nationalist ethos in the Jewish democracy. In R. O. Freedman (Ed.), *Israel's first fifty years*. Gainesville: University Press of Florida.

Peleg, I. (2004). Israeli foreign policy under right-wing governments: A constructivist interpretation. *Israel Studies Forum* 19(3), 1–14.

Peleg, I. (2009). The Israeli Right. In R. O. Freedman (Ed.), *Contemporary Israel: Domestic politics, foreign policy, and security challenges*. Boulder, CO: Westview Press.

Peres, S. (1965). *The next step*. Tel Aviv: Am Hasefer.

Peres, S. (1970). *David's sling*. London: Weidenfeld & Nicolson.

Peres, S. (1979). *From these men: Seven founders of the State of Israel*. New York: Wyndham Books.

Peres, S. (1993, September 13). Remarks by Foreign Minister on Occasion of the Signing of the Israeli-Palestinian Declaration of Principles, Washington DC.

Peres, S. (1995). *Battling for peace: Memoirs*. London: Weidenfeld & Nicolson

Peres, S. (1996). Vision and reality. *The Brown Journal of World Affairs* 3(2), 57–64.

Peres, S. (1998). *The imaginary voyage with Theodor Herzl in Israel*. New York: Arcade Publishing.

Peres, S. (1998). *For the future of Israel*. Baltimore, MD: The Johns Hopkins University Press.

Peres, S., & Naor, S. (1993). *The new Middle East*. New York: Henry Holt and Company.

Peres, S., & Naor, S. (2003, September 28). Peres at 80: Peace can be grasped. *The Observer*.

Peres, S., & Naor, S. (2009, January 6.). Peres: Europe needs to open its eyes. *The Jerusalem Post*

Peri, Y. (1996). Afterword, Rabin: From Mr. Security to Nobel Peace Prize Winner. In Y. Rabin (Ed.), *Yitzhak Rabin: The Rabin memoirs* (pp. 339–80). Berkeley: University of California Press.

Peri, Y. (2006). *Generals in the cabinet room: How the military shapes Israeli policy*. Washington, DC: United Institute of Peace Press.

Petty, R. E., Wegener, D. T., & Fabringar, L. R. (1997). Attitudes and attitude change. *Annual Review of Psychology 48*, 609–47.

Pillar, P. R. (1983). *Negotiating peace: War termination as a bargaining process*. Princeton, NJ: Princeton University Press.

Pipes, D. (2002, August 26.). The privatization of peacemaking. *The Jerusalem Report*

Pressman, J. (2008). *Warring friends: Alliance restraint in international politics*. Ithaca, NY: Cornell University Press.

Pundak, R. (2001). From Oslo to Taba: What went wrong? *Survival, 43*(3), 31–46.

Pundak, R. (2001, March). The Israeli-Palestinian Peace Process: Lessons of Oslo. Paper presented at conference, Colgate University.

Quandt, W. (1993). *Peace process: American diplomacy and the Arab-Israeli conflict since 1967*. Washington DC: Brookings.

Quester, G. H. (1970). War prolonged by misunderstood signals. *The Annals of the American Academy of Political and Social Science 392*, 30–9.

Rabin, L. (1997). *Rabin: Our life, his legacy*. New York: Putnam's Sons.

Rabin, Y. (1985, July 18). Lecture at the National Security College. Transcript 6940.

Rabin, Y. (1985, July 28). Lecture at the National Security College. Transcript 6539.

Rabin, Y. (1995). *Rodef Shalom: Neumay Hashalom Shel Rosh Hamimshalah Yitzhak Rabin [Pursuing peace: The peace speeches of Prime Minister Yitzhak Rabin]*. Tel Aviv: Zmoorah-Beitan.

Rabin, Y. (1996). *The Rabin memoirs*, expanded ed. Berkeley: University of California Press.

Rabin, Y., & Goldstein, D. (1979). *Pinkas Sherut [The Rabin Memoirs]*. Tel Aviv: Ma'ariv.

Rabinovich, I. (1999). *Waging peace: Israel and the Arabs at the end of the century*. New York: Farrar, Straus and Giroux.

Randle, R. (1970). The domestic origins of peace. *The Annals of the American Academy of Political and Social Science 392*, 76–85.

Rasler, K. (2000). Shocks, expectancy revision and de-escalation of protracted conflicts: The Israeli-Palestinian case. *Journal of Peace Research 37*(6), 699–720.

Remnick, D. (1998, May 25). The outsider. *The New Yorker*, 80–95.

Reiter, D. (2009). *How wars end*. Princeton, NJ: Princeton University Press.

Rokeach, M. (1960). *The open and closed mind: Investigation into the nature of belief systems and personality systems*. New York: Basic Books, Inc.

Rokeach, M., & Bonier, R. (1960). Time perspective, dogmatism, and anxiety. In M. Rokeach (Ed.), *The open and closed mind: Investigation into the nature of belief systems and personality systems* (pp. 366–76). New York: Basic Books, Inc.

Rosati, J. A. (1987). *The Carter administration's quest for global community: Beliefs and their impact on behavior*. Columbia: University of South Carolina Press.

Rosati, J. A. (2000). The power of human cognition in the study of world politics. *International Studies Review 2*, 45–75.

Rosati, J. A., Hagan, J. D. & Sampson III, M. W. (Eds.). (1994). *Foreign policy restructuring: how governments respond to global change*. Columbia: University of South Carolina Press.

Rosenblum, M. (1998). Netanyahu and peace: From sound bites to sound policies? In R. O. Friedman, (Ed.), *The Middle East and the Peace Process: The Impact of the Oslo Accords*. Gainesville: University Press of Florida.

Ross, D. (2004). *The missing peace: The inside story of the fight for Middle East peace*. New York: Farrar, Straus, and Giroux.

Rubin, B., Ginat, J. & Ma'oz, M. (1994). *From war to peace: Arab-Israeli relations 1973–1993*. New York: New York University Press.

Rubinstein, A. (1979, August 24). Interview of Yitzhak Shamir: Coping with parliamentary pandemonium. *The Jerusalem Post Magazine*.

Rynhold, J. (1999). Identity, Values, and Culture Change: Israel, the United States and the Palestinian Question since Camp David. PhD diss., London School of Economics, International Relation Department.

Rynhold, J. (2003). Making sense of tragedy: Barak, the Left and Oslo. *Israel Studies Forum 19*(1), 9–33.

Rynhold, J., & Waxman, D. (2008). Ideological change and Israel's disengagement from Gaza. *Political Science Quarterly 15*, 11–37.

Sarig, M. (Ed.). (1999). *The political and social philosophy of Ze'ev Jabotinksy: Selected writings*. London: Valentine Mitchell.

Sarsar, S. G. (1984). The Effects of Defense and War Costs and Personal Traits on Change in Foreign Policy Orientations: A Case Study of Sadat's Egypt, 1970–1977. PhD diss., Rutgers University.

Sarsar, S. G. (2005). From conflict protraction to peace actualization in Palestinian-Israeli relations. *Peace and Conflict Studies* 12(2), 69–87.

Sarsar, S. G. (Ed.). (2009). *Palestine & the quest for peace*. Washington, DC: The American Task Force on Palestine.

Savir, U. (1998). *The process: 1,100 days that changed the Middle East*. New York: Random House.

Scham, L. P. (2006). The historical narratives of Israelis and Palestinians and the peace-making process. *Israel Studies Forum* 21(2), 58–84.

Schechtman, J. B., & Benari, Y. (1970). *History of the revisionist movement, 1925–30*. Tel Aviv: Hadar Publishing House Ltd.

Schelling, C. T. (1966). *Arms and influence*. New Haven, CT: Yale University Press.

Schemann, S. (1997, November 23). Outside in. *New York Times Magazine*.

Schemann, S. (1993, November 24). Shamir: Kshenachzor Lashilton Nimtsa Derech Leshanot Hahescem [Shamir: When we return to the government we'll find a way to change the agreement]. *Chazash*.

Shamir, Y. (1993). *For the sake of Zion, vision and faith: Addresses and speeches* (Hebrew). Tel Aviv: Beit Yair-Stern House.

Shamir, Y. (1994). *Summing up: An autobiography*. New York: Little, Brown.

Shamir, Y. (1996). Israel and the Middle East today. *The Brown Journal of World Affairs* 3(2), 65–70.

Shamir, Y. (2008, November 13). Peres: Arab peace plan – A serious opening for real progress. *Ha'aretz*.

Sharon, A. (1999). Security and coexistence: An alternative approach to breaking the deadlock between Israel and the Palestinians. *Likud Archives* 12/1372. Tel Aviv: Jabotinsky House.

Sharon, A., & Chanoff, D. (1989). *Warrior: An autobiography*. New York: Simon & Schuster.

Shelef, N. (2010). *Evolving nationalism: Homeland, religion, and identity in Israel, 1925–2005*. Ithaca, NY: Cornell University Press.

Shimko, L. K. (1991). *Images and arms control: Perceptions of the Soviet Union in the Reagan administration*. Ann Arbor: The University of Michigan Press.

Shindler, C. (1995). *Israel, Likud and the Zionist dream: Power, politics and ideology from Begin to Netanyahu*. New York: I. B. Tauris.

Shlaim, A. (1996). The Likud in power: The historiography of Revisionist Zionism. *Israel Studies* 1(2), 278–93.

Shriver, D. W. (1995). *An Ethnic for Enemies: Forgiveness in Politics*. New York: Oxford University Press.

Smith, B. M., Bruner, J. S., & White, R. W. (1956). *Opinions and personality*. New York: Wiley.

Snyder, G. H., & Diesing, P. (1977). *Conflict among nation: Bargaining, decision making, and system structure in international crises*. Princeton, NJ: Princeton University Press.

Snyder, J. (1984). *The ideology of the offensive: Military decision making and the disasters of 1914*. Ithaca, NY: Cornell University Press.

Snyder, J. (1991). *Myths of empire: Domestic politics and international ambition*. Ithaca, NY: Cornell University Press.

Snyder, J., & Jervis, R. (1993). *Coping with complexity in the international system.* Boulder, CO: Westview Press.

Snyder, J., & Jervis, R. (1999). Civil war and the security dilemma. In B. F. Walter & J. Snyder (Eds.), *Civil wars, insecurity, and intervention.* New York: Columbia University Press.

Soyinka, W. (1999). *The burden of memory, the muse of forgiveness.* New York: Oxford University Press.

State of Israel Press Bulletin. (1977, December). A Compendium of Hate: Palestinian Authority Anti-Semitism Since the Hebron Accord. Government Press Office.

State of Israel Press Bulletin. (1998, March 31). Palestinian Incitement, Threats of Violence Continue. Government Press Office.

State of Israel Press Bulletin. (1988, April 27). Arafat Invokes 1974 Phased Plan Calling for Israel's Destruction, Compares Oslo to Temporary Truce. Government Press Office.

State of Israel Press Bulletin. (1998, May 4). Four Years of Israeli Concessions and Palestinian Violations. Government Press Office.

State of Israel Press Bulletin. (1998, May 6). Further Redeployments in Judea and Samaria. Government Press Office.

Stedman, J. S. (1997). Spoiler problems in peace processes. *International Security* 22(2), 5–53.

Stein, J. G. (1994). Political learning by doing: Gorbachev as uncommitted thinker and motivated learner. *International Organization* 48(2), 155–83.

Susser, L. (1997, November 27) How vulnerable is Bibi? *The Jerusalem Report.*

Susser, L. (1998, February 5). Unity finale for Netanyahu's three stage balancing act. *The Jerusalem Report.*

Susser, L. (1998, June 22). History repeating itself? *The Jerusalem Report.*

Susser, L. (1999, June 7). Picking up the pieces. *The Jerusalem Report.*

Susser, L. (2001, May 7). Ever the peacenik: Shimon Peres still believes he can create a new Middle East. *The Jerusalem Report.*

Susser, L. (2003, December 1). Administration angst. *The Jerusalem Report.*

Susser, L. (2003, December 15). Preventing the unthinkable. *The Jerusalem Report.*

Susser, L. (2004, March 8). Why Ruby lost his sparkle. *The Jerusalem Report.*

Susser, L. (2010. April 12). Crunch time for Netanyahu. *The Jerusalem Report.*

Sylvan, D. (1998, July). Assessing the Impact of Problem Representation Upon Israeli-Palestinian Conflict and Cooperation. Presented at the 21st Annual Meeting of the International Society of Political Psychology, Montreal, Canada.

T'Hart, P., Stern, E. K., & Sundelius, B. (1997). *Beyond groupthink: Political group dynamics and foreign policy-making.* Ann Arbor: The University of Michigan Press.

Tamir, N. (2009, August 12). Pondering American-Israeli relations. Full Text of Letter.

Tesser, A., & Shaffer, D. R. (1990). Attitudes and attitude change. *Annual Review of Psychology* 41, 479–523.

Tessler, M. (1994). *A history of the Israeli-Palestinian conflict.* Bloomington: Indiana University Press.

Tetlock, P. E. (1983). Cognitive style and political ideology. *Journal of Personality and Social Psychology* 45, 118–26.

Tetlock, P. E. (1984). Content and structure in political belief systems. In D. A. Sylvan & S. Chan (Eds.), *Foreign policy decision making: Perception, cognition, and artificial intelligence*. New York: Praeger.

Tetlock, P. E. (1986). A value pluralism model of ideological reasoning. *Journal of Personality and Social Psychology* 50(4), 819–27.

Tetlock, P. E. (1991). Learning in U.S. and Soviet foreign policy: In search of an elusive concept. In G. W. Breslauer & P. E. Tetlock (Eds.), *Learning in U.S. and Soviet foreign policy*. Boulder, CO: Westview Press.

Troen, I. (2003). *Imagining Zion: Dreams, designs, and realities in a century of Jewish settlement*. New Haven, CT: Yale University Press.

Troen, I. (2011, July 18). The consul who dared. *Haaretz*.

Thompson, W. R. (1995). Principle rivalries. *Journal of Conflict Resolution* 39(2), 195–223.

Vardi, R. (1997). *Mi Ata Adoni Rosh Hamimshala? [Benjamin Netanyahu: Who are you Mr. Prime Minister?]*. Jerusalem: Keter Publishing House Ltd.

Vasquez, J. A. (1993). *The war puzzle*. Cambridge: Cambridge University Press.

Vertzberger, Y. I. (1990). *The world in their minds: Information processing, cognition, and perception in foreign policy decisionmaking*. Stanford, CA: Stanford University Press.

Walker, G. S. (1977). The interface between beliefs and behavior: Henry Kissinger's operational code and the Vietnam War. *Journal of Conflict Resolutions* 21(1), 129–68.

Waterman, H. (1993). Political order and the "settlement" of civil wars. In R. Licklider (Ed.), *Stopping the killing: How civil wars end*. New York: New York University Press.

Watts, W. A., & Holt, L. E. (1970). Logical relationships among beliefs and timing as factors in persuasion. *Journal of Personality and Social Psychology* 16(4), 571–82.

Waxman, D (2006). *The pursuit of peace and the crisis of Israeli identity: Defending/ defining the nation*. New York: Palgrave Macmillan.

Weber, S. (1997). Prediction and the Middle East peace process. *Security Studies* 6(4), 167–79.

Wittman, D. (1979). How a war ends: A rational model approach. *Journal of Conflict Resolution* 23(4), 743–63.

Wolfers, A. (1962). *Discord and collaboration: Essays on international politics*. Baltimore, MD: The Johns Hopkins University Press.

Wooten, J. (1995, January 29). Meddler, moralist, or peacemaker. *New York Times Magazine*.

Zaller, J. R. (1992). *The nature and origins of mass opinion*. Cambridge: Cambridge University Press.

Zartman, I. W. (1985). *Ripe for resolution: Conflict and intervention in Africa*. New York: Oxford University Press.

Zartman, I. W. (1993). The unfinished agenda: Negotiating internal conflicts. In R. Licklider (Ed.), *Stopping the killing: How civil wars end*. New York: New York University Press.

Zeruvabel, E. (1991). *The fine line: Making distinctions in everyday life*. New York: The Free Press.

Israeli Labor Party Publications

(1974, July 29). Meeting of the Labor Party Leadership Bureau.

(1974, September 4). Meeting of the Labor Party Leadership Bureau.

(1974, September 29). Meeting of the Labor Party Leadership Bureau.

(1975, May 20). Meeting of the Labor Party Leadership Bureau.
(1975, May 25). Meeting of the Labor Party Leadership Bureau.
(1975, May 26). Meeting of the Labor Party Leadership Bureau.
(1975, August, 27). Meeting of the Labor Party Leadership Bureau.
(1975, November 27). Meeting of the Labor Party Leadership Bureau.
(1976, March 29). Meeting of the Labor Party Leadership Bureau.
(1976, April 22). Meeting of the Labor Party Leadership Bureau.
(1990, July 26). Meeting of the Labor Party Central Committee: Document #177.
(1990, July 26). Meeting of the Labor Party Central Committee: Document #291.
(1990, August 9). Meeting of the Labor Party Leadership Bureau: Document #182.
(1990, September 6). Meeting of the Labor Party Leadership Bureau: Document #1262
(1991, January 31). Meeting of the Labor Party Leadership Bureau: Document #278.
(1991, February 7). Meeting of the Labor Party Leadership Bureau: Document #1009.
(1991, February 14). Meeting of the Labor Party Leadership Bureau: Document #288.
(1991, March 27). Meeting of the Labor Party Central Committee: Document #1053.
(1991, May 13). Meeting of the Labor Party Central Committee: Document #1111.
(1991, July 4). Meeting of the Labor Party Central Committee: Document #1156.
(1992, January 19). Meeting of the Labor Party Central Committee: Document #569.
(1992, July 1). Meeting of the Labor Party Central Committee: Document #4076.
(1992, July 12). Meeting of the Labor Party Central Committee: Document #4076

Israeli Likud Party Publications

(1997, November 11). Meeting of the Likud Party Central Committee: Document #170/2.
(1998, December 27). Meeting of the Likud Party Central Committee: Document #166/2.
(1998, October 28). Meeting of the Likud Party Central Committee: Document #165/2.

Lectures

Hochschild, J. (1998, August 7). Lecture at the Summer Institute in Political Psychology in Columbia, OH.
Migdal, J. (1998, April 13). Lecture at Columbia University.
Pundak, R. (2001, March 24). From Oslo to Taba – What Went Wrong? Speech at Colgate University Conference, The Israeli-Palestinian Peace Process: Lessons of Oslo.

Television Programs and Interviews

(1999, April 13). Debate between Benjamin Netanyahu and Yitzhak Mordechai on Israeli Television. *Israeli Broadcasting Authority, Channel Two*. Program titled "Mishal Ham."
(2000, October 8). Interview with Shimon Peres on *Face the Nation*.
(1993, November 19). Interview of Yitzhak Rabin. *Al Hamishmar*.
(1997, December 7). Mishaal, N. Interview of Yitzhak Shamir and Shimon Peres on Israeli Television. *Israeli Broadcasting Authority, Channel One*. Program titled "Poplitika," Aharon Goldfinger, producer.
(2000). Richards, D., & Percy, N. (Directors). The 50 Years of War: Israel & the Arabs. *PBS Video*.
(2005, January 25). Interview of Ehud Barak on *Charlie Rose*.
(2007, March 26). Meeting with MK Yossi Beilin. *Meretz USA Weblog*.

Government Documents

(1978, September 25). Knesset Records: 4067–71.

(1992, October 26). Knesset Minutes: 23, 24.

(1993), September 21. Knesset Minutes: 143.

(1994, February 28). Knesset Minutes: 4910.

(1994, April 18). Knesset Minutes: 6244, 6247, 6248, 6251.

(1995, September 28). Signing ceremony of the Israeli Palestinian Interim Agreement, Israel Foreign Office Website.

(1998, May 4). Israel Government Press Office Press Bulletin. Four Years of Israeli Concessions and Palestinian Violations.

(1998, May 6). Israel Government Press Office Press Bulletin. Further Redeployment in Judea and Samaria.

(1999). Ministry of Foreign Affairs Information Release No. 16. Wye River Memorandum: Status of Implementation as of February 1.

(2001, April 30). Report of the Sharm el-Sheikh Fact-Finding Committee.

Interviews Conducted by Author: See Appendix B

Index

CPSIA information can be obtained at www.ICGtesting.com
Printed in the USA
BVOW05*0309230514

354233BV00016B/29/P